THE GOOD NEW ZEALAND BEACH GUIDE
NORTH ISLAND

We hope this book helps you find a beach just right for you!

Compliments of

MITSUBISHI MOTORS

Bay City Mitsubishi

140 Cameron Road, Tauranga   Phone 07 578 0039
www.baycitymitsubishi.co.nz

clean media

First published in 2011 by:
Clean Media Ltd
94 Upper Wainui Rd
Raglan.
027 447 4853

www.cleanmedia.co.nz

Copyright © in text: Tim Rainger
Copyright © in photographs: Tim Rainger
(unless otherwise stated below)
Kelly Weeds: Tapuaetahi Surf 41
Joe McPhee: Piha Surfer 113
Dave Elley: Hot Water Waves 148
Greta Kenyon: Paddling Girls 159
Sandy Britain: Tolaga aerial 174, Makarori aerial & Wainui aerial both 177
Taranaki SurfDaze: Fitzroy & Back Beach both 182
Cory Scott: The Spit 183 & Rolling Stones 185
George Santorik: Aotea Reef 204
Paul Kennedy: White Rock 199 & Lyall Bay 231

Copyright © Clean Media Ltd.

National Library of New Zealand
Cataloguing-In-Publication Data:
Rainger, Timothy
The New Zealand Good Beach Guide: North Island
ISBN no: 978-0-473-18680-7

Written, photographed, art directed and published by Tim Rainger/Clean Media
Graphic Designer: Edith Woischin
Layout Assistant: Kelly Clarkson
All maps plus wind and swell rose diagrams:
Brett Beamsley/MetOcean
Printed in China through Colorcraft Ltd., Hong Kong.

All rights reserved. No part of this book may be used in any format, reproduced, stored in any retrieval system or transmitted in any form or by any means, electronic, mechanical, photocopy, recording or otherwise, without the express permission of the publishers and copyright owners.

The representation in this guide of a road is no proof of the existence of a right of way.

Surfing, fishing and swimming are potentially dangerous and highly addictive pursuits. The author and publisher takes all care but accept no responsibility for either injury or loss of life, job or wife as a result of using the information contained within.

THE
GOOD

NORTH ISLAND

media

Medlands beach

INTRODUCTION & ACKNOWLEDGEMENTS

Aotearoa/ New Zealand has roughly 18,000 kilometres of coastline, more than any nation of comparable area on Earth. Its geological forms and topography vary immensely, but what stands out so clearly to the naked eye, glinting in the sharp South Pacific sunshine, is the unbelievable variety of beaches that make up one third of that coast.

From the intensely white silica sands of the Far North, to the imposing cliffs and rocks of the Wairarapa; the shingle strewn coast of Cook Strait, to the purple-black sands of the west coast, its beaches are a perfect example of the incredible diversity and beauty of our South Pacific paradise. The seas that surround this wondrous creation also teem with life. Our oceans are home to over half of the world's whales and dolphin species, while eighty-six of the world's 360 species of seabirds call New Zealand home. That is just the start.

Over the years, this country was settled by waves of the hardiest seafarers to have ever sailed the oceans, both Polynesian and European. And with nowhere more than 130 kilometres from the sea, it is hardly surprising that beach culture inhabits a space at the absolute centre of the New Zealand psyche. Put simply, Kiwis live for the beach. Likewise, for the majority of tourists who arrive on these shores, bursting with expectation, the beach is one of the first places they head, attracted by the allure of some of the most spectacular and pristine coastline on the planet.

This book is an attempt to convey some of the variety and depth of experience available. It is the first edition of a two volume set, which will soon include a companion edition covering the South Island. Through words and pictures it offers a glimpse of this spectacular country that I have explored since my childhood, and am fortunate enough to call home.

I hope my words help stimulate a conservationist ethic amongst those who use it. Our coast is facing many serious pressures, some of which I have attempted to define in the ensuing pages. I don't wish to seem to be overly negative, but when you fully realise the extent of the problems we have created, and know how preventable many of them are, it is impossible not to speak out. We all need to stand up and protect this wonder of the world if we want our children to enjoy it as we do today.

While I have included details of all beaches accessible by car, there is no way I could visit every kilometre of the North Island in the two years it has taken to compile this guide. That would be neither necessary nor desirable. After all, there has to be something left to find for the intrepid beachcomber. I have also left many inner harbour beaches unreported, due to their lower recreational value. Equally beaches requiring access through private land are generally ignored for obvious political reasons.

I know there will be discussion surrounding some of my observations and I should point out this is just one person's view of the world. I know it won't be perfect, but I have called it as I see it. I welcome any constructive criticism and input into any aspect of this publication. Comments may be sent to the author tim@cleanmedia.co.nz or lodged on the facebook site www.facebook.com/thenzgoodbeachguide

I owe my deepest thanks to a huge number of people who have given their unflagging support and assistance during the course of this project. Firstly and most importantly, Sarah and Robin Rawstorne, and my son Finn Rainger. Gavin Melgren and Patti Mitchley who made me so welcome in their home over such a long period. Cindy Barrett who provided me with unconditional friendship and a bed whenever I was in Auckland. Cam and Suzie Williamson for their warm hospitality in Wellington. Sally MacIntosh who helped me with many design issues over the course of the project. Paul Bateman and the staff of David Bateman Publishing, who offered me advice and assistance way above and beyond the call of duty. Dave Thorpe from McLeod's Books for sage advice and support. Richard Kotch, my good friend, for your invaluable friendship and inspiration over many years. Gazza, my fishing guru, and the saltiest person I know. Harry and Viv Hill who always made me feel like this was a project worth persevering with, and who housed me and fed me many, many times. Brett Beamsley from MetOcean for all your technical assistance and dry humour in the face of adversity. Edith Woischin for your total professionalism at all times. Sealink for assistance with ferry travel. Air Discovery for flying me over Waiheke. Chris Harrison and Bernie Griffen for keeping me sane in their own unique ways. Sebastian, Andraina and Maurice Horat, my intrepid Swiss travelling companions. Malibu Hamilton for your friendship and an Iwi perspective. Scott Macindoe and all the others who offered me advice and information along the way; there were a lot of you and I couldn't have done it without you. And last but not least my parents for giving me such a rich childhood immersed in the sea.

Julie Rainger may you rest in peace and be proud of this work.

20

76

122

CONTENTS

10. New Zealand weather and sea conditions
14. Weather and swell forecasting
16. Threats to our coastal integrity

20. THE FAR NORTH
22. CAPE REINGA TO NORTH CAPE
24. 90 MILE BEACH AND AHIPARA
28. THE HOKIANGA
32. THE AUPORI PENINSULA EAST COAST
34. THE KARIKARI PENINSULA
36. DOUBTLESS BAY
38. THE CAVALLI COAST
42. THE BAY OF ISLANDS

46. NORTHLAND
48. RIPIRO BEACH
52. THE OLD RUSSELL ROAD
54. WHANANAKI COAST
56. THE TUTUKAKA COAST
60. WHANGAREI COAST
62. BREAM BAY

64. RODNEY COUNTY
66. MANGAWHAI TO GOAT ISLAND
70. THE WARKWORTH COAST
74. MAHURANGI TO OREWA

76. THE AUCKLAND REGION
78. THE WHANGAPARAOA PENINSULA
82. THE NORTH SHORE
88. INNER WAITEMATA
92. EASTERN BEACHES
94. THE SEABIRD COAST
96. WAIHEKE ISLAND
102. GREAT BARRIER ISLAND
108. MURIWAI TO TE HENGA
112. THE PIHA ROAD
116. THE MANUKAU HARBOUR

122. WAIKATO WEST COAST
124. FRANKLIN COUNTY
126. WHAINGAROA/RAGLAN

46

108

130

 168

 194

 208

- **130. THE COROMANDEL PENINSULA**
- 132. THAMES TO TE KOUMA
- 134. COROMANDEL TO WAITETE
- 136. COLVILLE TO FLETCHER BAY
- 138. STONY BAY TO KENNEDY BAY
- 140. NEW CHUMS TO RINGS BEACH
- 142. KUAOTUNU TO MATAPAUA BAY
- 144. MERCURY BAY
- 146. MERCURY BAY EASTERN BEACHES
- 148. HOT WATER BEACH TO PAUANUI
- 150. OPOUTURE TO WHIRITOA

- **152. THE BAY OF PLENTY**
- 154. WAIHI BEACH AND BOWENTOWN
- 156. TAURANGA HARBOUR AND MATAKANA IS
- 158. MT MAUNGANUI AND PAPAMOA
- 160. MAKETU TO PUKEHINA
- 162. THE WHAKATANE COAST
- 164. THE EASTERN BAY

- **168. EAST CAPE AND POVERTY BAY**
- 170. LOTTIN POINT TO EAST CAPE
- 172. TIKITIKI TO KAIAUA
- 174. TOLAGA BAY TO TATAPOURI
- 176. GISBORNE AND POVERTY BAY

- **180. HAWKE'S BAY**
- 182. THE MAHIA PENINSULA
- 186. WAIROA DISTRICT
- 188. NAPIER COAST
- 190. HASTINGS DISTRICT
- 192. CENTRAL HAWKE'S BAY

- **194. THE WAIRARAPA**
- 196. MASTERTON DISTRICT
- 198. SOUTH-EAST WAIRARAPA
- 200. THE SOUTH COAST

- **202. THE KING COUNTRY**
- 204. AOTEA AND KAWHIA
- 206. MAROKOPA TO MOKAU

- **208. TARANAKI**
- 210. NORTH TARANAKI
- 212. NEW PLYMOUTH
- 214. OAKURA TO THE CAPE
- 218. OPUNAKE
- 220. SOUTH TARANAKI

- **222. THE SOUTH WEST**
- 224. MANAWATU AND HOROWHENUA
- 228. KAPITI COAST

- **230. WELLINGTON**
- 232. MANA COAST
- 234. PETONE TO WAINUIOMATA
- 236. CITY BEACHES
- 238. THE SOUTH COAST

- 240. Beach index

 180

 202

 230

New Zealand weather

The main islands that make up New Zealand are located between 34°S and 47°S. They are bordered by the South Pacific Ocean to the north and east, the Tasman Sea to the west and the Southern Ocean to the south, and lie in a region commonly known as the "Roaring Forties". At these latitudes, the atmospheric circulation is directed west to east, and results in a predominantly easterly passage of weather systems, featuring troughs of low pressure revolving clockwise, separated by a series of anticyclones, that revolve anti-clockwise.

Summer is typically marked by a series of large anticyclones (regions of high pressure) that can sit over the country for days at a time, while areas of low pressure generally sit well beneath the country at this time.

Winter is marked by a decrease in frequency and duration of anticyclones, and an increase in size and a more northerly track for troughs of low pressure and their associated fronts.

Sea breezes are a common feature of New Zealand summer days, created by the temperature differential between sea and the land masses. Land heats and cools much quicker than the ocean, and warm days see winds flowing from the sea to the land as convection currents rise over warmer masses. Cooler evenings can result in a reversal of these winds, and the formation of what are commonly known as "land breezes." This effect though less marked in winter, still occurs on warm days and cool clear nights.

Tropical cyclones (also known as hurricanes or typhoons in other parts of the world), can also affect New Zealand's weather and beach conditions. The ones that affect us are those that form in the area of ocean between Queensland and Fiji. The Coriolis effect causes them to move along a curved path south by south-east, sometimes passing above the top of the North Island, occasionally tracking directly over us, by which time they are usually downgraded to ex-tropical storms. Their effects can often be seen well before their influence on weather is felt, with large long period swells arriving on many east facing beaches. They often bring intense rain when they cross the country, and generally occur between November and May when the Pacific is at its warmest. Some years there are hardly any, others, especially in La Nina summers, there can be up to a dozen.

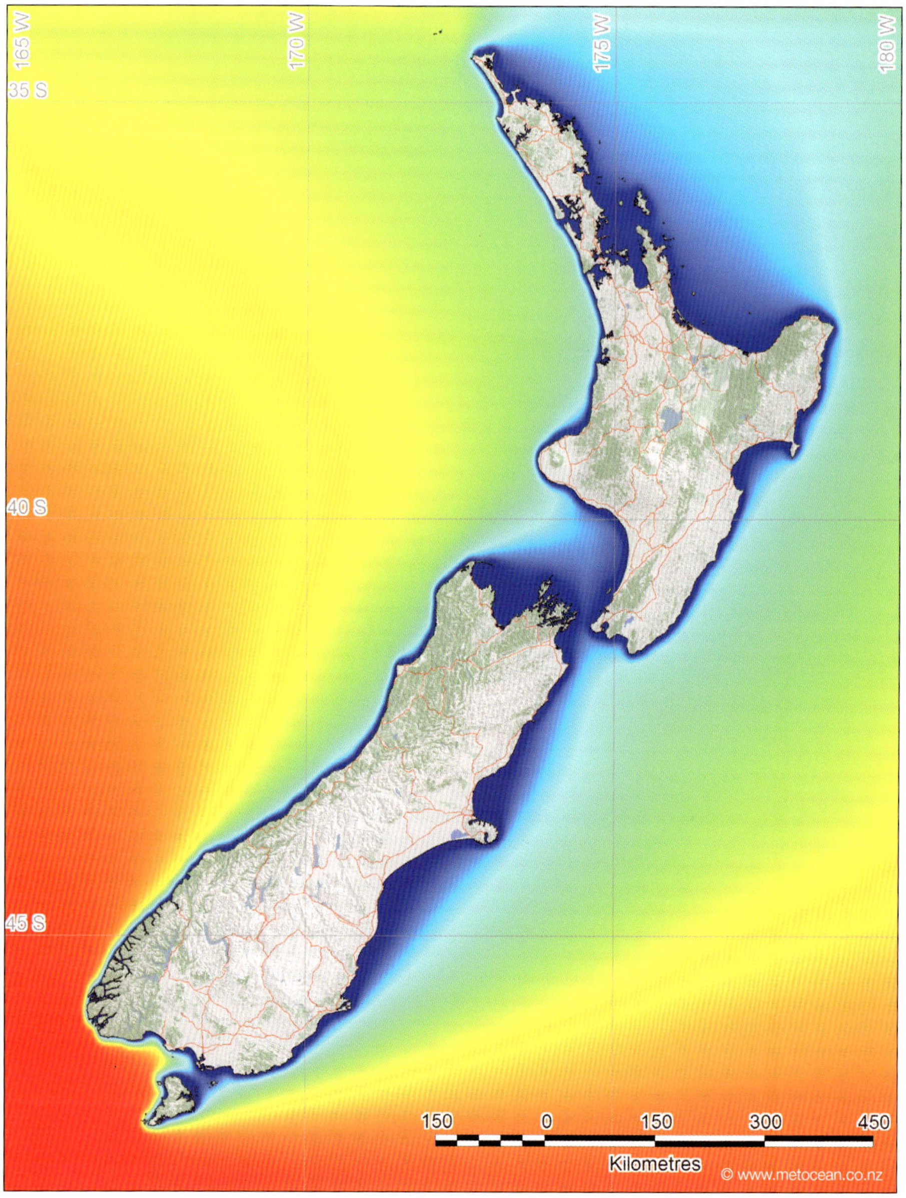

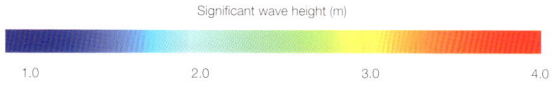

NEW ZEALAND MEAN ANNUAL WAVE HEIGHTS

The shape of the country has a huge influence on the weather patterns experienced on land. New Zealand's long, mountainous spine is essentially a speedbump in the way of the prevailing weather, intercepting westerly winds, and creating mountain-generated rain in the west, and leaving it drier in the east. This orographic shadow effect is particularly prominent in the South Island, and results in a large disparity between annual rainfall on either coast. The North Island also experiences this phenomena, to a lesser extent, with eastern areas experiencing less rainfall and higher sunshine hours.

The Birth of swell

Swell is created by strong winds blowing over the surface of the sea. The height that these waves reach is dependant on the wind's fetch (i.e the distance wind blows over) and speed. The period is dependant on how far from the generation zone the wave has travelled. As the distance travelled increases, the waves become more regular, long crested and become separated into well defined groups, or sets. The best surfing conditions feature long period waves created by systems far from the coast. In New Zealand, these conditions are most often produced by low pressure systems to the south of the country, but they are unable to reach many north and north-east facing beaches, because of the shadowing effect of East Cape, graphically illustrated in the chart opposite.

Along these stretches of the North Island, swell conditions are usually produced along the top of high pressure systems, where the wind fetch can be more than 1000 kms. A low pressure system such as an ex-tropical cyclone can intensify the wind speed and result in large waves striking the north-east coastline. These mechanisms for swell generation tend to result in smaller and less consistent swell conditions being experienced.

How does all this affect beach goers?

Surfers and fishermen usually seek areas of coast with offshore winds, which more often than not can be found on the east coast. Winds that blow from the land to the sea are preferable for general beach goers too, producing calmer sea surfaces inshore. Surfers, however, seek swell whereas fishermen and swimmers usually prefer none. The great thing about New Zealand is that with two coasts so close together, we have a choice of where to visit. If the weather forecast is for westerlies, then the east coast will be the logical place to look for calm conditions. If the forecast is for easterly winds, the west coast will have a groomed appearance. Local winds shouldn't be confused with swell, which is usually created by weather systems a long way from the shoreline (see above), but there are so many variables, it is difficult to account for them in a short introduction like this. With the amount of information available on the internet these days, it is easy to get an update of current conditions, and often very accurate predictions for up to a week out.

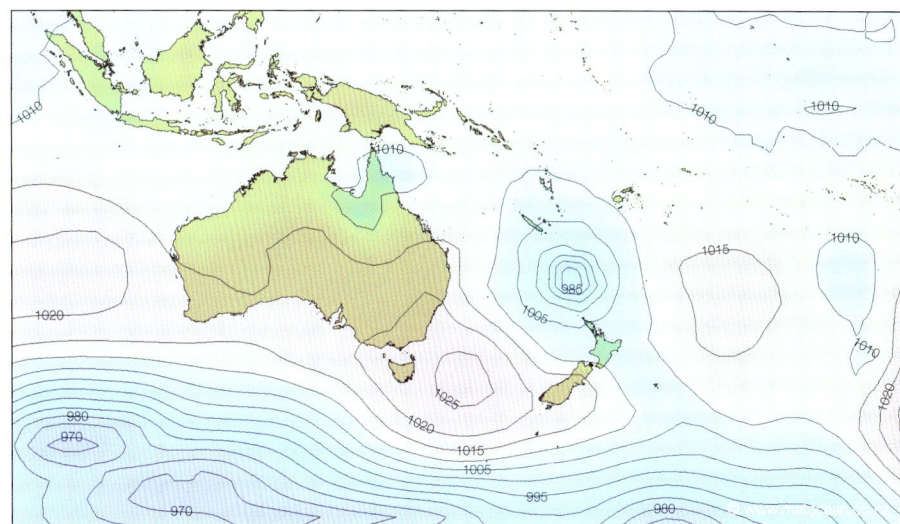
TROPICAL CYCLONE

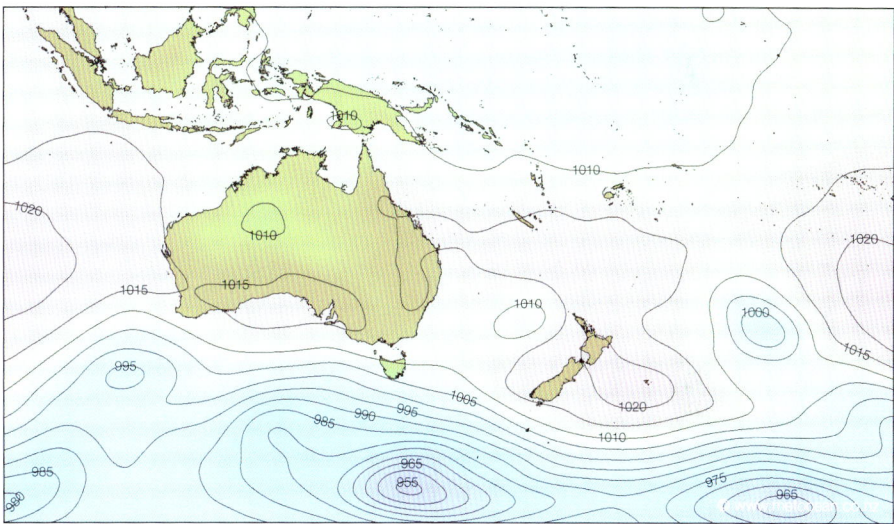
SOUTHERN OCEAN LOW PRESSURE

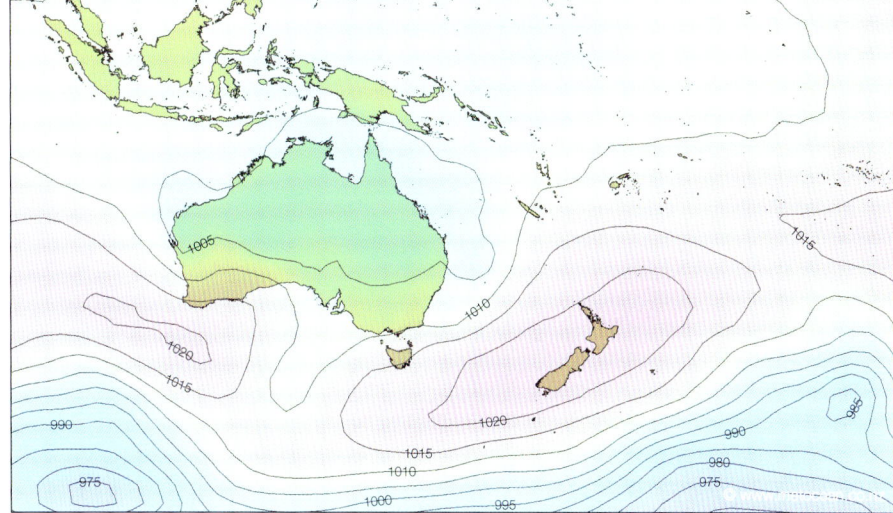
TYPICAL SUMMER HIGH PRESSURE

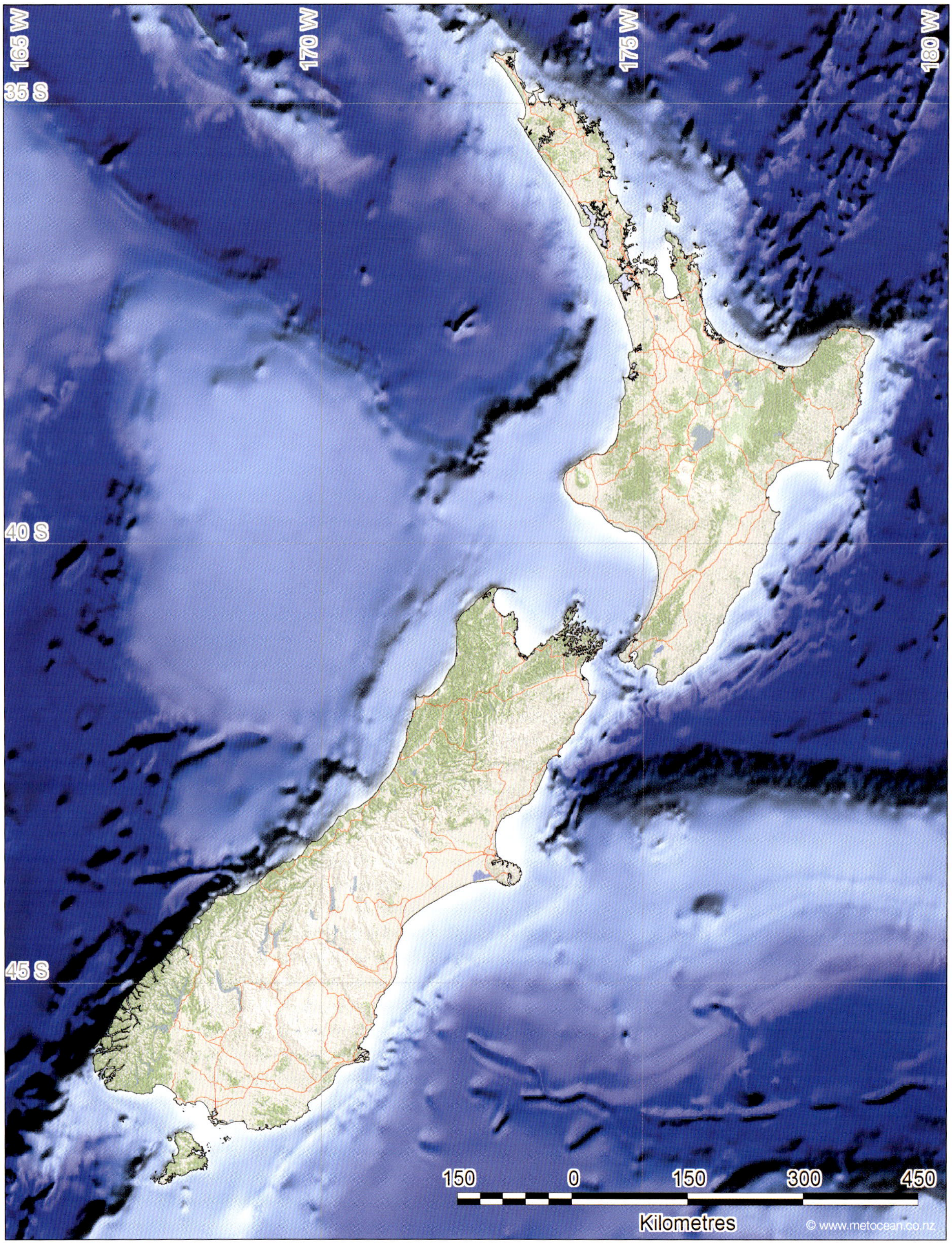

NEW ZEALAND BATHYMETRY

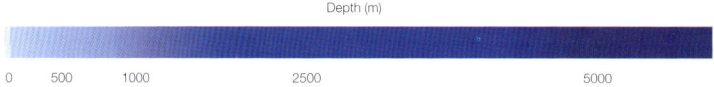

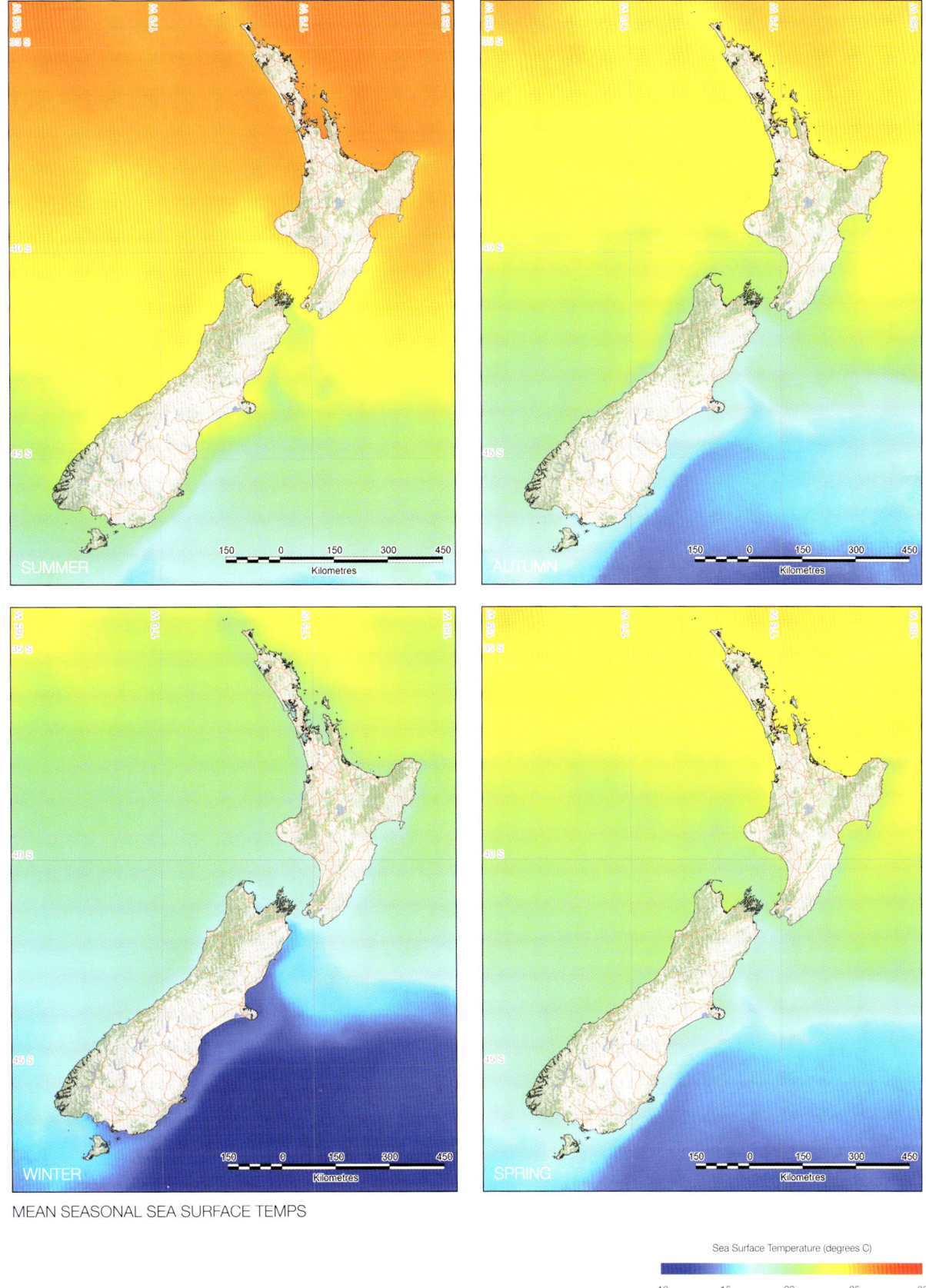

MEAN SEASONAL SEA SURFACE TEMPS

WEATHER AND SWELL FORECASTING

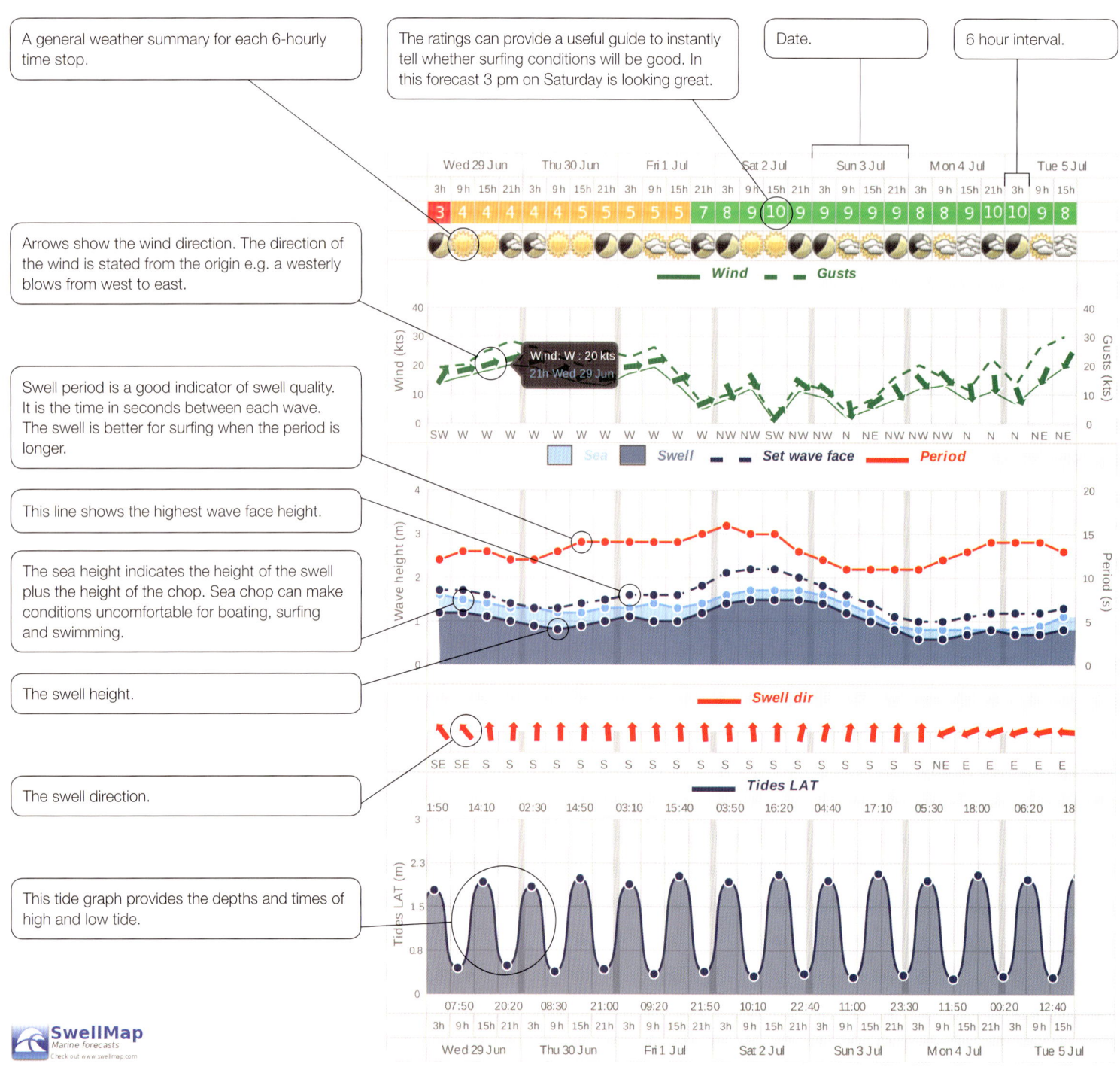

I use two primary meteorological sites, one for swell and wind conditions and forecasts, and one for general weather. They are www.swellmap.co.nz and www.weathermap.co.nz. SwellMap provides marine and weather forecasts for thousands of boating sites and beaches in and around the world. The forecasts are presented in user friendly formats; including charts/maps, graphs and tables. The maps are a great way to see the passing weather patterns; the graphs present data for a chosen site that can interpreted at a glance; and the tables are useful for picking out individual statistics for specific times from a chosen site.

SwellMap takes into account the main features that influence New Zealand's weather, for example the oceans, mountain ranges and other topographical features. Marine weather conditions can vary drastically along New Zealand's twisting and rugged coastline and it is important to capture local factors in any forecast. SwellMap's high resolution analysis takes these factors into account and factors them into forecasts for specific sites.

Coarse global data is initially obtained from the National Oceanic and Atmospheric Administration (NOAA), which allows the model to forecast weather conditions 7-days out. Observational data is used to initialize the atmospheric model; ensuring that the model as faithfully as possible captures the actual weather conditions.

SwellMap's wave model uses regional and local scale bathymetric features (ocean depths) to provide marine and beach forecasts that are more representative of the local conditions. It does this by using state of the art atmospheric and oceanographic numerical (computer) models that take observational data and coarse global data down to regional and local scales – increasing the resolution of the data by several orders of magnitude.

SwellMap updates 4 times a day providing 7 days of weather data at 6 hourly intervals so you get the latest and most accurate forecasts. The website also provides quality ratings for surfing and boating making it easy to identify when conditions are likely to be good for that activity at a particular site. The ratings are scaled from 1-10 (1=poor, 10=excellent) and colour coded. Now you don't have to be a local or knowledgeable about a particular location to know when conditions are going to be right for your chosen activity!

THREATS TO OUR COASTAL INTEGRITY

Aotearoa/New Zealand was for many years quite rightly called "Godzone," referring to its outstanding natural beauty, unique bio-diversity and benign climate. Successive governments and tourist authorities have nurtured our reputation as a clean green paradise, with the globally recognized "100% Pure" campaign promoted internationally as a core component of our national brand. Sadly, as I write this piece, this reputation is under serious threat, because despite all the rhetoric, the truth is that we are collectively as bad or worse than most nations on the planet in our reckless disregard for our God-given resources.

I don't write this to score a cheap shot, but in the hope that upon reflection, this may force some awareness from all who use this book, and lead to the realisation that we cannot take out natural heritage

for granted as we have been. Repetitive over-use of resources is a recurrent theme, and one that's fast becoming a national tragedy, which is at risk of making us a laughing stock in the international community. They will laugh at us for the extent of the lie we are attempting to propagate, and at the mindless way which we are squandering our natural wealth, with little appreciation of its true long-term value.

There will be some who disagree with these statements, but if you ask any septuagenarian, they will tell you the extent of the decline in our environmental integrity. I don't have all the answers, but there are many people out there working on them. I have listed a top line appraisal of some of the primary problems we are facing below. For a fully researched title on this and other relevant coastal subjects, Raewyn Peart's "Castles in the Sand," published by Craig Potton Publishing is an excellent starting point in the search for an objective appraisal of our current situation.

Sewage and effluent run off

Two of the most prevalent, insidious and potentially dangerous forms of coastal water pollution are: (1) human sewage, and (2) farm run-off (consisting of both animal waste and agricultural chemicals like fertilizers and sprays). Both are widespread problems in New Zealand now.

Human waste can contain a wide range of hazardous bacteria and cause a number of both minor and major health issues, ranging from ear, nose and throat infections, to Hepatitis and other serious illnesses. The most common causes of contamination occur from faulty septic tanks or poor public wastewater disposal; either through under-capacity of systems, or poor effluent discharge by design. There is usually a simple solution to these types of problems and they involve repairing or upgrading existing facilities in affected areas. This costs money, and it is this expenditure, coupled by a lack of political will, that are the primary obstacles to solving these problems.

Animal waste, and other agricultural run-offs, (primarily caused by intensive dairying), when combined with siltification from eroding land, also have a crippling impact on the health of our inland waterways, many of which discharge at the coast. As well as the downstream human health implications of these discharges, they also have a serious impact on surrounding shellfish populations, which in turn has a negative impact on local fish stocks.

Animal waste is allowed to enter waterways through poorly fenced streams or other indolent farming practices, and while there is a voluntary operational code called "The Clean Streams Accord", which attempts to offer best practice solutions, few farms adhere to it, and little is done to enforce it.

New Zealand is the only country in the OECD not to have a National Environmental Reporting Act, meaning information on water quality is left to local councils. Consequently, the majority of our inland waterways are now polluted by farm effluent, and where these waterways arrive at the coast, they should be avoided.

Large urban areas present a different set of problems, and this remarkably honest appraisal of the current situation taken from the Auckland City website, gives a good snapshot of what conditions are like across the country. Ironically, it first states how much we "value" the bathing water resource we have inherited, yet goes on to catalogue how we have abused it with under-investment in infrastructure. "Bacterial concentrations are monitored at many popular swimming areas around the Auckland region. Auckland's waterbodies (including beaches, lakes and estuaries) are highly valued and extremely popular for recreation during the summer months…A closer examination of the data shows that exceedances of the Red threshold tend to be greater on beaches that are close to highly urbanised catchments. Bathing beach water quality north of Whangaparaoa and on the northern side of Waiheke rarely, if ever, exceed the Amber thresholds. In contrast, beaches within the metropolitan urban limits (MUL) regularly experience levels of microbiological contaminants that are potentially harmful to human health. Exceptions to this pattern are a small number of freshwater sites near the Waitakere Ranges coast, which regularly exceed the guidelines. The surrounding catchments do not have reticulation systems and the contamination is therefore likely to be as a result of septic systems failing."

Given that many coastal regions in NZ do not have reticulated sewage, the implications are clear. Avoid

Doubtless Bay

stream mouths in populated coastal areas, especially after periods of rain. The bad news is that these problems are now widespread. The good news is that most can be solved with social pressure, political will and capital expenditure. But it is up to us as the voters of New Zealand, to ensure that governments and councils spend our money in ways that will guarantee our future as one of the finest places in the world to be on the coast. The simplest way to make a difference is to exert pressure on your local Mayor and MP.

The bathing water monitoring regime

Coastal bathing water quality testing for microbial contamination is carried out to ensure that public health is not put at risk from pathogens, including bacteria, viruses and protozoa. The risk to health from all 3 of these is inferred from the bacterial counts. Enterococci are used to assess saline waters, while E.coli are used to assess freshwater contamination. When high counts occur, monitored swimming beaches may be closed, and shellfish gathering banned. The safety of shellfish for harvesting is monitored by the New Zealand Food Safety Authority. Monitoring the state of our bathing water is the responsibility of regional councils, yet while this is suggested by central government, there is no firm requirement for them to do this, and little or no punitive enforcement when the recommended standards are not complied with. Consequently, the response varies across the country, ranging from good to non-existent, with some, like Waikato District, deciding not to bother testing at all. This is a disgrace, and represents abject disregard for public safety. Regular monitoring of all populated bathing beaches, especially those with known problems, should be mandatory, and the results should be clearly displayed for reasons of public health.

Relevant MFE Guidelines

The Ministry for the environment set the guidelines for bathing water standards, and they are available for public examination at the following sites:
www.mfe.govt.nz/publications/water/microbiological-quality-jun03/index.html

1. Coastal bathing water quality
www.ew.govt.nz/Environmental-information/Environmental-indicators/Coasts/Coastal-water-quality

2. Estuarine water quality
www.ew.govt.nz/Environmental-information/Environmental-indicators/Coasts/Coastal-water-quality/Estuarine-water-quality

Bathing water quality from local bodies
Northland www.nrc.govt.nz/upload/3465/Coastal%20Water%20Quality.pdf
Auckland www.aucklandcouncil.govt.nz/EN/environment/Land_water/beach_water_quality_safeswim/Pages/latest_monitoring.aspx
www.monitorauckland.arc.govt.nz/natural-environment-and-heritage/coastal-management-home/bathing-beach-water-quality-for-contact-recreation.cfm
Waikato/Coromandel www.waikatoregion.govt.nz/Environmental-information/Our-coast/Coastal-water-quality/Coastal-water-quality-for-swimming/Coromandel-Peninsula-coastal-water-quality-monitoring-map
Bay of Plenty www.envbop.govt.nz/Environment/Swimming-Water-Quality.aspx
Gisborne/East Coast www.gdc.govt.nz/environmental-monitoring
Hawkes Bay www.hbrc.govt.nz or 0800B4USwim
Taranaki www.trc.govt.nz/Environment
Manawatu www.stuff.co.nz/environment3097651/Manawatu-River-among-worst-in-the-West
Wellington, the Wairarapa and Kapiti Coast
www.gw.govt.nz/recreational-water-quality-2009-1
www.gw.govt.nz/kapiti-2
www.gw.govt.nz/wairarapa-3
www.gw.govt.nz/wellington-4

Our aquatic assets

Our seabed is a vast repository of wealth in many forms, both living and inanimate. Despite our poor understanding of its nature, man has exploited its potential in small ways since the beginning of time. New Zealand's economic zone covers 5.8 million square kilometres of ocean. It is the fifth-largest national resource of its kind in the world.

Aside from the fish stocks that generate large national revenue, there is also a range of mineral wealth in the sea bed. Given the rising values of global commodities, many organisations have been looking at ways to generate income from this massive asset.

In a recent article, Rod Oram had this to say:
"Currently, our oceans generate only $3.3 billion of GDP a year, of which $1.4b is exports of seafood and oil. Other values are harder to quantify. For example, some two million tourists a year engage in saltwater activities; and 90% of us live within 50km of the sea. The Ministry of Fisheries estimates our oceans deliver to us ecosystem services that would be worth $184b a year if we had to pay for them. That's a greater value than we generate in GDP each year. These services come in four categories: provisioning, such as food production; regulating, such as climate control; supporting, such as nutrient cycles and sewage disposal; and cultural, such as recreational benefits."

"Although offshore oil exploration has already hit the headlines, there are plenty of other contentious initiatives coming. For example, Widespread Energy, a local company, is proposing to seabed-mine for phosphate nodules on the Chatham Rise for use as farm fertiliser. In the near future expect even more challenging ideas such as extracting minerals – or even organisms which might have therapeutic value – from hydrothermal vents deep on the ocean floor." The Sea Bed and the Sea Flaw, Rod Oram/Sunday Star Times, 20/06/11.

Seabed Mining

Seabed mining comes in many forms, some with negligible effect on the marine environment, and some that can prove catastrophic. Sand itself is now a precious resource, used amongst other things in the manufacture of cement and glass, and also to replenish urban beaches in many regions.

Maintaining the sand levels on Auckland's city beaches has already had catastrophic consequences for the foreshore of Pakiri Beach. Sand mining for concrete mix has irretrievably altered the integrity of the Kaipara Harbour, and both continue unabated as you read this. While we use cement and glass, we need sand, and the harbours are the easiest places from which to gather it, but they are not infinite resources, so clearly another sustainable solution needs to be found.

In New Zealand, we also have a range of precious metals in the seabed, but currently the one being targeted on a broad scale is iron. The black sand which is a unique feature of the west coast beaches of the central North Island, is washed down the streams which scour Mt Taranaki and is carried up the coast and deposited in the inshore seabed by the littoral drift which accompanies the prevailing swell and wind. The black/blue colour of these beaches is due to the presence of a mineral known as titomagnetite, a base metal from which iron ore is made. Its extractive potential has been recognized since the 1800's, and it has been mined commercially from the dunes around Port Waikato and Kawhia for many years. But the greatest amount of it is to still to be found in the seabed.

Recent technological advances, coupled with the soaring price of steel world-wide, have made these vast supplies of iron economically feasible to mine, using giant vacuum cleaners that can suck up as much as the top 5 metres of the seabed. Crown Minerals has issued permits to huge swathes of the North Island coast, and as you read this, some of the world's largest mining organizations are looking at how they can extract this resource.

The impact of large scale mining of the seabed would undoubtedly cause catastrophic damage to the aquatic ecosystems of the west coast, and potentially cause serious erosion of the foreshore. It is an unfolding national tragedy, that ironically will create few jobs and return comparatively little income. For more information, visit www.blacksands.org

Overfishing

Another problem faced by most nations now, is the dwindling number of fish in the ocean. New Zealand still supports a fishery to envy, though numbers are vastly reduced from what they were before the advent of purse-seine netting and bottom trawling, and while some stocks in some areas seem stable, other species are still in rapid decline.

Commercial fishing is largely responsible for a majority of the damage to our fish stocks, with destructive and indiscriminate catch methods still being employed around our coast. A propaganda war is being carried out with the tacit support of successive responsible ministers, to make us believe that our fishery is being harvested sustainably; yet if you talk with any recreational fisherman, they will provide anecdotal evidence to the contrary. Perversely, the current Minister of Fisheries, Phil Heatley has recently indicated that the national government he reperesents supports an increase in quota numbers for the commercial sector.

The NZ Sport Fishing Council keeps catch records from all its clubs, and as an example, yellowfin tuna catches have declined from well over 2,000 per year in the mid 1990s to a mere 69 in 2009. The Whakatane Sport Fishing Club has had to rename their annual fishing tournament to take "tuna" out of the title after two consecutive years of no tuna catches.

A tragedy of the commons is playing itself out, with recreational and industry groups squared off against each other and no-one prepared to sacrifice catch numbers.

> "WE CAN'T ALL KEEP HAULING FISH OUT OF THE SEA AT THE RATE WE CURRENTLY ARE AND EXPECT IT TO BE SUSTAINABLE. IT'S NOT."

If we want our children to enjoy our fishery in any form similar to what it is today both recreational and commercial quotas of all stocks should be reduced from current levels. Some real leadership needs to be shown; and greater vigilance and co-operation between recreational angler groups, local iwi, fishing media and MFish should be initiated.

The concept of catch and release, especially focusing on breeding stock, must be promoted and encouraged, as it is overseas. We can't all keep hauling fish out of the sea at the rate we currently are and expect it to be sustainable. It's not. Penalties for those that transgress existing rules should be increased, and greater efforts put into enforcement of legislation relating to every sphere of the industry. Catch numbers vary across New Zealand. For information about fish limits in your area, go to www.fish.govt.nz. If you become aware of anyone illegally harvesting shellfish or abusing their recreational catch limits, **MFish** has a confidential hotline **0800476 224 or 08004poacher**.

But one principle should remain firm at all times. The historical practice of being able to put food on the table by recreational anglers should be put first in any list of priorities. Please support any groups that are working to ensure the rights of individual anglers like Option 4 www.option4.co.nz

Inappropriate Coastal Development

The last thirty years have witnessed an almost unrecognizable transformation of large areas of the New Zealand coast. The rise in popularity of beach culture, better transport links, faster cars and a change in social make up have all contributed. The baby boomer generation has exploited lax planning laws and over-worked and under financed councils, who have generally buckled in the face of legal challenges to their fragmented planning codes.

Case by case mitigation rather than a bigger picture perspective, has led to many sensitive areas being over run by new developments that in many cases have completely altered the social and environmental make-up of what were once small tight knit communities. Often investment in infrastructure has lagged behind population growth, and some outstanding coastal areas that should forever have remained as wilderness have disappeared under acres of ugly subdivisions.

Raewyn Peart summed it up well In an article written in The Sunday Star Times: "The foreshore and seabed debate has highlighted the close attachment that New Zealanders have with the coast. The ability to access and enjoy our fantastic coastline and marine area is seen as a national birthright. But we have failed to put in place an effective mechanism to ensure that this strong public interest is reflected in day-to-day management decisions." Shifting Sands. Raewyn Peart, Sunday Star Times,16/08/09.

With the announcement in 2010 of a National Coastal Policy Statement, there has at least been some recognition of the need to introduce over-arching guidance around issues of coastal development and protection. Of particular note to recreational users of the coast is the recognition and protection afforded to a list of 20 well known surf spots around the country.

Policy 16, gazetted on 3 December 2010, which states: "The Surf breaks listed in schedule 1, which are of national significance for surfing, shall be protected from inappropriate use and development, by: (a) ensuring the activities in the coastal marine area do not adversely affect the surf breaks, and (b) avoiding

adverse effects of other activities on access to, and use and enjoyment of the surf breaks".

"Schedule 1" lists the following surf breaks: Ahipara (Peaks, Supertubes, Mukies 1, Mukies 2); Raglan (Manu Bay, Whale Bay, Indicators); Stent Rd (Stent Rd, Backdoor Stent, Farmhouse Stent); Whangamata (The Bar); Gisborne (Makarori/Centres, Wainui/Stock Route, Wainui/Pines, Wainui/Whales; Tuamotu Island); Maungamaunu (Meatworks), Otago (The Spit, Karitane, Murdering Bay, Papatowai).

While all this sounds like good news, it is yet to be tested in law. Already gross infractions against it are being carried out by Port Otago in dredging of the harbour and depositing of the resulting spoil, which is interfering with the quality of Aramoana Spit, one of the listed breaks.

Recognition of the status of surfbreaks as cultural, recreational and economic assets has largely been driven by the efforts of The Surfbreak Protection Society, a small organisation led by committed Kiwi surfers. They need your ongoing support to continue their good work, as do the other organisations working in this field.

Surfbreak Protection Society www.surfbreak.org.nz and Lost Waves www.lostwaves.com

One man's meat is another man's murder, and obviously a piece of cure-all national legislation covering all aspects of coastal development would be a near impossible task, but positive developments like the Coastal Policy Statement, which is in effect a set of guidelines available to all councils, is a good starting point, and would have in no small part been a result of efforts by Gary Taylor, Raewyn Peart and the team at Environmental Defence Society www.eds.org.nz

Coastal Litter

Due to our distance from large population centres in the northern hemisphere, we suffer less from the problems of flotsam and jetsam than than those experienced in many other regions of the Pacific. But we still do find trash on our beaches, deposited from a variety of sources. Stormwater drains near urban areas are primary culprits, and both of Auckland's harbours suffer quite badly after rain, with large amounts of plastic objects washing off city streets to end up on beaches, or drifting out into the Hauraki Gulf, where it typically ends up on the south-western shores of the islands. Other cities and towns near the coast suffer similar isues on a smaller scale. Additional sources of beach debris are fishing boats and other commercial marine trafffic, and to a lesser degree, lazy beach goers leaving waste after a day at the coast. All of these problems are preventable.

Many beaches have volunteer clean-up groups, who spend long hours picking up other peoples rubbish. Their activities are often unrecognised by the wider population, but they do have a significant effect. There are several charitable groups who organise large-scale beach clean-ups, like Keep New Zealand Beautiful, The Sir Peter Blake Trust and Sustainable Coastlines.

Since early 2008, Sustainable Coastlines has motivated over 12,500 volunteers to remove more than 670,000 litres (95+ tonnes) of rubbish from our coastlines. They have also educated over 14,800 school students in person across the country in efforts to reduce the amount of rubbish that makes it to the coast in the first place.

After each clean-up event they collect detailed rubbish audit data, often with assistance from Department of Correction's community workers. Results are provided to schools, media and their supporters and make for staggering reading. For example, with 1,200 people in one day they removed 201,003 individual pieces of rubbish from the uninhabited Rangitoto Island, including 23,260 plastic bags, 3,531 drinking straws and over 8 cubic metres of plastic bottles.

In December 2010 they spearheaded 'Love your Coast', which initiated a series of massive clean-up events around New Zealand. This involved over 5,500 people working hands-on, and established www.loveyourcoast.org This is a free event planning tool and social network that helps communities to tackle the issue themselves. Since the launch, dozens of clean-up events have been independently created and numerous schools have adopted what they learned, building it into their ongoing curriculum.

You can use www.loveyourcoast.org to plan your own clean-up today. Or, to get involved, ask questions or support the projects Sustainable Coastlines has in store, head to www.sustainablecoastlines.org, www.loveyourcoast.org or www.facebook.com/loveyourcoast

Epilogue

This quote from the first edition of the Silver Surfer, from August 1968, written by Jack Kirby/Marvel Comics, seems like it was written specifically for us New Zealanders, and is as poignant now as it ever was then.

"In all the galaxies, in all the endless reaches of space, I have found no planet more blessed than this, no world more lavishly endowed with natural beauty, with gentle climate, with every ingredient to create a virtual living paradise! Possessed of rainfall in great abundance, soil fertile enough to feed a galaxy! And a sun, ever-warm, ever-constant, ever symbolizing new life, new hope. It is though the human race has been divinely favoured over all who live! And yet in their uncontrollable insanity, in their unforgiveable blindness, they seek to destroy this shining gem, this softly spinning jewel, this tiny blessed sphere, which men call earth."

THE FAR NORTH

The Far North is just that. It's as far as you can go without a boat. Geographically, it's generally taken to mean the area north of the Bay of Islands, and encompasses some of our most inviting coastal landscapes including the Karikari Peninsula, the Aupori Peninsula, and The Capes. The sheer magnificence and salty, almost sensual pleasure of being in the Pacific Ocean at its warmest point in NZ, is something you really should experience at least once in your life, though the Tasman is also extremely inviting this far up. Climatically the most friendly area in New Zealand, it is truly sub-tropical, often dry, and also lightly inhabited. The generous dollops of space and peace you'll get "up-north" are a direct payoff for the distance you have to drive to get here, and while not all whims can be catered for, you'll satisfy most with interest. The ocean provides endless opportunities for beach goers, while some of the coastal walks are also unrivalled in New Zealand, and though sadly much of the east coast is privately owned with many closed roads and locked gates, it's still a region you'll relish to visit, and are unlikely to ever leave disappointed.

Travelling After the bustle of the Bay of Islands, time starts slowing down the further north you drive. There are not too many facilities away from the main areas, so it's a good part of the country to be self-contained. www.farnorthtours.co.nz offer just what they say they do. www.topofnz.com is a privately maintained tourist website. www.fndc.govt.nz

Wreck Bay

Surfing Two coasts lying so close together, in the warmest part of the country, that receive waves from every direction is a useful quirk of nature, that always made nice noises in my head. It is great to be able to switch coasts with relative ease as the wind changes. The west coast gets a continual lashing of swell, and loves a north-east wind, except Shippies, which prefers a south or south-west flow. The east coast really only fires properly in cyclones or mid-latitude lows, with offshore winds from the westerly quadrant. With all those options and a bit of driving, you can generally surf every day somewhere up here.

Swimming There's no better region in the country for those who love to swim in clear, still water. There are very few water quality concerns, but remember there are no lifeguards anywhere. The west coast in particular should be treated with caution.

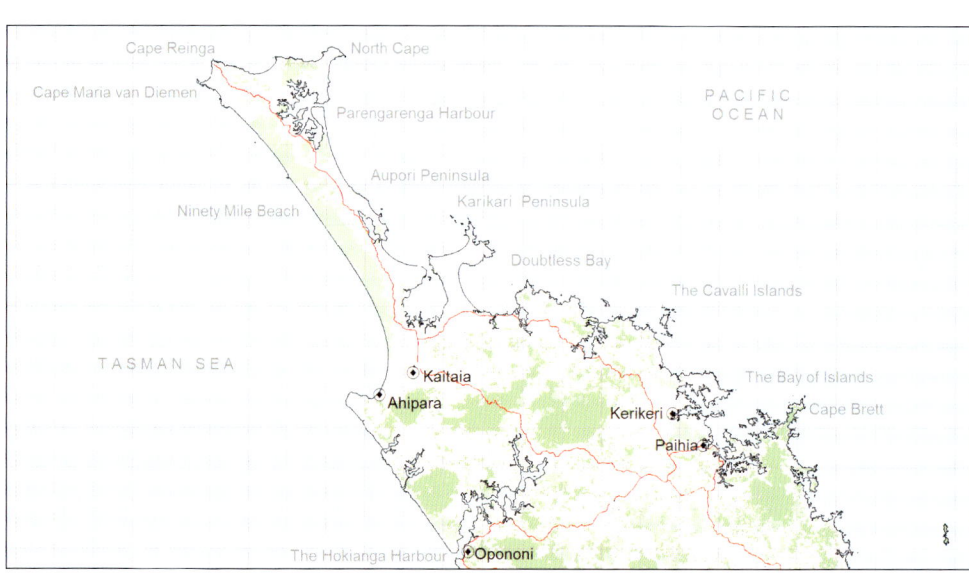

Cape Reinga

Karikari Peninsula

Fishing This is one of New Zealand's premiere destinations, in particular for those chasing big pelagics and billfish, but also snapper, trevalley, kahawai, and multiple shark species. Hundreds of exceptional land based locations exist close to deep water. Several extremely fertile harbours present an array of altogether different fishing scenarios. And then there is the world class beach fishing offered on 90 mile beach. But let's get real; due to its popularity and long season, fish stocks have been hammered over the years up here, and the onslaught shows no sign of abating. It is a natural wonderland deserving utmost protection. Please respect the quotas, and ask yourself if you really need to keep those trophies, or whether a photo, and the memory of an encounter with a huge fish might be the best thing to take away.

Tapotupotu Bay

Cape Reinga to North Cape

The northernmost part of the New Zealand mainland is a long, almost desert-like peninsula, capped by a clutch of rocky headlands, divided by a succession of spectacular and widely differing white sand beaches. Each has a unique exposure and character, and for the beach lover who prefers solitude to company, this may prove to be the singularly most appealing part of the entire country. Devoid of habitation but swathed in sand, the visually surreal stretch of coast reaching from Scott Point to East Cape offers a huge amount to explore, and whether you are a fisherman or a simple beachcomber, if you like your nature 100% pure, you won't be disappointed. This oceanic wonderland is home to vast schools of fish, the beaches littered with semi-tropical shells, and rarely do you find footprints other than your own along its shoreline.

Travelling The road to Cape Reinga is now sealed, though not to the beaches, with no public transport other than bus tours. The last shops are at Waitiki Landing, where there's a small supermarket, bar and internet cafe. They also sell gas, bait and most basics. The area covered by this map is a part of the Te Paki Recreational Reserve and dogs are forbidden.

Surfing You'll get consistent waves at the north coast beaches plus Te Werahi can get absolutely huge and epic, but it's a long walk down there and pretty sharky!

Fishing This area is one of the premier land-based destinations in the country, but the decline in the fishery is more noticeable every year, with more recreational fishermen, better road access and greater publicity. If there is a fishery that needs a catch and release culture to survive, this is one of them.

Swimming Some of the most pristine water and squeaky white sand you will ever see, plus brilliant free-diving around all the ledges, so bring your cozzie.

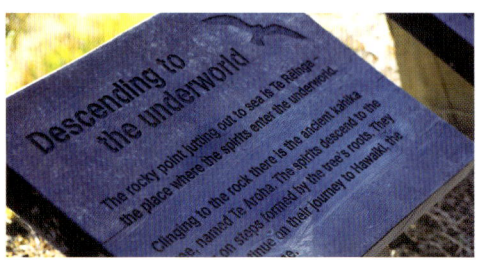

1. Twilight Beach
Twilight Beach is accessible only with a determined two hour walk from the Cape Reinga road, or alternatively a shorter hike from Kahokawa Beach, at the northern tip of 90 mile beach. At its southern end is Scott Point, a legendary and challenging rock fishing spot renowned for big fish of many species. This beach faces west/south-west, so cops almost all the prevailing swell and weather, but in north-east winds it can be absolutely idyllic.

2. Te Werahi Beach
An eerily beautiful ribbon of sand separates Cape Reinga and Cape Maria Van Diemen, that is surely one of the most isolated spots in the country. It takes five hour return to walk from Cape Reinga along Te Werahi to Cape Maria Van Diemen (the most westerly part of the North Island) and back, though only an hour down to the beach from the visitor centre. Very few people have been to this beach, which for some I guess, is a massive part of its wild appeal.

3. Cape Reinga
Maori consider Cape Reinga the departure point for the spirits of their people, as they leave this life

WIND ROSE

SWELL ROSE

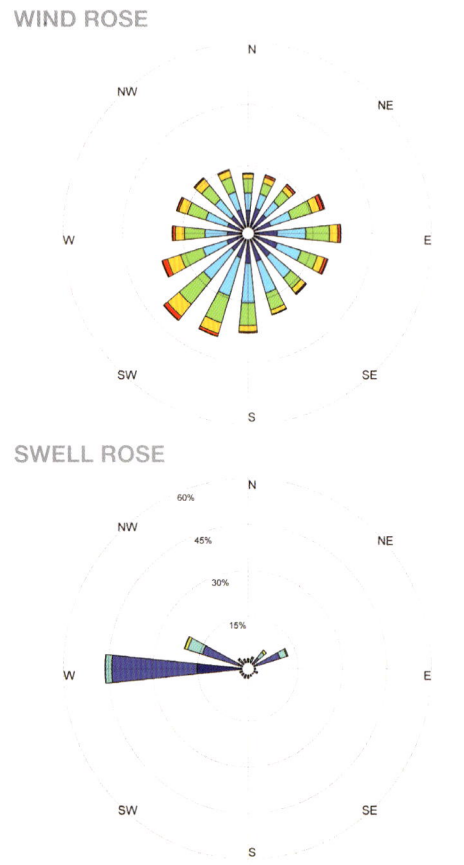

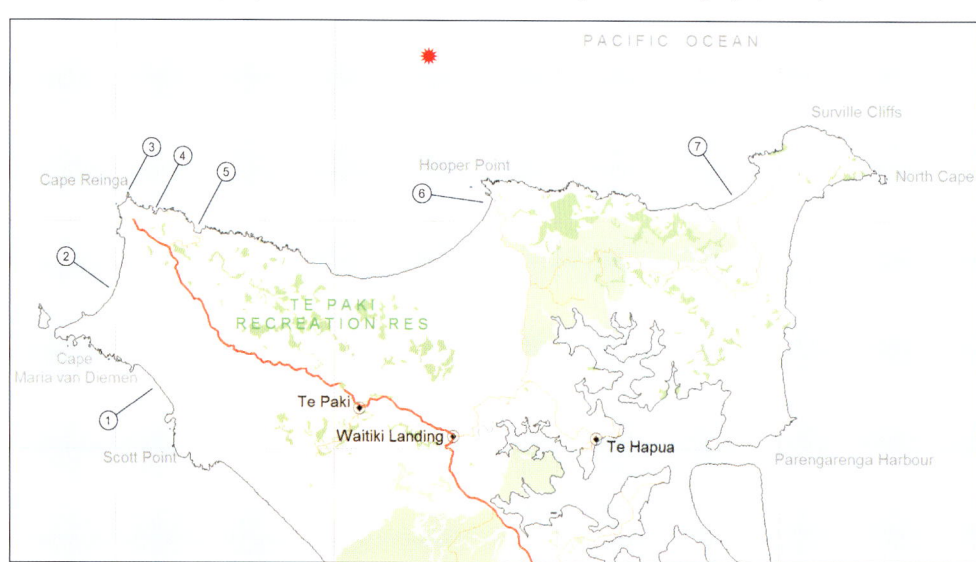

Te Werahi

Cape Reinga

for their spiritual home in Hawaiki. At the tip of The Cape is an 800 year old pohutakawa tree down which the spirits are said to slide. This is one of the most sacred sites in the country to Maori and should be treated reverentially. Stay away from the tree, and understand that eating and drinking near it are also culturally insensitive acts. Cape Reinga is where the Tasman Sea meets the Pacific Ocean, and the race formed by the meeting of the two waters can be seen clearly from the road. The well-appointed visitor centre has loos and fantastic displays, but it is one of the busiest places in the Far North. There's a beach below the cape, but its an ill-advised placed to swim.

4. Sandy Bay
Reached by walking east for an hour from Cape Reinga, or west from Tapotupotu, Sandy Bay is just that; a small sandy beach facing almost due north.

5. Tapotupotu Bay
This pristine and compact beach is flanked by headlands on either extremity, with native bush falling into the sea. It's one of New Zealand's hidden jewels, and a sheltered spot for a swim or a picnic in anything other than a northerly wind. Equally, it is an anglers paradise, home to many large species of fish with convenient rock shelfs at either end. It fishes best in a west or south-west breeze, when it is well sheltered by the cliffs above the rocks on the western edge of the bay. Some big fish have been landed from around this bay, and large pods of orca and dolphins are commonly visible from the beach. The surf can also be good, with consistent wrap-around swell from the west coast, and predominantly offshore breezes. There is often a good peak in the south-west corner of the bay. The only amenities are the DOC campsite with toilets and cold showers.

6. Kapowairua/Spirits Bay
As its name suggests, a trip to Spirits Bay is often a lot more than a standard trip to the beach. Something about this evocative 12 km sweep of squeaky white sand gets deep below the skin of even the most seasoned beach veteran. Known as a Mecca for New Zealand land-based fishermen looking to land that big kingie, it can get pretty crowded at Bucks Ledge or Rod Holders, the two main fishing spots out on the point to the east. There are a number of other spots including the island just off the beach, and the best time to fish here is in easterly winds, when the point is sheltered. It is possible to launch small boats in the river, and hump them over the final hundred metre stretch of sand, but they need to be light tinnies or inflatables. Kayaks are also a useful tool here, allowing access to other structures and less fished ledges in the area. The beach itself also fishes well in morning and evening, with the odd big snapper and plenty of kahawai landed. Waves are hard to pick. The beach can be good; or a close out from hell, with wrap around west swell getting in, and direct exposure to north and north-east swell. Offshore is anything with south in it. It's home to another legendary DOC campsite with water, cold showers and toilets, which is busy at the main times, and quiet the rest of the year. Sand flies and mosquitoes can be evil here, so be warned and come prepared.

7. Tom Bowling Bay
Apparently named after a local from Te Hapua, called Tame Porena, it is another of those spots that keen adventurers love to say they have been to, though few have, as you need to know someone who knows someone to get through the gates. Either that, or go by boat from either Spirits Bay or Parengarenga Harbour. But there it is; empty, untouched, waiting!

Tapotupotu Bay

Spirits Bay

90 Mile Beach and Ahipara

The west coast of the Aupori Peninsula is a beach-goers dream; a vast sandy domain with almost no signs of human habitation down its entire length, backed by pine forests and high sand dunes, and battered by the Tasman's relentless swell. Despite being called Ninety Mile Beach, it actually only extends for 90 kilometres, from Scott's Point to Ahipara, with just The Bluff to interrupt its length. It is famous for its fishing competitions, for the bus tours that run up and down its length on their way to The Cape, and for its empty, imperious feel. There are only a few access points (listed below), despite the existence of paper roads on the map, which are generally private forestry tracks and are locked most of the time. Shipwreck Bay marks its southern extent, with a little goldmine of waves and sheltered aspect that has given rise to the only substantial settlement on the beach.

Travelling Dargaville is nearby and supplies all basic needs including a good supermarket, auto repairs and a few cafes even, but dont expect much nightlife. **Harrisons** are the main bus company offering tours to the cape www.harrisonscapereingatours.co.nz (09)408 1033, I-Site Kaitaia (09)408 0879 kaitaia@isite.org. www.topofnz.co.nz

Surfing "Shippies" is one of the best winter surf spots in the country, offering a range of waves and clean conditions in the hugest of south-west storms. 90 mile beach can also get good in north-east winds and smaller summer swells, though is rarely surfed. The further north up the beach you go, the bigger the swell gets. **Ahipara Surf School** (09)409 4189 www.ahiparasurfschool.com. Kitesurfing lessons and accomodation 021 02417794 www.90milekite.com

Fishing 90 Mile is New Zealand's most celebrated fishing beach, with thick tuatua beds attracting some monster snapper into the channels and guts. As a consequence, it is also home to the country's richest surfcasting competition, www.snapperbonanza.co.nz. Demonstrator **Far North Charters** (09)409 8900. **Karizma Charters/Robbie Matthews** (09)409 4826 offer all types of fishing www.karizmacharters.co.nz

Swimming All the spots on 90 Mile beach can get pretty wild and woolley. If it's a safe dip you're after, Shipwreck Bay is usually the calmest spot, but there are no lifeguards here either, so exercise caution.

Driving the beach While it's famous as a beach that can be driven along its entire length, this is a popular pursuit I don't endorse for many reasons, including the damage it does to the shellfish beds and the intertidal zone. Practically speaking, it's not as straightforward a proposition as it seems either, and many vehicles get caught by the incoming tide and swallowed by the sand. There is a road running parallel to the beach, and I suggest you use it, but if you wish to chance it, a power-hose at The Kauri Kingdom is the place to wash your car afterwards.

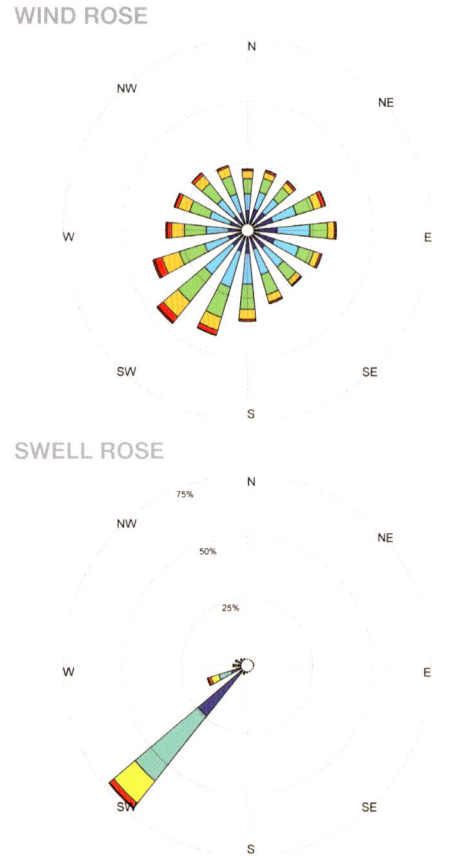

WIND ROSE

SWELL ROSE

90 Mile Beach

The Bluff

1. Scott Point
The northern extent of the beach is marked by Scott Point, a rocky bluff three or four kilometres north of Te Paki stream, that's a legendary fishing spot, attracting large snapper and trevalley, plus a host of other desirable species. It's pounded by swell, so can be dangerous as hell, but equally this makes it a great spot to look for waves when the beach is small and the wind is blowing from the north-east. Access is by driving along the beach, with no amenities.

2. Te Paki Stream
The northernmost vehicle access point onto 90 Mile beach is reached by driving down the Te Paki stream, located a few miles from Waitiki Landing. Here's where you'll find some of the biggest dunes in the country, which are now home to a dubious but popular recreational pursuit called sand-boarding. The road turns into a stream-bed for the last few km's, which is fairly firmly packed, and believe it or not, can get pretty busy. Stay in low gear and don't stop on it, is the official advice. **Ahikaa Adventures** (Sand boarding and kayak fishing) (09)409 8845.

3. The Bluff
This geological oddity is the only break to the sandy continuum of the beach and as you would expect, attracts both fish and waves. To get there take Te Ahu Rd off the highway. Follow your nose till you see a gate by number 321 with a sign saying "Private Road" and "gold coin koha for entry," with a tin nailed to the fence. Drive west and there are a couple of roundabouts. Go slowly through them, due to the logging trucks in the area. Once at the beach, you'll find a small reserve area for camping, with a long drop toilet. You're unlikely to get on to the beach or the campsite here without a 4wd, but can park adjacent to the sand and walk over the low dunes. It is an amazing fishing platform that has accounted for many large specimens over the years, and can be a busy place when the weather is good. Desirable fishing conditions are similar for those sought by surfers i.e. smaller swells and north-east winds, which make it an excellent place to find uncrowded waves, with good beach peaks either side of the rocks.

4. Hukatere/Whalers Rd
A gravel road leads out to the coast just south of Houhora, and it ends in a sandy track through the dunes. **Hukatere Lodge** 021 884145.

5. Waipapakauri
A fairly motley collection of a few dozen baches tucked away behind the dunes, constitute the only settlement near the beach north of Ahipara. You'll find a campsite and a grass reserve with a public toilet and a few baches for rent, but no shops or other facilities. It is a popular vehicle access point onto the beach, close to the main drag, so don't be surprised to find the odd big bus steaming past you. This is also usually the start point for the 90 mile beach fishing competition held in March. **Ninety Mile Beach Holiday Park** 0800 367 719 www.ninetymilebeach.co.nz **Fish Far North** offer homestays and beach fishing (09)406 7772 www.fishfarnorth.co.nz

6. Ahipara

An eclectic seaside town that's steeped in Maori history, is located 15 km from Kaitaia and offers a range of activities including sheltered swimming, access to the nearby waves and fishing spots further west, plus a good shop and campsite. The town has grown in leaps and bounds over the last decade, with a wide range of accommodation options springing up, designer homes built, and a marked increase in tourist numbers. This is the southern end of 90 Mile Beach, with a few scattered bits of reef just north of Shipwreck Bay being the last rocks you will encounter before the Bluff. **Ahipara Motor Camp** 0800 888 988 www.ahiparaholidaypark.co.nz **Ahipara Adventures** offer quad bike hire, long boards, blo-carts, kayaks, sandboards etc. 0508 ahipara or (09)409 2055 www.ahiparaadventure.co.nz. **Ahipara Horse Treks** (09)409 4122 www.truenz.co.nz/horsetrekking. **Coastal Cabins Budget Accommodation** (byo linen) (09)409 4839. **Foreshore Lodge** Studio and 2brm unit (09)409 4860. **Bellovista Accommodation on the Beach** (09)409 4534 www.bellovista.com. **Luxury beach side accomodation** (09)409 4007 www.beachfront.net.nz. **Endless Summer Lodge Beachfront Backpackers** (09)409 4181 www.endlesssummer.co.nz

7. Shipwreck Bay/Te Kohanga

"Shippies" as it is affectionately known by the surf community, is a small sheltered bay over the hill from Ahipara and signals the start of an extensive series of point breaks that wrap around the huge headland that extends many kilometres to the west. Known as Te Kohanga (the Nest) by local Iwi, it is a special place with a rich history that offers ample protection from big winter swells, and is a popular surfing, fishing and boat-launch spot as a result. The Pakeha name comes from the wreck of the HMS Favourite that foundered here in 1870, remnants of which can be still seen protruding from the sand today. Surf-wise, Shipwreck Bay is the first spot you see. It's a sand bottom point, and due to its north-easterly orientation, it receives the most shelter from south and west winds. Consequently it is always the smallest, but can get really good, and breaks at all tides depending on swell size. There are a number of other surfable points heading west of Wreck Bay. The most sought after spots are all around the first point, but you can only access them below half tide as the sea comes right up to the base of the cliffs in sections. It is possible to get some of the way around at low tide with a 2wd car, but many sections on the beach are impassable and the locals get pretty bored dragging people out of the sand. "Peaks" is the first, offering some of the

Ahipara

longest rides in New Zealand, with waves breaking through to the main beach when the swell is good. Keep going and you come to "Mukies 1", "Mukies 2", "Supertubes" and "Pines". Further west of the stream you'll come to "Blue House". All can be epic on their day, mostly from low to mid-tide, (though Blue House can get good at high). Way out on the end of the point, past the seaweed gatherers huts, you'll find "The Box". It is a right reef that spits and growls in small swells and east winds, though rarely surfed. While the main points close to Wreck Bay can get busy in primetime, the takeoff spots are numerous and the length of rides and strong sweep in a proper swell, especially on outgoing tides, tend to have a thinning effect on crowds. It is usually a happy place to surf if you dont go looking for stress. The fishing off the rocks is good at many spots around the coast, though there is a rahui on shellfish collection out on the tip, of Tauroa (Point, with signs clearly indicating its extent. The campsite on the beach front at Wreck Bay is pretty basic and operated by local Iwi. It's open from November till late April, but there are no other facilities, so even if you want to use the loo, you have to head back to Ahipara, where there are public amenities on the foreshore. **Te Angaanga ATV Club** also offer rudimentary camp and van sites on the foreshore year round 021 158 082.

Wreck Bay

Sihppies

The Hokianga

Hokianga is an abbreviation of Hokianga nui a Kupe, which translates as "The returning place of Kupe", and was reputedly his base during his time in Aoteaoroa, as well as the spot where he departed from on his return voyage to Hawaiki. It remains the last frontier in Northland; a wild and raggedy region stretching from The Whangape Harbour down to Mangonui Bluff. There are very few roads out to the coast, but around these iconic waterways lies a wealth of Tasman treasure that's locked up for those with a bit of adventurous blood running through their veins to discover. Reefs and points stud miles and miles of empty golden sand, that's regularly pounded by Tasman swells. With an offshore wind blowing, it can offer a beach experience that's unrivalled, ranging from Kawerua's house size waves to Omapere's gently lapping shoreline, with every conceivable stop in-between. If you add an abundance of sea life, in a region backed by some of New Zealand's most spectacular native forests, you'll find yourself agreeing with the locals, who so proudly proclaim that the Hokianga has got it all.

Travelling With vehicle access to the open coast at only two points, it's not the easiest area to enjoy, but ideal for those who like to walk. Accommodation and public amenities are a mixed bag, centred around Omapere/Opononi. The Hokianga I-Site is at Opononi (09)405 8869 www.hokiangatourism.org Footprints Waipoua offer night tours of the Waipoua forest www.footprintswaipoua.co.nz 0800 687 836

Surfing Despite the extensive coastline, there are only a few surf spots and none of interest to beginners, with access issues and a really challenging nature, plus nobody around to help if you get in trouble.

Fishing Firstly there's some excellent fishing in the harbours, with wharves to aid casual land-based anglers. If you can get out on a boat into the Tasman, you'll find it is one of the country's most exciting and fertile fisheries, with big snapper all year and excellent gamefishing in late summer. Extreme Measures Fish and Dive Charters (09)439 7612 operate big game charters and west coast diving out of Omapere www.extrememeasures.co.nz

Swimming Omapere and Opononi offer calm inner-harbour bathing options, and Mitimiti has a large and beautiful lagoon, but other than that, it's the wild Tasman Sea, with no lifeguards.

1. Herekino Harbour
Herekino was named on some charts as "False Hokianga" due to the similarity of the entrances, as

WIND ROSE

SWELL ROSE

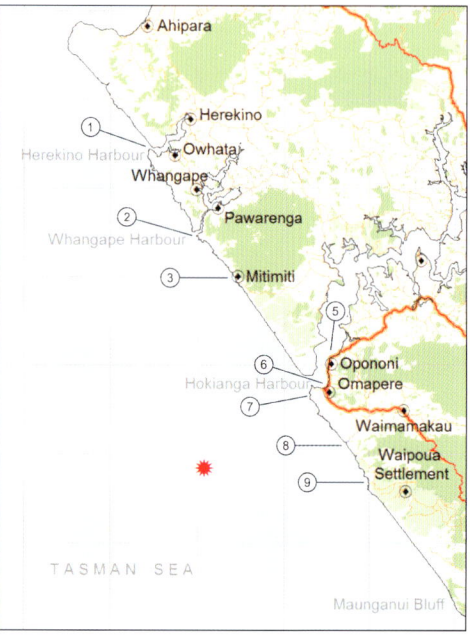

Whangape Harbour

Mitimiti

the northern heads used to be an extensive sand dune until they planted pine trees. It first made European history with the wreck of the brig HMS Osprey in 1846. Her captain mistook the Herekino Heads with the entrance to the Hokianga, due to misty weather and the similarity of the two features, and she was driven ashore on the shallow sand bank just north of the headland. No lives were lost, but wreckage is still visible today. The harbour features significant mangrove forests in the upper reaches, with access to the coast limited to a walking track from the end of Owhata Rd, where there's a marae and a few private homes. There's no boat launching potential, nor are there any facilities here. Both Herekino and Whangape are almost time forgotten, flanked by huge hills and lightly populated, with little to offer travellers who arent searching for pigs, fish, or an experience of the NZ wild frontier, because this is it. **Tui Inn Adventure Accommodation** (09)409 3883 is located midway between the harbours, with basic camp facilities on a rustic old farm property.

2. Whangape Harbour

This historic waterway is formed by the confluence of the Awaroa and Rotokakahi Rivers, which course out to the sea through a remarkably long, narrow, fjord-like inlet. According to Maori traditions, the waka Mamari, captained by Ruanui, settled the Whangape after being driven from the Hokianga. They established a large fighting pa at Pawarenga, but were attacked by a war party from the south, which greatly outnumbered them. They (Ngati Ruanui) stacked manuka around the pallisades and set it on fire, before escaping across the harbour, hidden by the smoke. They eventually settled much of the far north, becoming known as Te Aupouri ('au' means current and 'pouri' smoke) after this event. Whangape settlement became an important timber port in the late 19th and early 20th century. Whangape Rd leads to the north side of the harbour, and ends in private land just before the entrance, and whilst it isn't a harbour that's conducive to pleasant swimming, there are several easy access points for launching small boats and kayaks beside the roadside here, for those who want to enjoy what must be at times sensational fishing. The southern access is from Pawarenga Rd which ends at Pawarenga; a populated Maori settlement, but again one with no facilities. The track out to the sea, known as "the Golden Stairs" leads from here.

3. Mitimiti

One of the farthest-flung, most "out-there" beach communities in the North Island, is a collection of raggedy old shacks, mixed in with a few normal baches and homes, and a stunning Marae and Church. Notable for being the place where Ralph Hotere grew up, it features two long stretches of sparkling white sand, separated by a lagoon and a series of reefy outcrops, and backed by steep, native bush-clad hills. It's an ancient and extremely powerful place, staring straight at the Tasmans waves, that can be hallucinogenically beautiful on a fine day, and absolutely desolate in bad weather. To get there, it's a twenty five minute drive down a gravel road after the seal ends, and this fact manages to deter most casual beach-goers, which isn't a bad thing really. There are a range of surfable waves in the bay plus miles of surrounding beach peaks, and for fisherman there's the usual fare to be gained off and around west coast rocks and beaches. The only public amenities are a long drop toilet at the south end and a couple of private accommodation options. **Mitimiti Beach House** (09)409 5347 is a self contained three bedroom bach www.beach-house.co.nz
Andrew from **Sandtrails** (09)409 5035 also offers b&b accommodation. Further up the beach there's an odd **backpackers** 021 150 2912 run by Rob Penney, who also offers guided horse-treks up to the Whangape Harbour entrance and The Golden Stairs Ngatuna@yahoo.co.nz

4. Rawene

Not a beach, but a pivotal thoroughfare on the west coast highway, Rawene is a harbourside town of some historical repute, with several cute little shops and cafes. **The Rawene Car Ferry** (09)405 2602.

Hokianga North Head

Omapere

5. Opononi

Opononi rocketed to international fame in 1955/56, when it was adopted by a dolphin called "Opo", who entertained the crowds and obligingly let children take rides on her back. These days it's quite a busy little tourist thoroughfare in summer months, with a couple of sandy inner harbour beaches and a bustling wharf and boatramp, with a store, pub, café and tourist info centre, plus campsite and numerous private accommodation options. The wharf is a popular place for the local kids to do "bombs" off, and the adjacent fish and chip shop is legendary. Swimming can be okay here, but beware the dropping tide near the wharf, as the water can rip along at a fair rate of knots, presenting challenges for less confident swimmers. You will undoubtedly sit there and stare at the massive dunes across the harbour, and for those interested in exploring them, a company based at Mitimiti offers a unique dune buggy experience **Sandtrails** (09)409 5035 www.sandtrailshokianga.co.nz. **The Hokianga Express** (09)405 8872 runs from the wharf, offering transport across the harbour and a fishing charter service.
Crossings Harbour Cruises 0800 687 836 offers guided tours of the Hokianga www.crossings.co.nz
Opononi Holiday Park (09)405 8791.
Globetrekkers Lodge (09)405 8183 is the local backpackers www.globtrekkerslodge.com

6. Omapere

Twinned with Opononi, it is difficult for the uninitiated to differentiate between them, the one merging seamlessly with the other. Omapere is the closest beach to the harbour entrance, consisting of a kilometre or so of steeply shelved sand that offers beautiful swimming above mid tide, but which can get fairly rocky about the low tide mark. There's an old wharf near its western fringe (located down Old Wharf Road) that's the easiest place in the area to throw a line into the water, and has seen a few good kahawai and even the odd kingie in its day. Adjacent to it are good public facilities including the children's play area at Freese Park, and one of the most popular access points onto the beach. The others are further east. The rest of the beach features private homes adjoining the sand. **Hokianga Haven B&B** (09)405 8285 offers self-catering waterfront accommodation www.hokiangahaven.co.nz.
The Copthorne 0800 808 228 offers a bit of luxury on the waterfront www.milleniumhotels.co.nz. **www.omapere.co.nz** for general information.

7. South Head/Arai Te Uru

This is one of the most spectacular and well visited spots in The Far North, offering an unobstructed view over to the sand dunes that mark the northern entrance of the Hokianga. It is a popular tourist spot

and rates as one of my favourite places in the country to eat fish and chips, assuming you can wait that long. It's a ten minute walk out to the coast from the carpark, and when you get there you can accesss two beaches. Martins Bay faces north into the harbour, with a well signed track leading down to it. It's a bit rocky at low tide, but sheltered from south winds, and not a bad place to fish. Heading west, there is a beach at the entrance that's punctuated by reefs at high tide but gorgeous at lower tides. With nobody around to help you, beware tidal currents. The coastal walkway to Waimamaku leaves from here.

Ti-Kouka B&B (09)405 8622 offers B&B and self-catering accommodation.

8. Waimamauku

One of only two ocean beaches that you can actually drive to in the entire region, Waimamaku sits at the mouth of a broad river, 4km from the main road, with vehicle access to the northern side. It is a wild and exposed section of coast that receives a fair lashing of swell, but its steep profile means it's a surf spot that takes a fair amount of size to work. Offshore winds are from the north-east, with wave quality dependent on the sandbanks, which change constantly. From here you can walk an hour or so south to the Waipoua reefs and Kawerua, though you have to cross the river which is easiest at low tides. Access is from the carpark located a few hundred metres from the beach, with a track running down to the water. Sadly there have been many reported incidences of vehicle theft from here, so quiet times of the year leave one feeling distinctly uneasy, especially as you can't see the carpark once you get to the beach. Leave nothing to steal, and make sure you're insured. The headlands both north and south can produce good kaimoana, but there are no facilities of any kind here.

9. Kawerua

This historic location used to house 600 residents, who survived off the kauri gum extracted from the hills around here. Nowadays, only the dilapidated shell of the old hotel remains. The dense native forest has been supplanted by pine trees, and the private logging roads in are locked from the Waipoua settlement. The coastline features a collection of finger reefs protruding into the Tasman, which are renown for holding waves of monster proportions. Access is generally by jet ski though a few hardy souls walk down from Waimamaku. There's also good land-based fishing and diving when the swell is small, if you can deal with the access issues. There's a long drop toilet behind the beach near the old hotel.

West coast reef break

The Aupori Peninsula East Coast

Stretching from North Cape to The Rangaunu Harbour, this exceptional piece of coastline offers a staggering variety and richness of marine geography, habitats and life-forms. The beaches are some of the whitest anywhere in the world, demonstrated most evidently at Parengarenga, whose shimmering silica dunes seem almost unreal in the blue light of summer. The Pacific Ocean is a placid body of water, compared to its rowdy neighbour across the peninsula, and still well endowed with a vast array of marine life; yet despite the abundance of natural riches, the region remains remarkably unspoilt by coastal development. Rolling farm and conservation land backs onto most of the beaches, each with a distinct character. You can only gain access to a few points by car, and the few holiday homes in the area are at Hendersons Bay and Pukenui/Hohoura. Those with a passion for empty spaces will look at all this in a celebratory light. Those of a more social disposition will probably move on.

Travelling Accommodation options revolve around Pukenui (if you're looking for a solid roof over your head), or the campsites at Hohoura and Rarawa. The roads are good and supplies can be bought at a few places, though Pukenui is the best equipped.
Far North Horse Trekking (09)409 8232

Surfing There are some classic spots in a north-east swell that are well known, like Henderson Bay, and Hohoura Heads, and there are a few more to find, if you're feeling adventurous.

Fishing All of your options are pretty incredible up here. The harbours are prolific, hosting large fish of many species. Land-based choices are equally good, especially if you like doing a bit of walking. Pukenui or Paua are the main boat launching spots, giving access through two extremely beautiful waterways to the open sea beyond, where you'll find some of the country's finest game-fishing grounds. Hohoura Big Game and Sports Fishing Club (09)409 7755
Demelza Charters (09)409 8292.
Rob Parker Guaranteed Fishing 021 056 2582.
NZ Fishing Charters 027 453 5258
www.fishingnz.net.nz

Swimming All the main beaches offer exceptional swimming conditions, with beautiful white sand and crystal clear water, but again, there are no lifeguards anywhere.

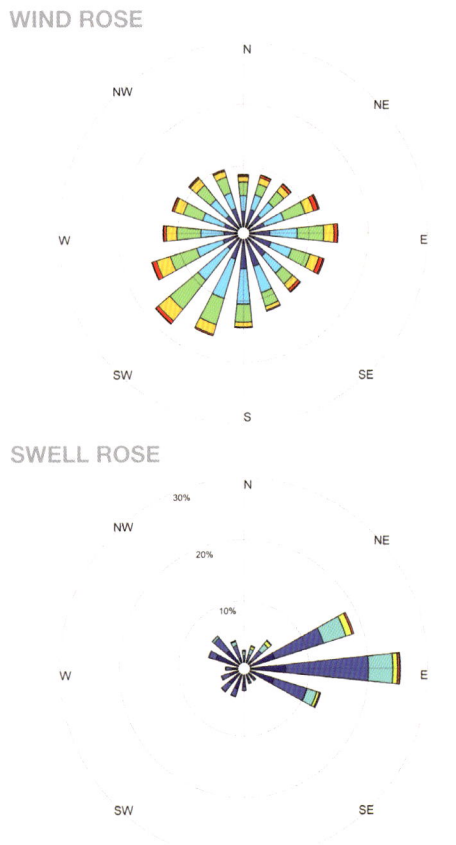

Pukenui wharf

Henderson Bay

1. Parengarenga Harbour
It gained notoriety in recent times as the location where the Rainbow Warrior terrorists smuggled their explosives into New Zealand by boat, but geographically is most famous for its massive deposits of some of the world's purest silica sand, heaped in huge dunes that protect this expansive and fertile harbour. It is home to all sorts of hard fighting fish, which despite its shallow bottom, has seen some magnificent kingfish and trevalley hauled onto it over the years. Free public access is limited to the wharf at Te Hapua. The other option is the ramp and campsite located at Paua, but it's on private land. Obtain permission, make payment, and receive a key from the whanau at the shop by the Paua Rd turnoff.

2. Rarawa Beach
Rarawa is so clean it squeaks, but aside from the sound of your feet scrunching in the sand, the only other noises you're likely to hear are the birds and the ocean. It is one of Northland's most tranquil and beautiful spots, with an access road that splits in two a kilometre or so before the beach. The right fork leads to the **DOC Campsite** at Paxton Point, which offers walking access to the south end of the beach. The left fork ends in a carpark of sorts in the dunes nearer the middle of the beach, with no amenities of any kind. There are a few houses on the hills a fair way behind the bay; other than those, it's empty. Waves here can be good, though it doesn't have the steep shelf like Hendersons Bay, and picks up slightly less swell. The campsite is a typical DOC set-up, with toilets, cold showers and no on-site manager.

3. Henderson Bay
You'll need to drive 6 km off the main road to find one of the best beach breaks on the east coast; with its reef studded bottom and steep shelf producing fun, hollow waves whenever there's a swell. "Hendo's" as it's usually known, is also an excellent fishing beach, with a wide variety of options for land-based anglers that usually deliver a feed, including rock fishing at either extremity and good holes and rips along the beach to throw a bait into. It is one of the few beaches up this way with houses anywhere near it, though they're strung out along the last kilometre of the gravel access road, and when you're on the beach, you are usually there alone. The limited accommodation options and lack of public amenities are somewhat of a deterrent. **North Wind Lodge Backpackers** (09)409 8515. **Sea Toys** offer quad-bike rental, plus surfboard and body board hire, plus they have an apartment for rent near the beach (09)409 7742 www.hendersonbayrentals.com

4. Pukenui
The settlement of Pukenui is what most people consider to be Houhoura. It consists of a wharf and shops, with a hundred or so baches and homes, adjacent to the harbour some kilometers from the mouth. It is one of our seminal fishing towns, offering a safe anchorage and the last fuel and amenities for game boats heading up to, or returning from the Three Kings, or fishing the waters around North Cape. It is also a highly respectable land-based spot in its own right and probably the most prolific fishing wharf in the country, with multiple species feeding on the baitfish attracted to the sponges and almost tropical marine life around its piles, not 50 metres from State Highway 1. The shops are well supplied and the café is a fun place to enjoy a proper coffee, a meal and a beer. The pub a little further north, is one of the country's oldest and most colourful, and if you enjoy a beer, it's an experience not to be missed. **Pukenui Lodge Motel and Backpackers** (09)409 8837 www.pukenuilodge.co.nz
Hohoura Holiday Cottage (09)409 8166.

5. Hohoura Heads
The old Subritzky Homestead and Museum used to be a real highlight for visitors to the north, with a wide collection of local artefacts from early settler and whaling days. Sadly it is no longer, though the building remains and an impressive whale oil ("try") pot, and old wagon hint at its history. The carpark here offers access to the foreshore, which is tidal and not ideal for swimming, though an extremely pretty place to picnic. There's a public launch ramp that isn't too bad at high tide, for those with small boats or kayaks, wishing to sample the fantastic fishing near the mouth. In huge east and north-east swells, there's also a sandbar at the entrance of the harbour that is reported to hold significant sized and well shaped waves. **Wagener Holiday Park** (09)409 8564 www.northlandholiday.co.nz

6. East Beach
This perfect gaping crescent of totally empty sand stretches from the mouth of the Hohoura Harbour, all the way to Rangiputa, backed by swampland and a protected zone incorporating East Beach Reserve and the Kaimaumau Scientific Reserve. Access is from Hohoura Heads by foot, or south from Kaimaumau, where the private road turns into a 4wd track. It is a great beach to fish or swim from, and one that must get a pounding in north and east swells, though little information exists regarding the wave quality. One thing is for sure, it is a highly tapu in parts, with many burial grounds behind the dunes, and access from the south is only by kind permission of the local Iwi Ngai Takoto, whose land the road crosses. Respect this fact and their beach, and this will continue, though there have been many issues of late as it becomes more popular. There are no amenities of any kind so pack your trash out and stay off the dunes!

Rarawa

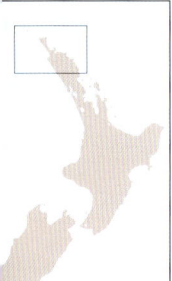

The Karikari Peninsula

The geographical description would refer to its unique, finger-like profile, jutting into the sea and forming a protective flank for the Rangaunu Harbour to the west; fringed with a succession of the whitest beaches and the clearest waters in the country. All this is true, but sadly mans efforts on land have reduced what was surely one of the wonders of the world into a denuded feeling piece of land that is the scene of some of the scariest coastal subdivision in the country. The carnage is ongoing, with the epic Karikari beach campsite recently lost to a foreign developer. As a result of all this, the local Maori are obviously and understandably disaffected, so don't expect a warm welcome from them. The beaches themselves are all fantastic if you can get over the ambience.

Travelling It is a gravel road off the main highway all the way to Matai Bay, which is as far as you can go without entering Maori land. The shop above Tokerau Beach sells gas, bait and food. **The Rusty Anchor** has tourist info/backpackers and tent sites above Tokerau Beach www.rustyanchor.co.nz 0800 787892 www.bachman.co.nz for local bach rentals.

WIND ROSE

SWELL ROSE

Surfing Both Karikari and Puheke beaches get waves in a north-swell, and Tokerau in an easterly, but it is not a well known surf destination. **Water Cowboys Stand-Up Paddle Board** offer lessons and board rental www.watercowboys.co.nz (09)406 7787. **Airzone Kitesurfing School** (09)408 7129 www.kitesurfnz.com

Fishing Fishing is one of the main reasons people are attracted to this region. The beaches are popular kontiki spots, and the deep water just offshore brings a whole other dimension to what can be caught close-in here, with all the obvious species, plus the fact that it is high on the list for potentially snaring a land-based marlin. **Reel Rods** is a local custom fishing rod maker and tackle supplies outlet, with years of local knowledge. Kieron 027 4861 019 www.reelrods.co.nz. **Freespool Charters** (09)406 7735 www.freespoolcharters.co.nz

Swimming Unquestionably some of the most gorgeous places to swim in the country, with pure white sand, warm water and minimal crowds. **Karikari Kayaking** (09)408 7575 offer kayak and wetsuit hire.

1. Rangiputa

A small coastal village just inside the amazingly fishy Rangaunu Harbour features a handful of baches and a basic holiday park. It appeals mainly to fishermen and their families, looking to exploit the calm waters of the harbour, and a laid back atmosphere. It has recently become a popular kiteboarding spot as well, but there are a lot of big bronze whalers in this harbour, so I am not sure what to recommend for those wanting to get in it rather than on it. There have been no fatalities that I am aware of. **White Sands Apartments** (09) 408 7080 www.whitesands.co.nz. **Rangiputa retreat Fish and farm Stay** (09)406 7735 www.rangiputaretreat.co.nz

2. Puheke

Thankfully Puheke has escaped the attention of the developers, and remains in a pristine state, stretching for a couple of kilometres from end to glorious end, with public access at the north. Fantastic beach fishing, squeaky white sand and clear waters make it one of my favourite spots, and there are rumored to be good waves here too, but it has no amenities.

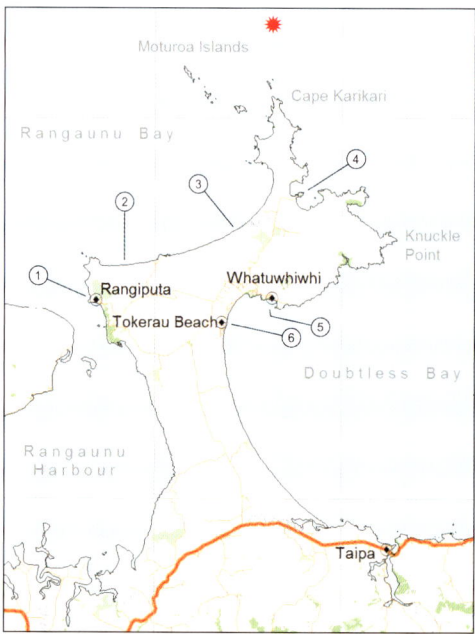

Puheke

Karikari Beach

3. Karikari Beach

A gravel road just past Matai Bay leads down to a small access way and carparking area on the north side of this beautiful, shell-lined stretch of sand. Fishing off the beach and the rocks at either end can be good, and it will also produce waves in a north-east swell. There used to be a fantastic campsite here but it was purchased by a foreign developer, and the surrounding land cut into sections which are currently being sold, despite objections from the local Iwi. Sadly, this is another prime example of how we are being robbed of some of our best beaches, and right-thinking people should see it as an example to learn from in the future. You can also reach the beach on foot from the south, near the base of the fabulous Mt Puheke, where there are some lovely coves that are sure to offer privacy, fish and waves in a swell.

4. Matai Bay

One suspects this would have been a very busy place in pre-European times. For a people who lived off the sea, it would have been an absolute gold mine, with two east-facing, semi-circular bays, divided by a promontory that offers sweeping views both ways over an incredibly fertile and sheltered piece of ocean. Nowadays there is a **DOC campsite** and day-use area to the north that can get very busy over summer months, and a large expanse of Maori land stretching south, with a few homes set up in the dunes. Matai Bay is a popular beach-launch spot for trailer boats, and a fabulous place to enjoy a sheltered swim and a picnic, but there have been quite a few issues surrounding car break-ins here, so be warned.

5. Whatuwhiwhi

A beautiful little bay with some of its character left intact, facing south, and thankfully protected by the headland from Tokerau's garish subdivisions. There aren't a lot of homes here, and the bay is dominated by the campsite, but it's a good spot to find shelter from north and east winds, with some good fishing

Whatuwhiwhi

off the rocks either side.
Whatuwhiwhi Top 10 camping ground (09)408 7022 www.whatuwhiwhitop10.co.nz

6. Tokerau Beach

It would have been an amazing place once, when there were some trees and no people, but now it makes one want to cry for our stupidity and greed. It is nearly 10 miles long curving around to the south-east in a spectacular arc, and thankfully the homes are all clustered at the north end, where you'll find acres of half-empty subdivisions (that are a total blight on this beautiful beach) lining most of the flat land plus the the hills behind it. All that aside, there is still fabulous fishing and swimming on its gloriously sandy shoreline, but the settlement totally lacks any planning sensitivity. Tokerau Beach Rd is the main coastal access from the north and Simon Urlich Drive takes you along the foreshore past the Waiotariri Reserve with its toilets, kids play area, norfolk pines and picnic tables. **Tokerau Beach Campsite** occupies a prime beachfront location (09)408 7055 www.tokeraubeachmc.co.nz. Heading south, Dick Urlich Drive is a short gravel track that ends at a grassy turnaround, offering 4wd or foot access onto the beach. Ramp Rd is home to a small cluster of a dozen or so baches and a fantastic reserve area with toilets, bins and bore water available. There is a "no camping" sign here, yet it seemed like a massive free-camp site, with a collection of motorhomes and buses owned by retirees and fishermen that were in no hurry to go anywhere when I visited.

Tokerau Beach

Doubtless Bay

You'll read this comment a few times, but there's only so many ways to say it: this is a stretch of coast with phenomenal variety. It occupies a privileged position in one of the most spectacular parts of the east coast, facing north into the Pacific, and sheltered from many of the difficult winds that blow over the coast. There are headlands and harbours, big beaches, small beaches, rocks and sand, plus shelter for boats, and all this is of huge appeal. But sadly, much of it has been trampled without regard by waves of development, the desire to exploit it's substantial charms almost erasing them from view. The main road hustles and humps along, often directly behind the beach, with a distinctly Californian feel. Despite the invasion, Mangonui remains timelessly interesting, and HiHi still has an off the beaten-track vibe. Off-season is the best time to visit, but even then, don't expect too much privacy.

Travelling Accommodation options are many and as the road passes most of these spots within view, it's hard to miss much. www.doubtlessbay.co.nz

WIND ROSE

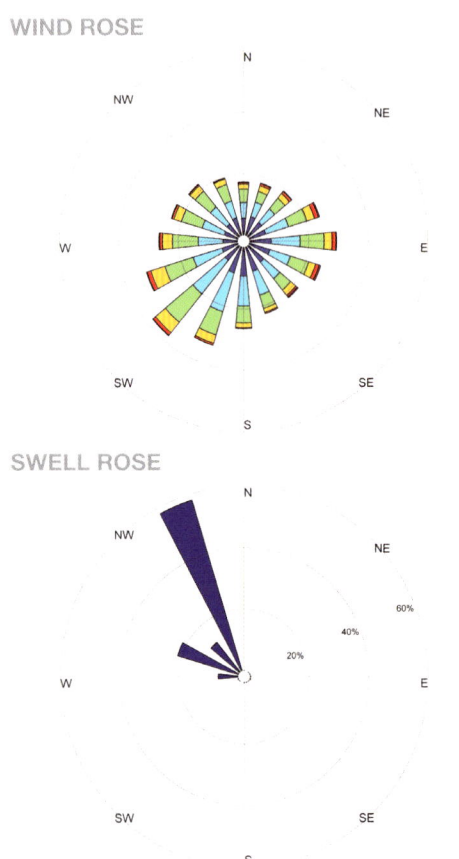

SWELL ROSE

Surfing There are some good waves to be ridden at Taipa in a big northerly swell, and probably a few peaks around Cable Bay also.

Fishing Significant shelter and varied land formations offer good land-based opportunities, with excellent boat fishing also to be had. **Doubtless Bay Sport Fishing Club** (09)406 0229. **Kiwa Kayaks** (09)406 1110. **Castaway Boating** (09)406 1102 offer fish and dive tours or you-drive boating packages www.castawayboating.co.nz. **NZ Fishing Charters** (09)406 7680 www.fishingnz.net.nz

Swimming All these beaches offer exceptional swimming; just avoid the streams. Swim with dolphins 0800 732 432 www.dolphinrendezvous.co.nz

1. Taipa

The beach itself is amazing; 2km of golden sand, with a river mouth and estuary to the east, and a rocky headland to the west. You will find the sailing club and launch ramp behind the estuary entrance, and public loos by the reserve near the centre, plus all the gas and booze you could ever want along the main road. It is historically an important place for Maori, but the proximity of the busy highway and the presence of some hideous architecture dulls the mystique somewhat. Ngati Kahu road to the north-west leads you to a quiet grassy area that's an ideal spot for a picnic, then continues along to meet up with Foreshore Rd and the busier, south-eastern end. The rocks at the west are a great place to throw out a line, as is the river mouth, though the presence of boat traffic from the launch ramp by the yacht club can make this latter choice a bit complicated. The best waves break off the point at the western end in a north or north-east swell, with peaks along its length.

2. Cable Bay

Little Cable Bay is the Chihuahua of the region. Sandwiched between Taipa and Coopers Beach, it is really just a couple of short stretches of peachy coloured sand, wedged between scattered rocks, flanked by rocky outcrops, with only a Four Square and the busy main road for company. Many pass by without stopping as Cable Bay offers not one skerrick of privacy; but the grassy reserves at either end, plus toilets and park benches, make it an okay spot for a picnic, and a convenient spot for a dip. **Driftwood Lodge** 0800150175 www.driftwoodlodge.co.nz **Golden Sand Apartments** (09)406 0475 www.goldensand.co.nz

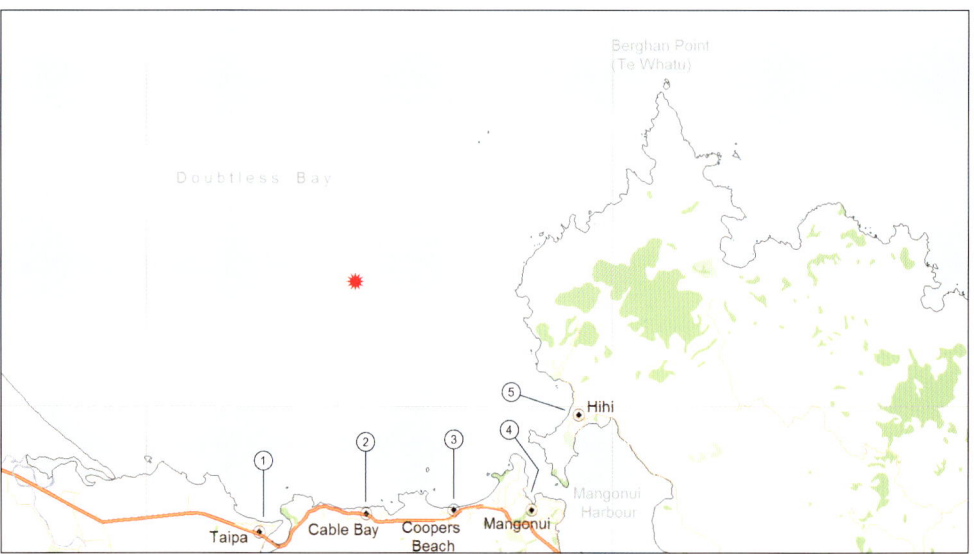

Taipa

3. Coopers Beach

Coopers Beach occupies a significant portion of Doubtless Bay, with homes packed behind the beachfront and extending both sides of the main road that passes along its length. It is the commercial hub of the east coast, offering a wide range of both shops and commercial services of all kinds. The residents who occupy the prime beachfront locations must love it, but for those passing through it has less appeal than many of the other stretches of the Northland coast. It has definitely got the wow factor when you are down on the beach, with huge pohutakawas sprawling onto the sand, and acres of space, but personally I find it annoyingly exclusive and a great place to drive through on the way to somewhere less developed. Still, it's a good spot to launch a kayak and has some excellent fishing in the bay and around the nearby points and islands, plus offers safe swimming. If you're there after a big northerly storm, it's not uncommon to find the beach strewn with scallops. There are three access points. The first is opposite the bowling club, where you find the Taumarumaru Recreational Reserve, which occupies the north-western end of the beach and the headland with its historic Marae sites. It is a bit of a walk from the carpark to the beach, but worth it for the peace and space afforded at this end of the bay. The main public access is visible from the road heading south from the main shops, where there's a large parking space, childrens playground, and toilets beside the stream. The eastern access is the most difficult to find. Follow signs down Kupe Rd to San Marino Lodge, which is right on the beach. There's not a lot of parking here and the road is steep, so it's not ideal in peak times or for campervans. **San Marino Motor Lodge** (09)406 0345 www.sanmarino.co.nz.
Beach Lodge (09)406 0068 www.beachlodge.co.nz.
By The Bay self contained apartments (09)406 1268 www.bythebay.co.nz

4. Mangonui

Mangonui is one of our classic old whaling ports. It features a collection of colonial buildings set in the crook of a beautiful harbour that's now home to an armada of moored pleasure crafts, some lovely baches, a couple of drinking establishments plus one of the best fish and chip shops in NZ; so it's definitely worth a detour. There aren't a lot of places to swim around the town, but no guide to the coast would be complete without a reference to its salty charms. The **Mangonui Hotel** has been described as our most beautiful hotel, with some justification, and is an Historic Places Trust protected building (09)406 0003. **Mangonui Fish Shop** (09)406 0478. **Sanctuary in the Cove** is absolutely idyllic (09)4061707 www.sanctuaryinthecove.co.nz. **Puketiti Lodge** is down the scale but spectacular value (09)406 0639 www.puketitilodge.co.nz. For self contained baches and homes **www.mangonuiholidayhouses.co.nz**

5. Hihi

Just a wee slip of a beach, literally two hundred metres long at low tide. It's flanked by cliffs to the south-west and a rocky headland to the north that eventually leads out to Bergen Point (a renown kingie and snapper spot). Hihi faces almost due west, and as such is a great place to escape strong easterly winds. The campsite is right opposite the beach and totally set-up for fishermen, with a smoke house, gas bbq's and all other amenities. It's an absolutely classic piece of Kiwiana, that can get mad at Christmas, but for much of the rest of the year reverts to its normal sleepy pace. **HiHi Beach Holiday Camp** (09)406 0307 www.hihicamp.co.nz. **Butlers Point Whaling Museum and Historic Home** (09)406 0307.

Mangonui

Hihi

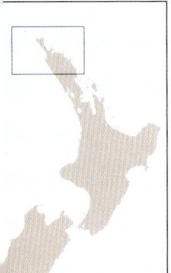

The Cavalli Coast

The coastline between Doubtless Bay and Kerikeri isn't easily categorised, and doesn't fit neatly into a small homogenous group, with extensive variety and a broad geographical range, so I have named it The Cavalli Coast for reasons of ease. It encompasses some of our most striking coastal landscapes, with beaches and bays facing in all directions, and sprinkled with offshore islands, of which the Cavallis are the best known. There have been a series of protracted wrangles about the beaches north of Kerikeri over the years that highlight the confusion that exists in this country concerning basic rights of access. It is particularly problematic in this area as there are few open sea beaches in the first place, and the closure of Elliots Beach, Takaou (now reopened) and Tapuaetahi was a slap in the face for the beach going public. Responsibility in many cases lay with the council for lack of leadership, but private interests drove these events, so somehow it was a failure all round that would be sad if it were allowed to spread as an example across the rest of the country.

Travelling The road from Matauri Bay to Tauranga Bay is called the "Million Dollar View Road", as the vistas over the Cavalli Islands are literally worth gold; though the entire loop road to Whangaroa is spectacular. Waipapa/Kerikeri or Doubtless Bay are the closest places to buy provisions and gas.

WIND ROSE

SWELL ROSE

Surfing Heaps of north-east swell hits this coast, but considering the vast amount of territory, there are only a few surf spots, and access to many of the best ones are either prohibited or restricted in one way or another. Takaou and Elliots are the most exposed, Tapuaetahi holds the most size, and Taupo Bay is the most beautiful. **Isobar Surf School** and lodge at Taupo Bay (09)406 0719 www.isobarsurf.co.nz

Fishing There are some exceptional land-based fishing spots around this section of the coast, including Flat Island off the Mahinepua Peninsula, which is a reknown kingfish location, and a spot where land-based marlin are being targeted. Most of the bays also have productive headlands. **Dive HQ** at Waipapa is a good place to get diving and fishing knowledge and supplies (09)407 9986 www.divehqboi.co.nz

Swimming Not a lifeguard in sight, but acres of sparkling white sand and crystal clear water, with a choice of both sheltered and exposed beaches, make this a pretty desirable place to spend time. www.dolphinrendezvous.co.nz

1. Motukahakaha Bay/Paradise Bay

As you drive down the Taupo Bay Rd, you come to a one way bridge and just after it, an unmarked gravel road heads up to the left. It winds up and around and after a few kilometres offers a glimpse over one of Northlands untouched jewels. As you drive down the hill, the road forks in three, with access to a Maori owned block to the left, and right to what's known by Pakeha as Paradise Bay. It seems a pretty apt name given the delicious variety on offer on this uninhabited, north-facing slice of heaven.

Paradise Bay

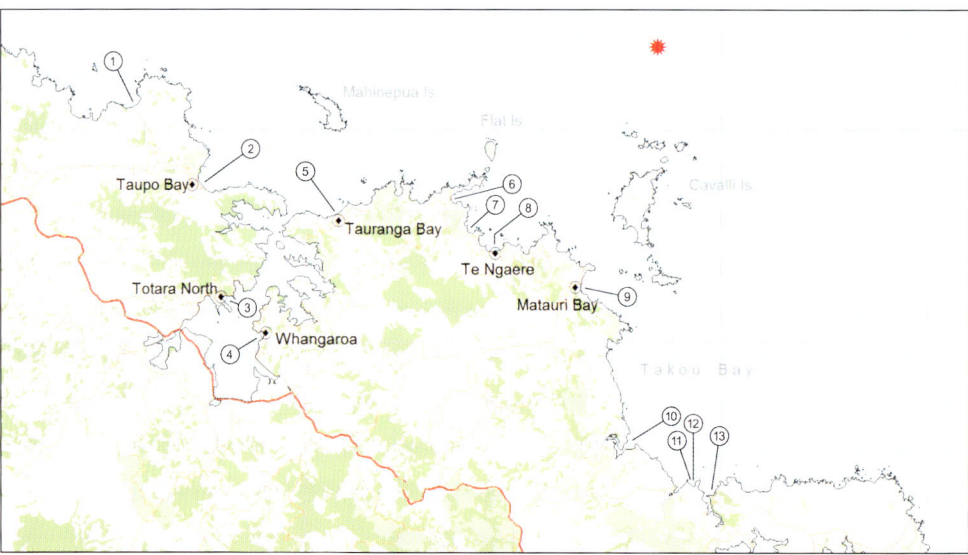

Taupo Bay

There are actually several bays punctuated by fringe reefs, all well-sheltered from east wind and swell by an extensive headland. Mahinepua/Stephenson Island sits just offshore, and no doubt it holds good fish, crays and a few mussels. The sad thing about all this is that it is on private land and you can only access it by asking permission from the local farmer. For the surf community, it's possibly worth the effort in a north swell and a southerly wind.

2. Taupo Bay
God was having a good day when he or she designed Taupo Bay, conjuring up a glittering kilometre of the purest sand, backed by improbable and spectacular cliffs that could have been cut and pasted from the backdrop of a Sergio Leone film. It is 13km off the main drag to get there, and the road twists and winds, but after about 10 kms, you come round a bend, see the cliffs with the sand sparkling at their feet, and can't help but gasp. The beach itself has an intimate, enclosed, almost fjord-like feel, but the spectacular rock faces rising straight out of the sea lend an epic sense of scale. Boats launch off the sand at the north-western end, and the swimming is good all along its length. On its day Taupo Bay can also have some of the best beach waves in the Far North, breaking off both ends, depending on the wind and swell direction. In particular the right point at the south is renown for fast, ledging walls and the odd barrel at higher tides. A south-west wind is offshore, but south or south east winds can also be tolerable, aided by the shelter offered by the cliffs. Walking around either headland at lower tides can be fruitful in your hunt for a fish or some mussels. Facilities include a campground with a small shop open in summer. **Beachfront Holiday Homes** Jan Turner (09)406 0943 is the local real estate agent. **Marlin Lodge** **Private Bach** 021 470 076 www.marlinlodge.com. **Taupo Bay Motor Camp** (09)406 0315 is open all year www.taupobayholidaypark.co.nz

3. Totara North
It is home to a very abandoned old timber yard, a bunch of other old derelict factories, and a gritty, commercial wharf, with little to offer the drifting beach-comber other than some okay fishing and a convenient place to throw your boat into the water.

4. Whangaroa
This equally boat-focused settlement is infinitely more salubrious than its neighbour across the harbour, with extensive marina facilities, a waterside hotel and a large and famous game fishing club. It is a boat owners place through and through, offering sheltered anchorage with access to some spectacular fishing grounds offshore that have produced many good sport fish over the years. You can also get a feed of many species in the harbour itself, including snapper, flounder, kingies and crays, which is a great fallback option when the open ocean is too rough. **www.whangaroa.co.nz** is a community website with heaps of good info. **The Marlin Hotel** (09)405 0347 is the old classic by the marina. **Kingfish Lodge** (09)405 0164 is another well-known luxury lodge, with boat access only www.kingfishlodge.co.nz. **Sunseeker Lodge** (09)405 0496 www.sunseekerlodge.co.nz. If the land-based accommodation options dont appeal, you can even rent a houseboat **www.houseboatrentals.co.nz**

Whangaroa

Matauri Bay

5. Tauranga Bay

"Welcome to Tauranga Bay Holiday Park. Get away from it all and enjoy a kiwi beach holiday the way it used to be. No traffic noise or high-rise resort buildings – just a stunningly unspoilt beach, beautiful views and soft golden sand. There are precious few places left in New Zealand where you can holiday right on the beach. The Rush family are proud to offer you an absolute beachfront break at Tauranga Bay Holiday Park." Well that's the copy from the brochure, and it is so bang-on I didn't bother changing a word. There's good rock fishing off either end, plus mussels and no doubt a few crays too. Dramatic and deserted Stephensons Island sits just offshore with its own bays and beaches.
Tauranga Bay Holiday Park (09) 405 0436
www.taurangabay.co.nz

6. Mahinepua

A little piece of Northland that has quite happily remained in the hands of local Maori, and consists of ample grassy land set behind a tiny cove-like bay, at the base of the peninsula of the same name. There's only an urupa and a section of private land set aside for camping, that gets fairly busy with Iwi in peak season, but was empty save for a local caretaker in March. Facilities are very basic, but it's a beautiful spot, with sheltered swimming and spectacular walks on both sides, plus it's a great place to launch a kayak or small tinnie. Camping is by permission of local Iwi for a small koha if you're polite and respectful.

7. Wainui Bay

It's a magical little cove that's on private Maori land, and while it isn't encouraged, day use is allowed if you ask the owners nicely. Some of the most beautiful trees in the country grace the foreshore here.

8. Te Ngaere

Simply stunning, little Te Ngaere is a sandy beach facing north, quietly tucked away out of the wind, and protected from swell by a small island just off the beach, a headland to the east, and the sheltering influence of The Mahinepua Peninsula and Flat Island to the north-west. A small stream flows onto the beach at its eastern border and it is at this end of the bay that locals launch their boats. The rocks at either end are a joy to explore and snorkel around; with a little cove to the east, which can be accessed by walking over the stream and following the track past the old boat shed, harbouring a private beach and a few good land-based fishing spots at low tide.

Putetawa

There're only a few dozen baches, so Te Ngaere rarely gets crowded, even at peak periods. Public access to the beach is gained in the centre of the bay, where the main road passes adjacent to the foreshore, with parking beside a grass reserve, where you'll find the public loos. It is a sheltered and convenient spot for a picnic if you're driving the loop road, and a delightful place to swim in clear, sparkling water, but none of this does justice to its intimate charms. It's the kind of spot where you wish you had a house, though few people are lucky enough to be able to make that claim.

9. Matauri Bay
One of Northland's best known and finest beaches faces due east in a long arc, looking straight out at the Cavalli Islands just offshore, and on a clear day they appear so close you feel you could almost swim there. It is more than a kilometre long, but wide open to the elements, with only a few trees down its length for shade, and a denuded hinterland that's been carved up for development in what has been a protracted and difficult saga for all involved. Public access to the beach has been made more difficult by the pushing back of the foreshore reserve, resulting in a hundred metre walk from the car, but despite its somewhat plundered character, and the convoluted access issues, it is still a stunning beach with tuatuas in the intertidal zone. One of the country's finest waterside campgrounds occupies a prime position at the northern end, tucked beneath the large headland that frames its boundary. There's a small Maori settlement down a private road to the south, but few other homes in the bay as yet. It receives all east swell, so is worth keeping on the radar if you're in the area, though it's a flat beach so rarely has standout surf. For the rest of the time, it's a convenient place to launch a boat or kayak from, with some good fishing in the Cavalli Channel and around the rocks nearby. For divers, there's the lure of the wreck of The Rainbow Warrior on the Cavalli Islands just offshore, and if you don't have a boat, the campground runs dive trips out there. Over the saddle at the northern end, you can walk to beautiful Putetawa Bay, which is a sheltered spot for a swim and a snorkel if there is a swell running. **Matauri Bay Holiday Park** (09)405 0525 has both a store and takeaways www.matauribay.co.nz.

10. Takou Bay
Thankfully the Takou Trust has recently reopened Takou Bay after nearly a decade of closure. Access is through the Otaha settlement and down a steep, private gravel road. There is a 20km speed limit for the safety of children, and to reduce dust nuisance, with a $5 per car charge levied to help maintain the road. Takou Bay whanau have established a rahui from Takou Taumatangi (Pink Beach) to Tohoranui River (Elliot's Beach), to prevent over-harvesting of kaimoana. Takaou is one of the most exposed beaches in Northland, picking up all east and north-east swell, with assorted beach peaks along its long extent.

11. Elliots Bay
One of the area's best surf spots remains difficult to access but for those that can be bothered with the walk, a legendary right point break awaits. It works in a north-east or big east swell, and the bonus is that it's somewhere you'll be guaranteed to find a bit of peace. Access is off the DOC walkway signposted on Hewitt Rd. Walk to Taronui Bay and go north.

12. Taronui Bay
This bleached white jewel, sheltered by a reef just offshore, was designated a DOC reserve in 2007, but it's a hike to get there, which almost certainly guarantees privacy. The 7.5 km track leaves from Hewitt Rd, passing through a mix of farmland and bush, with three stiles to cross, and takes between 45 minutes and an hour each way.

13. Tapuaetahi
A privately owned peach with nearly a kilometre of glorious sand, backed by a few dozen baches, that's surrounded by rocky reefs at either end. Sad to say, it is a gated community, so unless you have friends, there is no vehicle access (unless the gate happens to be left open), though there is a DOC walkway for day-users from the top of Hewitt Rd, giving access to both Elliots, Taronui and Tapuaetahi. It takes about 30 minutes, and leads you to the river estuary at the southern end of the bay. Whilst the snorkelling and swimming is good, that may not be a good enough reason to suffer the hike; however the extremely high quality of the waves in and around the bay probably is. When people refer to the Kerikeri reefs, this is what they mean; with a left and right reef in the middle of the bay, a left point that can hold solid swells to the west, a smaller right reef to the east, and a mysto bombie off the eastern headland. North swells are best. There are no public facilities here, not even a bin; which is what caused the closure of the road, as locals complained of litter and mess from day trippers and campers. I find it incredible that the local council let it come to this, but that's another matter.

The Bay of Islands

Celebrated globally as one of our maritime treasures, which it is in many ways; yet The Bay of Islands has less to offer the land-based visitor than one might expect. You'll find views a plenty and a powerful sense of being near an aquatic paradise, but quality beaches accessible by car are few. Thankfully, these are concentrated around Russell and Paihia, the two primary tourist destinations, though as a consequence, the experience is not exactly a private one. But it seems most tourists to the north make a pilgrimage to here at some stage, and the concentration of foreigners creates its own unique dynamic, that isn't without appeal. Just don't expect peace and quiet, because you won't find it until you head out to the fringes.

Travelling Russell and Paihia are the two main centres, but are separated by a large inlet. For those who want to drive between them, the car ferry from Opua is a short, half hourly service that makes it significantly quicker than driving the long way around. Accommodation options in Russell and Paihia are too numerous to start to list, but there are several websites to help: www.bay-of-islands.nz.com or www.bay-of-islands.co.nz or www.bayofislands.net or bayofislandsinfo.co.nz. **Live Aboard Tours** operate a beautiful old sailing launch www.ocean-eco-tours.co.nz 0800 773 569. For a Maori cultural experience www.taimaitours.co.nz 0800 wakatours (09)405 9990. **Fullers** developed the original ferries in the bay, and are still the biggest name in local transport 0800 653 339 www.dolphincruises.co.nz

WIND ROSE

SWELL ROSE

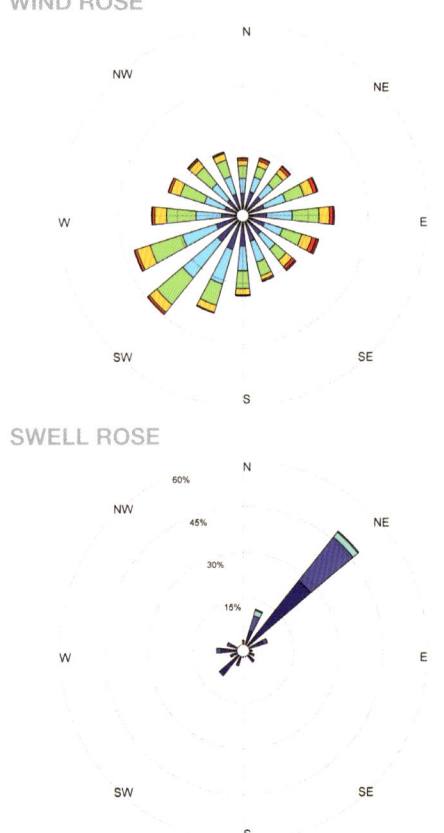

Surfing Waves in the bay are rare, but on a massive north swell, there are a few spots like Long Beach, and the reefs off Waitangi that are worth a look. Brampton Reef in the middle of the bay is a mysto tow-in spot, but it rarely breaks. **Russell Boardriders** (Kent Thwaites) 021 403 255

Fishing Obviously the Bay has a reputation as a fishing Mecca, which began with Zane Grey's early forays from Urupukapuka Island in search of marlin. The reputation was well deserved, and the marlin fishery continues to be a prime drawcard for visitors to these waters. It has also seen many good table fish landed over the years, however if you're fishing from shore, you have to get out to the extremities to really get amongst the good stuff. Tapeka Pt and Rawhiti are favourite spots due to deeper waters. A kayak launched near these spots would be dangerous!

Swimming Strangely enough, the best swimming is around Paihia and Russell and out on the islands, as most of the beaches in the middle of the bay are highly tidal and muddy.

1. Opito Bay

Opito Bay is way out at the head of the Kerikeri Inlet, and the northernmost vehicle-asccessible spot in the Bay of Islands. If you're a trailer boatie, you'll find yourself in good company here, as it's one of the most popular launching locations in the bay, with an excellent concrete ramp at its northern end. The beach itself is fine, dark, shingly sand, that shelves steeply, so is a good place to swim at all tides. Public loos, a large grassy foreshore and ample shade trees along the shoreline, also make it a good place for a family picnic. The walkway to the Ake Ake Point scenic reserve and some good land-based fishing, is located at the end of the beach by the boatramp. Just before you get to the beach, you'll see The Kerikeri Cruising Club, with its large marina conveniently situated close to the head of the Kerikeri inlet.

Te Ti marae

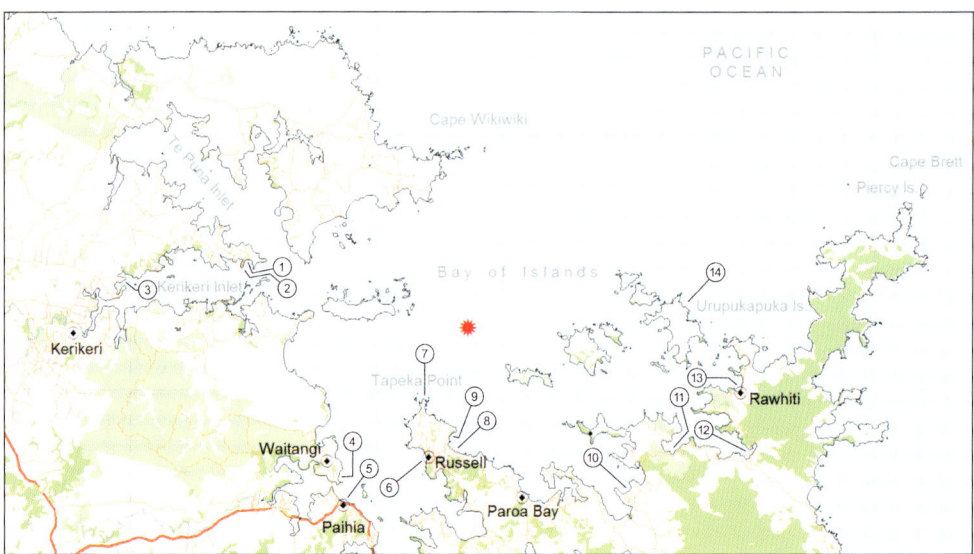

Opito Bay

2. Doves Bay

Take the road to Doves Bay and near its end there's a hard left turn down a gravel road. You end up on the foreshore overlooking the Kerikeri boating club marina. It's a shingle and mud beach, but a pretty spot nonetheless, surrounded by trees and very sheltered from the wind, with one cute house but no amenities. If you had carried on instead of turning left at the top of the road, you would have come to a grass reserve with a sign saying "pedestrian accesss to beach and ski lane." A short steep bush walk through some fantastic manuka stands, delivers you to another unnamed shingly bay facing west, that shelves steeply so is a good spot for a swim, is protected from easterly winds, and is usually empty.

3. Skudders Beach

It hardly deserves its name as a beach, as it is just a section of a muddy inlet that runs alongside the road, with a pretty pathetic attempt at a boat ramp that would be no good for launching a dinghy, even at high tide; but there it is, Skudders Beach, marked on the map, and surrounded by houses. Very onomatopaeic.

4. Waitangi/Hobson Beach

There is a short patch of sand between the reefs, where Governor Hobson came ashore to sign the treaty, out in front of the Waka and the Copthorne Hotel. Not many people swim here, but believe it or not, on a big north-east swell, there can be a few waves here. **The Waitangi Treaty Grounds** are open daily (09)402 7437 www.waitangi.net.nz

5. Paihia

Paihia's beachfront extends for a few kilometres from the causeway leading from Waitangi, eastwards to the ferry terminal, broken by a headland. To the west is Te Ti Beach, which is a cool place to swim, though not private at all. It's backed by the road and Te Ti Marae, and offers easy parking with amenities staggered along its length. There is a good boat ramp just over the causeway. Horotutu Beach is the short shingly patch of sand with a few upturned dinghys adjacent to the main shops. Further east towards the **Opua Ferry**, there's another quaint wee beach called Taiputuputu that's backed by pohutakawa trees, with parking at either end. **Bay Beach Hire** (Bikes, Kayaks, Boats) (09)402 6078. **Bay of Islands Dive** and water taxis www.diveops.co.nz 0800 387 892. **Waitangi Holiday Park** (09)402 7866 www.waitangiholidaypark.co.nz. **Coastal Kayakers** 0800 334 661

Horotutu Beach

Russell

6. Russell Main Beach

Russell was formerly known as Kororareka, and though at one time was the nation's capital, it was widely regarded as "The hellhole of the Pacific," and a veritable den of vice and debauchery. These days it's a far more genteel and less dangerous place to visit, with a beautiful beach and wharf, backed by some cool cafes and several fabulous little eating and drinking holes, including the legendary **Bay of Islands Swordfish Club,** and the equally renown **Duke of Marlborough Hotel**. It is one of the most popular anchorages for yachties in the country and is a town that really knows how to party. **The Eagles Nest** won best coastal resort in the World Luxury Hotels Awards in 2010 (09)403 8333 www.eaglesnest.co.nz. **Russell Top 10 Holiday Resort** offers beds at the other end of the scale (09)403 7826 www.russelltop10.co.nz

7. Tapeka Point

Head over Flagstaff Hill from Russell, and you will end up on Tapeka Point. There is a beach on either side of this craggy little promontory. Du Fresne faces west, and features a hard boat ramp, grassy reserve picnic tables and spectacular Norfolk pines dating back to 1830. Rocky Bay faces east, and it is an apt name, with some shingly sand between the reefy outcrops, though hardly a beach. **The Anchorage** is a delightful spot with apartments and b&b all with sea views (09)403 8410 www.anchoragerussell.co.nz

8. Oneroa/Long Beach

If you drive along Wellington St east of Russell and head over the hill, you come to a spectacular beach extending for at least a km, with a dead end road passing along its length. There's a grassy bank behind the foreshore, a few strategically placed trees for shade, and a couple of dozen holiday homes watching proceedings. It offers the best swimming in this part of the bay, with spectacular views out to the islands and the cape. There are public loos at the western end where you'll also find a coffee cart in season. Believe it or not, it even gets waves in a huge north swell, though they aren't likely to set the world on fire.

9. Waitata Bay

A track runs from the western end of Oneroa around Tapeka Point all the way to Russell. It passes through private land that's protected by the QE2 trust, but for much of its length, is only accessible below half tide. There are a few spots to enjoy along the way but Waitata or Donkey Bay as it is known by many, is the first, easiest to access, and the only real beach. It is a short stretch of sand that's clothing optional.

10. Jacks Bay

Once one half of a happy duet with adjacent Jills Bay, which used to house a popular camping ground. Private ownership changed all that, but Jacks Bay can still be accessed by the public down a short walking track, and while it feels like a private beach, the foreshore reserve remains in the public domain. It is a shingly bay with huge pohutakawa trees down its length and offers stunning views over Motukauri Island, but there are no facilities of any kind. It isn't the best beach in the north, but one that offers peace and quiet, good swimming and a sheltered spot for a picnic, (though the owners of the few expensive homes above it probably don't want you to know this). Jacks Bay B&B (09)403 7887.

11. Te Uenga Bay

Just east of Waipiro Bay, which offers no public access, is Te Uenga Bay. Unlike some of the flat, muddy and tidal inlets in the area, it offers some pretty decent sand, good trailer-boat launching and has a dozen or so tasteful baches dotted along behind it. It is completely sheltered from most but north-west winds, but sadly has no public amenities.

12. Parekura Bay
It is tidal, muddy and of no real interest to travellers, but just past here you will find the access point to the Whangamumu Scenic Reserve, and DOC walkways to the old whaling station (1 hr 15), and the Cape Brett Track via Te Toroa Bay (3 hrs 30 mins). Bookings for the track must be made prior to departure with **DOC Russell** (09)403 9005. Guided tours are also available with **Cape Brett Walkways Ltd** (09)403 8823. An adjacent property, located just before the walkway, offers private off-road parking for those who want extra security. Costs $3.00 per day/$8.00 over night. Probably a good investment.

13. Rawhiti
It isn't a single beach as such, but an area with several beaches, all with a strong Maori presence and featuring a formidable Marae. It is probably the most spectacular part of the whole bay in my opinion, with sweeping views over the many little islands just offshore, plus some of the best sandy beaches, coupled with very few people. Kaimarama Bay is the easiest to access, located at the end of the road, and though it's privately owned by the proprietors of the small, family-run campsite by the carpark, you won't be denied access unless you start causing hassles. There's also a popular concrete boat ramp and grass reserve here, and it's a great place to launch a vessel close to some spectacular fishing territory. **Rawhiti Airfills** offers dive bottle fills, petrol, diesel, bait and ice and a couple of small, rustic baches and caravans. Della Snowden-Hartwell (09)403 7248

14. Urupukapuka Island
The only of the islands with a regular ferry service and featuring two **DOC campsites**, this is where Zane Grey set up his first NZ fishing camp, and where NZ sportfishing had its international baptism. A fantastic restaurant and bar is named after him at Otehi Bay **www.zanegrey.co.nz**. There are several fine beaches on the island and good land-based fishing off the rocks. The campsites gets very buy over peak periods so reservations are essential www.doc.govt.nz. **Fullers Urupukapuka Island Adventure** runs regular ferries 0800 744 487.

Rawhiti

NORTHLAND   GLISTENING   EXOTIC   ABUNDANT

Northland is a province with two completely distinct faces. Its boundaries are the Bay of Islands to the north and The Brynderwyns to the south, but despite a legitimate claim as a bona fide coastal paradise, this is predominantly a lightly populated farming region, with few permanent residents. It just happens to be peppered with some of the most exotic and desirable sections of coastline in the country, that for many of us, is where the Kiwi dream is played out. There are the spectacularly beautiful, and by-and-large, up-market east coast beaches and resorts, all pohutakawa-clad and glistening, featuring superb harbours, offshore islands and an indented coast with thousands of tiny bays, white sand and glamour. Then there's the raging west coast; straight, swell-battered and foaming. The two are like chalk and cheese, but it doesn't matter which coast you're on, Northland is never boring, offering a feast of aquatic options on any particular day. The weather is kind, the water warm, and the oceans on both coasts are alive with fish. The surf can be excellent on either shoreline, and with two to choose from, it can be hard thinking about work if you're distracted by good waves. Its proximity to Auckland means the crowds are building at many spots, though there are still plenty of nooks and crannies where you'll find yourself alone if that's what you prefer. To put it more simply, if you love beach culture, Northland will probably pop all your lights.

The East Coast
There will be few people who are unaware of the popularity of Northland's east coast. Bream Bay is a warm-up before the main event, which starts with the stunning Whangarei coastline. You then have the myriad delights of the Tutukaka region to choose from, before the little visited Whananaki area. The Old Russell Rd follows, and how it has escaped significant attention over the years, I will never know. It is phenomenal! They're all sensational. Go for a "Tiki-Tour" sometime and you will see what I mean.

The West Coast
It's one straight, wind-battered beach, with a big rock (Manganui Bluff) to the north, and a mangrove fringed harbour to the south, facing directly into the prevailing wind and swell. Unsurprisingly, the west coast has not seen the explosion in numbers witnessed 100km across the island. There is no glamour here mate! Cafe culture hasn't overtaken this coast. There is no shopping to do, and no glitzy marinas for million dollar gin-palaces. You're struggling to get a cup of tea even. Yet what this coast

Otumare

Daisy Bay

lacks in glitz it makes up for in true grit, with epic waves on its day and an abundance of fat snapper. The people are fantastic and the hospitality legendary.

Travelling The twin coast highway skirts the west coast. The east coast isn't as closely served by state highway one, and until you hit the Old Russell Rd, you have to deviate substantially to get to the ocean. Aside from Whangarei and Tutukaka, facilities are few, and shops at the coast sparse and rudimentary.

Surfing The west coast is one long beach break that likes smaller swells and north-east winds. With few rocks and thus little variety to the wave type, it doesn't appear to offer as much as the east coast, but what it does have up its sleeve is constant swell. It's just a case of getting it offshore and finding a bank. The east coast on the other hand offers almost infinite variety, featuring a series of harbour bars, beach breaks and the odd point break and reef thrown in for good measure. Sadly swell is inconsistent, and swell checking can be an arduous affair due to the tortured nature of the coastline. But somehow between the two, there always seems to be somewhere to surf if you've got the time and the gas money to go looking.

Fishing Warm water and a steep shelf off the east coast brings large fish in close. There are many top spots; too many to name really, but the snapper are plentiful, pelagics are everywhere, especially in late summer, and every headland will give you a kahawai or two. The scallops are abundant, there are mussels and tuatuas to feast on if you know where to look, and you'll find kina around most rocks; so really, it's a gigantic larder. The west coast is a whole different cup of tea, but no less productive.

Swimming A mind-boggling array of choices present themselves on the east coast, and while the long stretch of Ripiro beach isn't the most inviting, it shouldn't be ruled out. **Northland Regional Council** environmental hotline 0800 504 639.

Glinks Gully

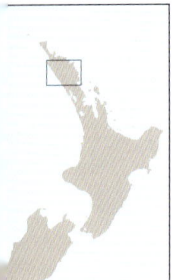

Ripiro Beach

One long beach leads from Maunganui Bluff to the entrance of the Kaipara Harbour. It is a classic "lee-shore" that can be hideously tortured by howling westerlies for months on end. With no sizeable land features or even any trees behind the beach to arrest the winds flow, in the wrong conditions, it can feel both plain and downright inhospitable, yet proves a landscape that offers much more the more you look into it. The dune and cliff geography behind the foreshore is totally unique and changes substantially, depending on which section of the beach you are on. The sand is pale gold. There are very few people around. Go there on a fine day with the wind offshore and it's as enchanting as anywhere in the country and one of my absolute favourite places to spend time.

Travelling There are very few people on this beach and the only public ammenities of note are at Baylys Beach. Dargaville is the main service centre and the privately run I-site is a mine of useful information (09)439 4975 www.kauriinfocentre.co.nz

Surfing This is one gigantic straight beach break, featuring all the vagaries of beachies everywhere. The sand banks change regularly and the only way to get the best waves is to drive the beach and snoop. What makes that a fraught proposition is the fact the best waves tend to be found at higher tides when the beach is almost impassable, even driving four wheelers. The main access points all seem to have decent banks on their day, possibly due to the streams which formed them. While it appears straight, it isn't, with more westerly orientation to the north. Small swells and north-east winds are required. John Matich Surf Shop (09)439 8380.

Fishing The big scallop shaped bays that appear at low tide along Ripiro offer a multitude of rips, guts and channels which will all hold fish, especially in late summer and autumn. The favourite period seems to be below mid-tide, when the beach is more sculpted. Daytime is productive in the often stirred up water, and night time can also offer tight lines. Obviously the best winds are offshore north-easterlies.

WIND ROSE

SWELL ROSE

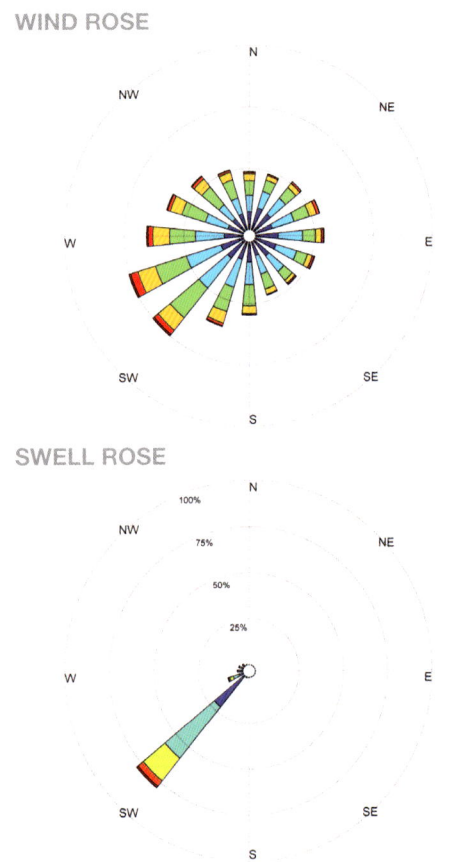

Glinks Gully

Aranga Beach

Beach fishing

Swimming This is an unpatrolled coast. Exercise caution on dropping tides and in strong swells, when rips are more pronounced. High tide is always safer. Avoid areas where no waves are breaking.

Driving the beach Ripiro is a listed highway and one of those places where old Subarus go to die at the hands of fired-up young surfers and fishermen seeking spots to themselves, or simply exercising their demons on the country's longest driveable stretch of beach. While it doesn't necessarily require 4wd, there are only a couple of access points suitable for 2wd vehicles. The speed limit is 30km/h and all road rules apply, though rarely seem to be adhered to. From low to mid tide it is relatively safe and firm, but driving at high tide is extremely hazardous and requires a good 4wd, steely nerves and a certain disregard for the state of your car. The sweeper sets which pound right up to the cliffs in some parts are going to get you one day, and there are other obstacles along the beach, like sections of lignite, which become exposed by the tide. Care should be taken at all times, but extreme caution exercised if travelling on the beach at night.

1. Aranga Beach/Maunganui Bluff

Maunganui Bluff is a land feature of significance and beauty, rising to 460m directly from the ocean, marking the northern extent of Ripiro Beach. The walk to the top takes around an hour, but the spectacular views both ways that await you once there, make all the sweating worthwhile. Aranga, as the settlement and stretch of beach to the south of the bluff is known, consists of a rough access point onto the beach, a few dozen baches and a fairly ripe longdrop, and sadly there's no accommodation for travellers. That said it is a magical spot offering good beach fishing, some kaimoana off the rocks, and good waves when it's on. There is even a rock ledge to fish off for any mountain goats that can get up and down the near vertical track running down the nose of the bluff. It is strictly 4wd access onto the sand here, due to the sad state of the last 50m of road.

2. Omamari Gap

A little less remarkable geographically; one could even say featureless, Omamari is a broad "gap" in the dunes and hills created by what must once have been a fairly sizeable river, and is the next stop south on this beach. There are no baches here, though it is well used by many local folk, especially fishermen, but somehow Omamari offers less of the charm and intimacy of the spots north and south. A popular beach-launching location for the west coast trailer boat guys, it's often inaccessible to 2wd vehicles due to the depth of the stream at the mouth. Many of the locals do cross it though; as a few of the youngsters were only too happy to shout out, amidst peals of laughter, as they roared through the metre deep water, "no sweat for us bro…we're Maoris!" Amenities include a very raw long-drop toilet, plus bins and picnic tables at the little reserve where the road joins the beach.

Baylys Beach

3. Baylys Beach

The most populous of the Kauri Coast spots, Baylys has a rapidly expanding collection of holiday homes, a cafe, holiday park and a shop even! For this part of the world it could even be described as occasionally busy, and on a fine day you will find a steady stream of cars driving down beside the stream which leads onto the beach, and parking up for a picnic on the hard sand, or venturing both north and south for a fish or surf. Due to the close proximity to the deeper waters off the Kaipara Trench, good all round fishing, easy access onto the beach, and the hard sand at lower tides, Baylys is a popular launching spot for trailer boaties who can read weather and swell maps. From January till April you will find quite a few guys from around Northland chasing marlin from here. Likewise the ease of access often sees a committed crew of local surfers here at high tide, when there are often good banks. The Funky Fish Cafe is a charming source of refreshments near the coast and while there are public toilets before the beach, they were pretty rough.

Baylys Beach Campsite and quad bike rental (09)439 6349 www.baylysbeach.co.nz. **Sunset View Lodge** has six self-contained cabins (09)439 4342 www.sunsetviewlodge.co.nz. **Baylys Beach Horse Treks** www.baylysbeachhorsetreks.co.nz.
Skydome Observatory www.skydome.org.nz

Glinks Gully

4. Mahuta Gap

It is a strangely sensual experience driving down to Mahuta Gap. An enchanting, broad valley filled with raupo and cabbage trees converges into one little gap in the hills that takes you down the path of the stream which formed it. As a consequence of this convergence, access to the beach here is only advised for 4wd vehicles, though it is sometimes possible for two wheelers. There are a handful of tiny baches tucked into the south side of the dunes on the sea front, but no public facilities of any kind.

5. Glinks Gully

Glinks gully is a tiny but deeply charming settlement of 50 or so baches and a campsite, located just south of Dargaville. It's a real family community with deep roots and a timeless air that's a popular spot for the local beach fishermen, which also produces good waves on its day. The campground is one of the prettiest in New Zealand when the wind is blowing from the east, with spectacular views south-west down the beach; however when the wind switches around to the west or south-west you would probably find me heading to the east coast. Public facilities include toilets and bins, with easy vehicle access onto the beach. There is also a reserve with bins and picnic tables at the south end. **Glinks Seaside Holiday Camp** (09)439 0712 or (09)439 4713.

Glinks Gully

6. Pouto

The section of beach south of Dargaville is on a long finger of land known as the Pouto Peninsula, that forms a storm barrier for the Kaipara Harbour. The road turns to gravel half way down and eventually ends at Pouto Point, which is a tiny collection of dinky homes with an unusual campsite, in what was the old customs house. The main attraction is the fishing from the foreshore and the unusual dunes and historic lighthouse at North Head. **Pouto Sand Safaris** offer 4wd and quad-bike tours; book at the info centre in Dargaville.

North Head

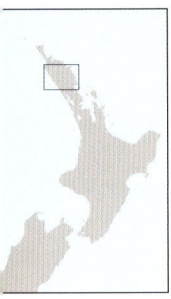

The Old Russell Road

This once important highway is a backroad of sorts now, but it passes by some of the most enchanting spots in Northland, all of which seem to have retained a traditional kiwi beach community feeling, perhaps due to their relative isolation. Maori influence is still strong, and the variety of coastal environments is huge, with rocky shorelines giving way to some of the finest sandy beaches in the country. I don't want to rave too much lest I start a goldrush, but it is a pretty special section of a pretty special coast.

Travelling When it was a gravel road, few people venturied down this road. Nowadays it's sealed and a lot more accessible, but there still aren't too many accommodation options available, with Oakura the most likely, also having groceries and fuel. An epic backpackers which is central to all these spots is **The Farm** (09)433 6894 www.thefarm.co.nz

WIND ROSE

SWELL ROSE

Surfing Ironically not the most wave-rich section of the Northland coast at first glance, though I suspect a thorough examination during a solid swell would turn up some pleasant surprises.

Fishing It is a primo fishing area, with a million deliciously fertile reef systems, and some pronounced headlands and points offering deep water drop-offs, plus some easily accessed, empty stretches of coast. A kayak is a useful weapon to deploy up here. **Oakura Bay Fish Dive and Cruise** 0800 652 872.

Swimming Richly endowed with swimming spots of all kinds, plus some stunning inshore reefs and rocks close to the road to snorkel around.

1. Elliots Beach

After the enclosed and somewhat claustrophobic feeling of driving around the Bay of Islands, seeing Elliots is a huge breath of fresh air for most. You drive over the hill, and there it is, spread out below you like a feast; quaint, picturesque and invitingly empty for most of the year. With its sparkling white sand, ramshackle old farm buildings, pohutakawa trees, and the little island separating it from miles of empty coastline stretching north, it is one of those quintessentially Kiwi spots that literally define who we are. For rock fishermen, there's lots to get excited about in the wider area, and for surfers, Elliots is a consistent fall-back option when there's a small east coast swell, picking up every little burp in the ocean.

The adventurous amongst us will benefit from taking a stroll up the coast to the north. If you're looking for either fish, waves, or just some solitude, you won't be disappointed. There is a limited amount of accommodation behind the beach. **Elliots Bay Cabins and Beachfront Accommodation** (09)433 6607 elliotbay@ubernet.co.nz

Elliots Bay

2. Taupiri

Just south of Elliots you'll find two delightful little coves, carved out of black Northland reef, that are minute slices of paradise. At the first one, there's not a house in sight, but equally no amenities either, which makes it a lovely picnic spot, but not an overnight option. Parking is a bit tight on the side of the main road, and access is via a track down between the sprawling pohutakawas. Taupiri proper, which is a little further south, has a few homes behind it and easier parking, but with the same pohutakawa dripping beauty. A bonus is that it offers the possibility of launching a kayak with relative ease.

3. Bland Bay

While it may lack a bit of variety on land, without too many trees and a very low key ambience; the beach and it's surrounding coastline is anything but bland. It is long and sparkling, curving around in a massive arc, with a fairly narrow opening to the sea making it particularly hospitable for swimmers. This, and the shelter offered by Motuhi Island, almost guarantees swell-free launching here, making it popular for kayaks and other small craft, offering access to some stunning coastline, in particular north towards Home Point. The beach profile is flat, so doesn't offer the best waves in Northland, but in a big easterly swell you can surf here. Bland Bay has a tiny community, without too much in the way of private accommodation, but it does have a large campground. **Bland Bay Motor Camp** (09)433 6894.

Bland Bay

Oakura

4. Oakura

Another of Northland's amazing surprises, Oakura is a bit of a mission to get to, but worth every twist and turn in the road. It's a sculpted crescent of flat smooth sand, that's hands down the most popular spot on this section of coast, offering an expansive open beach, with multiple coves and sheltered bays all around it. Quite a few lucky families call this fine beach theirs, but bach culture here hasn't become too stuffy, with a down to earth ambience which is becoming increasingly rare these days, that always drags me back. Boat launching is best done by tractor or 4wd in the lee of the wee island at the north of the beach. You'll find petrol and supplies, plus takeaways at the small shop in the middle of the beach. There is a campsite at Whangaruru, the small beach over the hill to the north of Oakura. **Whangaruru Beach Campsite** (09)433 6806. **Robins Nest Luxury Accommodation** (09)433 6035 offers something at the other end of the scale.

5. Mokau

Deeply Maori, intensely beautiful, but not really a public place; this is a cultural centre for local Iwi (Ngati Wai), with a large area of land that's Wahi Tapu behind the beach. Asking permission to use it will guarantee a better reception.

6. Helena Bay/Mimiha Reserve

A small cove-like bay with a modest pull-over for parking, and a handful of pretty basic shacks. There are no public amenities, but it is still a pretty spot for a picnic and a swim, though it shelves steeply, which is good news for surfers but less appealing for younger children or weaker swimmers when there is a swell.

7. Teal Bay

Another little gem that's well populated, but retains a private feel, with public access at either end and boat launching to the south. It's a steeply shelving beach with a mix of old and some more modern homes, with tons of character, but no public ammenities.

8. Ngahau Bay/Paparahi Point Reserve

A divine, if lonely bay with access down a gravel road at the north end where there's a small parking area set back from the beach. It is wide open with a grassy foreshore that's punctuated by old pohutakawas and puriri trees, but no toilets or other public facilities. Little Waihihi Beach, located just north, can be accessed by walking around the rocks or over the hill.

9. Mimiwhangata

A stunning DOC maintained farm on a peninsula with beaches on both sides offers an array of marine opportunities regardless of your preferred activity. Okupe Beach is the main publicly accessible spot. It's a long expanse of sparkling east-facing sand, with rock reefs to the north and south, that offers gold for both swimmers and fishermen. For surfers, it's an epic spot in an east to south-east swell, with good exposure to both. It also allows foot access south, past a range of smaller bays to Paraparea. There is a range of accommodation available in the **DOC Reserve** (09)433 6554, including a well-appointed lodge, and simpler but comfortable cottage and beach house. An extremely popular tent-only campsite, is located on the west side of the peninsula at Waikahoa Bay, where there's also great swimming and fishing.

Helena Bay

Whananaki

There's a 30km loop road to get in and out of Whananaki, and it's not on the way to or from anywhere else, which lends an isolated, time-forgotten feel to this stretch of coast; but if you've ever been here, you'll never forget it, as it is pure magic! There are several vastly different bays and beaches grouped together in the area, each with its own unique feeling and aspect, offering a range of swimming, surfing and fishing options. There aren't a huge array of flash houses and very few public amenities, but for many, that only adds to the appeal. The quid pro quo is that there are unlikely to be swarming hordes to interrupt your experience of this special piece of Northland, and even the Christmas madness seems a little less mad here.

Travelling The only public facilities are near the estuary, with only two public loos, so bear this in mind. All the prime beaches are adjacent to the main road, so there's little difficulty locating them.

WIND ROSE

SWELL ROSE

Surfing All the exposed beaches get rideable waves, but by far the stand out is the Whananaki Bar, a world class left on its day, though it breaks infrequently, requiring a huge south-east swell, and north-west wind, which is a rare event. The other spots break in standard east swells and west winds.

Fishing An array of reef systems begins here and continues up to the Bay of Islands, with small islands and craggy headlands at every turn in this convoluted coast. It is excellent kayak territory with quite a few obvious land-based spots too.

Swimming Plenty of delicious options in pretty much any weather pattern.

1. Pareparea

Beautiful, pohutakawa-backed Parepare (as it is known), is one out of the box, and while it is as delicious as anywhere in the country, the road from Moureeses is private, passes through Maori land and remains accessible by car only to whanau or those with connections. The waves at the northern end are legendary and it's the most consistent spot for miles, with lefts off the north point and rights off the reef which divides the beach in two. For those who don't mind a hike, the beach is accessible by walking down from Mimiwhangata, though it takes an hour either way. Best conditions are often at lower tides. Leave no trash. Respect the locals! No amenities.

Mangaiti

Rockall

2. Moureeses
An absolutely stunning cove-like bay, and like Parepare, Moureesees is divided in two by a rock reef. It is known as an okay surf spot, especially the southern end which is exposed to north-east swell, but the main concentration of baches are at the north, where there's a shady reserve under the trees, featuring a barbeque-pit and picnic tables. The points at each end both offer good fishing prospects, and the gorgeous sand invites a swim at any tide.

3. Mangaiti
A tiny cove looking out to a little island at the mouth of the bay, with a small parking space, a grass reserve and a picnic table. The beach is made of shingly dark sand and it's extremely protected from swell, but these factors just mean the water is mind bogglingly clear in most conditions and consequently a great place for a snorkel or swim. Again, there are no public facilities.

4. Rockall
Just over the hill from Mangaiti you spy Rockall Bay. It has been recently privatised with a subdivision of sorts restricting public access, but the beach itself isn't private and access can still be gained down the steps, which aren't that well signed but are well maintained. They are are adjacent to the Rockall Shores subdivision on the hilltop at the south, and are visible once you park, though there isn't much space for that on the side of the road.

5. Nikau Bay/Watkin-Powell Reserve
Heading south just before Otumare there's a DOC sign denoting the Watkin-Powell Reserve. The track from here leads you to beautiful Nikau Bay, which is a great place to escape people.

6. Otumare
A popular DOC campsite dominates this short stretch of Kiwi gold, though you don't have to stay there to get to the beach, with public access from the north end where a sandy track runs adjacent to the beach. **The DOC Campsite** is manned from Labour weekend to Easter (09)433 8402

7. Motutara Farm Park
Another absolute minter; Motutara farm covers most of the land leading out to the peninsula that protects the northern entrance to the estuary, adjoining the DOC reserve that covers the remainder of the headland. It is run as a private campsite from Labour Weekend till Queens Birthday, with more than 50 sites nestled in and around the surrounding hills and paddocks, encompassing two private beaches and offering access to a third further east. Barons Beach is the northern bay and Kings Beach lies to the south, separated by a rocky outcrop. While both face east with a relatively steep profile and good exposure to swell, Barons usually has the better waves. Access to the reserve further east is easy from the camp, and if you're adventurous and walk out to the end, you'll find the delightful lagoon set amongst the rocks that must rate as one of Northland's finest swimming spots. There is also some excellent rock fishing from the head of the peninsula, with alternative access from the town side being resolved with DOC as we go to press. **Motutara Farm Campsite** (09)433 8252 www.campingholiday.co.nz

8. Whananaki North
The main settlement on this coast is centred around the estuary at Whananaki North, consisting of a collection of classic Kiwi baches and a shop, with a school, marae and campground. The estuary is as lush as any in the country and offers safe swimming and good boat launch facilities, and the village provides all the basic amenities a traveller could want. From here you can look over towards the even more rustic collection of baches at Whananaki South, which is connected by the longest footbridge in the southern hemisphere. **Whananaki North Holiday Park** (09)433 8896 www.whananakiholiday.co.nz

9. Whananaki South/Grahams Beach
Take windy, gravel covered Hayles Rd for 8km down through the bush and farmland, then turn down Te Ara te Tunua Rd, and you end up at a large open expanse of grass behind a long stretch of totally empty ocean beach. This is the Whananaki Scenic reserve, and it's marked by an iconic row of old Norfolk pines. It's a mission to get here, which is why most don't bother. Consequently there are rarely people on the beach, which can have good surf on its day and also offers the prospect of a few fish, especially down the southern end off the rocks. This is also the best place to access the legendary Whananaki Bar, one of Northland's finest rivermouth breaks, that lights up in a large south-east swell, with accompanying west or north-west winds. Expect long dredging lefts wrapping down the sandbar if the sand is in good nick, but also expect crowds, as when it's on, half of Northland will know, and most will try and get there. Further along the road is the tiny collection of baches facing into the estuary. There are no amenities or toilets anywhere on this side sadly.

Whananaki Estuary

The Tutukaka Coast

Travelling It's located 30 km from Whangarei, down a twisty road with a fair bit of traffic, so drive carefully! There are imited groceries but a few good eating-out options at Tutukaka. www.tutukakacoast.co.nz 0800 288 882. Coastal holiday homes (09)434 4146 www.coastalholidayhomes.co.nz

WIND ROSE

SWELL ROSE

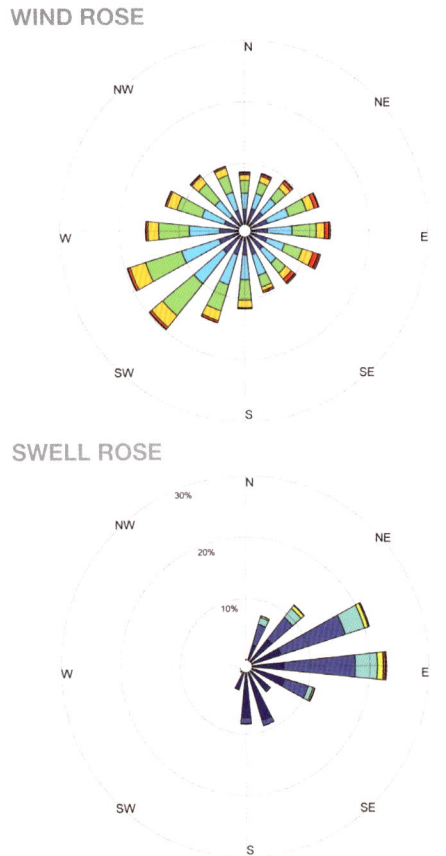

You could almost write a separate book on this small but spectacular slice of Northland. There is nowhere on our coast that features as many delightfully different beaches in such a compact area, offering so many recreational options, and a healthy swag of evening entertainment to boot. Add this all to a long and proud nautical history, dry climate, close proximity to the Poor Knights Islands, and chuck in a few good surf spots with an outrageous diversity of aspect and character, and you will see why there has been a virtual stampede to develop coastal property here over the last few decades. That stampede has significantly altered the social make-up of the area and caused a few environmental issues, more recently threatening the integrity of the Ngunguru Spit. But while some cracks are starting to appear, the primary qualities of the region are difficult to erase, no matter how hard the developers try.

Surfing Some classic surf on its day at Sandy Bay, which picks up all north-east and east swell. Woolleys can be a good learner spot, and Ngunguru Spit is a wildcard in a huge south-east swell. Tutukaka Surf Experience Shop and Surf School (09)434 3938 supply most basics and are super friendly www.tutukakasurf.co.nz. Ding Repairs Mark Weeler does fix ups at Woolleys Bay (09)434 4103

Fishing Tutukaka has one of the pre-eminent game fishing clubs in the country, with good launching facilities and a fantastic marina. The inshore fishery is also incredibly diverse, with some tasty land-based options and a couple of healthy estuaries for flounder and the like. As a fisherman, you can't ask for much more. Whangarei Deep Sea Anglers Club (09)434 3429 also has a restaurant and bar. Happy Hooker Charters 027 574 4136 www.happyhookercharters.co.nz

Swimming Absolute heaven. There are a myriad of safe swimming options regardless of wind and swell, due to the differing aspect of the various beaches. The epic diving out at the Poor Knights just caps it off.

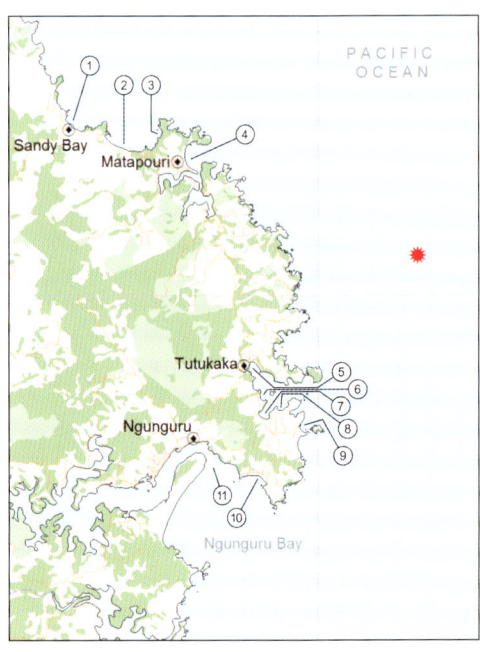

Sandy Bay

Woolleys Bay

1. Sandy Bay

Sandy Bay only has a dozen or so holiday homes, but on a fine day or when there's a swell running, you will struggle to get a carpark on the delightful shore front here. It is a fantastic beach with rocky points at both ends, a small stream in the middle, and good public toilets discreetly located just off the main road. Sandy picks up all north and east swell, claiming a favoured place in the local surf culture, and has been the venue for many fun surf competitions over the years, including a regular slot on the longboard tour. You'll normally find three main peaks down its length, with an extremely convenient rip at the southern end that offers a sure-fire, dry-hair paddle out, even on pretty large days. Strangely, it doesn't really like lined up or south-east swells, and high tide is often best, with offshores from south-west. In summer there's the delightful **Havana Cabana** selling coffee and Cuban donuts down McAuslin Rd, which also takes you to Daisy Bay, and the start of the fantastic Whananaki Walkway. This 2-4 hour coastal and farm side ramble leads all the way to Whananaki, past some stunning and empty bays.

2. Woolleys Bay

Nearly a kilometre long and backed by one of Northland's most picturesque coastal farms, Woolleys is one of the most under-rated of the region's beaches. Perhaps it's because there are few homes down its length, or possibly due to the popularity of surrounding beaches, but either way it is a place where you will rarely feel like you're in a crowd. Access points are at either end, with good public loos at the north in the ample grassy reserve tucked back from the beach. It's not a popular surf beach due to its sheltered aspect, though in a large swell you may find it a useful place to find manageable sized waves if you are a less competent surfer or beginner. There's good land-based fishing off the rocks either side, plus a few mussels around for those that know where to look.

3. Whale Bay

Many years ago, local Maori noticed a large floating object in the sea offshore. They used Mr Woolley's telescope to discover it was a dead whale, which they proceeded to tow ashore into this little cove-like bay. Located on the headland that separates Matapouri from Woolleys, it now seems to be a magnet for foreign tourists who have got wind of "Whaleys" subtle and intimate charms. It is a tiny but delightful west-facing beach located a ten minute walk through native bush, that's thick with Nikaus and Puriris, is totally sheltered from both swell and easterly winds, and which gets beautiful late afternoon light. When you get down there, the outside world ceases to exist. There's even a toilet down on the beach. Halfway down the path there is a look-out, a picnic table and a track that leads to a good fishing ledge. Sadly the piles of shattered glass in the carpark lend credence to the sign warning against leaving valuables in parked cars here, though recently installed cameras may have curbed the problem somewhat.

Whale Bay

Matapouri

4. Matapouri

Beaches don't come a lot better than Matapouri. A stunning horseshoe shaped bay, with the Te Wairoa Stream feeding out through a meandering estuary to the south, is protected by large headlands at each extremity and backed by modest dunes of golden sand. This is top-shelf coastal paradise by anyone's standards, made more popular by its enclosed, relatively sheltered, and intimate nature. Three main access points onto the beach between the holiday homes, all offer the casual beach-goer a grassed space to park and relax, with the reserve between Wehiwehi and Waetford St featuring a free gas barbeque and picnic tables. The estuary can also be a nice place to laze with the kids, and is where locals launch their boats, but it's a high tide proposition only, as the bar, which can have excellent waves in a large swell, gets too shallow to navigate at low tide. Sadly, the main beach rarely has rideable surf, and close-outs are its favourite demeanour. The bridge on the main road is a popular jumping and fishing spot at high tide, and if you head to the northern end of the beach, cross over the saddle and walk east along the rocks you'll come to the Mermaid pools, a delightful natural pool system flooded by the tide. Matapouri also has a good grocery store. **Matapouri Cedar Stone Lodge** (06)833 7552 www.matapouri.co.nz. **Pacific Edge Self Service Apartments** (09)438 2781. **Bluewater Cottages** (09)434 3423 www.bluewatercottages.co.nz

5. Tutukaka

The hills surrounding Tutukaka were notable for the abundance of kaka (native parrots); and a tutu was a tree in which snares were set, hence the name. Nowdays it is better known for it's excellent marina, renown game fishing club and good restaurants. It isn't a beach as such (though there is a small stretch of sand at the end of the marina drive), but is the social heart of the coast, with a variety of shops and accommodation options, and sells the only gas on the coast. The harbour wall is a popular spot to fish from with mixed results. **Tutukaka Holiday Park** (09)434 3938. **Pacific Rendezvous Motel** www.pacificrendezvous.co.nz. **Oceans Resort** (09)470 2290 www.oceansresorthotel.co.nz

6. Church Bay

If you take Ngunguru Ford Rd south of Tutukaka, you come to a selection of pretty beaches inside Tutakaka harbour. The first is Church Bay, facing north with its grass reserve and picnic tables. Accommodation at **www.seaviewbach.co.nz**

7. Kowharewa Bay

Another beach similar to Church Bay. Tiny, cove-like and a bit shingly, but charmingly intimate; it features a short concrete boat ramp and one or two baches,

Tutukaka harbour and Pacific Bay

Whangaumu Bay

Ngunguru Estuary

with a grass reserve and a public loo. **The Bach** offers absolute waterfront accommodation (09)434 3977.

8. Pacific Bay
The third of Tutukaka's north facing triplets, Pacific Bay is off the main road, down a steepish valley. It features more homes, and looks like it's going to get a whole lot busier soon, with the entire hill behind marked out for subdivision.

9. Dolphin Bay
If you really want to avoid people, take Dolphin Bay Rd to the end, where a walkway delivers you down onto a private, east-facing beach out on the tip of the peninsula, offering spectacular views out to the Poor Knights. **Pebble Cottage** self-contained accommodation (09)434 4995.

10. Whangaumu Bay
Another of the region's less visited and possibly under appreciated beaches is also known as Wellington Bay, but whatever you call it, it enjoys a beautiful, if south-facing aspect looking over the Ngunguru Spit, with views down towards Patau and Manaia. It is sheltered from all swell, and the lucky residents enjoy beachfront splendour and safe swimming for most of the year. A track out to the headland at the western end offers a fantastic vantage point over the Ngunguru Bar and sandspit, and is the entrance to the Ngunguru Walkway which follows the harbour banks past some sheltered coves and eventually to Ngunguru. You will find a great reef at the beginnning of the walkway, from where you can cast lures or bait into the estuary mouth, with the prospect of a few kahawai and snapper a fairly likely occurence. There are several easy vehicle access points to the main beach, plus a good set of public toilets at the eastern end. There's no shop and only a few private accommodation options.
Lookout Lodge luxury hilltop apartment (09)434 4503 www.lookoutlodge.co.nz.
The Sands Beachfront Motel (09)434 3747 www.sandsmotel.co.nz. **Ramoana B&B** (09)434 4406 www.ramoana.co.nz

11. Ngunguru
Ngunguru is another of a series of fantastic river estuaries which drain into the sea along the Northland coast, providing safe anchorage and an incredible diversity of marine life. It is a picture postcard cute little village, with some quaint old baches and a few shops that is protected by a large dune backed sandspit. Sadly, this unique ecosystem is currently threatened by an entirely inappropriate development proposal, with a long running fight going on in the courts led by locals who are trying to prevent it going ahead. The Ngunguru rivermouth can get fantastic waves in a huge south-east swell, though this is a rare occurrence, with short rights and longer peeling lefts, best at low tide. Further down the spit you will also find some good peaks, with access gained by paddling over the estuary and walking across the dunes. The lookout north of Ngunguru is a good place to check out proceedings.

12. The Poor Knights
While I haven't covered most of the inshore islands that dot our coastline, the Poor Knights are such a huge tourist drawcard that I felt it worth making an exception for them. One of the great conservation success stories in New Zealand is happening 23 km off the coast, where a vast marine reserve has seen the resurgence of a bewildering array of marine life, at what is perhaps the most popular dive site in the country. Jacque Cousteau described it as one of the 10 best scuba locations in the world, and while that's a matter of opinion, the experience is truly spectacular and easily accessible for even the most inexperienced snorkeller. **Dive Tutukaka** is the main operator, with a range of options accommodating everyone from seasoned veterans to children. Their base is at the marina in Tutukaka, by Snapper Rock Restaurant (09)434 3867 or freephone 0800 288 882 www.diving.co.nz

The Poor Knights

Whangarei Coast

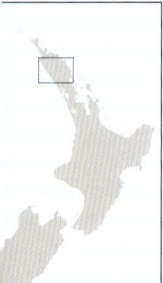

Working out what to do must be something of a dilemma for Whangarei's 50,000 residents, who wake up each day with such a wealth of world-class beaches on their back door step. Which one to choose from depends on mood, preferred activity and the wind direction; but no matter what your preference, or which way the wind is blowing, it's a fair bet your desires can be sated. Strangely overlooked by those flying through on their way to the more celebrated beaches further north, Whangarei is an absolute goldmine for ocean lovers, with some of Northland's finest coast right on its back door, and Mt Manaia imparting a powerful presence over the entire region. Spend a bit of time exploring the area and you will see what I mean.

Travelling The drive out to the Whangarei Heads is delightful, especially at high tide, with pohutakawas lining both sides of the road, reminiscent of the Thames coast. **Whangarei I-site** 92 Otaika Rd, Whangarei (09)438 1079 www.whangareiNZ.com

WIND ROSE

SWELL ROSE

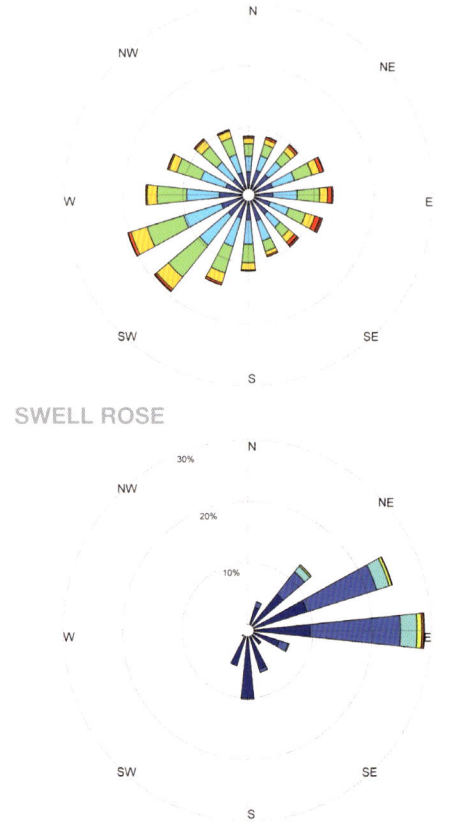

Surfing Ocean Beach and Pataua offer some of the best sand bottom waves in Northland. www.oceanbeachboardriders.co.nz (09)434 0744. Ding Repairs (09)436 1696 Murray Wood, 360 Whangarei Heads Rd, Waikaraka.

Fishing The diversity of habitat between Whangarei and Pataua includes most marine eco-systems, supporting a vibrant fishery. Bream Bay is one of the best pilchard grounds in the country, which attracts a multitude of other desirable species.

Swimming There are plenty of choices, though the beaches inside the heads are a pale shadow of those on the east coast, and water quality issues have plagued the inner harbour for years. **NRC Environmental Hotline** 0800 504 639 www.nrc.govt.nz

1. Onerahi
Beach Rd leads you around the Onerahi headland and to the first real beach of sorts east of Whangarei. It's a tidal and shingly stretch of sand facing south into the river, and home to the **Onerahi Yacht Club**, a popular small boat launch ramp, plus a kids play area. **Topsail** restaurant (09)436 2985 www.topsail.co.nz

2. Tamaterau
Another tidal, shingly beach of sorts that is home to the mangrove lined marine reserve that extends from the grassed reserve west of here.

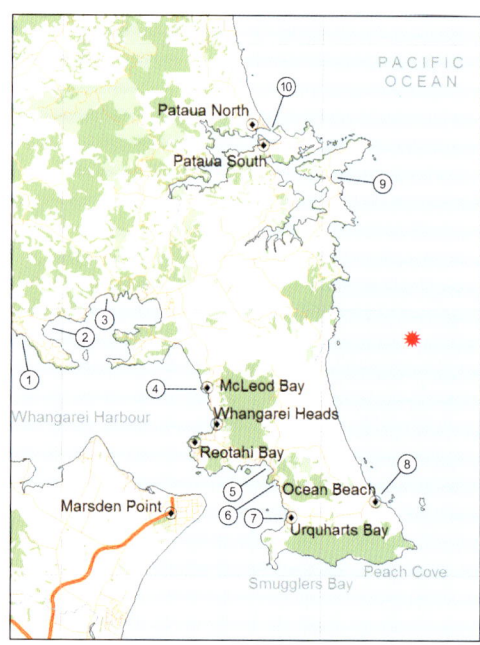

3. Parua Bay/Solomons Point
Solomons Point is the start of Parua Bay and the busiest of the boat launching spots in the Whangarei estuary. It's home to the **Whangarei Cruising Club**, the **Outboard Boating Club** and also a popular public ramp. The actual beach is further east, accessed

McLeods Bay

Ocean Beach

either from Wharf Rd or Richie Rd. It's not an epic swimming beach and is rapidly being built out, with private homes lining the foreshore. **The Parua Bay Tavern** dates back to 1902, and is a local landmark of some note, supplying fresh seafood and cold beers to locals and travellers alike.

4. McLeods Bay

This is what's known as Whangarei Heads and is stunning in a tidal, estuarine way. It's quite a long area of coastline, fringed with oysters, that sits at the base of Manaia Mt. The main swimming area is at the eastern end, where you'll find loos, picnic tables and a barbeque area, but like all the beaches in the area, it's shingly, tidal and shallow. **Whangarei Heads Holiday Units and Motel** (09)434 0793. **Mystic Mountain** luxury accommodation (09)434 0705.

5. Taurikura/McGregors Bay

A short stetch of sand just after the shops is the best place to swim, plus there's ample shade offered by the pohutakawas on the shoreline here. It's a highly sheltered spot which makes it perfect for families with young children.

6. McKenzie Bay

A sweet, enclosed, but private bay with no public access. **Appin Cottage B&B** is the only accommodation option.

7. Urqharts Bay

Urqharts extends in a sweeping crescent with several separate patches of sand, backed by houses. It's a sheltered swimming spot and the last car-accessible bay before Bream Head, that ends down Urqhart Rd, and ends in a turnaround and a small carpark. This is the access point for the Smugglers Bay walkway which leads around Bream Head to Peach Cove and eventually to Ocean Beach. These are both primo fishing areas for land based anglers, but require a bit of effort to get to.

8. Ocean Beach

One of Northland's finest, Ocean Beach has a wild and untamed feel, with a rocky promontory and a series of islets projecting off its southern fringe, and a smaller headland 1km to the north. There's a community of baches behind the beach and a well equipped surf life-saving club occupying a prominent position overlooking the coast at the south end, down Ranui Rd, which is where the main carpark and public amenities are located. Despite appearances, it continues north over the sand dunes and headland nearly all the way to Pataua, so if it's a bit of peace and quiet you're after, you will find it in spades there, and while locals call this northern beach Proctors, it's all part of Ocean Beach proper. Surf-wise, it's all good at OB, with its steep shelf, pronounced sandbanks and patchy reef giving shape to any swell. Proctors is known to pick up a bit more size but also hold its shape and is a popular spot for the local boardriders club competitions. Fishing off the rocks to the south looks to be highly productive for a number of species. The great thing about Ocean Beach, aside from its squeaky white sand, is the fact that it hasn't been gentrified by southern money. It still feels like a Kiwi beach town, and not some advertisement for indoor/outdoor flow. Long may it remain thus.

9. Taiharuru/McGregors Bay

A narrow, almost fjord-like inlet gives way to a broad scallop shaped bay. Houses line the cliffs to the east while farmland provides a buffer behind it and to the north-west. The bay itself faces south-east, but due to its large curve, there is almost always a place to find shelter from the wind. There's one main public access point at the south, where there's a grassy parking area, public loos and access to the beach for boat launching. It can be a bit tricky swimming at low tide due to the stones and reef remnants which appear in patches, but it's a pretty cool spot nonetheless, with only a handful of holiday homes and no real fuss or scene. Not a surf beach, but there looked liked some good land-based fishing ledges either side of the bay for those that don't mind a bit of a walk.

10. Pataua

Pataua is possibly the finest of Northland's lush river estuaries, with a beauty and fertility that is virtually unrivalled on this earth. It isn't until you've travelled around the world's oceans a bit that you can really appreciate this fact, but it's true. They don't get much more stunning than Pataua, with a sheltered little settlement on the south side of the inner estuary, and its seaside neighbour to the north. The two Patauas are connected by a footbridge, that makes for a great jumping spot at higher tides. Neither features more than 50 or so baches, and the only real public amenities are at the campsite with its shop that unfortunately only opens in peak summer periods. The beach at Pataua North extends way north towards Ngunguru, and holds some good waves when conditions are small. In a solid swell, you can expect good shaped rights off the river bar. Both sides of the estuary have launch ramps, though the south side features a hard concrete version, whereas to the north it's an onto-the-sand affair. Frogtown or Castaway Bay is an empty little beach to the south of the mountain at Pataua Sth, that is a beautiful swimming spot and also picks up a bit of north swell. Access is via the DOC walkway just past the campground. **Treasure Island Trailer Park** (09)436 2390 www.treasureisland.co.nz. **Surfpad** at Pataua North offers an apartment and surf lessons (09)436 2794 www.surfpad.co.nz. **Pataua Fishing Club** (09)436 0068 (North)Neville Brunker (South) Gary Hannam. **Tahi Ecosphere Retreat** www.tahinz.com

Pataua

Bream Bay

It looks like something took a massive bite out of the Northland coastline and what's left is Bream Bay. But that's not a bad thing, as its deep indentation offers a huge amount of shelter from wind and swell, and has conspired to produced a gigantic sandy playground for us lucky humans. Named by Captain Cook for the abundance of bream (snapper) in the bay, it is still a prolific fishery, yet the vast expanse of sparkling sand which extends from Marsden Point to Waipu cove has for many years been somehow overlooked by many who rush past it on their way to other places. This now appears to be changing, with a gradual increase in patronage over the years, and a range of new subdivisions popping up in various spots.

Travelling Main roads skirt most of its length, with a couple of good campgrounds but a dearth of private rental accommodation. The main shops are at Ruakaka and Waipu Town. www.breambay.co.nz

WIND ROSE

SWELL ROSE

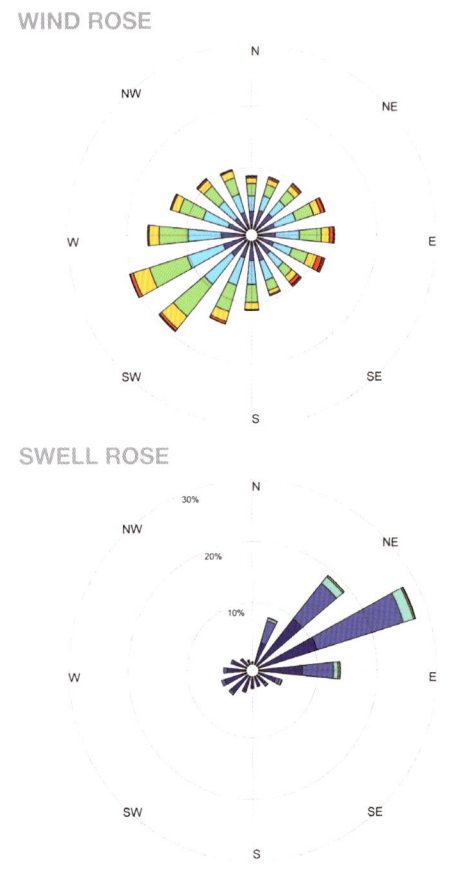

Surfing Its protection means it gets less size than some of the more exposed coast nearby, but that can work to its advantage in bigger swells.
Roger Hall Surfboards, 8 Kepa Rd, Ruakaka. (09)432 8110 www.surfline.co.nz.
Bream Bay Sliders are the local longboard crew, breambaysliders.blogspot.com.
Bream Bay is also a popular kiteboarding location www.ruakakitesports.co.nz (09)432 8347.

Fishing Bream Bay is one of New Zealand's richest pilchard hatcheries and also a prolific shellfish ground, which attracts a wide range of fish for most of the year. Birds diving and dolphins feeding just offshore, are both common sights. Few rocks, and calm seas make it a kontiki and small boat paradise. The islands offshore only add to the appeal.
Bream Bay Charters (09)432 7484.

Swimming You'll find beautiful white sand, and calm seas for most of the year, without too many people around. Ruakaka and Waipu have lifesaving clubs on patrol during weekends and peak holiday season, and Uretiti Beach offers the chance to escape the crowds and get naked, if that's your wish. **Ruakaka Surf-lifesaving Club** (09)432 7002 www.ruakakalifeguards.co.nz **Waipu Cove SLSC** (09)432 0564

1. Marsden Point

Take Marsden Point Rd to the end. Just south of the powerstation, Mair Rd leads you to the northernmost access point to Bream Bay proper. It's hardly the most romantic spot, dominated by the huge plant, but the beach itself is stunning; dune backed and sparkling. It is a fine fishing spot and also the most exposed to south-east swells, with good banks that the locals surf regularly. Not surprisingly, it is known as "Powerstations" to the surf community. It is also extremely popular with kiteboarders, with the north-east sea breeze usually at its strongest point in the bay here. Just south is the community of Marsden, originally built to house workers during construction of the refinery; but now a bit of a ghetto, if truth be known. Nonetheless there is a grass reserve and parking area with pedestrian access to the beach down the walkway through the dunesoff Sime Rd, but no toilets or other public facilities.

2. Ruakaka

A small, established coastal settlement is nestled south of the river mouth of the same name, with a shopping centre and surf club, plus all the associated facilities. It hasn't traditionally had the swank of other east coast settlements, though this is changing slowly, as it becomes harder to afford property in nearby areas, and also because it posesses the main asset of any good beach town: a strategic position in the middle of a fabulous white sand beach. The surf club is located at the main beach access point, which has a large reserve area and toilets, with plenty of public parking available. Princes Road takes you to the mouth of the river, and it too is a delightful spot, with a grass reserve and picnic areas. The rivermouth is a renowned and protected bird breeding ground, in particular attracting godwits and knots. The estuary has become a very popular kiteboarding spot of late, but restrictions apply especially during peak spring tides when the birds are known to roost here. You will see the signs showing restricted areas at the carpark by the surf club. **Ruakaka Reserve Motor Camp** (09)432 7590 www.motorcamp.co.nz.
Whitesands holiday unit 021 405 650.

3. Uretiti

Next stop south along this sparkling stretch of largely east-facing coastline is the Uretiti DOC Reserve, which is a fascinating and fabulous place to visit. There are two parts to it; the day area to the north, and the camp to the south, but both offer access through the beautiful dunes and on to the beach. The camp is a well maintained and popular resource, that's manned all year, and can take up to a thousand people in peak season, though for most of the time is remarkably quiet. The area south of the campsite is a renown nudist beach that can get a bit fruity, so be warned. If you are easily offended, stay to the north of the camp boundary. The day use area is a big parking space adjacent to the camp, set amongst the trees just behind the beach, with a fairly rough old longdrop toilet. The only vehicle access onto the beach at this end is off Uretiti Rd, 4wd access only. **Uretiti DOC Campsite** (09)432 1051.

4. Waipu Cove

The name is somewhat of a misnomer, as it isn't a cove in the strictest sense of the word, though the small rocky headland at the south-east corner does signal the end of the massive beach, which extends all the way from Marsden Point. Here the coast is angled around and faces almost north, which makes it a popular place to be when there's any south in the wind. The main public access is at the eastern end of the beach where there is a shop, takeaways, toilets, surf club and parking. There can be good surf off the point, and banks all along the beach here, especially at higher tides; best in a north-east or huge east swell with south winds. Given that the main road passes directly behind the beach, you cant miss it when it is pumping. There aren't many holiday homes to rent, but a couple of good camps. **Waipu Cove Cottages and Camping** (09)432 0851. **Camp Waipu Cove** (09)432 0410 www.campwaipucove.com

5. Laings Beach

More gorgeousness facing north into Bream Bay. Laings is stunning, though the most densely populated spot in the area, with houses on all sides and on the hills behind; yet strangely, it features no public amenities other than a set of toilets at the eastern end. Pohutakawas grace the foreshore for much of its length, but parking is very limited. This, the lack of public accommodation, and the somewhat rarefied atmosphere, make it less inviting for travellers. Nonetheless it offers great swimming, waves in bigger swells at lower tides, and good kayak launching. For fishermen, the major drawcard is access to some excellent rock fishing spots on either side, but especially east towards Bream Tail, where there are a few private bays to find. Ding Bay is a small cove to the west, accessed by walking around the rocks. It faces further east and often has the best waves in the area. **Melody Lodge B&B** (09)432 0939.

RODNEY COUNTY

Historically known as North Auckland, Rodney is a region of rolling farmland that is linked inexorably with the city to its south, yet despite the obvious associations, remains staunchly separate. As you leave Orewa and drive over the hills, the urban sprawl slowly releases you from its clutches, and you slip effortlessly into the arms of the myriad delights around Kawau Bay, Leigh and Matakana; before falling completely in love with Pakari and Mangawhai's captivating and pristine beauty. It is an affair that Auckland's residents can't seem to shake off, and probably never will. So close, so beautiful and so willing; why would they?

Travelling The road north of Orewa is probably New Zealand's worst for traffic snarl-ups at peak periods, and at times it can be gridlocked from Orewa to the Brynderwyns. I strongly advise not travelling at busy times for the sake of your mental health. **Warkworth I-Site** (09)425 9081 www.warkworthnz.com

Surfing Rodney county has some epic surf spots ranging from the world class river bar at Mangawhai Heads, to Orewa's gentle peelers, with most stops in between, and there's usually somewhere to surf in typical swells. Finding the right one is called "doing the east coast shuffle." In south winds, Tawharanui and Goat Island can be the places to look, when its north-west, Daniels is a good option. South-west and west winds are good for all the main spots.

Fishing Land-based fishing gets better the further north you go, as the water gets deeper. Kawau Bay has always been a very productive fishery for boaties as well as an easy place to access for kayakers and while the marine reserve near Leigh cuts out some useful terrain, the coastline either side is very good.

Swimming Most notable for the spectacular marine reserve at Goat Island, but it also hosts a range of pristine sandy beaches and good amounts of sheltered options in between the rolling surf beaches.

Orewa

Mangawhai

Surf carnage

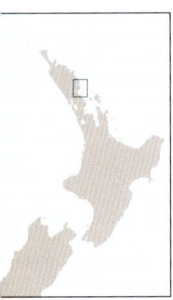

Mangawhai to Goat Island

Most people that have spent time here agree that this area is one of our coastal diamonds, offering some of the most pristine and beautiful beaches in the country, a marine reserve that is mind-blowingly alive, excellent fishing locations and some world-class waves, all within an hour and a half of Auckland. That it has, by and large, remained in a largely unexploited condition, is a testament to the old Rodney District Council and some well timed pressure by local environmentalists and scientists. Both Pakiri and Mangawhai/Te Arai beaches feature large, fertile, dune-protected estuary systems, that deserve the utmost care and preservation.

Travelling Mangawhai is the only place with real shops plus nightlife of a kind, though you can get basic provisions at the Pakiri campsite, but no fuel. The back roads between Mangawhai and Leigh are all gravel and pretty tortuous, so take your time.

Surfing This is one of the best places on the east coast, with somewhere handling most swell directions and sizes. What makes it even better, is the country vibe, but its proximity to Auckland means crowds are guaranteed in the weekends and holidays. **Aotea Surf School** (09)431 5760 or 027 250 7906 www.aotearoasurf.co.nz. **Bammas Surf and Leisure** (09)431 4660 is a good shop in the old village. **Supersession Surfboards** (09)431 5633.

Fishing Lots of good land-based fishing around the rocks and streams in the area, plus world class snorkelling at Goat Island Marine Reserve that's a huge tourist attraction and an absolute delight. **Ridgeback Fish and Dive Charters** 0800 347 467 **Hook 'Em Up** (09)431 4747 **R'n'R Charters Mangawhai** (021)954 241 www.rnrcharters.co.nz.

Swimming All the bases are pretty well covered, with sheltered options aplenty around Mangawhai and Goat Island, and a surf life-saver patrolled beach at Mangawhai Heads. Both Pakiri and Te Arai get swell, but are beautiful swimming spots nonetheless.

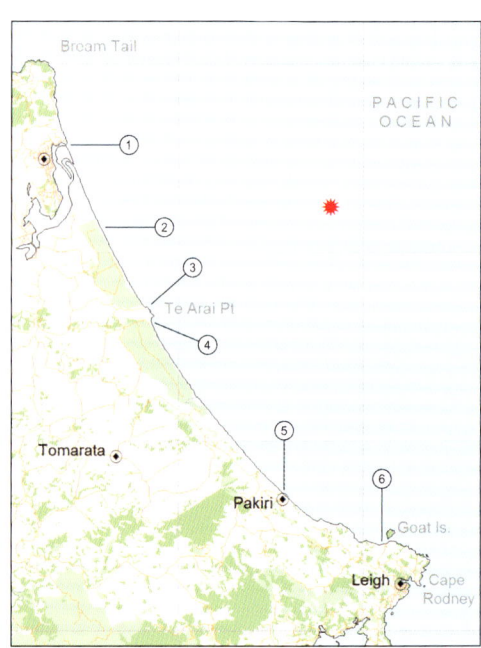

WIND ROSE

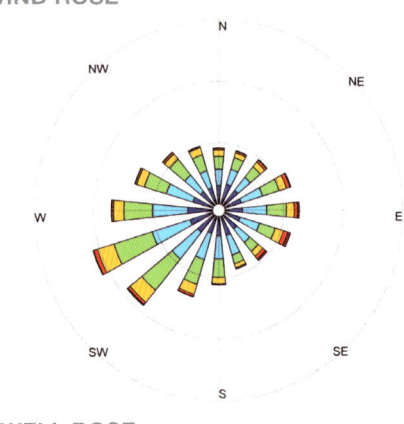

SWELL ROSE

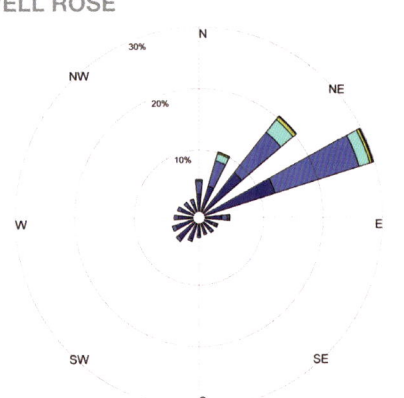

Mangawhai heads

Mangawhai dunes

1. Mangawhai

The name is an abbreviated version of Manga (where the streams meet), and Te Whai (the stingray). The stingray was a Ngati Whatua chief of the area, and his pa was at Moir Point, where several streams meet. It is another magnificent east coast rivermouth, with a spectacular rocky headland protecting the northern entrance, and vast shimmering dunes to the south. Mangawhai is a legendary surf town with a number of options, the most interesting being the wave that breaks off the south side of the harbour bar. It is predominantly a left that can get long and powerful in bigger swells, at lower tides, with an occasional short, punchy right off the peak. The beach between the north side of the heads and Bream tail can also be good, especially in smaller swells. It is where you'll find the surf club and is also a fab place to walk and swim. If the ocean is too violent and you want somewhere placid to take the family, the beaches inside the estuary offer calm swimming, especially Picnic Bay, located down a track from the main carpark at the heads. You can also walk here from town at low tide, but not at high. The settlement at the heads, which has grown rapidly in the last decade, is clustered on the north side of the river, while the old Mangawhai village sits at the head of the estuary some 5 km inland, connected by the causeway that was built in the 70's. Several of the roads off Molesworth Drive have walking access to the inner harbour, with boat ramps at Alamar Ave and Lincoln St, where there's a large reserve area with parking and shade trees. The shops at Wood St are excellent, with cafes, gas station, a fishing shop and the like. There's a fair amount of rental accommodation available at www.mangawhai.co.nz. **Mangawhai Lodge** (09)431 5311 www.seaviewlodge.co.nz. **Mangawhai Heads Motor Camp** (09)432 4675.

2. Black Stump

Te Arai Beach extends from Mangawhai all the way south to Te Arai Point, and Black Stump Rd offers the first easy vehicle access south of Mangawhai. It is a beautiful and usually private spot, that's a great place for a private swim and a sunbathe, plus usually has good waves at all tides, but no facilities.

Mangawhai estuary

Mangawhai bar

Te Arai

Te Arai

3. Te Arai Point

Te Arai Point Rd takes you to the headland that marks the southern extent of this spectacular stretch of sparkling white sand. It's a renown surfing, fishing and free-diving location, and a fantastic spot to day-trip that even has a small freedom-camping site with public toilets and bins. The point gets really good in a south-east swell at higher tides, but can work on most swell directions, while waves on the beach will be all about the condition of the banks, which are highly variable, as all beaches are. The rocks a few hundred metres offshore are surrounded by constant schools of baitfish, which is fantastic news for kayak fishermen and freedivers, and even if it's just a swim you're after, you can do a lot worse than Te Arai. The rocks between here and Pakiri hide a few little coves to explore and some good snorkelling spots also. It's gravel road in, no matter which way you choose to come, but well worth the dust on your windscreen.

4. Forestry

Just south of the Te Arai Point there's another access road through the pine forests leading to the north end of Pakiri Beach. It is almost a mirror image of Te Arai, with a cove-like feel, but without the campsite, and offers access to miles of glittering sand to the south with rarely a soul in sight. The surf can be great down the beach, with a left off the point that can smoke on a good day, best in a north-east or east swell, and again, there's good fishing off the rocks between here and Te Arai. The road in is gravel, and heavily potholed, but its worth the effort. There are no facilities at the beach, but there is a campground with toilets and hot showers at the top of the road. **Forestry Campsite** 027 233 6924.

5. Pakiri

Lovely Pakiri beach is as spectacular as it is long, with a substantial stream and estuary feeding into the southern end, which is where you'll find the campsite and parking areas. Most people surf this end too, though there can be peaks all the way up the beach, that are normally better in north-east swells. The best land-based fishing is generally off the beach further south towards Goats Island. Despite the ravages caused by advancing tides of city folk, who have transformed surrounding beaches with development, Pakiri has maintained her unspoilt character, with almost no noticeable changes in the previous twenty years. I say almost, because there has been one major issue and sadly it is pretty catastrophic; the loss of its sand dunes, almost certainly a result of the sand mining that has been performed to provide sand to replenish Auckland's city beaches. The Red Beach SLSC patrols the south end in weekends. **Pakiri Camping Ground** (09)422 6199 www.pakiriholidaypark.co.nz. **Pakiri Beach Horse Riding** (09)422 6275 www.horseride-nz.co.nz

Te Arai point

6. Goat Island Marine Reserve

This coast has long been inhabited by Maori. The bay was known as Whakatuwhenua and the island as Motu Hawere, and was a prolific fish, shellfish and crayfish gathering area. In the early part of last century, large snapper were caught from the beach and crayfish collected from rock pools by locals. They also removed large amounts of kelp that washed onto the beach after storms to use for fertilisers. By the 1950s and 1960s the marine life had been heavily reduced due to commercial fishing and collecting. A marine laboratory was established by the University of Auckland to the east of the beach in 1964. Staff at the university had the idea of creating a protected piece of coast so that their studies of marine life would not be affected. New Zealand's first marine reserve, commonly known as Goat Island, was created in 1975 and officially opened in 1977. It covers 518 hectares of coastal sea between Cape Rodney and Okakari Point. The best time to visit is when there is less than a metre of swell on the east coast, and no wind, or offshore wind from the southwest. After heavy rain, easterly swells or onshore winds, visibility is usually reduced. The marine reserve is ideal for children to experience snorkelling and see marine life in numbers not seen anywhere else on the coast. In a north-east swell and south winds, there's a good reef break here for surfers, that is rarely surfed. Facilities near the beach include toilets, changing rooms, a cold shower and information kiosk. **Glass Bottom Boat** (09)422 6334 www.glassbottomboat.co.nz.
Goat Island Dive/Outer Gulf Charters (09)422 6925 or 0800 348 369.
Seafriends (09)422 6212 hire snorkelling gear www.seafriends.org.nz.
Goat Island Camping (09)422 6185.

The Warkworth Coast

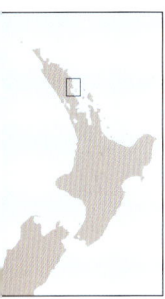

It encompasses the two broad areas of Omaha Bay and Kawau Bay, including Kawau Island; and again, this section of coast is incredibly varied, with a mix of rocky shores, flat muddy harbour beaches, and a couple of the finest sandy bays you'll ever encounter. The common denominator is that all are serviced and generally accessed within twenty minutes of Warkworth. It is something of a favourite short getaway spot from Auckland, and can get pretty busy with day-trippers, especially given the foodie appeal of Matakana and the patronage it draws. But it is popular for a reason; with so much in a small area, it caters to so many people's whims and tastes, with the caveat that you have to like crowds.

Travelling Lots to see and do, with a ton of variety for all types of beach lovers here. Everything is pretty close together. The tourist centre is at Warkworth (09)425 9081 www.warkworth-information.co.nz

WIND ROSE

SWELL ROSE

Surfing Omaha used to be legendary till they built the groines, though it still gets a few waves in bigger swells. Daniels Reef and Goat Island are the novelty waves in the north of the area, but Tawharanui the most consistent spot. All work in different conditions, though none are really world class.

Fishing Kawau Bay is an area where people are intensely focused on fishing and scallops, but most of the action is off boats; it being pretty shallow. The Leigh coast and the tip of the Scandrett Peninsula are the best land-based options.

Swimming Again plenty of fantastic swimming options in different wind and swell conditions, with the bonus of Goat Island Marine Reserve nearby, for the most interesting swim of all.

1. Leigh

Leigh is a charming little coastal town that has developed around the boat harbour and commercial wharf that are both set into a deeply indented bay just north of the village. The community is built on the cliff tops overlooking the east coast, offers a range of facilities, and is the social hub of the surrounding coast. It isn't a beach as such, though does have an excellent boat ramp and offers access to several beautiful spots, so I felt it was appropriate to give it a listing as you don't tend to visit any of the surrounding beaches without dropping in to Leigh to

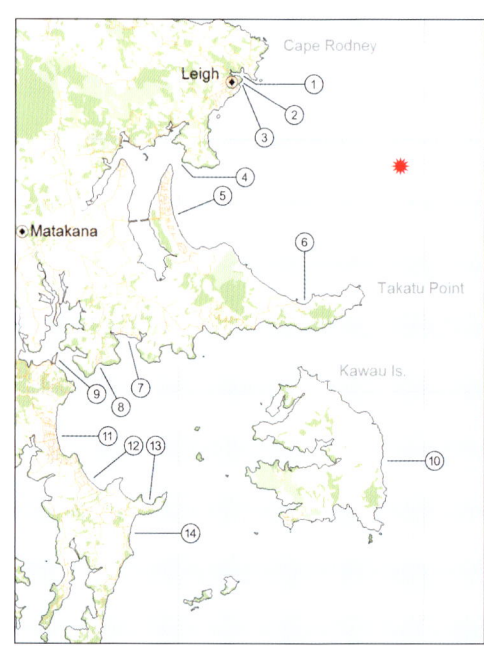

get gas, food, or stop by the **Sawmill Cafe** (09)422 6019 www.sawmillcafe.co.nz for coffee and varied night time amusement. **www.leighbythesea.co.nz**. **Leigh Bach** (09)422 6688 is an old style bach for rent. **Leigh Harbour Holiday House** (09)422 6559 www.nearleigh.co.nz.

Leigh Wharf

Mathiesons Bay

2. Daniels Reef
Daniels is a short, punchy right reef break, located below the cliffs south of Leigh. It's one of those spots that's much discussed but not surfed as often as you might like, as it only breaks well in the biggest east or moderate south-east swells, though it profits from being offshore in a north-west wind. Access is down the steps at the bottom of Wonderview Street, Leigh.

3. Mathiesons Bay
Mathiesons Bay is Leigh's beach, a beautiful and protected sliver of sand protected by headlands on either extremity and a reef system offshore that is a superb place to swim and dive. It has a fabulous domain behind the beach with lot of grass and a childrens playground, plus a raft moored 50 or so metes offshore that's a great place to laze on and jump off. The beach can be accessed down either of two roads: GrandView to the north and Mathieson Bay Rd to the south. The foreshore shelves steeply, which is fantastic for swimming in normal conditions, but can make it a bit treacherous in swell, though only the rare big south-easters get in here, with occasional rideable rights off the south-western point in those conditions.

4. Ti Point
It's just a small boat landing and simple wharf at the mouth of the Whangateau Harbour, which runs in behind Omaha. There's a great walk around the coast from Ti Point. **Ti Point Retreat** (09)422 6908 B&B or self catering www.tipointretreat.co.nz

5. Omaha
Omaha is one of the less homogenous beach resorts in the country, that's home to famous designers, the Prime Minister and a host of wealthy Aucklanders who over the past twenty years have colonised what was once one of NZ surfing's little secrets and a cruisey old beach town. It isn't any more, even though some of the old baches remain, but you'll feel right at home if rubbing shoulders with rich listers is what you want to do on your holidays. It has been described as "one giant koru lounge," which sounds about right, but still it offers a lovely long sandy beach that gets a few rolling waves on a decent north-east swell, and hosts a full range of facilities. Just don't expect to see many crusty old fishermen or rootsy surfers on the beach, because you won't. The most sought after waves break off the bar at the northern end, though there are also peaks down its length; but be warned, it has been heavily colonised by SUP's and longboarders. **www.omahabeach.co.nz**
Omaha Lodge www.omahalodge.co.nz
Omaha Bach 027 274 8488 www.omahabach.co.nz.
Omaha Boat House (09)422 9918
www.omahaboathouse.co.nz

Omaha

6. Tawharanui/Anchor Bay

To quote the DOC brochure, "Tawharanui Regional Park boasts some of the Auckland regions most beautiful white sand beaches, rolling pastures, shingle bays and regenerating wetlands. The 588 hectare park is NZ's first integrated open sanctuary, where farming, public recreation, and conservation of native species combine," which is a pretty accurate and concise summary. The park occupies the eastern tip of the peninsula of the same name, and the last 5 or 6 km of the road are gravel. I made the mistake of arriving once at 5.00pm on a fine summer Saturday, as half of Auckland seemed to be leaving, so every bend in the road felt like a game of Russian roulette. As you arrive, there is a south-facing shingle beach that is good for swimming and fishing, but north-facing Anchor Bay is the main attraction; so named after the anchor of HMS Phoenix, which was wrecked on this coastline in 1879. It is a stunning beach with intriguing rocks to the north, a shelf reef to the west, and another long stretch of sand that sits in front of the DOC campsite even further west. It is normally

Anchor Bay

Buckletons Beach

calm and sheltered and of particular appeal to those who want a controlled sense of wild. Surfers enjoy its northerly orientation and exposure to big north-east swells, with off-shores from the south and south-east that makes it pretty unique. The main waves are a range of beach peaks at all tides west of Anchor bay, and a high tide right that breaks off the reef that divides Anchor Bay from its neighbour. There are waves of varying quality all down to Omaha at lower tides, but generally, the surf is better between mid and high tides, though crowds can be intense, with heaps of learners and marginal wave quality a lot of the time. There are toilets at many spots in the park and camping is allowed in a sectioned off area adjacent to the beach west of Anchor Bay www.doc.govt.co.nz. **Sandpiper Lodge Boutique Hotel** (09)422 7256 www.sandpiperlodge.co.nz

7. Baddleys Beach/Cambells Beach

These two conjoined twins both face into an extremely shallow and tidal inlet on the northern side of Kawau Bay, and are almost a mirror image of each other, with a clutch of holiday homes in the centre of each beach and a public boat launch ramp and toilets at one end. On Cambells it's at the east and Baddleys it's to the west. There's plenty of picnic space at both, but they're really only fun for swimming at high tide.

8. Buckletons Beach

Together with Baddleys and Campbells, these very British sounding beaches all share a very British conuntenance. They're all very tidal and quaint in a "look at me, I am cute" kind of way, but aren't really a great base for super active types, as there's only a beach for a few hours a day; then it's a muddy thing like the English east coast. There's a beautiful pohutakawa clad reserve along the entire length of the bay (only a few hundred metres), plus a boat ramp to the east that gets a bit of use at high tide, but there are no public loos or obvious rental accommodation.

9. Sandspit

Sandspit is the departure point for the ferry to Kawau Island. It has a motor camp on the shores of the harbour and several property owners both in Sandspit itself and up the hill above Brick Bay, who provide bed and breakfast or lodge-style accommodation options. Because Sandspit is situated along an estuary (fed by the Matakana River), large numbers of sea birds congregate here. There is a small, sandy beach and an all-tide boat ramp. The large wharf houses the booking office for Reubens cruises. **Reubens** (09)425 8006 www.reubens.co.nz. **Sandspit Holiday Park** (09)425 8610 www.sandspitholidaypark.co.nz

10. Kawau Island

Kawau Island was purchased from the Maori in 1840 for sheep farming, but manganese and copper were discovered later and more lucrative mining began. The remains of the mine's brick pump-house chimney, and a tunnel, can be explored near Bon Accord Harbour. New Zealand's first governor, Sir

West of Anchor Bay

Snells Beach

George Grey, bought the island in 1862 and turned the 10-room mine manager's house into his beautiful two-storey home, which became known as the Mansion House. Later the property was reinvented as a popular hotel. Today, the house is open to the public, administered by the Department of Conservation, and is still home to many of the former Governor's treasures. Grey, a keen amateur botanist, introduced many species of exotic plants and animals to the island. A few of these species remain such as kookaburras and wallabies (and possums!). Kawau can be accessed by boat from nearby Algies Bay, Martins Bay, Sandspit and Snells Beach. There are no roads on the island, so Reubens Water Taxis operates the well-known Royal Mail Run, which departs daily from Sandspit for Mansion House, via the north-eastern bays and Bon Accord Harbour. The 3 hour cruise delivers mail and freight to many of the island's residents and features an informative commentary and optional lunch. The company also operates shuttle services several times a day and a water taxi. Vivian Bay is the best beach on an island without too much sand, though there are no public amenities. **Kawau Lodge and Island Experience** can provide transfers from Sandspit as well as fishing trips, and offers hosted luxury accommodation at North Cove. Other accommodation includes **The Coppercabanas/ Cedar Lodge**. There's an outdoor education centre, **Camp Bentzon**, that's used by community groups.

11. Snells Beach

Snells is a wide, shallow, extremely tidal stretch of sand and mud at the head of Kawau Bay, and a fairly popular small boat anchorage due to the shelter offered by Kawau. It is densely populated with a mixture of holiday homes and permanent residences, with multiple access points between the homes to the beach, where you'll find a broad grass and pohutakawa-backed foreshore extending for much of its length. It is only really okay to swim here at full tide and even then it doesn't get very deep, which may appeal if you have very small children. The only thing of any real interest to travellers is the extensive shopping centre on the ridge above the beach.

12. Algies Beach

There's little clear separation between the two communities of Snells and Algies, but Algies is a far smaller bay to the south, with a concrete boat-ramp that's good at higher tides. The facilities behind the beach are also good, but the swimming remains a high tide only affair.

13. Scandrett Regional Park

Another of the former ARC parks offering camping opportunities, sits on the north-facing arm of the peninsula jutting into the south channel of Kawau Bay. It was once an early settler farm, now frozen in time, with the old homestead, farm buildings and boatsheds on the shingly foreshore preserved as a museum of sorts. It's an ok place to swim at high tide but probably of more interest to land-based fishermen who like to fish off Mullet Point, chasing snapper and a range of other species at the southern entrance to Kawau Bay.

14. Martins Bay

A deeper bay, an extremely popular camping ground, better boat launching, and a handful of older baches, make Martins Bay more appealing for general beachgoers than Snells and Algies. It faces east and is located halfway out along the peninsula, with a turnoff before you get to Scandrett Regional Park. The rocks to the south offer good land-based fishing.

Martins Bay

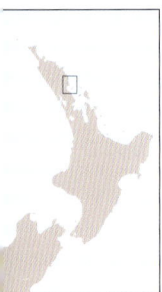

Mahurangi to Orewa

These are the last beaches before the Whangaparoa Peninsula and the Auckland region, and while they serve as an opportunity for short day trips away from town, they possibly offer less appeal for visitors than the sparkling sections of coast further north. Nonetheless, it is a unique and beautiful section of the country, with its high sandstone cliffs, large rivers, and views out to Great Barrier and Kawau Islands. Access to the beaches on this map is easy, as all are close to the road, but the quality they share is that all are relatively shallow, with a large tidal range.

Travelling Close proximity to Auckland means they get pretty busy on weekends, but strangely, with the exception of Orewa, there aren't a huge amount of accommodation options.

WIND ROSE

SWELL ROSE

Surfing East coast storm-surf and large north-east ground swells produce rideable waves at Orewa and in the hugest conditions, Waiwera and Wenderholm too. The Orewa longboard club is highly active, and meet on the first Wednesday of the month at the surf club www.orewalongboardclub.com (using up large amounts of wax since 1993).

Fishing Not great land-based fishing around here, though morning and evening high tides may produce the odd fish off the headlands and stream mouths.

Swimming They're all lovely swimming spots, but other than Orewa, all are relatively flat shelved and shallow, so best at higher tides.

1. Mahurangi

The sheltered bays, native bush, open pasture and historic sites of Mahurangi Regional Park straddle the entrance to the beautiful Mahurangi Harbour, which gives the park its name. The park is divided into three "fingers" – Mahurangi West, Scott Point and Mahurangi East. Mahurangi West provides a backdrop to three pohutukawa-fringed bays: Sullivan's (Otarawao) Bay, Mita (Otuawao) Bay and Te Muri Bay. Scott Point includes the historic Scott Homestead, while the remote Mahurangi East is only accessible by sea. The park is a favourite stop for boaties all year round. It takes on a festive air during Auckland Anniversary Weekend in January, when hundreds of classic vessels revel in the Mahurangi Old Time Regatta. Turn into Mahurangi West Rd then right into Ngarewa Drive and follow to the end of the road. Scotts point can be accessed from past Snells Beach. Camping info www.aucklandcity.govt.nz

2. Wenderholm

Wenderholm sits at the mouth of the Puhoi River and has a colourful European history both as a boat building location, and as a "bohemian settlement." The beach is on an isthmus protecting the sprawling river estuary, that features a well-used, all tides boat ramp. One of the country's finest and largest remaining stands of Pohutakawas extends imperiously for acres behind the beach and foreshore, and exists as one of the first examples of environmental protection in our history, saved for us by a local farmer who had

Waiwera

to fight to keep them from ending up on the fire. Nowadays they form a protective shade curtain for picnic goers and those enjoying the Auckland region's oldest park; a hugely under-appreciated little gem, right on the city's fringe, that offers a pristine coastal experience, yet is less than an hour from the CBD. There is a campsite attached to the park plus a limited amount of van sites for overnight stays. www.aucklandcouncil.govt.nz

3. Waiwera
For hundreds of years, local Maori were aware of the healing properties of the mineral springs at Waiwera, calling them Te Rata – "the Doctor." In 1842 after observing the locals soaking in hot pools on the beach, and hearing stories of the cures attributed to the waters, a Scottish doctor named Robert Graham bought land at Waiwera and established a hotel for the accommodation of "invalids, travellers and pleasure parties," giving birth to the country's first spa and tourist facility. One English businessman, a cripple for 15 years, was testimony to Waiwera's properties. He declared himself cured after six weeks at the resort, dispensed with his crutches and walked the 38 kilometres back to Auckland. Hmmm. "Miracles" such as this helped put the spa on the map, and by 1875, the healing powers of the water were being lauded internationally. To satisfy demand, Graham added 50 more rooms to his existing accommodation and barged in cottages and an entire hotel from the Coromandel, then a 400m wharf was built in 1905. With extensive grounds, tennis courts, croquet lawn and gardens, it had a distinctively European flavour, but met an untimely end in 1939, when the kauri hotel burned down in a blaze that could be seen from Auckland. Today, artesian bores 1500m deep feed purpose-built pools, capturing the hot water before it reaches the beach. Aside from the pools, there is occasionally good fishing at the stream mouth to the north end and okay swimming at high tide. **Waiwera Infinity Thermal Spa Resort** 0800 924 9372 www.waiwera.co.nz

4. Hatfields Beach
Best known as the place where former Prime Minister Robert Muldoon, had his holiday home, rather than for it's aquatic qualities, it's yet another bay like its neighbours, but in miniature. There's a small stream to the north, with headlands at either end, and a row of pohutakawas behind the foreshore, with a concrete slipway onto the beach at the southern end for beach-launching boats. It is a lovely if flattish beach, but the presence of the main road directly behind it, while making it a convenient picnic stop on the way north or south, somewhat detracts from the ambience.

5. Orewa
Orewa was once a small seaside holiday town adjacent to the main highway north, but more recently it has evolved into the last satellite suburb of Auckland. It still retains a holiday feel with its iconic campsite at the south by the river, and an extensive grass reserve behind the foreshore, but it is hardly a "getaway from it" kind of place. It's usually extremely busy and bristling with people and cars, a little reminiscent of Mt Maunganui, with its high rise apartments, and a slew of recent developments all around the seafront. Despite exposure to swell, it is a great swimming spot, with nearly 3 km's of ruler straight sand, that is an excellent place to let off some city steam. Orewa is known as a surf beach, and hosts a thriving longboard club, with an active lifesaving club also, but in truth it rarely gets anything more than a shoulder high waves, and even that is infrequent. The sandbars at the rivermouth usually have the best shape, but you better be prepared to fend off the SUP brigade that have claimed it for their own. It takes a big north-east swell and west or south-west winds to work, and while frustrating, isnt a bad learners spot. www.orewabeach.co.nz. **Orewa Top Ten Holiday Park** (09)426 5832 www.orewabeachholidaypark.co.nz. **Orewa Beach Surf Life-Saving Club** (09)426 5058 has a bar and bistro plus a webcam to check current conditions www.orewasurfclub.co.nz

Hatfields Beach

Orewa

Rodney County | 75

AUCKLAND

The Auckland isthmus is sandwiched between two of the most fertile harbours on the planet, with the roaring Tasman Sea washing its western coastline, and the sublime Pacific Ocean to the east. It is a city of coastal people that has always been linked to boats and boating, and the reason is blindingly clear, when you consider the beauty and strategic value of the Waitemata Harbour and the Hauraki Gulf, with its vast array of islands just offshore. Then once you factor in the Manukau, just a hop skip and a jump away, with its own sublime qualities, your head begins to spin. People think of Auckland's beaches and maybe Tamaki or Mission Bay come to mind, but there is so much more than just the waterfront to explore, with the huge number of excellent sandy bays on the Whangaparaoa Peninsula and the North Shore, Herne Bay's hidden surprises, Waiheke and Great Barrier to the east, and some of the most spectacular sections of the restless west coast, all waiting to receive visitors by car or by boat. There's a good reason that Auckland is New Zealand's biggest city, and a lot of it is down to the embarrassment of riches on the coast all around it. It's not a perfect city, but you don't often hear Aucklanders complain about their beaches.

Travelling Given the huge amount of territory covered by the Auckland region, it's hard to single out any specific theme, but obviously the inner-city beaches are busy places, especially in the weekends, and if you want to find peace and quiet, you need to head west or get out to the islands. I haven't covered all the islands in the gulf, but have focused on the two main ones that you can get to with a car, Waiheke and Great Barrier. www.aucklandnz.com is the official visitor website. www.aucklandcity.govt.nz is the council website.

The East Coast
They don't come much more diverse and spectacular than the bays of the Hauraki Gulf and Waitemata Harbour, so its hard to simplify things with a one paragraph description. Put simply, it is an oceanic treasure, with every type of sand, rock, beach and bay imaginable, offering sensational fishing, some phenomenal waves, excellent boat harbours, and sublime swimming beaches. It is just a case of choosing your preferred activity, and finding the best beach for that in the current weather conditions.

The West Coast
Auckland's west coast breaks down into three distinct and separate sections, with the inner-Manukau displaying all the characteristics you would expect of a west coast harbour. Its coastline is shallow, tidal and shelly, and while beautiful, not the best for swimming. Then there are the famous beaches accessed off the Piha Rd, sitting at the feet of the dramatic Waitakare ranges, that plunge into the sea with unmistakable drama and grandeur. Further north you'll find a coastline in transition, with the foothills of the Waitakares shaping Bethells like its southern neighbours, before Muriwai signals the start of hundreds of kilometres of sand, that stretch all the way to Cape Reinga, with few interruptions.

Mission Bay

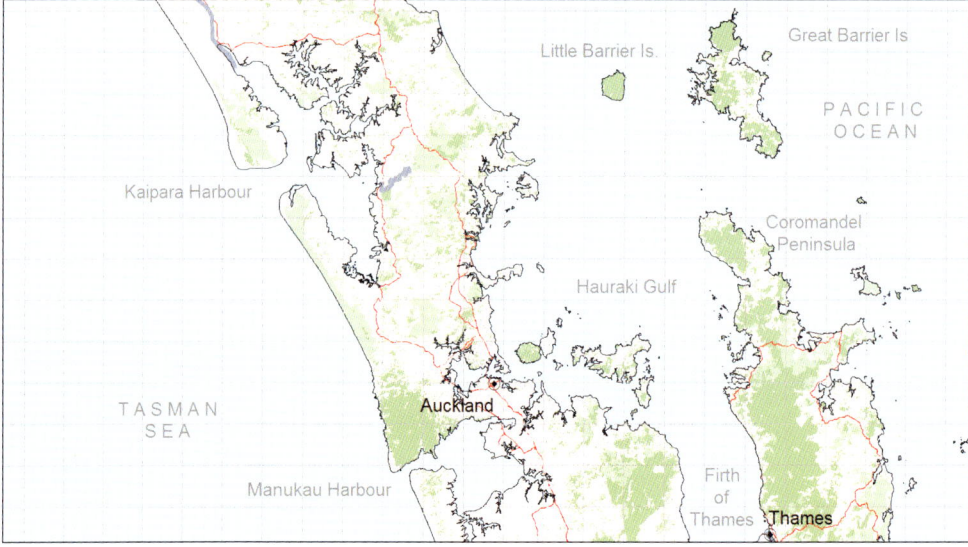

City skyline

Surfing Surf on both coasts and not a lot of territory to cover switching between them, makes the Auckland region as good as anywhere in the country in terms of daily options. That said, it is the biggest city in New Zealand, with a large surf population, so it's a bit tricky finding waves to yourself. The basic rule of thumb is that the west coast likes small swells and north-east winds, and the east coast likes large north-east swells and south-west or west winds.

Fishing Aucklanders are blessed with a massive amount of fish and shellfish on their back doorstep, with twin harbours and twin oceans each offering vastly different eco-systems, and completely separate weather and tidal conditions. Land-based options are numerous. If you own a boat, it becomes hard to find time to work, especially in summer and autumn, when both coasts are firing.

Swimming There are so many beaches, with so much variety on two oceans, that if you like to swim in the sea, you'll never regret coming to this city. There are some water quality issues in the most populated areas, but plenty of places still offer sparkling clear water.

Rangitoto Island

Auckland | 77

The Whangaparaoa Peninsula

A long thin peninsula juts 11 km out from the mainland, 25 km north of Auckland, marking the northern boundary of the city. Whangaparaoa means "Bay of Whales" in Maori, though the relevance seems tenuous, as the shallow waters around this peninsula would be an unlikely whale ground. It has more recently been dubbed the "Hibiscus Coast," alluding to the temperate climate that's a big part of its appeal to the large numbers of retirees and lifestylers who have made it their home. What used to be a rinky-dink holiday destination is now a satellite suburb of Auckland, with homes on nearly every square inch of it. The coastline features sandstone cliffs and a succession of broad bays, sharing some similarities to Waiheke and Great Barrier Islands; with one coast boasting golden sand beaches while the other features a more tidal, shingly disposition. Notable features include The Shakespear Regional Park and Tiritiri Matangi Island, a successfully regenerating wildlife sanctuary off its eastern tip.

Travelling Remarkably there are very few public accommodation options here, other than a campsite at Red Beach and another at the Shakespear Regional Park; plus a few baches for rent from the various commercial websites. There is no dedicated tourism web portal and relatively few genuine tourists.

WIND ROSE

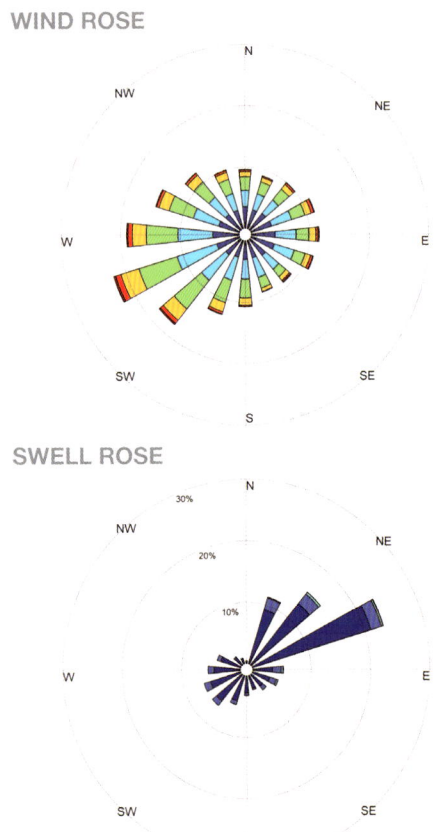

SWELL ROSE

Surfing While not renown for its waves, unlike Orewa and parts of Auckland, large north-east swells do get into the exposed bays with the odd good day. Red Beach Surf Life-Saving Club (09)426 5006 www.redbeachslsc.com

Fishing Options are many, though relatively shallow water means land-based fishing is marginal and generally only successful in late summer.

Swimming You'll find some fabulous swimming beaches, and though the north side is generally deeper and gives greater protection from south winds, its varied aspect offers multiple choices, no matter which direction the wind is blowing from.

1. Red Beach
On the other side of the Orewa River is a small headland and a set of rocks. Red Beach begins to the north of them. The main public access is off Ngapara Ave, that runs along the foreshore, with parking adjacent to the beach along its length. There are two other smaller pedestrian access points to the east, off Marellen and Chelverton Roads, where there is a large grass reserve. It is a great beach for all types of activities, but when there is swell running, swimming is safer at other places on the peninsula. It faces east/north-east, which explains why it receives almost as much swell as Orewa, but while the long finger of reef projecting off the western end of the bay can sometimes hold good banks, the beach is generally one long close out that's popular with surf-skis, SUP's and beginners. That said, it can be cleaner than Orewa in a south wind. Pinewoods Motor Park (09)426 4526 www.pinewoods.co.nz

2. Stanmore Bay
Relatively unknown by those off the peninsula, Stanmore Bay has huge appeal to all kinds of beach-goers due to its sparkling sand, broad mix of amenities and the range of options afforded to visitors. The main public facilities including the boat club, skate ramp, soccer ground and public parking are at the Stanmore Bay Park, opposite the Leisure Centre at the eastern end of the Bay. From here you can walk around the rocks to the east and at low tide get to Manly Beach if you're keen. The western section of the bay can be accessed from the reserve at the

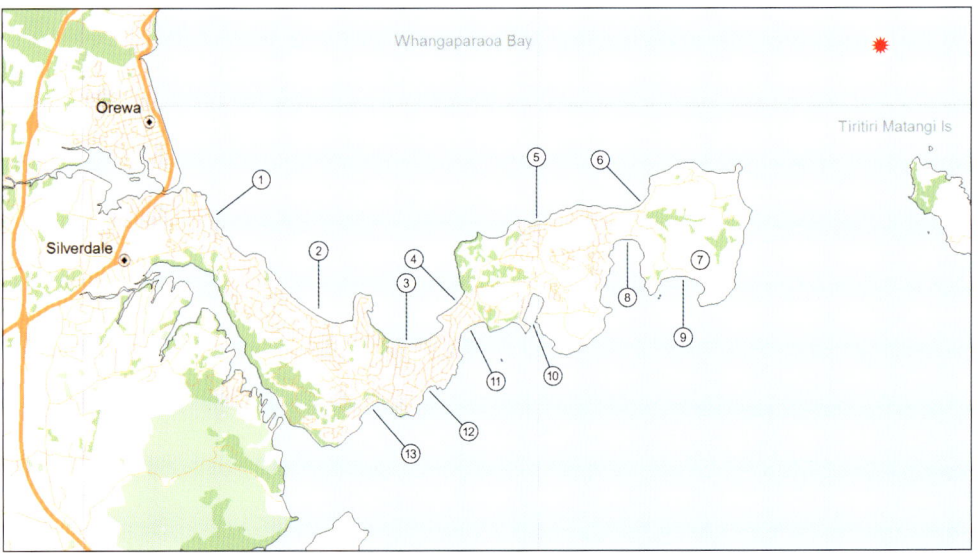

Red Beach

bottom of Coopers Rd, with a good carpark, public loos and a paved ramp for small boats. This end of the beach offers much greater privacy, plus some large pohutakawas offering useful shade, as well as a set of rocks to the west to fish off, but the carpark is locked between dusk and dawn. There is also another small pullover and public toilets at the bottom of Kauri Road. Believe it or not, Stanmore Bay gets a few waves, and in a huge northerly or north-east cyclone swell, you'll get beach peaks plus a good right that peels down the point at the eastern end of the bay, that can get hollow on its day. Hibiscus Coast Boat Club run monthly fishing competitions on the first weekend of each month, plus offer a range of other group activities. They also have tractors for boat launching and house the local coast guard boat (09)424 0952 www.hibiscuscoastboatclub.com

3. Big Manly
Set in the broad sweep of Waiau Bay, Big Manly has been a coastal community for over a hundred years and is the biggest and most heavily populated location on the peninsula. Once known as Polkinghorne Bay, it was renamed after an apparent likeness to its Australian namesake. Dubious call that one. Manly features a large headland to the west and a false point leading to Tindalls Bay to the east. The bay itself faces almost due north and due to the large headland beyond Tindalls, is extremely protected from most swell and wind. As a consequence, it is popular with boaties, with several moorings in the bay and a well patronised centreboard yacht club located near the boat ramp in the middle of the beach. Other facilities include public loos and a large grass reserve and picnic tables behind the yacht club. Laurence St runs nearly the entire length of the bay one block back from the beach, with a narrow lane called The Esplanade running adjacent to the foreshore, where there are a few picnic tables on the low dunes. Despite its recent growth spurt, it is still a fabulous family beach offering great swimming conditions at most stages of the tide. Fishing in the bay is okay, but the rocks only really allow access at lower tides, though you can catch snapper off both ends in late summer. The western side of the beach leads around under the cliffs to a protected cove that you can walk to at lower tides called Swann Bay, that's really an extension of Manly. Access by car is off Swann Beach Rd, where there is a small reserve with a ramp down to the seashore. In a strong westerly, it's very protected here. **Manly Sailing Club** www.manlysailingclub.org.nz. **Whangaparaoa Lodge-Motel** (09)428 4666.

Stanmore Bay

Big Manly

Tindalls Beach

4. Tindalls Beach
A headland divides Big Manly from Tindalls Beach, and despite the fact they are very nearly conjoined neighbours, they are separate communities with a completely different character. It's another beach named after an early farming family, but Tindalls is only a hundred or so metres long and for most of its length, private homes occupy the foreshore, with public access points at each end and a boat ramp, toilets and cold showers in the centre. The western end of the bay is more private and sheltered, with big pohutakawas on the foreshore and no homes. At low tide you can walk around the point to the north-east and a few other small stretches of beach open up. It is a pretty place to go rock-hopping and also to fish.

5. Fishermans Cove
After Tindalls Beach there is a long stretch of cliffy coastline with only one small access point before Army Bay. Called Fishermans Cove, it is a tiny chink in the cliffs and features a small, steep boat ramp, with a reserve on the hillside above it and a tiny carpark.

6. Army Bay
Someone once told me that Army Bay reminded them of Gallipoli, which by all accounts is a fairly sparse bit of coast. Sparse would be a good description of Army Bay, which was the site of an Army camp in WW2, hence its name. The military firing range nearby reinforces its accuracy. The homes end well before the beach and a long stretch of grass on the cliffs to the west signals the start of the Shakespear regional Park. The shoreline is backed by a series of parking areas, with public loos and a boat ramp at the eastern end. If you keep walking under the cliffs to the west of the main carpark, several sheltered stretches of coast open up at lower tides, offering both isolation and lots of protection from south winds. Army Bay has a steep shelf and despite its north aspect does get some waves in large swells, but generally none worth surfing.

7. Shakespear Regional Park
The end of the peninsula is divided between the Army, who use it for artillery practice and the regional park that occupies the southern side. It was once farmed by the Shakespear family, hence its name. There are a series of popular walkways, and a wide range of other facilities to draw the visitors. As at Tawharanui, they are attempting to create an open sanctuary in the park by installing a predator free fence, coming into operation as we go to press. There are two main beaches, both on the south side, with a gate opposite Army Bay that's open during daylight hours. Land-based fisherman will find good opportunities by walking out to the end of the park.

8. Okoromai Bay
A deeply indented bay that suffers from being extremely shallow, making it popular for wading birds but less so for swimmers. It is backed by a wide strip of grass and a regenerating wetland, with a few Norfolk pines and small pohutakawas giving shade. Good for a dip at high tide only, lower tides are strictly for cockle gathering, which is popular here.

9. Te Haruhi Bay
Another wide bay facing south-east, it's backed by farmland and a broad grassy hinterland that's

Army Bay

Gulf Harbour

extensively planted with young pohutakawas, making one gigantic picnic area complete with tables, gas bbqs, and water fountains. The beach itself is a lot steeper than Okoromai Bay, so it's a better place to swim. **The Shakespear Campground** occupies the eastern section of the foreshore, tucked in the base of the hill (09)366 2000, with the Park HQ located at the western end of the bay. There is also an excellent **YMCA hostel** on the hillside west of the beach, that has a sailing school and a range of other facilities including a climbing wall (09)424 7111 www.ymcaauckland.org.nz/outdoors

10. Gulf Harbour
A subdivision sprouted up around this highly impressive marina complex, that boasts all the usual expected facilities. Sadly, it is a monument to dodgy architecture built with zero sensitivity or style, that could have been amazing, but somehow feels a bit tacky, though it's a great place to keep a boat.

11. Matakatia Bay
Named after a Pa that was once situated above the bay, it is similar to Okoromai in many ways but with a slightly steeper profile. It is covered in cockle-shells and backed by a thin grass strip and a broad belt of homes directly across from the foreshore. A series of shallow reefs lie at either end, with the middle of the beach generally better for swimming. There's a popular ski-lane to the east of the boat ramp, that leads onto the beach here.

12. Little Manly Beach
Due to its southerly aspect and the sprawling pohutakawas that completely dominate the foreshore, Little Manly offers plenty of shaded areas to escape from the sun on a hot summers day. The main access point onto the beach is by the concrete boat ramp at the western end of the bay, where you'll find good public loos, with limited parking on the roadside. The beach is directly adjacent to the road, so it lacks a bit of atmosphere as a result, but if privacy is what you're after, take Tiri Tiri Rd, then South Ave, off which there's a walkway to the east of the beach. It also offers access to a tiny sandy cove just east of Little Manly that's deep at most tides and has a great rope swing into the water, with parking in the reserve at the top of the walkway.

13. Arkles Beach
Arkles Strand runs the entire length of the foreshore of this charming, south-east facing bay. The road in is one-way off Arkles Drive, meaning you have to drive the loop back to the Whangaparaoa shopping centre to exit, not that that should be foremost on your mind, as Arkles can be a good place to escape the crowding of some of the other beaches on the peninsula during peak periods. Crown Reserve at the western fringe leads down to some beautiful shade trees, with sheltered swimming. There are no shops but a set of loos are set back from the beach.

Okoromai Bay

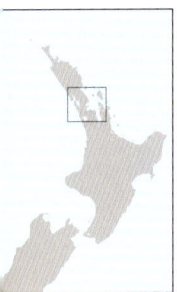

The North Shore

One of Auckland's defining characteristics is its huge mix of coastal geography, and the North Shore provides some of the better pieces of the jigsaw. It is a quintessential part of the city, connected by "the coat hanger" to the south side of the isthmus, yet there have always been subtle differences between the people and the cultures on either side of the bridge. A wide selection of easily accessible beaches, which offer almost every type of ocean sport you could hope to pursue, give the local residents significant lifestyle benefits. Consequently beach culture is far more ingrained on this side of town, which may explain the differences. Though as built up as their neighbours across the harbour, the beaches facing into the Rangitoto Channel all tend to be steeper shelving and deeper than those on the Inner Waitemata, a bathymetric quirk that gives them more appeal from a recreational perspective. There are a number of inner harbour beaches on the shore that I understand are loved by local residents, but that I have omitted as they have little appeal to those outside their local catchment.

Travelling There's an excellent coastal trail that starts at Devonport and ends at Torbay for those who want to explore the shore without a car. Maps of it, as well as info on accommodation, are available at the I-sites at Takapuna and Devonport, with high and low tide variations marked. www.teararoa.org.nz also has downloadable maps. www.tourismnorthshore.org.nz

Surfing The North Shore actually gets quite good surf in big north-east swells, which squeeze in the narrow swell window to the north of Rangitoto. A range of reefs around Takapuna can get hollow on the right conditions, plus a couple of the beaches can offer rideable waves, though quality is variable and overhead days are rare. West winds are offshore and crowds almost guaranteed, though for a novelty, it's worth trying to get a wave here at least once.

Fishing You'll find lots of interesting land-based options, starting with the Devonport wharves, North Head and all the successive headlands, especially in mid to late summer, when snapper are in close in numbers. There is also a wide array of boat ramps for boat owners to use.

Swimming The options are many and generally all good. Water quality is generally better than the inner harbour beaches, though recent issues with toxic sea slugs have caused consternation and confusion. It's always best to avoid the sea in a suburban area for a few days after heavy rain.

WIND ROSE

SWELL ROSE

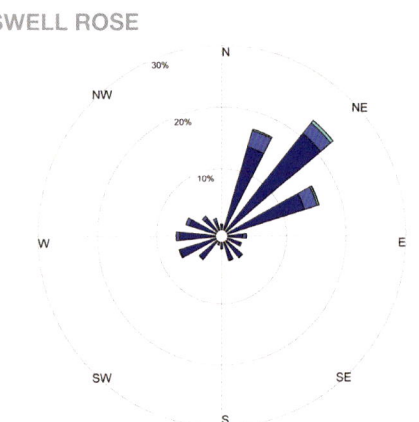

Long Bay

1. Long Bay Regional Park

This area is all within the Okura Marine Reserve and consists of three bays, if you include Grannys and Pohutakawa Bays that lie to the north of Long Bay. Nearly 2km long and rightfully named, Long Bay is the most easily accessible of the three. It is surrounded by huge grassed areas, pohutakawas, bbqs, picnic tables and little private picnic spaces with multiple parking areas dotted down its length. The main beach starts at the northern end of Beach Road, where there is a small public car-park outside the park gates for dog walkers to access the beach. Walkways through the dunes at regular intervals all down its length give foot access at many other spots. It is fairly exposed to north-east swell, and the point at the south side can get really good in the right conditions, but these are rare as for the rest of this coast. The beach itself consists of firm golden sand with a flat profile, so even when there are waves, it is still a pretty safe swimming destination. The beaches further north can be easily reached by walking around the coast at lower tides and are sure to offer greater privacy, but high tide access requires a longer walk across the cliff top. Pohutakawa Bay is a clothing optional beach. **Long Bay Restaurant** on the beach is open 7 days from 11.00am (09)473 5436. **Sir Peter Blake Marine Education and Recreation Centre** (09)473 0714 www.merc.org.nz

2. Winstones Cove

A sandy cove hardly 25 metres in length can be accessed down a short walkway off Grey St. It is totally surrounded by pohutakawas offering significant shade onto the beach, so if you wanted a swim but were sun-phobic, this could be the spot for you. For fishermen, it offers access to some pretty good ledges at the southern extremity of the marine reserve that begins at Toroa Pt, just north of here.

3. Torbay/Waiake Beach

It's namesake in Devon is nothing like our version, however Torbay is indeed a bay rather than a beach. There are in fact two beaches here that become separated at high tides. The main section of the bay is directly adjacent to Beach Road facing east, and backed by a low seawall and wide strip of grass where there are a few seats, picnic tables and a public loo. It is a pretty spot though the proximity of a busy main road so close to the water detracts somewhat from the serenity. A hard ramp onto the beach allows small boat launching, though most eschew this option for the other ramp at the northern section of the bay, which sits in the lee of "The Tor," a small sandstone islet just off the northern headland. This minute beach faces south, is highly sheltered and offers ample shade. It features a popular launch ramp and the surrounding streets are often littered with cars with trailers on fine summer days. Vehicle access to the north is off Rock Isle Rd. **Tides Restaurant and Café** is behind the beach (09)473 7870.

4. Browns Bay

Faintly reminiscent of parts of the Gold Coast, this wide open bay features a kilometre of golden sand, is lined with tall Norfolk pines, with a busy shopping mall directly behind the beach. There are a multitude of cafes and public amenities on the narrow lane separating the beach from the shops, which gives it a lively, if commercial feel. On a fine weekend it absolutely hums here, with people relaxing on the grass and filling the cafes and restaurants, kids playing on the extensive playground on the reserve between the shops and the beach and a host of others enjoying the long expanse of sand and sparkling ocean. There's a popular launch ramp at the north side of the bay and another in the middle of the beach, where you'll also find the **Browns Bay Boating Club** www.bbbc.co.nz. The local community has a website with local listings www.brownsbay.co.nz.

5. Rothesay Bay

A pretty spot, that's backed by an open expanse of grass reserve, it's not huge at high tide, though at lower tides large expanses of coast open up either side of the main beach, offering space to explore, and allowing walkers to get around to Browns Bay to the north. There's a narrow ramp onto the beach for small trailer boats, and public loos in the grass reserve which backs the beach, but not much else. Access can be gained off both Rothesay Bay Rd (where there is ample space to park), or Masterton Rd further north (with far less space for cars), but both are a bit off the main drag, which keeps the crowds down somewhat.

6. Murrays Bay

Not a big beach but one oozing character, with low cliffs at either end and large Phoenix palms and pohutakawas set behind the foreshore, giving it an exotic feel. Murrays Bay and Mairangi Bay to the south are connected by the excellent coastal walkway that gets pretty busy on fine days. Like Torbay, Beach Rd's proximity does somehow detract from the appeal. Murrays Bay's most unique feature, apart from the highly respected yacht club, is the long wharf projecting from its northern cliffs, that offers a fantastic jumping platform for the local kids at high tide, and also a great fishing spot that is usually fairly busy, especially mornings and evenings. The beach is backed by a small park, with some beautiful old pohutakawa trees, a children's play area and public loos adjacent to the clubhouse. **Murrays Bay Sailing Club** (09)479 4180 www.murraysbay.org

7. Mairangi Bay

In 1880 Joseph Murray bought the land we now know as Mairangi Bay from a Maori called Tommy, a mussel fisherman. Less than two hundred metres long, it features a U-shaped road leading down to and along the foreshore, with a convenient shopping centre behind the beach www.mairangibayvillage.co.nz. **Mairangi Bay Surf Lifesaving Club** has been around since 1954, though they don't get too much surf to practice in (09)479 4717 www.mairangibayslsc.org.nz

8. Campbells Bay

Private homes line the shoreline for most of its length, so access is restricted to three points. They are firstly off The Esplanade, where there's a limited

amount of public parking and a cold shower; and secondly off Huntly Ave, which has a public toilet block but less parking. The Possum Ladder is an intriguingly named set of steps, from a public walkway between houses off View Rd, on the north side of the bay. Few use this option. To the south are the cliffs leading to Back Beach, while the northern boundary features a cliff line leading to Red Bluff.

9. Back Beach/Kennedy Park

If you're prepared to walk down nearly two hundred steps to get some quiet time on the beach, then Back Beach is possibly the one for you. It suffered bad water quality for many years but since the new sewage outlet pipe was located further north and further out to sea, this has become less of a worry. It sits at the base of high cliffs between Rahopara Point and Red Bluff, and is popular for both dog-walkers and the more adventurous amongst us. Kennedy Park is a large stretch of grassland on the cliff tops, with some abandoned World War 2 tunnels.

10. Castor Bay

It's not more than one hundred metres of sand facing south-east. A large area of grass with a children's play area sits behind it, with shade trees to the south and a rock groyne structure to the north, where there are also a set of public loos. Parking is limited but in a northerly wind it's a great place to find some shelter and is rarely super crowded.

11. Milford

Milford is one of the longer beaches on the shore; a fabulous sweep of sand with several different public access points. The main public park with a big grass reserve, ample parking, picnic tables, shade trees, childrens playground and public loos, is at the northern end off Craig Rd. There's a patch of reef by the stream that also comes out here, so swimming is likely to be better further down the beach. Milford Rd in the centre of the beach has drive-on access to the beach for those launching boats, but has limited parking. Cecil, Saltburn, Ocean View and Muritai all take you to the beach at the south of the bay. It also features some good waves on a decent swell, with peaks off the reefs at the southern section of the bay that usually break best at higher tides. Milford is known to suffer from dodgy water after rain.

12. Thornes Bay

One of the North Shore's hidden treasures, Thornes is a cove-like beach cut into the reef system that marks this portion of the coast, and is accessed by the coastal walkway from Takapuna or either of the nearby streets like Minehaha or Tiri Ave. There are no facilities here.

13. Takapuna Beach

The best known of the North Shore's many beaches, Takapuna extends for over a kilometre from The Promenade at the north end, down to Hauraki Rd at the south, with a number of alternative access points along its length. "Taka" is hugely popular with vast numbers of people, who enjoy it as a place to swim, run, walk, paddle-board, or surf. You name it, you can do it on Takapuna. It is backed by a busy shopping centre, featuring a huge array of eating and drinking establishments. There are a number of public conveniences including a small park in the middle of the beach plus a boatramp and cafe on the point at the northern end that both get extremely busy. Taka gets some good waves in huge north-easterly swells, with two main spots: "Taka reef" which is directly in front of the boat-ramp, and O'Neils reef, 200 metres north of Takapuna reef, accessed off O'Neils Road. When they're breaking, both are likely to be busy. On a cultural note, Bruce Mason's classic play, "The End of the Golden Weather" was set here.

Takapuna I-Site 49 Hurstmere Rd (09)486 8670.
Takapuna Beach Holiday Park is a conveniently located campground at the north end of the beach (09)489 7909 www.takapunabeachholidaypark.co.nz.

14. St Leonards Beach

There isn't much here at high tide, with the water lapping almost up to the cliffs, but as the tide drops a long section of coastline becomes exposed to both the north and south, with large stretches of sand and a number of small coves. It is a stunning spot, that's highly protected from west winds by the high cliffs, and renown as a clothing optional location. Access is by walking south from Takapuna at lower tides, or down a steep but well maintained concrete path from the bottom of St Leonards Rd. Parking is extremely limited though, and there are no public facilities here.

15. Narrowneck Beach

Old Lake Road passes directly behind the grass reserve that backs onto this fabulous stretch of sand. This popular beach has a relatively steep profile offering deeper water than some of the other beaches nearby with the added bonus of good rocks at either extremity to explore and fish off. It allows easy access and perhaps more importantly, has a good carpark adjacent to the main road, that's a major drawcard in a city where parking is difficult. All this combined with an abundance of facilities makes it a great place for a family picnic. As well as a beach cafe, adventure

Narrowneck

Cheltenham

playground, picnic tables and gas bbqs, Narrowneck is home to the famed **Wakatere Boating Club**, one of the country's oldest and finest. Founded in 1926, it remains a cornerstone of the NZ sailing community, hosting large centreboard regattas and producing several world champs in many classes (09)445 2618.

16. Cheltenham Beach
One of the grand old dames of Auckland beach culture, with some of the loveliest villas in the city adjacent to the water and in the surrounding streets; it lies at the feet of North Head to the south, and Takapuna Head to the north. The bay itself is only a few hundred metres long, but is charming and intimate, with several public access points. Bath St at the northern end is a small public reserve with a children's playground. Arawa Rd, Matai Rd and Cheltenham Rd at the extreme south all offer reasonable beach access, but all have very limited parking. Balmain Park in the centre of the beach has the only public loos.

McHugh's of Cheltenham (09)445 0305 is a cute beachfront restaurant www.mchughs.co.nz

17. Devonport
A suburb of deep historical significance, it was named after one of the most famous naval bases in the British Empire (Devonport Royal Dockyard in Plymouth), and has always been the base for the NZ Navy, with the dockyard at Calliope once the biggest in the southern hemisphere. French explorer Dumont d'Urville landed here in 1827 and a memorial to the arrival of the Tainui waka from Hawaiki about 1300 AD, can also be found here. There are two separate swimming areas. Torpedo Bay, located just before North Head, was named after the naval torpedo boat housed here in the early 1920's. It is actually a couple of scallop shaped sections of sand, separated by rock groynes, with a patch of reef at the western end. This is an excellent bay to swim at, due to its remarkably steep profile, and also a popular place to launch boats, but suffers from a fair bit of wash from passing vessels.

Devonport Beach is a 25m patch of sand to the east of the Ferry terminal. It is backed by a grassy park that leads onto the main street, so it's hardly a private spot. As a curiosity, there is a small 1m deep tidal swimming pool that was built for convalescing sailors last century, that's suitable for toddlers, hidden away behind the navel museum. Walk east past the wharf and you'll see it at the base of the cliffs. **RNZN Museum** (09)445 5186 www.navy.mil.nz. Devonport has an I-site in the shopping centre on Victoria Rd and a separate website with multiple accommodation options **www.devonport.co.nz**

18. Little Shoal Bay
They say that "Little Shoal Bay is where old bis and tris go to die," referring to the flotilla of multihulls in various states of repair that inhabit the bay. It is extremely tidal, making it unsuitable for swimming at all but high water, but is backed by a big grass reserve and is a pretty place for a picnic, with heaps of parking, public loos, a gas bbq and picnic tables.

Torpedo Beach

Little Shoal Bay

Inner Waitemata

The word Waitemata loosely translates from Maori as "sparkling water", though Auckland is known internationally as the "City of Sails", and grew as the country's major seaport, primarily due to the Waitemata Harbour's gloriously sheltered nature, offering a safe anchorage in the days when sea traffic was the primary transport mode. Its assets are as appreciated today as they were then, though the thousands of people who use the harbour now, mainly do so for pleasure. The beaches that grace her shoreline offer a whole different set of reasons to live in this spectacular city from those that attracted the early settlers, and while all are shallow and tidal, they are extremely accessible and allow ample opportunities to de-stress after a long day battling paperwork or slugging it out on the motorways.

Travelling The biggest problem for all these beaches is parking. Tamaki Drive gets crazy with cars on a hot summer day, as does Point Chevalier. It just goes with the territory. www.aucklandnz.com

Wairangi Wharf

Point Chevalier

WIND ROSE

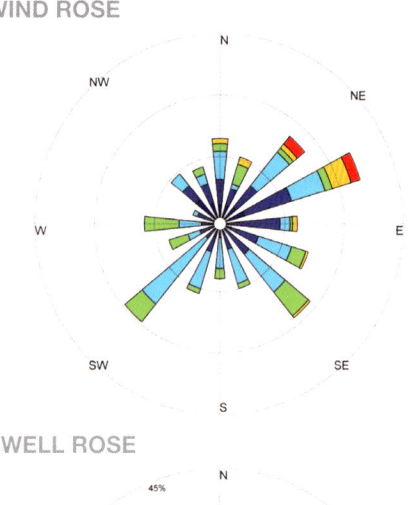

SWELL ROSE

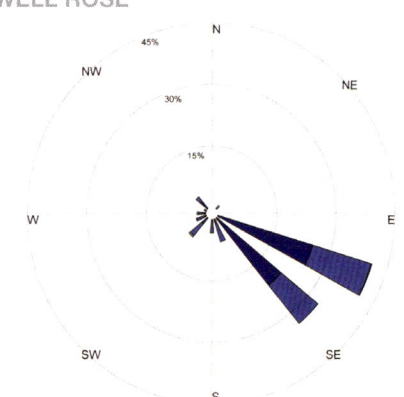

Surfing About the only thing you can't do in the ocean south of the bridge is go surfing, but kiteboarding and windsurfing are both really popular at Pt Chevalier, which picks up the full force of any southwesters, and offers flat water and easy launching.

Fishing Other than the often spectacular boat fishing in the harbour, there are some quite convenient land-based options, including the various wharves, though don't expect too many trophy fish.

Swimming The inner Waitemata is a fairly shallow body of water, and swimming at all the beaches is better at higher tides. The further west you head up the harbour, the shallower it gets, especially once you pass under the bridge. Water quality at most spots can be dubious after rain due to a chronic lack of investment in infrastructure over many years. The Auckland Council publishes water quality reports on its website, and generally posts signs advising of issues as they arise www.aucklandcouncil.govt.nz

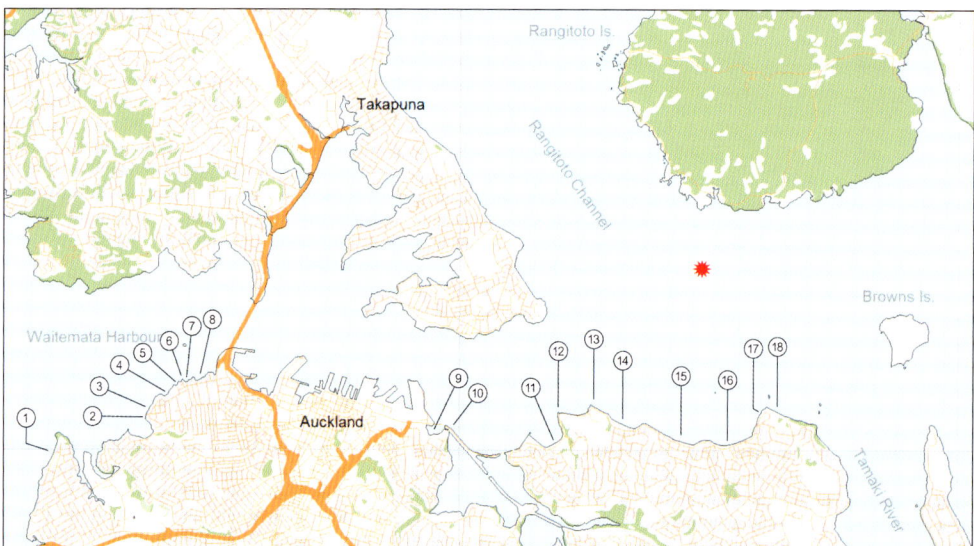

1. Point Chevalier
"Pt Chev" used to be a real working-class suburb, and its beach was long neglected by Aucklanders, but since the recent gentrification of the area it has become more popular as a place to walk and swim, especially at high tide. Being in the upper reaches of the harbour, it's even more tidal than the city's other beaches, but it's still a beautiful place for a lazy summer dip, though low tide is a pretty muddy affair. Weekends are a cosmopolitan joy, with many Pacific Island families setting up huge picnics, playing guitars and singing under the immense pohutakawas that line the extensive park sloping up to the main road from the beach. Pt Chev is another beach that is resupplied with sand from Pakiri, and it never fails to confuse me seeing scallop shells on what was an oyster bed. Sadly it is another spot that's blighted by dirty water after rain, be warned. Public loos and gas bbqs are the only amenities. The nearby yacht club is a popular kiteboarding location, picking up the strong southwesters, with flat water and easy launching. Point Chevalier Sailing Club (09)815 1379 www.sailptchev.org.nz

2. Bella Vista Rd Beach
It isn't a beach at all at high tide, just a set of steps leading straight into the sea; very odd indeed but somewhere else to swim at high tide.

3. Marine Parade Reserve
Just west of Herne Bay there's a short set of steps leading to a cute little boatshed. There's a 10m strip of sand at high tide and no amenities, but it's an enchanting spot for a dip. Located at the intersection of Marine Parade and Annan St.

4. Herne Bay
Herne Bay's beaches are probably Auckland's best-kept secret and this is the most popular of them. Again, it's not extensive, but at high tide is absolutely gorgeous, with its little boat shed, pohutakawas offering shade, two good public loos and relatively easy parking on the streets behind, putting it up there as one of my top swimming spots in the city. At low tide it's a dud, but so are most of Auckland's city beaches. Access is down steps at the bottom of Herne Bay Rd, with parking on the streets behind it.

5. Cremorne Reserve
A tiny beach at the bottom of Cremorne Road, with huge pohutakawas sheltering most of its 25 odd metres of sand from the midday sun. Usually empty.

6. Wairangi Wharf
Just to the west of Home Bay at the bottom of Wairangi Rd is a fabulous fishing wharf, that's a popular place to catch kahawai, sprats, piper at low tide, no doubt a stingray or two and even the odd snapper and kingfish in summer.

7. Home Bay
Another delightful spot at high tide, with no facilities; but good shade offered by the pohutakawas and easy parking on the streets behind the beach.

8. Sentinel Beach Reserve
The last of Herne Bay's gems is found at the bottom of Sentinel Rd, where a set of steps leads you down to another short stretch of sand, sheltered by a small sandstone point to the west and three impressive old boatsheds to the east, with their own private slipways. The great thing about Sentinel Beach, other than its northerly aspect and uncrowded feel, are the excellent amenities, including four classic 70's sun loungers, outside showers and well maintained loos. Shelter from the ample pohutakawas and a fabulous view towards the Harbour Bridge completes a rather spectacular and inviting inner-city vignette.

9. Judges Bay

You can swim at Judges Bay, but only at high tide. It has a lovely park behind it with plentiful shade trees that makes a great place for a family picnic, but the water quality is extremely dodgy after rain.

10. Parnell Baths

It isn't a beach, but the Parnell Baths fulfil a similar role for many Aucklanders and they are salt water filled, so I have opted for their inclusion. They are one of the greatest swimming pools in the country, right on the waterfront, with spectacular views, and a groovy 60's ambience, that I have enjoyed at many times during my life. They're not actually filled with seawater, but that's forgiveable. Access is from Judges Bay or across the walkway off Tamaki Drive.

11. Okahu Bay

One of the flattest and shallowest of the city beaches, Okahu Bay sits inside the wave barrier extending from the Orakei wharf across to the marina and boat ramp to its west, with hundreds of moored sailboats bobbing just past the low tide mark. The beautiful grassy bank and pohutakawas behind the beach make it a popular picnic spot, but the swimming is only good around high tide. Nonetheless it's a popular spot. **Fergs Kayak Rentals** (09)524 9460 offer rentals and guided trips into the harbour and more www.fergskayaks.co.nz

12. Orakei Wharf/Kelly Tarlton's

Again not a beach, but two well used resources that are iconic Auckland landmarks and are both accessed from the same car park east of Okahu Bay. One is a popular place to catch fish and the other a popular place to go and watch fish. **Kelly Tarlton's** (09)531 5065 www.kellytarltons.co.nz

13. Tamaki Beach

Tamaki used to be a great little beach when I was a child, and I fondly remember summer days with mum, lazing in the sun and jumping off Bastion Point. Sadly the sand has all gone and all that's left is a gnarled, rocky foreshore that's of little use to man nor beast. There is still a boat ramp by the car park, and you'll still find optimistic fishermen casting lines off the point at high tide. **Romfords of Tamaki** (09)528 6463 www.romfords.co.nz. **Tamaki Yacht Club** (09)528 5662 www.tyc.org.nz

14. Mission Bay

It is a cliché to call it an icon, yet that's what it is; popular because it is one of the finest, and probably the busiest of our city beaches, with its fabulous fountain and convenient grass reserve (known as Selwyn Domain) backing onto the beach, plus a host of cafes and eateries across the road, drawing a cosmopolitan and lively crowd on most fine summer days. **Mission Bay Watersports** Anton Ashcroft 021 686 735, offers a range of activities including windsurf, SUP and kite-board hire www.windsurfauckland.com

Okahu Bay Wharf

16. St Heliers
Te Whanganui o Toi, the great bay of Toi, is now known as St Heliers. The last of the drive-to beaches, this is in many ways my favourite, as it always seems a little less crowded than Mission Bay, is a bit deeper and has the interesting rocks to the east that can be good to walk around and swim off.

17. Ladies Bay
Ladies bay sits at the base of the cliffs that mark the end of St Heliers Bay, and is accessed by following the road to the look out on the hill top and walking down the track from there. It's small, but possibly the best swimming spot in Auckland at lower tides.

15. Kohimarama
The name Kohimaramara once applied to the whole foreshore area from Bastion Point to Gower Point including Mission Bay as well as "Kohi," as it's known. The name refers to the gathering of woodchips from the carving of waka, which must have been a prolific activity for local Maori back in the day. It is similar in many ways to Mission Bay, but without the grassy foreshore, and features some well disguised man-made groynes shaped like fingers of reef, that protrude off the beach to assist with holding the (imported) sand in place. **Kohi Yacht Club** is one of the country's best youth focused centreboard clubs located at the eastern end of the bay www.kyc.org.nz

18. Gentlemans Bay
If you walk around to the east from Ladies Bay and climb over the rocks facing into the Tamaki Estuary, you come to Gentleman's Bay, which is the city's naturist beach. At low tide you can walk a fair way but there isn't much beach at high tide. It gets morning sun but loses it early due to the cliffs.

Eastern Beaches

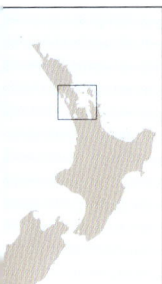

There is a whole section of coastline east of the Tamaki Estuary that's an integral part of Auckland, yet remains unknown to many of the city's residents. It sits directly in the lee of Waiheke Island, and falls fairly neatly into two distinct halves. Firstly, there are the beaches around Howick and Pakuranga that lie to the east of the Tamaki Estuary and end at the Mangemangeroa Stream. Then there is the Beachlands/Maraetai area, known by many, with some validity, as the Pohutakawa Coast, culminating in the Duder Regional Park. If there is a common denominator for all of them, it is the cockle-shells which line this coastline in thick middens, testament to its shallow, but fertile disposition.

Travelling The Howick/Pakuranga area is suburban to the core, densely developed with space at a premium. On the other hand the Beachlands coast is less built up, though the signs of suburban creep are all there.

WIND ROSE

SWELL ROSE

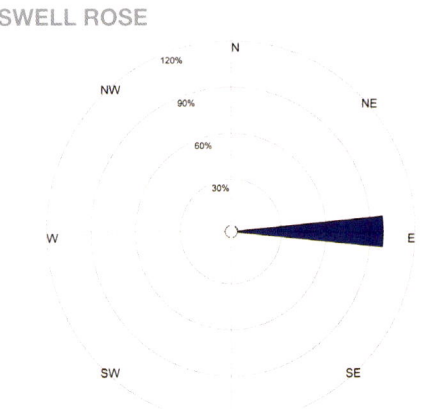

Surfing Not a hope in hell of getting a wave on this coast, but Bucklands Beach is highly popular with kite-boarders and windsurfers due to its exposure to south-west winds and easy launching.

Fishing Land-based fishing is very productive in a few spots, with several good boat ramps and boat clubs in the area and some well placed headlands and wharves. The water is relatively shallow all around the inshore region, so the points are best around higher tides and the channels at lower tides. **Howick Coastguard** emergency number (09)303 1303.

Swimming Some of the shallowest, most tidal bays in the Hauraki Gulf are found on this coast, yet there are a couple of steeper beaches among them, offering acceptable all tides swimming.

1. Bucklands Beach

A long finger of land projects out into the sea at the mouth of the Tamaki Estuary, that marks the eastern border of the Waitemata Harbour. Bucklands Beach occupies its west facing coast and consists of two distinct halves, divided by a headland that houses the Bucklands Beach Yacht Club. The southern portion, known as "Little Bucks," is a crescent-shaped bay with an enclosed, almost intimate character; a reinforced seawall along its length, and a walkway from the southern end across to Half Moon Bay Marina. It is a popular windsurfing and kite-boarding spot due to its south-west aspect, easy launching and good parking. The northern section of the bay, known as "Big Bucks", drops off steeply into deep water, with a row of yachts and pleasure craft moored alarmingly close to the beach. Musick Point at its northern extent features a popular golf-course, with a walkway from the carpark down the cliffs to the tip of the headland, where there's a useful land-based fishing spot. **Bucklands Beach Yacht Club** (09)534 3046 www.bbyc.org.nz. **Bucklands Beach Waterfront Motel** (09)537 4437 www.waterfrontchalets.co.nz

Little Bucks

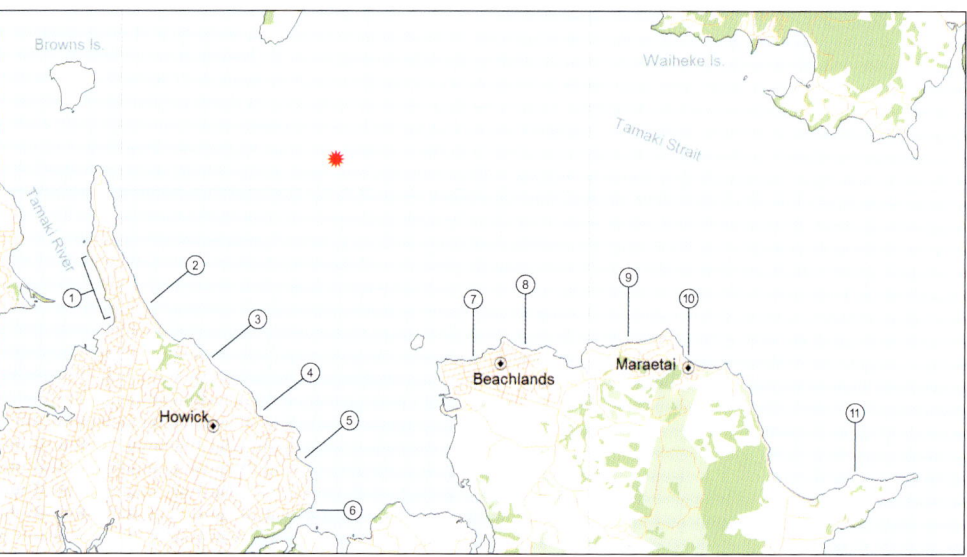

Mellons Bay

Maraetai

2. Eastern Beach
Three spectacular kilometres of fine golden sand, facing north-east and backed by an extensive row of homes, lie on the opposite side of the peninsula from Bucklands Beach. A midden of cockle-shells around the high tide mark attest to their presence in the mudflats here, but there's a total ban on collection of shellfish from this beach. You'll find a good boat ramp with public loos in the little reserve at the south end. A set of steps leads down the cliffs from the north, off Clovelley Rd, to an area known as Back Beach. **The Esplanade Restaurant and Bar** (09)534 1989.

3. Mellons Bay
This wide expanse of sand backed by high cliffs, extends for two or three hundred metres to the east of the carpark at the bottom of Mellons Bay Rd. Its charm comes from the lack of significant housing along the coast, making it popular with day-trippers and picnicking families from around the area.

4. Howick Beach
A row of pohutakawa trees lines the foreshore above the reinforced seawall that backs Howick Beach, with a carpark, the local coastguard building, a ramp onto the beach and the sailing club amongst the land-based features here. The bay is extremely shallow and flat with several sections of exposed papa rock in the sand along its length, and a large flat reef off the headland to the west, that locals are attempting to protect. Walking on it can damage life forms, as can vehicle traffic, which is prohibited. Be aware and respect their concerns. **Howick Sailing Club** (09)534 6687 www.howicksailingclub.co.nz

5. Cockle Bay
Similar in size and orientation to Howick beach, but featuring a thick midden of crushed cockle shells above the mid tide line, which is hardly surprising given its name. The low tide mudflats are thick with the live variety, and during the open season that runs from 1st May till October, you'll see many people knee-deep at low tide, digging in the mud for their allocation of 50. The beds were seriously depleted by overfishing a few years back, but the appointment of honorary fishing officers and the introduction of a closed season seems to be heralding a comeback which is great news. A row of pohutakawas grace the foreshore above the reinforced sea-wall, with an excellent playground and a petanque court to add to the list of attractions. **Windross House** offers fine dining in a beachfront colonial cottage (09)535 8720.

6. Shelly Park Beach
Sandspit Rd ends in a cul-de-sac at the top of cliffs, above a prominent sandspit that marks the entrance to the Mangemangeroa Creek. A reserve of the same name that features a large stand of old-growth, broadleaf native trees, leads several kilometres up the creek bed, with a popular walkway along its length.

7. Sunkist Bay
Above half tide there isn't really a beach at all here, with the ocean lapping up to the reinforced seawall that runs the length of Sunkist Bay, but this is Beachlands main beach, and a great place to swim due to the depth of water, with several sets of steps offering access into the sea. The foreshore is part of a reserve, with gates that are locked during the hours of darkness, and which is home to the Beachlands Boating Club. There is a little wharf and boat ramp at the eastern end. The wharf can be a very productive fishing spot, with kahawai and the odd kingie landed here over the years. The walkway leads around to the west and it's also common to see fishermen out on the point here too. Nearby Schnapper Rock, off Ealing Crescent, features a set of steps leading to a small island at the head of a hidden bay. It's connected to the mainland by a thread of reef, and was given its name for a reason, with good fishing ledges off its northern point. Access is a bit tricky at high tide.

8. Shelly Bay
What it lacks in size it makes up for in character, and the fact that Shelly Bay isn't visible from the road, has kept it a bit of a local secret. But the short walk down the path from the Shelly Bay reserve shouldn't put you off if you're looking for a private little oasis. Pohutakawas unfold onto the cockle shell and sand beach, while low cliffs in either direction offer protection from south and south-west winds.

9. Omana Beach
Omana Parade meanders behind a couple of kilometres of indented coastline, punctuated with several strips of sand, backed by a grass reserve along its length. To the east, private homes sit behind the road, while from the bottom of Campbell Rd, which is the entrance to the Omana Regional Park, you'll find a wide expanse of grass and a park, with an array of public amenities including a camping site, picnic areas, bbq pits, playgrounds and loos. At high tide it is stunning, but as the tide drops you have to walk a fair old way to get wet here. There are fish to be had off the eastern point, before the coast bends around into Te Pene Beach, which is just a short patch of sand that's okay for swimming at higher tides too.

10. Maraetai
Waiheke looks so close, you feel you could almost swim there from Maraetai. Understandably popular for a number of good reasons, not least because it retains a reasonable amount of water depth at lower tides making it one of the best places to swim and launch a boat in the eastern bays. The wharf in the middle of the bay offers a great place to fish and swim from, while its other qualities are its sparkling sand, sheltered aspect and the extensive parkland at either end of the bay, an excellent children's play centre, and three cafes just opposite the beach. As you head south around the coast road, there's another series of small bays offering good swimming and shelter from west winds, plus another excellent fishing wharf at Magazine Bay. **Maraetai Beach Boating Club** (09)536 6649 www.maraetaiboatclub.org.nz

11. Duder Regional Park
The Duder Regional Park is a 148-hectare coastal farm park located on the pohutukawa-fringed Whakakaiwhara Peninsula. While there are a couple of beaches, they are all a bit of a walk from the car, but the views are spectacular.

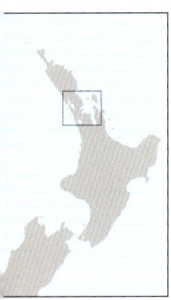

The Seabird Coast

Calling it a part of Auckland may be a bit of a stretch, but it defines the eastern border of the Auckland Isthmus, so there you have it, and my apologies to the separatists. This unusual and unique stretch of coast faces eastwards into the Firth of Thames and over towards the Coromandel Peninsula, which sits just across the water. It is shallow, highly tidal, and often rocky. There are only a few coastal communities with holiday homes, and consequently few holiday-makers, but it offers a charming and accessible escape from the city's chaos, just an hour or so from the CBD. It's named for the spectacular congregations of seabirds to be found in abundance at the southern end. If you're a twitcher, then you'll love this area.

Travelling The highway skirts the coast for much of its length, though the best spots, like the regional parks, are all a wee drive off it. There aren't too many accommodation options or shops.

WIND ROSE

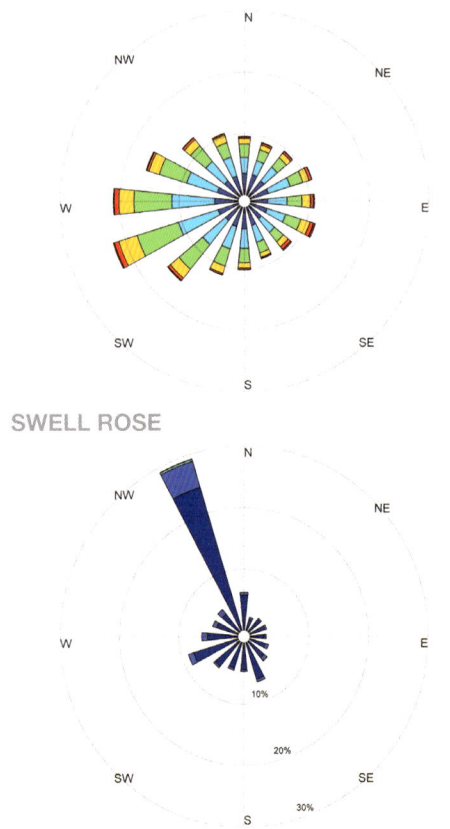

SWELL ROSE

Surfing Strangely enough, you'll find some okay waves breaking on the shingle and rock points around Orere, on a huge north or north-east cyclone swell. Though few have surfed it, wave quality can be high, but swells tend to be of short duration.

Fishing Beach fishing would best be described as marginal, though the rocky promontories at the north of the coast can be productive in late summer. Kawakawa Bay Boat Club, Commodore Drew Hayward (09)292 2131 www.kbbc.co.nz

Swimming Like its neighbour across the Firth, it is shallow and rocky, with just a few sandy patches, though normally sheltered from ocean swells, making it a good place for families with small children, or less proficient swimmers. The best time to visit is at higher tides in a westerly wind.

1. Kawakawa Bay

A busy bay with a long crescent of shingly beach; the high tide mark is lined with masses of bleached white cockle-shells. Kawakawa Bay is home to one of Auckland's biggest boating clubs, and on a busy summer day it can feel a bit like downtown, with a multitude of boat owners jostling to get out into the Gulf. While there have been issues in the past, a new wastewater collection plant has significantly

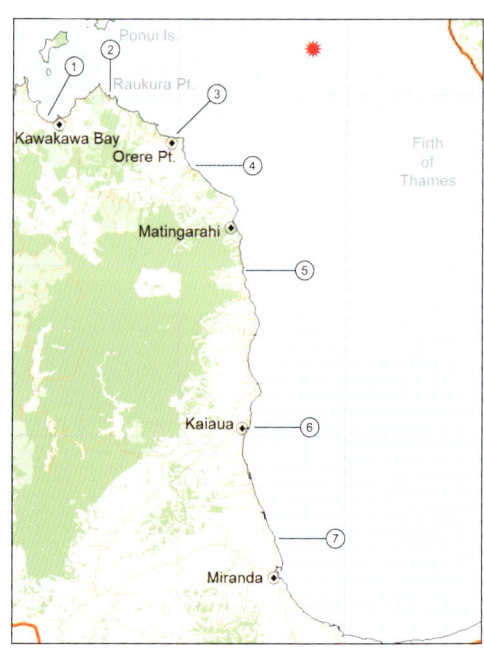

improved water quality in the area. Facilities include the beachfront store and public toilets, with plenty of parking along the foreshore. The Kawakawa Bay coast road, that extends beyond the boating club, is one of

Kawakawa Bay coast

Splore Festival, Tapakakanga Regional Park

the gems of the Firth, with a multitude of rock and sand coves below the road housing a couple of the best beaches in the area. Choose one and park. www.kawakawabay.org.nz

2. Tawhitokino
Between Papanui Point and Orere Point township you'll find a series of beaches that are probably the best in this region, but also the least accessible. Tawhitokino, the more north-westerly of them, is a fairly straight and unbroken stretch of golden sand more than a kilometer long. Taiwawe beach to the south-east is about 750 metres long and broken into two parts. Continue to Waiti Bay at the end of Kawakawa Bay Coast Rd. From there follow the Tawhitokino track on foot around the rocks and over Papanui Point to the beach, though this is only possible at lower tides. You'll find a campsite with longdrop toilets, but no water.

3. Orere Point
It's a small beach "resort" with a popular campground and a substantial reserve, with spectacular Pohutakawa trees that offer ample shade on a hot summers day. The beach itself is a mix of shingle and sand, with a good trailer-boat launch facility, giving easy access to the bottom of Ponui Island and into the Gulf. There's a store and takeaways, and even a library of sorts, plus a popular market on Saturdays. Oddly, there are no public loos. **Orere Point Top 10 Holiday Park** (09)292 2774 www.orerepointholidaypark.co.nz. **Tui Cottage B&B** tel (09)292 2189.

4. Tapakakanga Regional Park
One of the Aucklnd regions finest parks, a huge and sprawling patchwork of open spaces divided by some of the country's most spectacular pohutakawa trees, it backs onto a shoreline that may not be the sandiest, yet still offers safe swimming and oodles of character. The park is a truly amazing community resource, with an extremely widespread selection of camping options and plenty of facilities, that's just inviting you to take the kids and spend a relaxing weekend sheltered from the westerly winds. It is also one of the spots to go looking for a wave if you're on this coast during a cyclone swell, with a couple of shingly points and a half-respectable beach break.

5. Waharau
Another strange and yet quaint beach settlement with a cluster of baches and a reserve fronting the foreshore. Heading south, there are another couple of beaches further down the road with no names that would make a good picnic spot.

6. Kaiaua
Kaiaua is the main village on this coast. There's not much there, but it is famous for its award-winning fish and chip shop, and a well patronised wine and food festival. The coast gets extremely shallow and tidal here, so it's hardly the best area for swimming, though plenty of people fish off the coast here in boats. **Kaiaua Seaside Lodge B&B** (09)232 2696

7. Taramake Wildlife Reserve
The landscape flattens significantly here, with long tussock grass, intermittent wetland, sparse mangrove patches and layers of deep white shell middens lumped along the shore. It's not a spot I would choose as a place to swim, but for ornithologists it's an absolute goldmine, and the dense concentration of a wide array of wading seabirds is what draws the "twitchers" in their hundreds. A popular free-camping zone beside the beach seems to be drawing the ire of many local residents, due to the associated waste disposal issues. Something needs to be done about this one way or another: installation of public loos and bins seems the obvious answer.

Orere Point

Taramake Wildlife Reserve

Waiheke Island

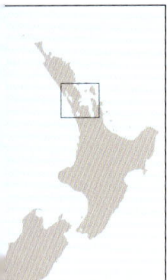

Once a sleepy backwater populated by a handful of farmers, tribes of hippies, and an oddball collection of stoners, solo mums and creative types trying to swerve the trappings of creeping urbanisation; in the last few decades it has become a vibrant epicurean and viticultural destination, drawing visitors from all around the world to its cellar doors, fine restaurants and sparkling beaches. This little subtropical oasis is located just 45 minutes from the CBD, and despite the inconvenience and cost of travelling to town on a daily basis, for many who choose to commute, the enviable lifestyle offered on the island makes it all worth it. There are two distinct halves to Waiheke: the densely settled west side, and the private farmland of the almost unpopulated east. The beauty of Waiheke is that there is something for just about everyone here, and whether it's a relaxing weekend eating and drinking, calm and sheltered swimming, or some top class fishing you're after, Waiheke can usually deliver.

Travelling Most people arrive by ferry from either the city or Half Moon Bay. The passenger ferry arrives at Matiatia while the vehicle ferry, which also carries foot passengers, comes in at Kennedy Point. **Sealink** run the car ferry from either Half Moon Bay or Wynard Wharf(09)300 5900 www.sealink.co.nz. **Fullers** also run a fast passenger-only service from downtown Auckland (09)367 9111 www.fullers.co.nz. There are a few tourist websites www.waiheke.aucklandnz.com and www.tourismwaiheke.co.nz. Air Discovery offer transport to the island and scenic flights (09)372 4480 www.airdiscovery.co.nz

Getting Around Once on the island, there's a bus service, various rental car companies and taxis, plus bicycles to rent for the energetic, **Waiheke Bike Hire** (09)372 7937. The western (populated) side of the island, is a maze of roads, and it's really easy to get lost. As one local so succinctly put it, "it's covered in goat tracks". Get a good map and use it. The **I-Site** is located in the main shops at Oneroa, and has a range of literature, though it has to be said they weren't very helpful to me (09)372 1234. There are several websites offering information regarding accommodation on the island including: www.waihekeunlimited.co.nz and www.waihekeholidayhomes.co.nz

WIND ROSE

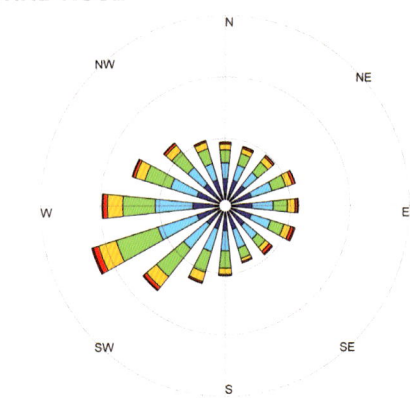

SWELL ROSE

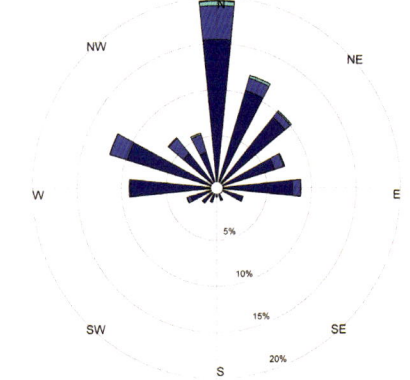

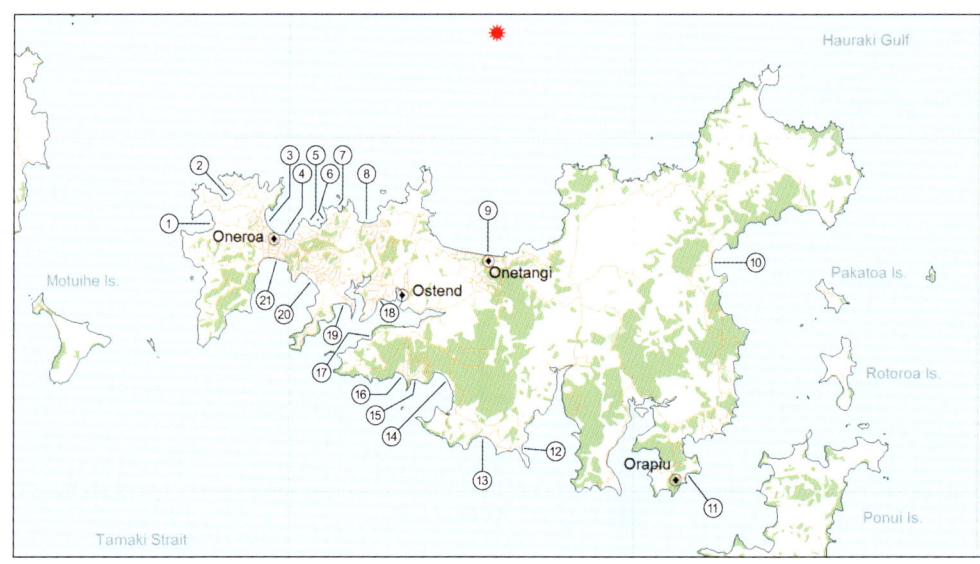

Waiheke and Ponui Islands

Surfing Onetangi is the main surf beach, though Oneroa also gets waves, and both can get good in a powerful north-east cyclone swell. Other spots on the north-east coast would undoubtedly hold waves though little information exists, and access issues present difficulties. **Out There Surf and Skate** is well supplied and well informed (09)372 6528.

Fishing As with surfing, the north coast offers vastly superior land-based fishing, with an array of headlands and rock ledges offering access to relatively deep water with comparative ease. A lot of good fish of many species are caught close-in, and a kayak also offers spectacular possibilities. There are a number of fishing operations on the island: **Kayak Fishing Safaris** (09)372 6660 www.kayakwaiheke.co.nz. **Fat Snapper Fishing Charters** (09)951 951. **Fishing Waiheke** (09)09 372 6237 www.fishingwaiheke.co.nz. **Waiheke Boating Club** (09)372 6104. **Mermaid Marine** Dave Collins 027 4951 065. **Adventure Fishing Charters**, Phil Scott (09) 372 6023. **Hamils Fishing Supplies** Oneroa (09)372 2399 www.hamilsnz.co.nz

Swimming The contrast between the two coasts couldn't be more marked. The northern beaches are vastly superior, with better sand and deeper water, while almost all of the south coast locations are extremely tidal and muddy, and relatively unappealing for swimmers at all but the highest tides.

Oneroa

Oneroa

1. Matiatia Bay
The wharf where the majority of passenger ferries disembark is located here, but as well as being a busy transport hub, the bay holds two beaches. One is at the south side in front of the large public carpark, the other, to the north of the bay, is part of the Matiatia Historic Reserve. They're both shingly and rocky, but you could swim here if you were desperate while waiting for the ferry. The bay is popular with yachties, with a huge number of moorings, and also a good boat ramp for smaller pleasure craft.

2. Owhanake Bay
Korora Rd leads from the western end of Oneroa down to a large grass paddock, where the public road ends. It's about a hundred metres from the carpark to the beach, which is a fairly unspectacular mass of shingle and stones, with a shallow shelf reminiscent of the south coast's tidal bays. It's probably of little appeal to the casual visitor, without facilities of any kind.

3. Big Oneroa Bay
Oneroa in Maori means "long beach". There are actually two Oneroas, and they are very different affairs. Big Oneroa is nearly 2km long and is the social and tourist heart of the island, with a wide array of cafes, shops and restaurants perched on the hill overlooking this gorgeous crescent of silver sand. Vehicle access to the eastern half is via a narrow lane that leads off Puriri Rd, along the foreshore, where a row of trees offers shade with intermittent parking in between. Beachside facilities include a block of public toilets, gas bbq and picnic tables near the middle of the bay. Due to the limited seafront parking, many choose to park and walk down the steps from the village. There is another access point into the western crook of the bay off Korora Rd, with a ramp onto the beach for boat launching, though limited parking.

4. Little Oneroa Bay
In contrast to its bigger neighbour, Little Oneroa is enclosed and intimate, with a fair amount of parking under the big macrocarpas at its eastern end, which is where you'll find the store, toilets, a gas bbq, picnic tables and a popular children's play area right beside the sand. Sadly the stream here has dubious water quality and should be avoided. The headland west of the carpark hides another little craggy cove with its own little sandy beach. A walkway on the hill above the bay connects the two beaches, and continues on to Big Oneroa, while another leads up the cliff-line and eventually to Hekerua Bay with a few deviations.

5. Hekerua Bay
Delightful Hekerua Bay will almost certainly offer both shelter from the wind and privacy; a result of the steep hill behind it, and the fact you can't drive there, despite the existence of a paper road on most maps. Access is by either walking around the rocks from Sandy Bay, or down the long stepped pathway at the intersection of Hekerua Rd and Queens Drive.

6. Sandy Bay
One of my personal favourites, this gorgeous enclosed gem faces north-west, and is protected from most winds by the headlands that extend off either end of the bay. A grass band behind the beach is home to a sea of kayaks, with a concrete ramp that offers easy trailer boat launching, giving access to some excellent fishing terrain nearby.

7. Enclosure Bay
A 50 metre wide crescent of sand and shingle, with rocky points at either extremity, is almost closed by a series of rocks forming a barrier to the open sea, with only three narrow openings. Whilst it is a bay in one sense, strictly speaking it is a gigantic rock pool, NZ's 2nd largest in fact, and for my money, it's one of the most delightful spots to swim in the country. Low tides can get a bit shallow, but above mid tide you'll find a delightful natural swimming pool with crystal-clear water and barely a ripple, that is ideal for children and less confident swimmers seeking a safe place to get wet. Whilst the local community have fought hard to preserve its integrity, the bay suffers after rain, with poor water quality as a result of old and leaking septic tanks in the surrounding valley.

Little Oneroa

Sandy Bay

Enclosure Bay

8. Palm Beach

So named after the Phoenix palms at various points along the beach, it's an intimate and highly popular north-facing bay, flanked by rocky headlands at either end. There are actually two beaches, Big Palm and Little Palm, though Little Palm is commonly known as "Nudie Beach", as it is well known as a clothing optional location, and has gained quite a reputation, and a fair bit of media exposure over the years. Big Palm is about 500 metres long, with three access points. At the eastern end is a small grass reserve with picnic tables, gas bbq, and toilets. There's another in the centre with loos, cold showers and a children's play area, and a further option to the west with no facilities. Little Palm can be reached by walking from the western end of the bay, though at high tide this involves scrambling over the rocks. Alternatively there is a well marked, but steep pathway from Cory Road, with limited parking on the roadside. Services include a popular store and a fish and chip shop behind the beach. The headlands and island off its shoreline offer good fishing terrain close by. **Palm Crest** clifftop accommodation (09)372 4500. **The Last Resort B&B** (09)372 9683 last_resort@xtra.co.nz

Palm Beach

9. Onetangi
An almost ruler straight strip of sparkling white sand extends for two kilometres from rocky point to rocky point, with a foreshore road extending along most of its length, and access onto the beach for boat launching at either extremity. Onetangi is the most popular surf beach on the island, with the eastern end generally producing better banks, due to the stream and headland there. It fires when a cyclone spits a north-east swell through the window between the barrier and the mainland. A line of homes and a few cafes sit adjacent to the foreshore road, with some spectacular coastal architecture on show, testament to the desirability of this north-facing gem. Facilities include public loos and free gas bbqs near the centre of the bay, while there is a petrol station, fish and chip shop and a dairy one block back from the beach.

10. Man'o' War Bay
There are two beautiful coves on the north coast when heading east on the Loop Road after Onetangi, called Garden Cove and Owhiti Beach; though access to them is through private land and this is prohibited with no easment for the public. The only beach that's publicly accessible by car on the eastern side of the island is Man'o'War Bay, which features many of the characteristics of the south coast i.e. shingly, tidal and shallow. A private wharf marks its northern boundary, and a long headland with a jagged point extends out to the south. The road runs right down its length, offering easy access. Facilities include a public toilet and gas-fired bbq, located where the road meets the beach at the north end. The Man'o'War Winery has a small cellar door operation adjacent to the beach, offering free wine tastings and sales in the weekends and during peak holiday periods. The south point offers good land-based fishing opportunities.

11. Orapiu
A small settlement at the south-eastern tip of the island is set into a horseshoe-shaped cove, that's shallow and again highly tidal, without anywhere easy for the public to swim. The main visitor drawcard is a highly popular wharf that attracts a range of fish, including kahawai and good sized kingfish, as well as the odd snapper; with sprats and mackerel livebaits fairly easy to come by using sabiki rigs. There's a set of public loos and ample parking out by the wharf. A gravel road leads from here, over the hill, to another isolated spot called Otakawhe Bay, that is shingly and steeper, but highly exposed to south winds.

12. Awaawaroa Bay/Deadmans Bay
The road past Whakanewa ends in a small carpark above the bay, and despite the existence of a paper road, it appears from the signs that the last 100 metres down to the beach are private, making access difficult without knowing a local. It is shingly and tidal with an oyster farm in the south-west corner.

13. Woodside Bay
A flat beach with farmland backing on to it, that may not be the best swimming spot on the island, but that looked like a good spot to launch a kayak, from where you could gain access to some interesting fishing waters in the vicinity.

Deadmans Bay

Ostend

14. Whakanewa
The broad, open expanse that is Whakanewa lacks intimacy and a certain charm, when compared to many of the beaches on the north coast, though it does offer the only camping site on the island. There are actually two halves to the beach, with a well equipped campsite located on the foreshore at the south end. For reservations and the combination to the gate (09)301 0101. It is an Auckland Regional Council reserve and aslo an extensive breeding ground for the endangered dotterel, with much of foreshore behind the northern section of the bay being roped off. The beach is only a good place to swim at high tides, but is popular with kite-boarders in westerly winds which blow straight in here. You'll find public loos at either end of the beach.

15. Omiha Bay
This is a very popular boat mooring, and home to the Rocky Bay Memorial Cruising Club, with its ultra-quaint club house. A more charming anchorage you will struggle to find, offering protection from westerly and south-westerly winds, though a due southerly would blow straight in here. There's a public parking area above the reinforced seawall in the crook of the bay, with a public toilet hidden under the trees.

16. Kukurau Bay
The prettiest of all the south coast beaches, there is a busy little community in the hills surrounding the bay, and a large grass reserve behind the beach, with picnic tables, a gas bbq, and toilets under the pohutakawas which are dotted along the foreshore. This is what most people refer to when they talk of Rocky Bay, and it offers slightly deeper water than those nearby, thus good family swimming.

17. Otoka/Dead Dog Bay
A west-facing bay that is relatively undistinguished, except for the sculpture park in the private wetland and tropical gardens just above it. Entry costs $10.00, which possibly puts a few people off. Beach access is gained via the walking tracks off the roads that lead towards the coast at either end.

18. Anzac Bay
Another extremely tidal spot below Ostend, it serves as an anchorage for a dozen or so boats that languish on the mudflats at lower tides. It is also the site of a fairly extensive retirement village.

19. Putaki/Shelly Bay
Shelly Beach Rd leads down to another flat-shelved, muddy bay with an oyster farm to the west and an historic Pa site on the reserve to the east. There's a foreshore road with ample parking and a few Pohutakawa trees spaced along it, and a few boats moored offshore that lie beached on the mud as the tide recedes.

20. Surfdale
They don't come any more inappropriately named than Surfdale, which was apparently given its moniker in a competition by one Ethell Miller, who believed it had a reputation for wild surf. Quite how this misconception crept in I don't know, but it's fair to say that there has probably never been a decent, rideable wave at Surfdale. Not really a swimming beach at anything other than full tide, it would be more aptly named kiteboard-dale as it's the most common recreational pursuit on this beach these days, due to its exposure to the prevailing south-west winds, easy launching, and ample parking on the grass foreshore. Low tide isn't much chop, due to the long walk over the mudflats to get to the water.

21. Blackpool
Nearly a kilometre long, but possibly the shallowest and hence for casual visitors, the least appealing of all the beaches on the island; it does at least share some similarities with its namesake. It was a busy place in pre-European times, probably due to its large cockle beds and strategic location closest to the mainland, and is still home to the surviving Marae on the island, which is tucked into the base of the hills to the west of the bay.

Surfdale

Great Barrier Island

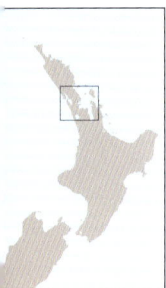

Also Known as Aotea Island, Great Barrier was once a part of the Coromandel Peninsula, and though now an island separated by the Colville Channel, it shares many of the Coromandel's geographical characteristics. Its west coast is a shoreline of rocky bays, deep harbours and steep cliffs, with one or two stretches of fine sand; while the eastern side features a collection of stunning white sand beaches that are pounded by Pacific swells, and backed by forest-clad hills. Dividing the two coasts is a mountain range with imposing peaks and bluffs, offering walkers a treasure trove of well maintained tracks and trails, giving spectacular views from nearly every ridge. Great Barrier seems like the last little slice of old New Zealand, with no mains power, a predominance of gravel roads, and a sparse cultural environment that appeals to hardy, self-sufficient types. This isolation led to the development of the world's first pigeon post in 1897, a shining example of kiwi ingenuity. But as a result of the distance to the city, fuel and food prices are high (often nearly twice the cost found in town), and sometimes supply is erratic. There are a collection of services and a few cafes and restaurants, but the mainland it is not. The quid-pro-quo for this isolation and the associated inconvenience, is the peace and pristine environment you find here. If you like that kind of thing, it's another one of those places that once you get there, you will never want to leave.

Traveling You can either get there by air or by boat. Ferries arrive at Tryphena and Port Fitzroy. **SeaLink** 0800732546 operates a car and passenger ferry from Wynyard Wharf in downtown Auckland. Their service runs year round between 3 - 6 days a week and their sailing time is just over four hours www.sealink.co.nz. Fullers run a fast cat from Queens Wharf to Tryphena at peak periods 0800 Fullers. **GB Air** 0800 900 600 or (09)275 9120 and **Fly My Sky** (09)256 7025, fly from the domestic terminal at Auckland airport to either Claris or Okiwi. It is possible to fly one way and ferry the other.

WIND ROSE

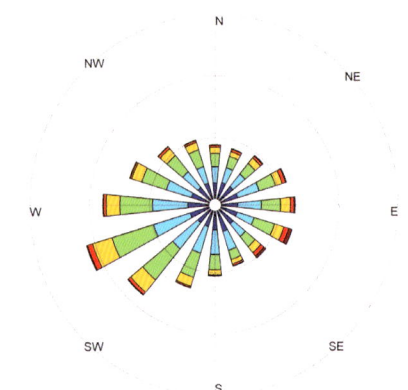

SWELL ROSE

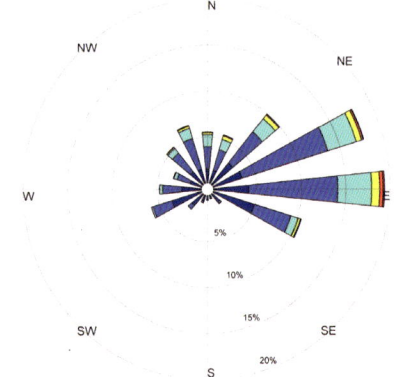

Getting around There are no bus services on the island and most visitors either take their own car on the ferry (which is often the best solution), rent a vehicle for the duration, or just get a taxi or shuttle to wherever they are staying; and either stay-put or hitch around. A shuttle van service operates from Fitzroy, bookings preferred **Great Barrier Shuttle/Mike Newman** (09)429 0052 or 021 876 296. The island has several rental car companies, the main two are **Aotea Car Rentals** in Tryphena (09)429 0474 or 0800 426 8332 and **GBI Rentals** in Claris (09)429 0062 www.gbirentacar.co.nz. Both have drop-off options at Port Fitzroy. Hitching is common, though car traffic is light. Tryphena and Claris are the two main shopping centres, providing most basic facilities, though Fitzroy also has a store, club, and fuel. To book the **DOC campsites**, (essential at peak times) (09)429 0044. Robin Grice is an agent for local homes (09)4290 955 www.islandaccommodation.co.nz. There is a tourist info centre at the rental car company near Claris. www.thebarrier.co.nz is a good website with heaps of local information. www.greatbarrier.co.nz also has tourist information.

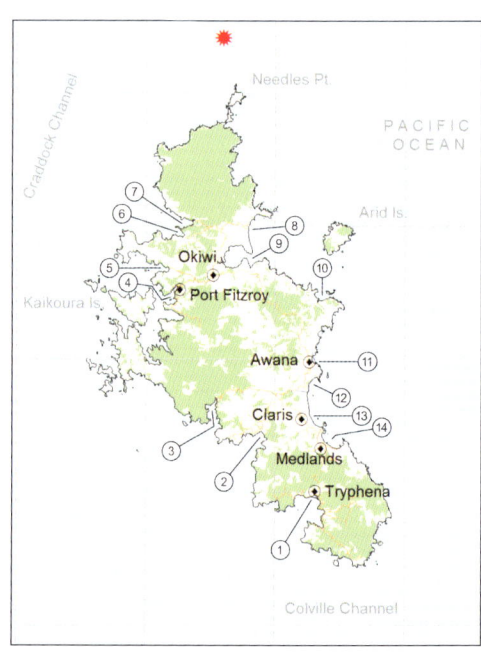

Kaitoke

Claris club

Patiki

Ocean bounty

Surfing Whilst it has four spectacularly exposed east coast beaches, the quality of the sand banks at all of them is highly variable. On the other hand, the rivermouth at Whangapoua is a world class right-hander and machine-like in north-east swells and south-west winds, which are the best conditions for most of the other spots too. Shark Alley is the exception, and works best in a huge south-east swell with southerly winds. **Aotea Surf School** (09)429 0293 operates from Medlands Beach www.aoteasurfschool.com. There is a small surf shop behind Medlands Beach down Masons Rd. Ilona at **Sun, Sea and Surf** sells basics like leggies, wax, boardies and bikinis (09)429 0352 sunseasurf@surf.co.nz

Fishing The Barrier is one of the best fishing locations in the country, with all major species available around the coast here for those that care to go looking. There is plenty of kai-moana too, and with two coasts so close together offering shelter in almost any wind, it's a hard destination to beat. Boat launching on the west coast is easy at all the main locations, with only **Medlands** on the east coast offering beach launching (at the south end). Hooked on Barrier Fishing Charters (09)429 0740 have a large boat and a fishing shop near Claris www.hookedonbarrier.co.nz. Surf Casting Safaris 021 238 3285.
Chaos Charters Tryphena 027 297 3141 www.chaoscharters.co.nz

Swimming For those who like gorgeous white sand with a bit of swell thrown in for good measure, there's the east coast with a range of conditions, but again no lifeguards should you get into trouble. For the less confident, Tryphena and Okupu offer sheltered conditions for much of the year, though are generally shallower. There are some delicious natural mineral pools in the Kaitoke Stream. It is a half hour walk off the Whangaparapara Rd along a dead flat track to get to them, with good parking off the road.

Mulberry Grove

Goosberry Flat

1. Tryphena

Tryphena is a broad, but relatively shallow bay, that contains a number of beaches and a wide selection of facilities and accommodation options. The wharf is in the crook at the southern end of the bay, and offers a good anchorage for visiting sailboats as well as being the main disembarkation point for most ferry passengers to the island. Travelling north off the ferry, you first see a very shallow, tidal and rocky cove called Shoal Bay, with a few homes and moored boats. Mullberry Grove is the first main beach you come to. The road passes directly behind the coast, which features a reinforced sea-wall, with stony seabed at both ends, and a narrow patch of sand in the middle of the bay. The best swimming spot is directly adjacent to the store, post office and gas station. **Mullberry Grove Store and Gas station** (09)429 0909. **Sunset Waterfront Lodge** (09)429 0051. Goosberry Flat is the next beach north, and probably the best of them all for swimming, with easy access and white sand but no amenities. The road then climbs over the headland to Pah Beach which is my favourite of the three. The southern section of the bay, adjacent to the **Stonewall Store**, **Curraghs Irish Pub** and **Wild Rose Cafe**, is a delicious sandy cove and a protected spot for a swim. The northern portion of the beach has a rocky bottom with a boat ramp adjacent to where the road forks. One way turns inland and begins its ascent over the hill to Medlands. The other follows the coast around to Puriri Bay, another rock-bottom section of coast with a few private homes along the foreshore. The best launch ramp in the bay after the one at Tryphena wharf is here, directly in front of Tipi and Bob's, and it can also be a great place to swim from, with a channel that's relatively deep and sandy at all tides. **Tipi and Bob's Waterfront Dining** and fishing charters (09) 429 0550 www.waterfrontlodge.co.nz. **Great Barrier Social Club** (09)429 0421 on the Medlands road, has bar meals, movies and sports activities; open Wed, Fri, Sat and Sunday nights. **Earthsong Lodge Fine Cuisine** (09)429 0421.

2. Okupu/Blind Bay

Okupu consists of several small beaches set within a deep, broad bay. As you arrive down the hill from Claris, Camerton Road splits off Blind Bay Road and leads down to the coast, under a spectacular canopy of some of the largest pohutakawas in the country. It is the sandiest spot on the west coast of the island, and while shallow, is a stunning and protected place to swim in most winds. The ramp onto the beach makes it a popular launch spot for trailer boats, and the bay also features good fishing and snorkelling in both directions, especially to the south. It is a popular location for kayakers, and you'll see a heap of old tinnies and assorted small craft overturned along the foreshore. A good set of public loos and some well-placed picnic tables on the grass reserve, make it an ideal place for a picnic. Continue around Blind Bay Road and you arrive at another small collection of houses and the Okupu wharf, which is a good spot to fish from at higher tides. There is another good boat launch ramp here, but no other public facilities. **Sunbeam Sanctuary** (09)429 0349 www.sunbeamsanctuary.org. **Bay Lodge** (09)429 0927.

3. Whangaparapara Harbour

Whangaparapara was once a whaling port, and still features a good wharf inside a relatively protected harbour, offering small boat access to the middle of the west coast, and some fabulous fishing terrain thereabouts. There isn't much here for the casual beach-goer though, just a 25 metre patch of shingle that you could call a beach at a stretch, but some would disagree with the claim. **Great Barrier Lodge** (09)4290 488 is located right on the waterfront here and offer fishing and dive charters, and operate a restaurant and bar www.greatbarrierlodge.co.nz

Okupu

Whangaparapara

Kawa

4. Port Fitzroy

This is the best anchorage on the island, a beautiful, almost fjord-like inlet that is the other main ferry embarkation point, and the busiest recreational boat harbour on the island, offering shelter from almost any weather. While it is popular all year, at Christmas and New Year, this harbour is absolutely jam-packed with yachties from all around the North Island partying their brains out, so be warned. Due to its popularity, there are a number of facilities in the bay including a general store and gas station with differing hours depending on season, plus The Boat Club, which has seen its fair share of carousing over the years. There are a couple of rocky coves within the broader bay, but there is no real sand anywhere and despite a good **DOC Campsite** at Akapoua, a rocky bay just west of the port, it is all spectacularly unspectacular if you are looking for a beach experience, and is only really of interest if you are either on, or looking to launch a boat. **Port Fitzroy Store** (09)4290 056. **The Boat Club Tavern** (09)429 0072. **Port Fitzroy Water Taxis** (09)429 0212.

5. Karaka Bay

Another rocky piece of shoreline, located down a tortuous gravel road just north of Fitzroy, it offers spectacular views east towards Little Barrier Island. There is very little sand on the beach and little else to attract travelling beach goers, but despite this, it has become populated over the years, and is now dominated by the Orama Christian Community, which is a camp of sorts featuring a collection of buildings, available for public use in conjunction with the Outdoor Pursuits Centre, which also operates from here. **Outdoor Pursuits Centre** (09)429 0762. **Orama Lodge** (09)429 0063 www.orama.org.nz

6. Kawa

Located down an even more tortuous gravel road than Karaka Bay, Kawa is the first of two bays on private Maori land. It consists of shingle and stones, with a Marae that's currently being rebuilt, and probably best left as a "visit on invitation" spot.

7. Motairehe

Also known as Catherine Bay, Motairehe is a rocky inlet at the mouth of a small stream on private land, and not particularly interesting for travellers other than the most hard core kayaker looking to get access to the north-west coastline. Visitors aren't necessarily discouraged, but nor are they encouraged, and respect should be shown to the local Iwi if you do end up down this way. You will find the island's biggest marae here, with public toilets, gas bbqs and a children's play area adjacent to the stony foreshore.

Port Fitzroy

8. Whangapoua Beach

Whangapoua Beach stretches for a couple of kilometres north of the estuary up to Waikaro Point. Vehicle access to the northern end is via Mabeys Rd, that runs from the township of Okiwi, ending in a large paddock behind a tall stand of pine trees, that dominate the skyline here. A track runs through them to the coast, arriving at a gloriously isolated and enchanting spot, though the only facilities here are the DOC maintained toilets. There can be some not bad waves in a south-east swell and northerly winds, though it is another shifty beach break. The north point offers spectacular fishing and snorkelling terrain if you can get around there.

9. Whangapoua Estuary

One of the most dramatic, fertile and beautiful river estuaries in the entire country, Whangapoua is notable for the grinding right hand waves breaking off its mouth, which is located at the southern extent of the bay. Desirable conditions are a medium to large north-east swell and south-west winds, best at lower tides. You'll find a good, but exposed **DOC Campsite** at the end of the airfield, offering toilets and cold showers as close as you can get to the bar. The walk over the river flats is fairly long, though a paddle down the stream on an outgoing tide can shorten the process. The fishing around here is also predictably good on flat days.

10. Haratonga Beach

The only really sheltered beach on the east coast, with Arid Island blocking most swell from getting in here, Haratonga features a fabulous **DOC Campsite** with good amenities, a hundred or so metres back from the coast. Large stands of trees offer generous shade in the camp, and the stream that flows out to the beach here allows relatively easy launching of kayaks and small boats into the ocean, within striking distance of some epic fishing grounds.

Whangapoua

11. Awana Bay

One of the more striking bays you'll ever see, Awana is dominated by a huge rock to the north and imposing headland to the south. It has the steepest profile of the island's beaches, and faces due east, so picks up any swell going. This makes it popular with surfers, but a relatively treacherous spot to swim for the less confident, featuring a pounding shore-break and strong rips. The best waves are often found at lower tides, though the banks are notoriously fickle. Smaller swells work best here; on larger days the bay can max-out easily. There is a small **DOC Campsite** set back from the coast at the north end of the beach, plus good public toilets and bins at the main beach parking area, adjacent to the road.

12. Palmers Beach

Palmers is a stunning stretch of sand, and really a continuation of the broad sweep of Kaitoke Beach. It is beautifully sheltered in north or west winds, though access is difficult. You can either walk from the gravel lay-by off the main road near its southern end, though it is a difficult track to find, and a bit of a steep hike. The other option is to walk around from the north end of Kaitoke. Both options take a bit of time, which is why it is usually deserted. The rocks here look particularly promising for snorkelling and fishing, so if that's your passion, it may be worth the effort. It is exposed to lots of south swell and is offshore with north winds, but while the surf can look appealing, the peaks seem to shift continually.

Haratonga

Awana

The Mermaid Pool

13. Kaitoke Beach

Nearly 2 km from end to glorious end, Kaitoke faces east into the Pacific, flanked by the Sugarloaf to the south, and a rocky outcrop to the north, which divides it from Palmers Beach. Kaitoke is a popular surf spot, with peaks at various points along it, often better near the south. It is a fab place to swim and laze in the sand, with a wide open, empty feel. Access is from three different points. The first and most commonly used is down Ocean View Rd; a small lane in the centre of the bay, just south of Claris township. It ends behind the dunes, offering a small amount of parking space on the road-side and a track onto the beach. At the south end of the bay, just before you cross over the hill to Medlands, is Sugarloaf Rd, which leads down to a grassy parking area under some big trees, and a privately run campground with a public access-way onto the beach. At lower tides you can walk from here around to the Mermaid Pool, a large rock-pool that is one of the most beautiful swimming spots you will ever see. **The Sugarloaf Campground** is run by the Blackwell family, another old established Barrier clan, who farm The Sugarloaf and surrounding area (09)429 0229 xtina@orcon.net. The other access point is down the stream that runs out to the ocean north of Claris. The road runs along its northern banks and ends a few hundred metres from the coast, requiring a short walk from where you leave your car. Be advised there is no turning space here and limited parking, so it isn't a popular option. The township of Claris lies in the middle of the beach with a shop, Post Office, gas station, cafe, medical centre, dentist, laundromat and the main airport. **Lazy Cow Cottages** (09)429 0773. **Barrier Bungalow** (09)429 0848. **Sugarloaf Cottage** (09)429 0229. **Claris Crossroads Backpackers** (09)429 0889 is at the intersection of Blind Bay Rd and Gray Rd. **Kaitoke River Kayaks** (09)429 0987. **Claris Texas Cafe** is open every day from 8.00am serving legendary coffee (09)429 0811.

14. Medlands Beach/Oruawharo Bay

Named after the family who farmed here for much of its European history, it is the most populated of the east coasts beaches, and yet another absolute stunner; a long crescent-shaped bay, facing predominantly north-east, punctuated by Memory Island in the centre. For such a big bay, it has an enclosed feeling, with the high Sugarloaf Hill and its rocky point to the north, and a false bay known as Shark Alley to the south. Shark Alley is protected by a long reef and distinctive headland, off which break some grunty waves in a huge south-east swell, though it isnt a wave that works regularly, and not for the faint hearted. The beach itself also has a reputation for good surf in a range of conditions, with consistent sandbanks either side of Memory Rock and along the length of the beach depending on swell size and direction. Fishing and snorkelling are both epic off the rocks at either end of the beach, with the ledges south around Shark Alley being particularly productive and accessible, and some large snapper and kingies have been landed here. The only boat launching on the east coast other than Haratonga, is off the beach at the south end by the stream. **Le Soleil Chalets** (09)429 0995 located down Mason Rd is a really beautiful place to stay, with several different chalet options. **Medlands Backpackers and Villas** (09)4290320 just behind the beach is the low cost accommodation choice www.medlandsbeach.com. **Foromor Lodge** (09)429 0335 offers a bit of modern luxury in the sandhills behind the beach. **Oruawharo Creek Recreational Reserve** is the DOC campsite at the south end of the bay, with good shade trees, a kitchen block, toilets and cold showers.

Kaitoke

Medlands

Muriwai to Te Henga

Te Henga/Bethells marks the northern fringe of the Waitakare Range, and signals a significant shift in coastal geography. Muriwai is the last of a series of flat straight beaches that continue almost unbroken all the way from Ahipara, while Bethells shares many similarities with the coastline accessed off the Piha Rd. Less patronized than the spots further south, but no less spectacular, these beaches offer a wide choice of character and a diverse array of recreational pursuits to go with it. In fact it's hard to find a coastal activity that you can't do out here. This region may not have the glam associated with Piha, but it has got a ton of soul and acres of space for everyone to do their thing, whatever that is.

Travelling The western motorway leads to Kumeu, and from there it's a pretty stress-free drive to get to all of these beaches. Accommodation and eating options are thin on the ground, with the cafes and campground at Muriwai the main public amenities.

Surfing Similar ocean conditions create waves as for the rest of the west coast: clean south-west swells and north-east winds. Maori Bay is particularly popular as is the north end of Muriwai in tiny swells. **Hard Core Surf Shop**, 16 Shamrock Drive, Kumeu. (09) 412 2233 www.hardcoresurf.co.nz. **Muriwai Surf School** 021 478 734 www.muriwaisurfschool.co.nz.

Fishing You'll find good, but hazardous rock fishing around Te Henga and at the south end of Muriwai, while the torpedo and kontiki guys have a field day further up Muriwai Beach, where they can escape the rocks. In particular the northern tip facing towards the Kaipara is a renown big snapper location, also accounting for large trevalley and sharks.

Swimming Muriwai is the beach with the second highest number of rescues in the country, due no doubt to its popularity, and the diligence of the surf club, but the point should be obvious. The Tasman is continually swell-exposed, and swimming at all these beaches should be well considered if you don't want to end up as a statistic.

WIND ROSE

SWELL ROSE

Muriwai sunset

1. Muriwai/Rangitira Beach

"Pummelled by waves, blustered by wind, blasted by sand, baked by sun. Sands ever-shifting, gannets ever-soaring, pohutakawas ever swaying, Muriwai… ever-changing." Whoever wrote this poem, that adorns the walls of the Muriwai visitor-centre got it dead right. In effect, a long peninsula protecting the southern shores of the Kaipara Harbour, Muriwai extends for nearly 50km from the cliffs at Maori Bay around to the tip of the Papakanui Spit. It is a long, flat expanse of black sand, backed by high dunes, that's become extremely popular due to the ease of access from Auckland city, coupled with the peace and space afforded by its vast expanse. The main access point is at the south end, where there are a few cafes, a store, ample parking and facilities, including the motor camp and surf club. A walkway from the end of the beach leads over the hill to Maori Bay, and you can also walk out to the flat platforms jutting off the headland here. These are probably the most accessible land-based fishing spots on the west coast, but they get pounded by swell, so be warned and wear a life jacket. The beach here rarely seems to have good surf banks, though one lives in hope. It is a listed highway, and four wheel drive vehicles and trail bikes are commonly seen, as are horses. Some use it for access to the surf and fishing spots towards the north, others just as a place to fang around for the hell of it. 4wd vehicle access onto the beach is provided off Coast Rd, that ends after the gap in the dunes, with a locked gate just after the surf club and camping ground. Access to the beach further north is restricted to one main entrance off Rimmer Rd, off state highway 16 before Helensville. As well as being a good place to avoid crowds on busy summer days, "Rimmers" is a renown small swell spot, and when the rest of Auckland's west coast is tiny, Rimmers can be relied on to provide a wave, featuring consistent banks and greater exposure to swell. If you have a 4wd, you can drive up the beach, and find your own bank before Rimmers. Generally the swell size increases as you head north, and if you want to get a wave to yourself in a small clean swell, this is a damn good place to start looking. The extreme tip of the beach culminates in a long sandspit facing into the Kaipara Harbour, which is one of the best fishing areas in the whole Auckland area, plus a significant bird watching spot, home to the endangered Fairy Tern amongst other species. Sadly this unique ecosystem is part of the RNZAF bombing range, and the land area is closed permanently. Beach access is still legal, but it too is restricted when live rounds are being fired. When this is happening, a red flag is erected on the beach at the 26 mile mark. **Muriwai Surf Lifesaving Club** (09)411 8055 www.muriwaisurf.org.nz. **Muriwai Motor Camp** (09)411 9262 www.muriwaimotorcamp.co.nz

2. Maori Bay

Maori called this bay Maukatia, referring to the grinding of stone tools in the area, though somehow it became Maori Bay. It is best known for the Takapu gannet refuge that's located on the distinctive rocks separating Maori Bay from Muriwai. The colony can be reached by walking from the carpark down the well-maintained walkway, from where you gain spectacular views both ways up and down the coast, which at sunset can be spectacular. It is also a magnet for the Auckland surfing community, with an array of peaks breaking on the sand south of the rocks. The banks change constantly, so optimum tidal conditions vary, but it can get epic with everything lined-up. There are a few waves to the south, including a left breaking off Shag Rock and another set of peaks way down the beach, but these are rarely surfed, though worth keeping an eye on. The beach itself is beautiful; protected by the cliffs from strong winds and offering an intimacy totally lacking at Muriwai. Granted you have to walk down a cliff path from the carpark at the top of the hill to get there, but it's a small price to pay for a bit of peace and quiet, as Maori Bay is rarely crowded; though at high tides there isn't a lot of sand compared to its neighbour over the hill. Oaia Island, just offshore, is a legendary fishing spot, and on the rare days you can get a kayak out, would be a likely spot to find kingfish, trevalley and good-sized snapper in the area. There are good public conveniences in the carpark at the top of the hill.

Gannet chick

3. Te Henga/Bethells Beach

The name Te Henga relates to the boards that run along the gunwales of a waka, that prevent water coming aboard. The reference is to the high dunes that provided shelter from strong westerly weather coming off the Tasman, for the original inhabitants of the valley behind the beach. The pakeha name was given to it by the Bethells family, who farmed here from the early 1860's, though Te Henga seems a more evocative and appropriate title. Whatever you call it, it is one of Auckland's most spectacular, yet underrated and least visited beaches. The fact it has remained somewhat of an enigma, may be due to its lack of facilities and relative isolation, though it is well loved by those who know it. Just over a kilometre long and facing south-west, Bethells features spectacular cliffs and points to the south, and the dominating presence of Erangi Point to the north. Erangi point is an extremely popular fishing spot with good ledges. It is flanked by a pair of islands, both privately owned, with Ihumoana, the southernmost of the two,

Te Henga/Bethells

O'Neils

featuring the cutest and most spectacularly located bach in the country. The surf can be good along its length, often better at higher or on incoming tides, as it can be badly current affected. The track to the beach leads from an extensive carpark where you'll find a caravan selling coffee and snack food on summer weekends. Just before you arrive at the beach, you'll pass a carpark on your left after Tasman View Rd, which is the start of the walkway leading to Lake Wainamu and the scenic reserve that surrounds it. Te Henga also has a surf life-saving club, though it is only manned in peak periods, and at weekends, from Labour weekend till easter (09)810 9381. There's a community website www.bethellsbeach.org.nz. Trude and John Bethell offer accommodation with several units (09)890 5981 www.bethellsbeach.com.

4. O'Neils

If you walk down the Bethells stream and head over the ridge at the north end of the beach, you come to O'Neils. Like Maori Bay, it is a great place to avoid strong winds and escape the madding crowd, also a good place to surf if you don't like getting dropped-in on. There are no facilities and often no people, so if you're going to swim, make sure you do it in the middle of the beach where there are generally no rips.

The Piha Road

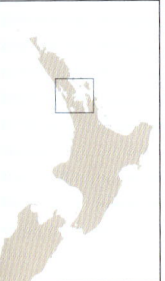

The 15 km road leading off Scenic Drive to the ocean is the gateway to some of New Zealand's best known beaches. These spectacular pockets of iron-sand lie recessed in the spaces between the many bush-lined ridges and points that hit the ocean here in contorted, black and green lines; with the Tasman's sea-spume sitting like a constant shroud, drifting up the valleys and hanging suspended between the ridges for days at a time. At times uncontrollably wild and violently beautiful, at others a shining, sparkling jewel; this coast enchants and challenges all who venture out into the hills, just thirty minutes west of Auckland city. It's the steepest and most dramatic section of the Waitakares, so predictably, the road can be pretty hectic, but what awaits you at the end of your journey makes the twists and turns eminently worthwhile. As well as the obvious locations, the area offers a couple of lesser known, but delightful bays that aren't accessible by car, but are easily found with some spirited walking. It is the coast where Edmund Hillary had his bach, and while not as challenging as the Himalayan peaks, if you're looking to ratchet up the adrenaline levels, it isn't a bad place to start, either on land or in the sea. Equally, it makes for a fabulous day-trip from Auckland, even if all you have in mind is a long walk, and to get some fresh air in your lungs.

Traveling All the roads are steep and winding, particularly Karekare Rd. Many people burn out their brakes by being impatient on the descents. Use your gears and don't be tempted to cut corners. There's no petrol after Titirangi or Swanson. **Piha Surf Shuttle** offers transport from Auckland (09)627 2644 or 0274 952 526 www.surfshuttle.co.nz

WIND ROSE

SWELL ROSE

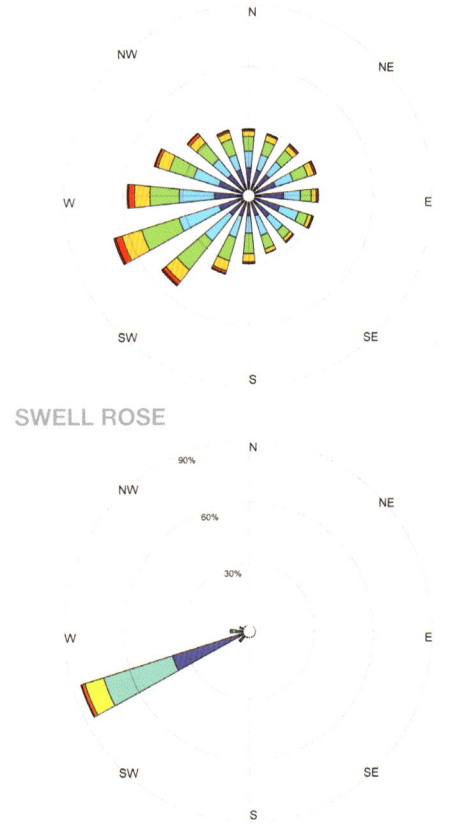

Surfing Some of the best waves in the Auckland region can be found down this road, and there's usually a place to surf for all ability levels somewhere, plus there are 2 surf shops of sorts at Piha in case you need stuff. The best conditions are a south-west or west swell up to 8 feet on the buoys, with a north-east wind. **Piha Surf Shop** (09)812 8723 www.pihasurf.co.nz. **Keyhole Boardriders** is the local surf club, contact Alistair Goodwin (09)812 8179. **Piha Surf School** (09)812 8123 www.pihasurfschool.com

Fishing There's some excellent rock fishing all around this coast, plus limited boat launching off the beach at Piha, but all precautions should be taken by those fishing on this coast. Many lives are lost each year by people turning their backs on the sea. Rogue waves are always a threat. **The Piha Deep Sea Fishing Club** holds meetings at 6.30pm on the first Tuesday of the month at the Piha RSA.

Swimming Statistics show Piha to be the most incident-prone beach in the country and vigilance is required at all these locations. The mix of urban folk who are unprepared for the sheer power of the Tasman's waves, plus the speed of the rips, power in the shore-break, and the relentless long-shore current, have all combined to cause many drownings in the past, and will continue to do so while people ignore all the warnings. Only swim between the flags when lifeguards are on duty. Never swim in jeans or other restrictive clothes. Dont even think about it if you've been drinking alcohol. Learn to spot rips.

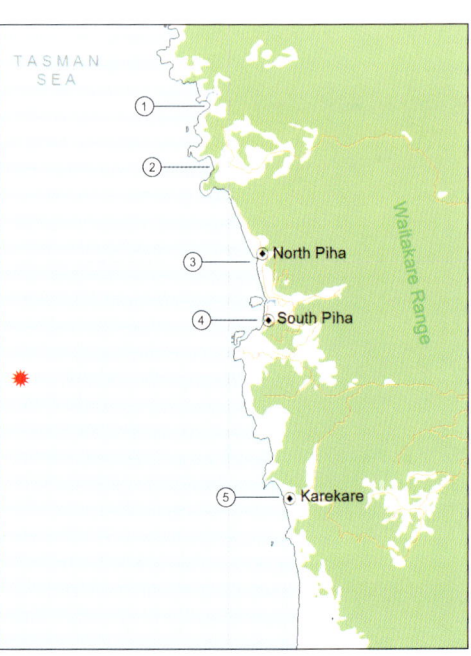

Anawhata

South Piha

1. Anawhata

It's about 20 minutes down a gravel road that leads off the Piha Rd, and another 20 or so to walk down to the beach, but if it is some natural rejuvenation and a dose of raw west coast beauty you're looking for, you will find Anawhata just the tonic. Whilst the road is windy, it is well maintained and fairly flat, plus offers spectacular views back over Piha that are almost worth the drive on their own. Wild is the right word to describe Anawhata, and given its isolation, and the absence of lifeguards, it should be treated cautiously by even the most experienced swimmers. The surf can be good, but has a tendency to get confused in all but the cleanest swells, though crowds are never a problem. Fishermen will find good ledges either side of the beach, with the one to the south usually producing the best, with trevalley, snapper, kahawai and rig regularly landed. The only amenity is the long drop toilet in the car park at the top of the hill.

2. Whites Beach

Head to the furthest carpark at North Piha, and walk towards the point. The near-vertical track to Whites Beach leads up and over the headland, down onto a rock ledge, and with a bit of a scramble down the hill, you're at the quaintest little cove on the west coast. There's nothing there except for a short strip of black sand. Enjoy it with abandon, but swim with caution.

3. South Piha

One of the most recognizable beaches in the country due to the striking profile of Lion Rock, and "that view" on the drive down the hill; it's actually two quite different feeling pieces of sand, separated by Lion Rock and the Piha Lagoon. South Piha is one of the cradles of the New Zealand surfing scene, and home to the busiest lifeguard tower in the country. It's also where most visitors begin their Piha voyage of discovery. I say that because there's a lot to discover. The hordes that congregate here are attracted by its charming and dramatic feel, and because it offers greater intimacy and shelter than its northern counterpart, plus convenient parking directly overlooking the beach. That said, it can be way more dangerous, with vicious rips at either end of the beach that have claimed many lives over the years. The one at the south end courses rapidly out towards The Keyhole, hugging the rocks, and ending way out to sea. Surfers and boaties use it as a conveyor belt, but less experienced swimmers should avoid it for fear of their lives. A similar rip runs out along the north of the beach, along the side of Lion Rock, and it can be equally dangerous. The middle of the beach is always safer. For surfers, there are a range of different peaks in the bay, but it is best known for the spectacular low tide lefts that peel off the sandbar at the south end.

"The Bar" as it is known, has been a crucible for both high-performance surfing and Kiwi board design over the years, and handles the biggest swells on the Auckland west coast. Access is by walking around the rocks and either paddling out through the keyhole, or jumping into the rip. At high tide the reform can also be legendary, though neither are what they were, due to a large influx of sand over the last decade. This is noticeable at the Blue Pool too, which used to be a wide basin of clear water, enclosed by rocks, that is now not much more than a spa pool. It is accessed by walking around the rocks to the south of the beach, and through the gap that's visible from the gorgeous and sheltered bay you find yourself in. Fishermen can usually be found over at The Gap, off Nun Rock, or off the rocks out towards the blowhole. There are a range of public facilities including two stores (one on the beach at South Piha and one on the main road between the two beaches) and two cafe's. **The Piha RSA** (09)8128 138 is a great place to get dinner and a beer on Tuesday, Thursday, Friday and Saturday, and the Surf Club at South Piha is also a good place to get a feed (09)812 8896 www.pihaslsc.com. It's also blessed with a really good campground **Piha Domain Campground** (09)812 8815 pihacamp@xtra.co.nz. Other self-catering accommodation can be found at www.pihabeach.co.nz and there is a **backpackers** on Glenesk Rd (09)812 8381 www.pihabeachstay.co.nz.

4. North Piha North Piha is a broad, open expanse of flat black sand that stretches for nearly 3 km, with Lion Rock to the south and Te Waha Point to the north. It is more exposed to the wind than South Piha, but its length makes it a fantastic place to let off some steam. If you're a surfer, you'll find North Piha as exasperating as any beach in the country; some days epic, others a total hoax, but generally better at high tide, though low tide can offer surprises when the banks are right. There are often good lefts off the north side of Lion Rock, a fairly consistent bank in front of the stream near the surf-lifesaving club in the middle of the beach, and occasionally exceptional waves at the far north of the beach. There can also be good fishing off the north point. You'll find walkways onto the beach at multiple points down its length, with parking on the grass beside the

Piha Sign

road. Ammenities include toilets just after Lion Rock, and at the surf club. North Piha has some of the coolest baches in the country and despite proximity to Auckland, has managed to maintain its wild ambience, and thus its timeless appeal. It is patrolled in sections during summer, but it pays to exercise caution at all times when swimming here, even though North Piha has its own separate lifesaving club www.unitednorthpiha.org.nz. A community website lists local water quality reports amongst other things www.piha.org.nz

5. Karekare
Odds-on favourite for the most dramatic beach in the country, Karekare has been a location for several films over the years, most notably Jane Campion's, "The Piano." It sounds like the ultimate writers cop-out, but its breathtaking beauty is almost impossible to put into words. You descend from the Piha Road down the steepest road in the Waitakeres, onto a bush clad valley floor and along to a wide basin behind the beach, where there is a large parking area with public loos and a few picnic tables. From there it is a walk over the stream and a few hundred metres through the dunes onto the beach, which is a wide expanse of open black sand, guarded by immense cliffs all around. Karekare is an abbreviation of Waikarekare, that translates appropriately as "Water of Rippling Surf". It is a wild, exposed bay that seems to amplify any swell and wind from the west, and you can both feel it and hear it from the moment you get out of the car. To the north is a huge bluff called The Watchman, which guards another section of beach before the north point with its headland. To the south the beach opens up to a long stretch of empty coast leading all the way to Whatipu. There is another access point from the top of The Watchman, that can be reached by taking a right just before the main carpark, over the bridge and up to park under the pohutakawas. From there it's a short walk to the top of the ridge and down the track to the beach. Waves can be excellent, but its exposed nature means it only really fires in the cleanest of conditions. There can be peaks down the beach and off either side of the island at the south end, plus the point at the north end can get really good when the sand is in the right place, which it hasn't been for some years. Offshore is north-east. The most common fishing spots are off the point, or from the beach down by the island. Other attractions at Karekare include the waterfall with its swimming pool just off Lone Kauri Rd, located a short walk above the main beach carpark. There's a small campsite at the bottom of the hill www.karekare.org. **Karekare Beach Lodge** offers self catering (09)817 9987 www.karekarebeachlodge.co.nz. **Equinox Lodge** is a luxury B&B (09)812 8078 www.equinoxlodge.com. **Wharepuka** quality 4 bedroom bach on Lone Kauri Rd 027 271 5733.

Karekare

The Manukau Harbour

The Manukau Harbour is New Zealands second largest, covering 394 square km, and holds a pivotal position in our maritime history. It is an oceanic wonder, that's probably the most underrated of any harbour in the country, offering a home to a huge amount of fish and shellfish, including mussels, cockles, scallops, snapper, gurnard, kahawai, kingfish and a range of sharks. It is also an important nursery for a number of species, including great whites, we are told. The Manukau has suffered much over the last 150 years from mans negligence and insensitivity. Being so close to the CBD, yet the less desirable of Aucklands twin harbours, it was for many years used as the city's toilet. Heavy industry in the Onehunga and Penrose area definitely had an impact on water quality. Precious landmarks like Puketutu Island were quarried for road metal and with the development of the Mangere sewage ponds, its fate was seemingly sealed. Yet even today, its waters still team with fish, and though its inner reaches are fairly unappealing for a casual visitor; when you head west down Huia Rd and explore some of the coastline there, you'll find yourself catching your breath from the beauty that surrounds you. The Waitakare Range and its cloak of native bush that plunges into the sea, pose a dramatic backdrop for a beach experience that can seem to be a wander back through time.

Travelling The coastline between Mangere and Titirangi is heavily inhabited and built up. As you leave Titirangi, the atmosphere changes dramatically, but there are still few accommodation options for travellers until you get to Whatipu.

Surfing The Ninepin at Whatipu, has waves in the hugest winter swells. It breaks infrequently, but worth remembering in the depths of winter when everywhere else is mental and a north-wester is howling.

Fishing There have been some huge fish weighed in here over the years, caught both inside the harbour, and out from the heads, where a finger of deep water is home to large tuna and marlin in season. It is home to an avid and unique angling community. **Manukau Sport Fishing Club** holds monthly meetings on the first Thursday of the month at **Dive HQ**, 5 Portage Road, msfc@ihug.co.nz. **Manukau Cruising Club** (09) 636 7177 www.manukaucruisingclub.com

Swimming It's not considered the greatest of places to swim due to its highly tidal nature, and at times dubious water quality, but many do, especially nearer the entrance, where it becomes deeper and less developed, with significantly cleaner water.

WIND ROSE

SWELL ROSE

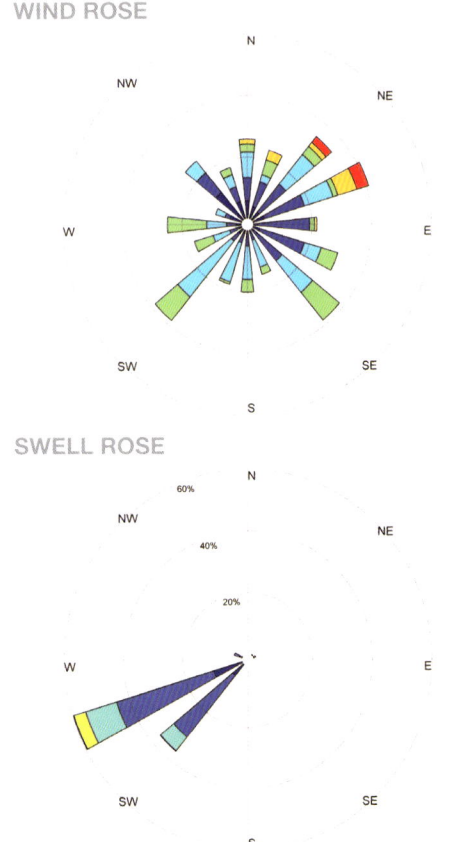

Huia

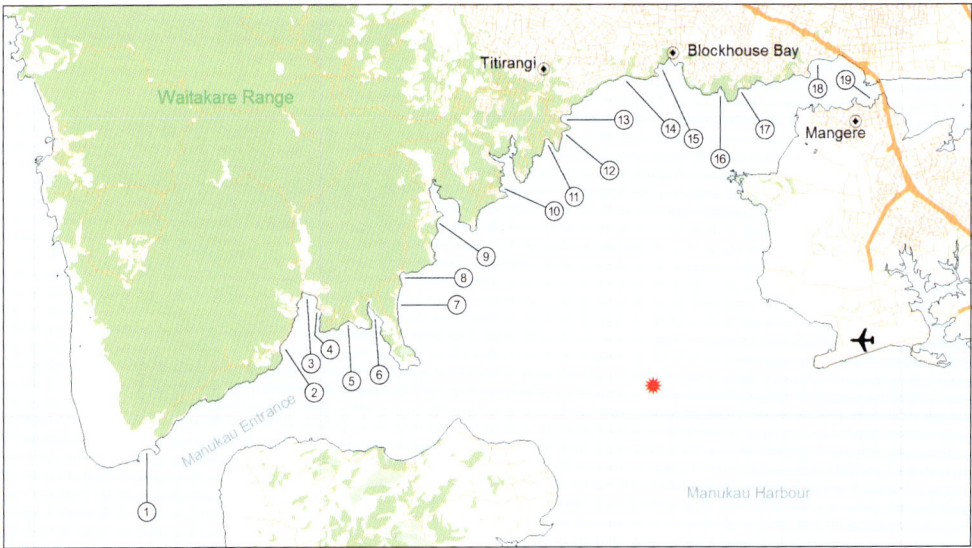

1. Whatipu

An 8km gravel and dirt road leads from Little Huia, over the hills to one of the most spectacular and unusual coastal regions in the country. The Whatipu Scientific Reserve features a huge sandy spit, covered in toi-toi, cabbage trees and flax, and backed by the bush-clad Waitakare Ranges. It marks the entrance to the Manukau Harbour, and the tumultuous currents formed by the filling and emptying of such a huge body of water, are clearly visible. To the south-east is Paratutae Island (which is actually connected to the mainland) and a lone rock known as The Ninepin, which sits off the sandspit's southern extent. There is one small beach just between the Ninepin and Paratutae that offers semi-safe swimming, but it isn't encouraged due to the currents and its isolation. In huge winter swells a wave can wrap around the Ninepin and in towards the bay, that's offshore in a north or north-west wind. Fishermen enjoy the area with several popular land-based spots including the beach to the north of The Ninepin, off the Ninepin itself, and also some good low tide ledges near the old wharf piles on the eastern side of Paratutae, though these are covered at high tide. The Whatipu Lodge and campground has provided accommodation for sightseers for nearly a century. The 'Lodge' is actually a collection of buildings, the oldest of which is the Gibbons homestead, that was built in 1867. At this time the shoreline was more than a kilometre closer than its present location. The old post office and a shed that once sat on a wharf alongside Paratutae Island, was also later shifted, to add to the complex. **Whatipu Lodge** (09)811 8660 whatipulodge@xtra.co.nz. There is another council-controlled **campsite**, with a solitary long-drop toilet, near the caves that can be found by the base of the cliffs to the west of the main bay. It is a twenty minute walk west from the carpark. Further info and bookings (09)366 2000.

2. Little Huia

At the western fringe of the bay there's a small beach, backed by a couple of very cute old colonial baches, with a boat-ramp and a weigh-station maintained by the Manukau Sportfishing Club. If you wanted a swim in Huia Bay, this would be the best place.

3. Huia

The name derives from a now extinct type of wattle bird with distinctive black and white tail feathers. Though it is a broad bay and backed by farm land with a few old homes, its shallow profile and slightly muddy nature makes it not the best swimming beach, and more likely to draw kite-boarders than those looking for a lazy dip. The foreshore offers a wide expanse of grass for picnicing, plus an adventure playground for the kids and a small half-pipe for skating. The Huia store and coffee bar is the only source of refreshments west of Woodlands Park.

Cornwallis Wharf

4. Foster Bay

It seems that Huia's locals all live at Foster Bay, a lively little community of about a hundred homes facing west, located just before you arrive into Huia proper. There isn't much to the beach, just a short stretch of cockle-shell and sand with no amenities, though it is a better swimming option than Huia itself.

5. Kaitarakihi

Perhaps the best actual swimming spot in this part of the Manukau due to the steeper profile of the shoreline, especially at high tide. Kaitarakihi is reached by following the signs to nearby Spragg's Monument, and taking a right turn along the shingle and clay road then following it roughly 2km to its end. As you drop down to the coast, your first thought is probably "jeepers the South Head looks close". It's as if you could throw a stone to the other side of the harbour, which isn't much more that 2kms away here. The beach faces south-west, but is protected from west and north-west winds by the cliffs and bush behind it. It's a popular shore-fishing spot, and the points either

Armour Bay

Cornwallis Beach

side are especially productive around the high tide. Beware of the current on the outgoing tide, especially if you aren't a strong swimmer. The access road is closed in the evenings at 8.30 pm with a fee for after hours call-outs. Facilities include well-maintained toilets and a picnic area.

6. Kakamatua

Also known as "The Dog Beach" by many local folk, Kakamatua was once the site of a busy sawmill, processing the trees taken out of the surrounding hills. Nowadays it's the most tranquil of settings and an ideal spot for a spirited walk for dog lovers from all over Auckland, who come to socialize (with) their dogs and let off steam. It's a beautiful five to ten minute stroll through native bush from the carpark adjacent to the Huia Rd. The track follows the stream for a few hundred metres through bush, before coming out onto the beach hinterland. Low tide is far better for walkers, as the headlands either side become possible to walk around, with some good land-based fishing at low tides if you head east. The only facilities are a bin for doggy waste at the carpark.

7. Cornwallis Beach

Cornwallis is one of the most popular places in the Manukau, a shelly beach facing east, extending a few kilometers along the peninsula which projects way out into the harbour. It's a lovely swimming beach with a good amount of sand through the tide, with deeper water and less mud than many of its neighbours. It is heavily sheltered in westerly winds, and backed by grassy areas with covered pavilions, trees and picnic areas that can be reserved for special occasions. The distance from the nearest homes and expansive surrounds offer a real sense of space and peace, which is why it is so popular. Historical accounts tell us it was the scene of a large scale swindle by the Manukau and Waitemata Company, who duped a boatload of settlers into parting with substantial amounts of money, and sailing across the world, believing they had bought into a viable and prosperous community that would rival Auckland in strategic importance. They were dumped on an empty beach and left to fend for themselves, and clearly, the enterprise wasn't successful. A community of sorts did spring up, and there were a handful of baches here for much of last century, though they too have now gone. You'll find two access points. Heading west, the first takes you to the main beach, with ample parking and facilities adjacent to the foreshore. The second delivers you to the wharf located at the end of the peninsula, that's separated from the main beach by a small headland. And what a great wharf it is. The original was built in 1826 at a time when there were no roads. In total there were eight wharves at various points on the Manukau, and ferries, tourist boats and flat-bottomed scows serviced the remote communities around its fringes. But as roads improved, their necessity diminished and most fell into disrepair and vanished. The current structure at Cornwallis was completely rebuilt in 1999 by SCOW, a community group working with the ARC. The reserve area behind the wharf and boat ramp is studded with huge pohutakawas, and is a fantastic place to park up and watch the fishermen, for whom the wharf is a genuine destination location, as proximity to the mouth, and relatively deep waters in the nearby channel means this structure is visited by many fish species on their migrations in and out of the harbour. **Park reservations** (09)366 2000.

8. Mill Bay

Another delightful spot facing south-east, with a beautifully maintained reserve and picnic area behind the beach, and stunning glades of nikau palms and other natives gilding the cliffs to the south. The beach at the high tide line is densely packed with white cockle-shells, but at lower tides it takes on a predictable shallow harbour feel. As with many of the other harbour beaches, it's strictly high-tide if you're looking for a swim. The usual picnic tables, toilets and bins are in evidence on the foreshore

9. Armour Bay

Armour Bay can be found off Armour Road, and it's quaint enough, though a bit more developed than much of the coast further west, with houses on the hills all around it. It is located in a huge park that gets locked in the evenings, and though it's not my personal favourite, it has a large grass area and picnic space behind it, and two good free ashphalt tennis courts that are open all year.

10. Laingholm
A charming cockle shell beach lies at the bottom of the twisty serpent that is Laingholm Drive. Facing east into Little Muddy Creek; it features a grassy foreshore with picnic tables and benches adjacent to the road. There is a store and takeaways for refreshments, plus the delightful **Laingholm Fishing Club** building that sits above the beach, and offers a bar and food on the weekends, with the added bonus of an opportunity to meet local fishermen. The beach has a shallow profile, and despite the number of homes in the area, it isn't the most popular swimming spot, due in part to regular water quality warnings. Most of the locals head west for a dip.

11. South Titirangi Beach
At the head of Paturoa Bay is Titirangi Beach. Due to the large park-like surrounds, beautiful stands of regenerating native trees on the steep hills which descend onto it, and the glades of nikau and kauri you pass through at the bottom of the road, there is a wild feel to this small, intimate bay that I personally find enchanting. Shallow and tidal like all the rest, it is nonetheless a great place to come and play with the kids, or to watch the sea at lunch-time. Sadly, water quality can be dubious after rain due to the overloaded drains in the hills above, which can flow into the stream that bisects the beach. Facilities include public loos, park benches and tables. Nearby Davies Bay and Herrings Cove offer alternatives further out along the point, but neither is substantial.

12. Otitori Bay/French Bay
Otitori Bay Rd leads down to the steepest of the Titirangi beaches, which makes it the most popular swimming spot in the area. As a result of the gradient and deeper water, it is also home to the French Bay Yacht Club and the Manukau Coast Guard buildings and a good concrete launching ramp. The main road skirts the foreshore without a grass reserve, though the row of pohutakawas and park benches provide a pleasant place to sit and have a picnic. The cottage where Colin McCahon's family lived between 1953 and 1960, is just above the bay. **French Bay Yacht Club** www.frenchbay.org.nz

13. Wood Bay
A well signed no-exit lane off Wood Bay Rd, leads to a grass reserve behind a flat, cockle-shell and mud bay, barely 50 m long. There is a playground and a few benches, plus ample parking, but other than the wastewater pumping station, nothing else. The council run reserve is open daily after 7.00 am, with closing hours changing seasonally (09)839 0400.

14. Green Bay
Portage Road ends just above the beach at Green Bay, which prides itself as the place where "the West" begins. A short set of stairs takes you down to a grass reserve backed by trees, with a public loo and picnic tables set back from the hundred or so metres of beach. A few people fish off the rocky point to the west, and there were a few kahawai landed when I was there. It faces south, so would cop a bit of wind.

15. Blockhouse Bay
Named after the "South Whau Blockhouse," a defensive fortification that was constructed during the Waikato wars, it features a short beach with a reinforced seawall, built during the depression to protect the reserve that backs on to it. There are two access points. Taunton Terrace ends with a walkway leading onto a grassy park on the hill at the western fringe of the bay, below which you'll find the yacht club, with its little boat ramp and a set of public loos. Direct vehicle access is off Blockhouse Bay Road, which leads to the main beach area. It is highly tidal again, but popular with kayak fishermen and small sailboats.

16. Wattle Bay
This beach is at the head of an indented bay, backed by an expansive and beautiful bush lined reserve. Access is from the grandly named Cape Horn Road where there's a walkway but limited parking, or from Canberra Ave.

17. Waikowhai Bay/Faulkner Bay
Another small beach and a fairly popular boat ramp, located at the bottom of a huge and beautiful park, but the bay is extremely tidal and turns into a gigantic mudflat at low tide.

Hillsborough Bay

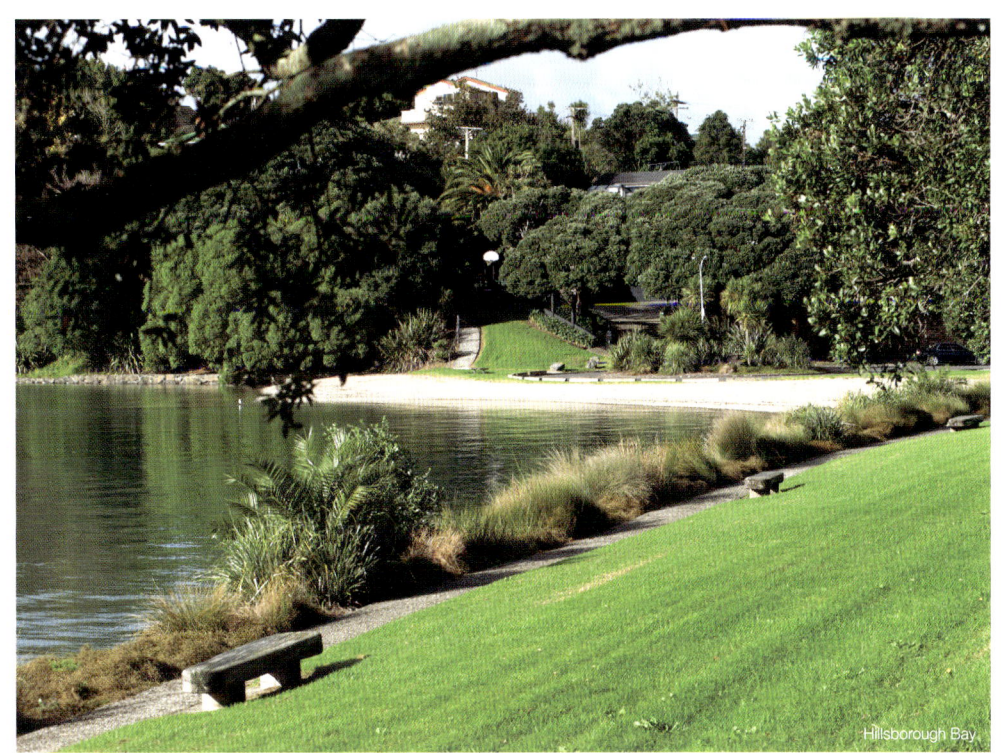

18. Hillsbrough Bay

A cove-like bay facing east, in the middle of a dense residential area, it features a 50m stretch of sand at high tide, with a kids playground and a large pohutakawa-clad grass bank to the north. It is a pretty spot, though the presence of the large pylons nearby is somewhat of an ambience killer.

19. Mangere Bridge

The old Mangere bridge is an iconic Auckland structure, heavily used by the locals from some of Auckland's nearby suburbs, who come here to catch a feed for their families; and no guide to the New Zealand coast would be complete without some recognition of this bridge and the colourful fishing culture that has grown up around it. Despite what you may think, it is a really friendly place to spend a bit of time, and besides that, a good place to catch kahawai and occasionally kingfish. The suburb of the same name to the south of the bridge has a small beach adjacent to Kiwi Esplanade, where you will also find the busy Mangere Boat Club, with its two launch ramps and weigh station. A sign near the beach proclaims that the water is tested regularly and is safe for swimming, though I would recommend caution. **Mangere Boating Club** (09)636 4673 www.mangereboatingclub.co.nz

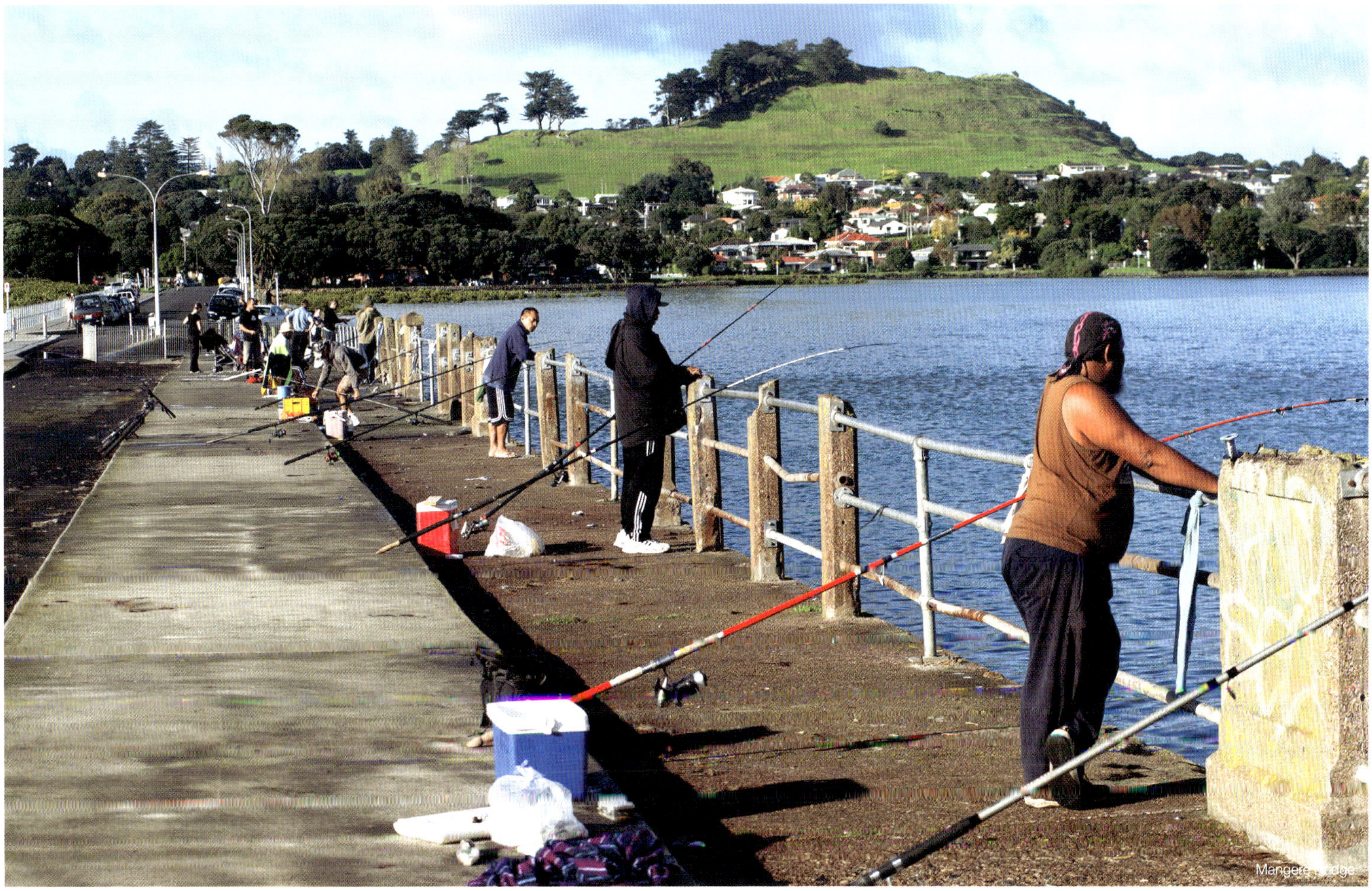

Mangere Bridge

WAIKATO WEST COAST

Despite being less than two hours from Auckland, for many years this was a neglected region, its black sand and constant swell seen as a giant turn-off for most. It was somewhere that Waikato farmers would come and brave the relentless swell, to pluck some hard won snapper from the sea; but foreigners were unheard of, and Jaffas thin on the ground. Not any longer. The explosion of the surf culture in NZ, coupled with the awareness of the numerous world-class breaks along its coast, have led to a huge increase in patronage by surfers from all corners of the globe. At the same time, advances in weather forecasting, and improved boat design have meant the Tasman is a far less threatening proposition for fishermen now. And as the east coast became increasingly crowded and populated, all the space and beauty out west suddenly became recognised for what it was. Raglan has soared in popularity, yet oddly, Port Waikato has remained a sleepy little backwater of sorts. The Awhitu peninsula is growing in appeal, though limited access to the west coast has hindered its development somewhat.

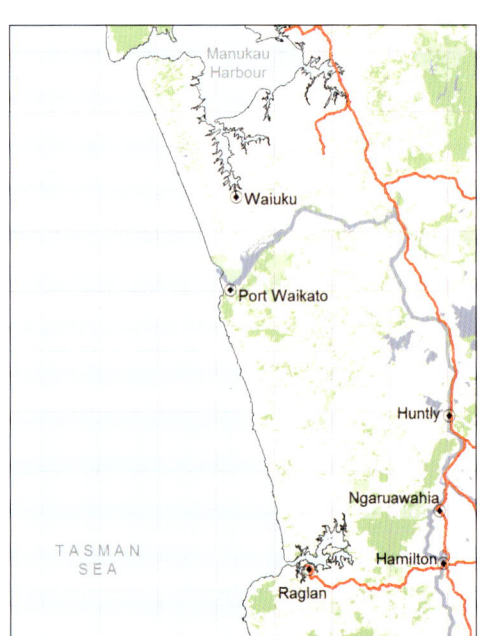

Travelling It is an easy drive from Auckland, with few traffic issues. Raglan has a ton of accommodation options, Port Waikato and the Awhitu Peninsula offer significantly less choices.

Surfing Constant west and south-west swells pound this coast. Raglan works in southerly and south-east winds, while most of the beaches like north-east or east winds. The Port reef is best in an easterly, and doesn't like anything with south in it. Both the Raglan and the Waikato River bars work in big swells and north-east winds. Raglan is New Zealand's single most popular surf town, with a phenomenal amount of surfable days in a year, though the crowds of visitors have also wised up to this fact, so quiet days are few.

Fishing Land-based fishing is a difficult prospect all around this coastline, with its constant waves and strong currents. There are opportunities inside the Raglan harbour and off various headlands near the tip of the Awhitu peninsula, but it is the boat fishing offshore that is the real drawcard for the fishing community, and it can be spectacular. Snapper are abundant with a few pelagics to hunt as well.

Swimming You'll regularly encounter dangerous conditions at many of the open ocean beaches, but sheltered water inside the Manukau and Raglan Harbours offers safer options. Both the Port and Raglan's main beach have surf life-saving clubs on patrol during peak periods, and in late summer with north-east winds, the Tasman can be very inviting.

Raglan north coast

Port Waikato

Franklin County

The Awhitu peninsula is the biggest coastal feature in Franklin County. A giant sand dune sandwiched between the Waikato River and the Manukau Harbour, it takes its name from the pre-European Maori settlement of Awhitu, which was located at the western end of Orua Bay. The word refers to the 'yearning' (awhitu) felt by Hoturoa, the commander of the Tainui waka, when he left the district. It offers a wealth of ocean environments, featuring beaches on both coasts, with its southern extent marked by the Waikato river mouth. For an area lying so close to Auckland, with such a diversity of coastline, it receives remarkably few visitors compared to the locations further north and south, but that doesn't bother the locals here, who enjoy the proximity to a big city without any of its drawbacks.

Travelling Waiuku is 40 mins south of Auckland. The top of the peninsula is another 40km, and while the roads are sealed, they're pretty windy. The only real shop on the peninsula is at Matakawau, offering most provisions, food and petrol. www.awhitu.com is a local website. Waiuku information centre (09)235 8924 www.franklincountry.com

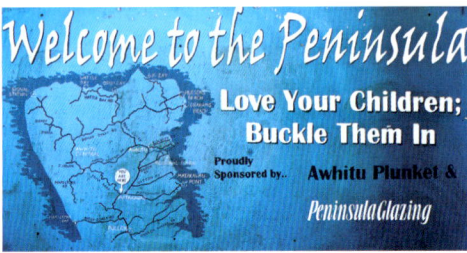

WIND ROSE

SWELL ROSE

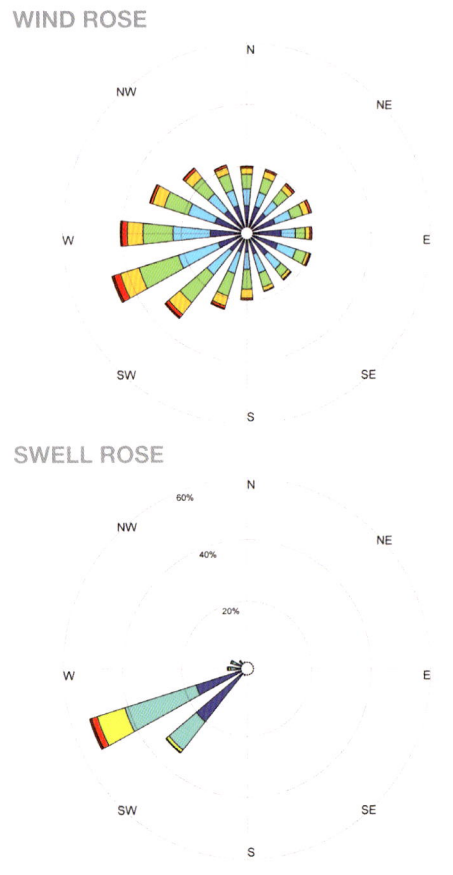

Surfing Epic waves at Port Waikato and the other west coast beaches on their day. The beaches like small swells and NE winds, while the Port prefers less north in the wind but can handle more swell.

Fishing A vast array of opportunities ranging from flounder, mullet and the other inner harbour species, to kahawai and snapper off the rocks at the Port and Hamilton's Gap.

Swimming It's a bit of a mixed bag, with very tidal inner-harbour beaches and tempestuous and often dangerous conditions on the west coast.

1. Wattle Bay
It feels like you could literally jump across to Little Huia on the northern shores of the Manukau from here. Certainly I have kayaked longer distances without breaking into a sweat. Wattle Bay has a sandy shelf, but the western end is fringed with flat reef that at higher tides makes a good fishing platform. Behind the beach there's a large grass reserve, with picnic tables, public loos and one or two old houses set well back from the beach. If you hike west at low tide towards the signal station, there's a tiny rocky outcrop called Cake Island, which can also be a great place to fish from. Further west from here is the lighthouse; it takes about 2 hours to walk from Wattle Bay, so time it right with the tides.

2. Orua Bay
One of the oldest beach settlements in the country, it was named by local Tainui after the sound of the water in surrounding sea-caves. It was notable as the location of the first iron sand smelters in the 1800's, once also having two wharves. Several of the original settler buildings remain, and it's now one of the peninsula's most densely populated beaches, with three access points. Orpheus Rd takes you down a stunningly fertile valley to the western end, where there is a ramp onto the beach. Dog Nose Point is a short walk west from the car-park, and was once the site of a wharf, signalling deeper water off the rocks here. Conveniently placed rod holders carved into the sandstone attest to its popularity as a fishing spot. Gap Road leads to a small children's play area, with public loos and another beach access point. Orua Bay Rd is the easternmost access and the best swimming spot,

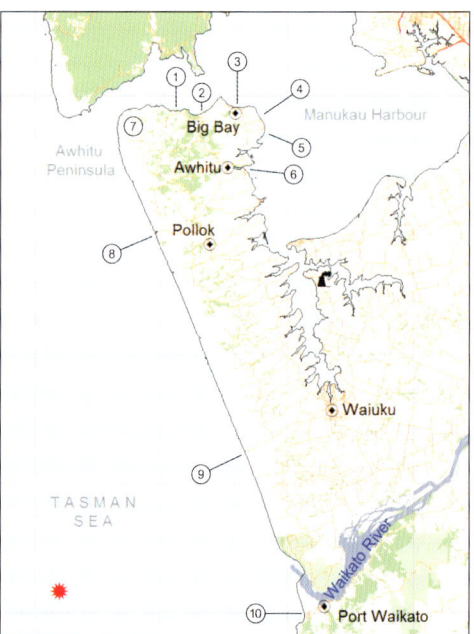

Signal Station

with a steeper shelf and cockle shell sand. From here you can head east and follow the coast in isolation for a couple of kilometres. **The Conifers** sleeps up to 4 adults sonja.potter@xtra.co.nz. **Orua Bay Motor Camp** (09)235 1129 www.oruabay.co.nz

2. Big Bay
The biggest bay on the peninsula, but compared to other "Big Bays" in the country, it isn't high on the leaderboard. It features two access points. The western one is home to a concrete boatramp leading

onto the beach that is a useful facility. There're also toilets, picnic tables and a well maintained grass foreshore with ample shade offered by the stunning pohutakawas here. The eastern one also has public amenities, a children's playground, and offers easy access to the coast further east. **Big Bay Motor Camp and Fishing Lodge** (09)235 1132 www.bigbayholidaypark.co.nz

4. Hudsons Beach
An absolutely charming high tide spot, with white sand, a well maintained foreshore offering play areas for the children, and a small boat ramp facing due east, with a collection of timeless old baches behind the beach. Low tide is a lot less inviting though.

5. Grahams Beach
A beach very similar to Hudsons, with sparkling white sand and good public amenities, but more homes behind the coast. Private 3 acre waterfront property contact **Treena Sixsmith** (09)235 2527.

6. Awhitu Regional Park
This is an ARC owned, working farm, with tranquil bays, rolling pastures and a rich history. Transformed wetlands lie behind the parks two long, sandy beaches (Kauritutahi Beach and Brook Beach), providing a wonderful habitat for the rare fernbird (matata), and banded rail (moho pereru). The pohutakawa-clad shoreline is a real treasure.
Park Reservations (09)366 2000.

7. Signal Station
Not a beach as such, but one of the most stunning coastal landmarks in the country; the views from the lighthouse at the south head of the Manukau Harbour are truly breathtaking, looking out over the bar and over to Whatipu. It is open between 9.00am and 5.00pm www.lighthouseawhitu.com. **Guiding Lights** (09)235 1458 offer historical tours of the whole peninsula.

8. Hamiltons Gap
West Coast Road follows an ancient stream bed through a cut in the hills that allows access to a short strip of the blackest sand you will ever see. The remnants of this historic watercourse feed into the Tasman, creating sandbars that look like they would hold some very tasty waves in a clean swell. A small headland with a reef structure protruding from it, offers some shelter from the south, which also seems like a bonus for both surfers and fishermen. The topography is steep here, with nearly vertical sand dunes behind the beach, making it a spectacular, if isolated place for a visit. The public loos are a piece of art sculpted by someone who loves their work; strange to see so much effort put into such an isolated location. Vehicles are prohibited from the beach here.

9. Kiritihere
It is only 0km from Waiuku, yet Kiritihere feels light-years from civilisation, stretching south all the way to Port Waikato, with a near permanent salt haze obscuring any sense of its northern boundary. Sadly it is as neglected as it is vast and primitive, and while there's a surf club, public loos and bins, it feels tatty, with a lot of vehicle traffic and a strong contingent of boy racers, who use it as a convenient place to practice doing donuts. Those of a more esoteric nature would more likely be found practising blo-carting, which is seemingly what this beach was designed for www.blownaway.co.nz. There's an award-winning conference centre on the hill above the beach (09)236 5041 www.castaways.co.nz

Big Bay

10. Port Waikato/Sunset Beach
One of the most undersold beaches in the country, Sunset Beach, or "The Port" as it is affectionately known by its friends, is a fairly low-key settlement at the mouth of the Waikato river, featuring a few miles of black sand protected by a headland and high cliffs, which lie to the south. In front of these cliffs break some of the heaviest waves in NZ. In a moderate sized swell and easterly winds, you'll find thick barrels out on Port Waikato Reef, and often long left beach peaks breaking across the channel directly in front of the surf lifesaving club. Access to the reef is by walking south around the rocks, but be warned, there are a couple of well known and mildly psychotic locals, so mind your p's and q's. High tide is usually better for the beach, while the reef can break through the tide. If something less dangerous is what you're after, Maraetai Beach inside the estuary is a safe swimming and kayaking option for the children. As you enter Port Waikato, and adjacent to the boat ramp and yacht club, on the site of the original wharf which gave the settlement its name, is the **Port Waikato Wharf Store**, which has all your basic essentials, including fishing gear and one lone petrol pump, but no diesel. **Waikatoa Beach Lodge** (09)232 9961 offers a range of accommodation www.sunsetbeach.co.nz. **Top Ten Camping Ground** (09)232 9857 www.portwaikatoholidaypark.co.nz

Port Waikato

Whaingaroa/Raglan

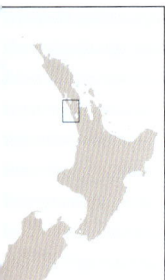

Since the arrival of Pakeha, the bustling township of Whaingaroa was a small fishing and farming town. Then came surfing. It first became noticed by the global community in Bruce Brown's iconic film from 1964, "The Endless Summer," and since then, it's been a powerful magnet for the itinerant surf tribes that encircle the planet. While the fishing is good, and sports like kite-boarding, para-sailing and land yachting are popular too, it is the three long waves which wrap around the base of Mount Karioi that have put Raglan on the map. But luckily for holiday makers with less treacherous pursuits in mind, it is also home to a selection of beautiful black sand beaches from the most tranquil, to the most tortured. The range of cafes, and some good shopping in town, has given it appeal to a broader range of people than ever before; to the point where you could almost call it cosmopolitan.

Travelling There're a lot of choices accommodation wise, ranging form backpackers to top end holiday homes. Info@Raglan (07)825 8690 www.raglan.tv. I-Site (07)825 0556 www.raglan.org.nz. **Sleeping Lady Whale Bay Lodgings** (07)825 7873 www.sleepinglady.co.nz. **Raglan Kopua Holiday Park** (07) 825 8283 www.raglanholidaypark.co.nz. **Raglan Kayaks** www.raglankayak.co.nz

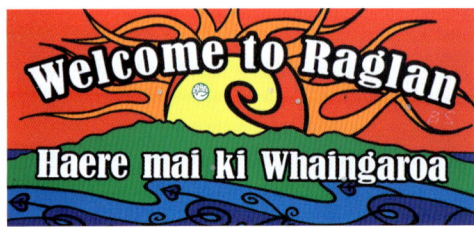

WIND ROSE

SWELL ROSE

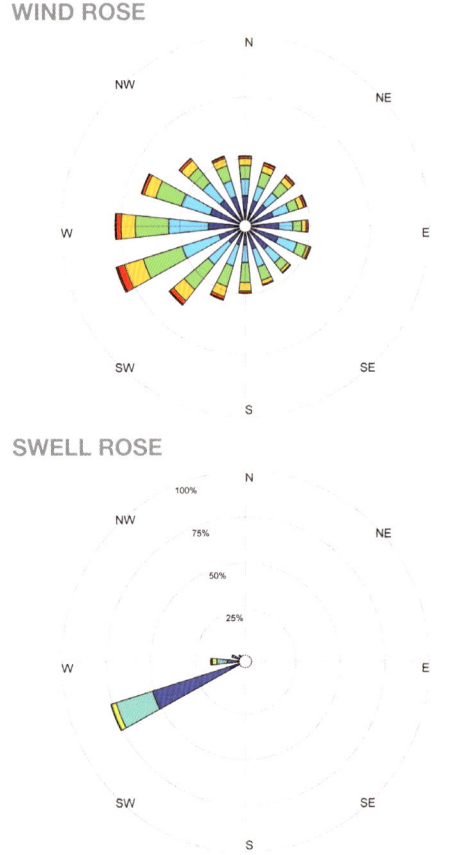

Surfing There is almost always swell of some kind, and surf up to 2m is very common, with occasional 3m days. The points are offshore in a south-east, which is a pretty rare wind, though a southerly is good and south-west, if not too strong, can be okay too. Any wind with north in it kills everything. Ngarunui Beach and Ruapuke both love a north-east, but both are bank dependent. Summer and Autumn are epic, winter okay and spring generally the worst season. However the crowds are becoming intense all year now, and it is a very rare thing indeed to get a quiet wave anymore. Add to this the fact that some of the locals are shameless drop in artists, and you sometimes wonder if it's worth it. So bring a relaxed mindset, you will need it. Getting in and out at all the points is hazardous, and dings and snapped fins are common. Raglan Longboards do the best ding repair service, located before the beach on Wainui Rd. **Raglan Longboards** (07)825 0544 www.raglanlongboards.co.nz. **Point Boardriders** (07)825 8997 is the local boardriders club. There are several surf shops in town: **Raglan Surf Co** (07)825 8898. **GAG Surf Shop** (07)825 8702. **Skyrider Kite Surf School** (07)825 7453. **Raglan Surf School** (07)825 7873 www.raglansurfschool.co.nz. **Kiwi Surf School,** Miles Ratima 027 4Raglan.

Fishing In the bay itself, the land-based fishing is difficult. I've seen people catching snapper down in the south-west hook of Ngarunui beach on low-tide mornings, and you get the odd kahawai around the boat-ramp. The harbour entrance is sometimes fished successfully with grapnel sinkers due to the fast current. Papanui Point near Ruapuke is a common spot, but can be hazardous. Both the jetty at the bottom of town and the Wallis St wharf are good for catching yellow tail and sprats for the kids. Boat fishing off Raglan is as good as anywhere on the west coast, with an active club and an excellent

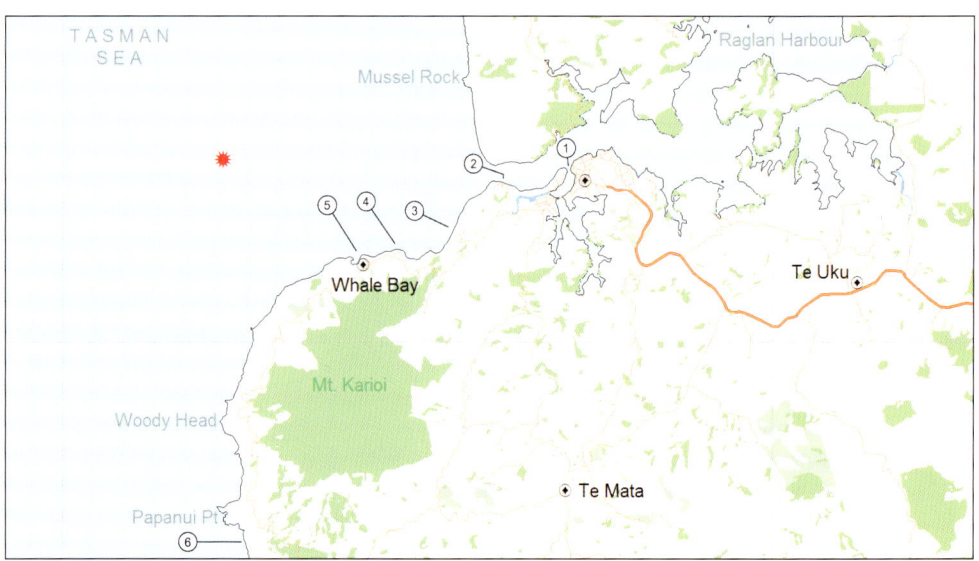

The old bridge

free launch ramp at Manu Bay, that allows stress-free launching outside the harbour bar in most conditions. **Raglan Sportfishing Club** (07)825 8867. **Islay Mist** 027 482 0662. **Megabite Charters** 027 473 1605.

Swimming The two most popular places to swim are at Ngarunui Beach, where there's an active surf life-saving club at peak times, or inside the harbour at the Kopua Domain. The Manu Bay boat ramp is also a good place for a dip.

1. Kopua Domain/Putoetoe Point
A walk bridge connects the two sides of the estuary that runs past the bottom of town. The stretch of sand adjacent to the camp located on its western side is where many local families swim with their young children. It is an inner harbour beach, with relatively strong tidal current at peak flow, so you have to be a little cautious on outgoing tides; but it is a really easy place to cool off for the littlies. Amenities include big shade trees, toilets, showers, a childrens play area and changing rooms, all just a stone throw from the village. The walk-bridge and the jetty at the bottom of Bow St are also popular jumping spots, but beware low tide at both, as water levels become dangerously low. The camp store nearby sells ice creams and drinks.

2. Wainamu/Ocean Beach
Once home to the local surf life-saving club, Ocean Beach is rapidly gaining fame as a world class kite-boarding location. The combination of exposure to the prevailing west and south-west winds, accompanied by flat water, easy launching and access to the waves breaking on the harbour bar, make it an action spot for the wind bogans. But conversely, these conditions are less than perfect for the average beach-goer. Add to this the fact that the harbour drains out here, with a six knot current sweeping in and out at peak tidal flow, and you will see why most people swim at either the campground, or at Ngarunui Beach, a few kilometres down the coast. There are toilets in the carpark at the end of Riria Kereopa Memorial Drive, and ample parking at the end of the road adjacent to the beach.

Ngarunui Beach

The Points

3. Ngarunui Beach

4km of surf-pounded black sand, stretch from the harbour mouth to Manu Bay. This is Ngarunui Beach, originally known as Bryant Home Beach, when access was restricted to a walking track from the Camp on the hill to the south. Since the new road and carpark was built, it has become extremely popular in summer, featuring the only lifeguard patrolled swimming in the area, and a range of good amenities including public toilets in the carpark and cold showers on the beach. It is also home to a couple of surf schools catering to beginners seeking initiation on the rolling whitewater. The waves can be epic, but the banks change constantly, and high tide is frequently best. Offshores here are north east. On a hot day, para-gliders circle above the steep cliffs which back the beach, and racehorses are often seen exercising in the early mornings.

4. Manu Bay

The first of the three legendary point breaks, works at all tides. At low tide The Ledge offers some of the sickest pits in the area, with a long inside section thats more forgiving. High tide is more playful and mellow, with shorter but less challenging waves. Regardless of the tide, it's always a bit of a zoo due to its easy access and the fact you can park up in front of the surf, with lots of learners groveling round in the

The harbour bar

Boneyards, Manu Bay

impact zone. Beware the evil rip formed on dropping tides in big swell. It runs from the boat ramp across to the bar, and has caught many people out. The park at the point has good facilities with toilets, showers, and ample parking, but don't be tempted to camp here, as there's a good chance you'll get ticketed by the aggressive park warden. Manu Bay also happens to be home to the only hard boat ramp on the west coast which allows boat launching outside a harbour bar. The boat ramp and small adjacent sandy beach that becomes exposed from low to mid tide, is also a fun place to swim on a warm day, and well protected from the south and west winds. **Solscape** (07)825 8268 offer eco-accommodation just above Manu bay www.solscape.co.nz.

5. Whale Bay

Whale Bay is a small cluster of about 50 homes located eight kilometers from town. It is the access point to both Whale Bay and Indicators, the two other lefts which made the town world famous. Whale Bay is the closest of them, and usually the slowest of the three points, though in a north-west swell, can get super hollow. It tends to break best from mid to high tide, and access is down the steps and out off the rocks behind the wave. "The Indicator" as it was originally known, or "Indies" as it's now generally called, breaks from the farthest headland, with three main sections: Outsides, Indies, and The Valley. Each have their own qualities and break best at different tides, but there is usually something to ride at one of these three spots. Access is either from the cove on the inside or by walking right around the lagoon and jumping off the rocks out the back. Its a 50/50 call what's quickest, but neither are risk free. All these spots are clearly visible from the lookout before Whale Bay. The lagoon which is visible from the car-park is a pretty place to swim at high tide,

but the area is backed by private land that is sensitive to local Maori and other landowners, so respect the queens chain rules, leave no trash, take nothing. There is a set of public toilets in the reserve off Calvert Rd. **Karioi Lodge** run by the surf school, offers a range of private accommodation options on and around the point. www.sleepinglady.co.nz

6. Ruapuke Beach

If wild and isolated is your cup of tea, Ruapuke will be a good brew. Ten km of battered iron-sand face the Tasman head on, and in the prevailing south-west wind, it can feel like a sand blaster has been turned on. But when the wind goes north-east, common in late summer, Ruapuke can be an unbeatable place to camp-out and experience true peace. The surf can be epic at many spots on the beach, but the north end carpark usually has a wave of some kind.

It picks up all swell in the Tasman, and if you can see waves at Manu Bay, Ruapuke will generally be too big. It's a popular fishing spot, in particular off the rocks to the north, but only accessible below mid tide. Kayak fishing close in on flat, late summer days, would be legendary and there are often kahawai in the surf zone that would take spinners or cut bait. Nearby Papanui Point, which you pass on the way from Raglan, is a popular land-based spot but a few people have lost their lives off this rock, so be wary of rogue sets. The gravel road from Raglan is spectacular but tortuous, with many blind corners and steep cliffs dropping hundreds of feet to the sea; beware of oncoming amped-up surfers and meandering campervans. Facilities include a long drop toilet at the north end and a small campsite at the south end that time has apparently forgotten.
Ruapuke Beach Motor Camp (07)825 6800.

Jump rock, Manu Bay

THE COROMANDEL PENINSULA

New Zealand's most famous peninsula is a mountainous and partially forest-clad region of intense contrast and drama that features over 400km's of tortured coastline, with the most idyllic bays and pristine sections of sparkling sand, liberally sprinkled with more than 100 offshore islands. Its bounty was first exploited by Kupe, the first Polynesian navigator to arrive in Aotearoa and successive visitors from Cook to Zane Gray have all found immense value in its vast array of natural resources, benign anchorages and teeming fisheries. Today it occupies a seminal space in our collective psyche, and unsurprisingly is backed by some of the busiest coastal subdivisions in the country; drawing more tourists per square km of beach than any other part of New Zealand. For many, that's reason enough to run in the other direction, but if you can brave the crowds and the traffic during peak holiday times, then there's lots of fun to be had here. Despite all the hype and the January madness, it still blows people away with its beauty, and ironically, for much of the the year it remains almost deserted.

The East Coast is the stuff of traveller's dreams, filling the tourist brochures with gorgeous pictures of sparkling white sand beaches, rolling surf and huge fish. Towns like Whangamata, Hahei and Whitianga are Kiwi icons that pulsate with happy crowds during the summer months, and many is the Kiwi who can recount one or more fun-filled holidays at them. Then there are the smaller communities like Onemana and Simpsons Beach; quiet and intimate, hardly known by outsiders. Despite its huge reputation and soaring popularity, the northern coast is still lightly populated, with huge sections inaccessible by road. While this may cause land-based visitors frustration, for boaties it's a goldmine waiting to be explored. Peppered with offshore islands that are a huge attraction for the diving and fishing communities, and receiving a healthy lashing of swell for the surfies, the Eastern Coromandel offers anything the ocean-lover could want, and then some.

The West Coast is quirky all the way to the top, sharing few of the features of its cousin on the east; with a shallow shelf, mangrove-studded harbours, shingly beaches and a multitude of inshore islands for much of its length. The quiet, almost estuarine waters of the Firth of Thames don't particularly endear it to swimmers. Neither is it a surfing coast. Yet the sublime beauty of its jagged coastline that's fringed with ancient pohutakawas, remains a genuine delight. Fishing is the primary recreational pursuit at most of the beaches here, and the harbours, islands and mussel farms scattered along its length all support a healthy bounty of snapper, kahawai and the like. The quaint old beach settlements near Thames, Coromandel's historic charm, and the alternative communities of Colville, are all a suitably intriguing backdrop to a well-loved shoreline. The gorgeous sandy beaches on its northern tip are the crowning glory, on one of New Zealand's least visited, yet at times most spectacular sections of coast.

Travelling Arriving at Te Kouma by ferry from Auckland is a great way to get there 0800 360discovery or www.360discovery.co.nz. Motorists need to realise there are lots of people around, the roads are windy and often steep, so sensible people drive slowly. The price of fuel gets higher as you head north. Tourism Coromandel www.thecoromandel.com

Tairua Ocean Beach

Otama

North Coast

Tairua Estuary

Cathedral Cove

Surfing Waves on the Coromandel are generated by cyclones and mid-latitude depressions in the Pacific, or off the squash zones between highs; with a swell window extending from north to south-east. Hot Water Beach, Whangamata and Waikawau Bay are the three most consistent beaches on the peninsula, and if there is even a burp in the ocean, you'll get a wave at one of these places. In a serious swell, there are a few champagne spots like Whangamata and some of the other harbour bars and reefs, that can really get the adrenaline pumping. Breaks that take a due north swell like Kuaotunu and Otama are great to surf, but also work rarely and are generally hellishly crowded when they fire.

Fishing Whatever you want to catch, you can generally catch it off the Coromandel coast, depending on your determination and the time of year. Tairua, Whangamata, Whitianga, Port Charles, and Coromandel are the main boat harbours, all of which support large fishing communities. There are good fish all around the coast for land-based anglers too, however years of over fishing means that the more difficult spots to access often produce the best specimens.

Swimming Some of the country's finest swimming beaches lie on this peninsula, and many of the main spots have busy surf life-saving clubs over peak holiday periods.

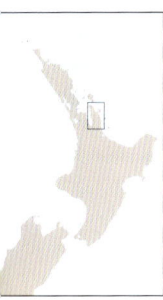

Thames to Te Kouma

Thames ushers the beginning of the peninsula's eastern shores, which aren't the kind you expect when used to images of Hahei and Cathedral Cove. This coast is shallow, tidal and craggy, with little sand. It shares the same kind of the charm of English fishing villages, that are quaint to look at, but don't necessarily make you want to tear your clothes off and jump into the sea. There are very few modern holiday homes, which has helped to maintain a timeless air, faintly reminiscent of the days when the buggys would bring holidaymakers and newly-weds up the line from Thames, which at one point was a bigger town than Auckland.

Travelling Whether you're eventually heading east over the range, or going all the way to the Cape, SH 25 is 50km of twisting, coastal road that isn't quick. Poor visibility and the fact the road reduces to one lane in many places, can cause frustration, especially on busy weekends and public holidays. Thames I-site (07)868 7284 www.thamesinfo.co.nz

Waikawau

WIND ROSE

SWELL ROSE

Surfing A bit of a joke, but after a huge westerly, you may see the odd wave break down the shingle spits.

Fishing This is an extremely shallow coast, but make no mistake, there are a lot of large fish caught in The Firth. I seem to recall a great white tangled up in a set net some years back, but on a more sporting note, kingies stray all around this coast in late summer and snapper and kahawai can be caught all year. It's a popular stretch of water in an east or north-east wind, but a south-west can lead to atrocious sea conditions pretty quickly, and the shallow water compounds the effect of wind generated waves. **Thames Angling Club**, Bev McKay (07)869 0407. Membership from Price and Richards Sports Shop in Thames.

Swimming Not a great coast at low tide, but at high tide, it sparkles like a jewel.

1. Kuruanui Bay
As you leave Thames and hit the coast, a small hook of sand projects out with a clutch of beachfront homes. It's the local high tide swimming spot and a little bit of "Bay Watch" in the Firth. The Thames beaches continue north to Tararu, where you'll find the Thames Sailing Club and Coastguard building. The little patch of beach to the north is called Tainui Cove. It is where the local iwi used to haul out their wakas and is also not a bad place for a swim.

2. Whakatete Bay
Whakatete has some nice sand and a steeper profile than some other beaches in the area, and at high tide would be a fine place for a dip. You see the odd fisherman here, and no doubt a few dinners are landed from shore.

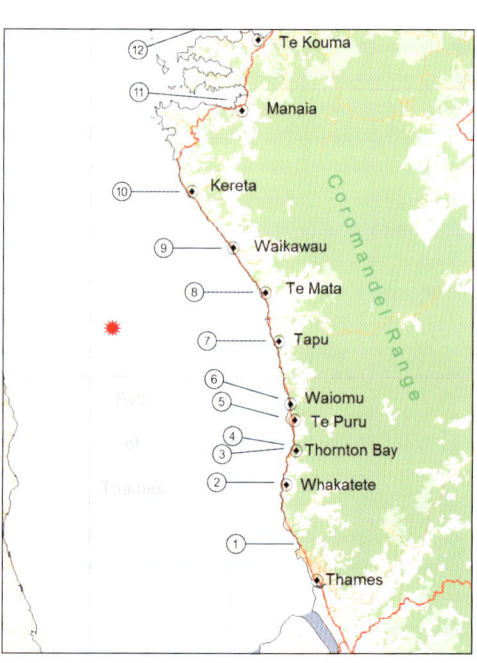

3. Ngarimu Bay and 4. Thornton Bay
These two beaches are separate communities but merge almost seamlessly. There are some stylish homes and some good swimming, in particular at the north end of Ngarimu and the south end of Thornton, which are almost completely rock free. Thornton seems to be the most popular beach in the area during summer, though neither have more than a dozen or so baches, nor do they have public facilities.

5. Te Puru
Yet another popular fishing hangout, with a large foreshore reserve and a long sandy spit. It is a substantial village, with a sizeable campsite, a useful high tide boat ramp (home to the Puru Boat Club), plus a store and takeaways. The best swimming spots are before the campsite, or as you leave town going north. Te Puru Holiday Park (07)868 2879 www.tepuruholidaypark.co.nz.

6. Waiomu
It has a popular waterfront domain with great facilities including toilets, showers and gas bbq's, but the foreshore is very rocky, making it fairly unattractive as a swimming spot. Other attractions include the Beach Cafe, a concrete boat-launching

ramp to the north, and **The Seaspray Motel** (07)868 2863 www.seaspraymotel.co.nz which is located right on the water. The intriguingly named Die Hard Stream is just north, plus Ruamahanga Bay further up the coast has an attractive sandy shoreline and a boat ramp that's sheltered in south-west winds. **Die Hard Creek Homestead** (07)868 4856.

7. Tapu
Another long shingly spit with a sandy beach in its lee, that's okay for swimming at high tide. There's a legendary old pub named The Royal Oak, a fantastic old-style campsite with a well stocked store, and a boat launch ramp down Wharf Rd. The river-mouth produces a mixed bag on its day if you're desperate for a fish but don't have a boat. There would have been cockles on the spit once, but it looks pretty fished out now. **Tapu Motor Camp** (07)868 4837.

8. Te Mata
Perhaps the biggest stretch of beach on the coast is lined with cockle shells and culminates in another long spit. There are a dozen or so baches here, but while it's a good swimming spot at high tide, there are no public facilities. You'll find a few coves with good swimming and rock fishing potential further north.

9. Waikawau
A small headland with a tiny beach in front, and a high tide boat ramp in the creek to the north. Just offshore is a mussel farm, that kayak or small boat fishermen love to fish around. The mussel farm marks the area where the water starts getting a bit deeper.

10. Kereta
Here you will find the ramp managed by the Thames Angling Club. It isn't the prettiest spot on the peninsula, but deemed appropriate for this task, and gets pretty busy in peak season, so parking can be tricky. It costs $5.00 for casual use, with an honesty box and an old longdrop if you feel the call of nature.

11. Manaia Harbour
Manaia is a beautiful stretch of enclosed water just south of Coromandel Harbour, but access is only possible through private land, or by boat. **Waimana Spa** (07)866 8971 www.waimanaspa.com

12. Te Kouma
This is a popular anchorage for pleasure craft, and the arrival and departure point for the extremely convenient Coromandel passenger ferry. **Te Kouma Holiday Cottages** have six separate dwellings www.tekoumacottges.co.nz. **Te Kouma B&B** (07)866 7971 www.tekoumabnb.co.nz

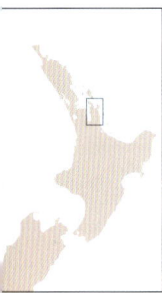

Coromandel to Waitete

In many ways one of the most mystical parts of the North Island coast, this is the start of the road less travelled. Facilities are few north of Coromandel town, and the sense of adventure deepens as the landscape steepens, and the road begins to wind into hills. It is twenty five kilometres to Colville, and the quaint settlements which stud its sandy stretches are again almost wholly focused on the fishing around the islands, that are so close in along much of this coast. Coromandel is picture postcard cute and alive with visitors, with several good restaurants, a pub or three, various tourist and camping shops, and no less than 28 historic sites of interest for those inclined that way.

Travelling Coromandel Holiday Park 636 Rings Rd (07)866 8830, www.coromandelholidaypark.co.nz. Once you leave Coromandel, campgrounds are the mainstay. www.coromandeltown.co.nz

Fishing Coromandel Kayak Adventures (07)866 7466 or 021 294 1694, offer guided fishing with all equipment provided. Guide Rob Fort is extremely good at what he does www.kayakadventures.co.nz. **The Mussel Barge** (07)866 7667 runs fishing trips to the mussel farms that are always a bit of fun. **Coromandel Smoking Company** do some pretty mean smoked fish and mussels!

Swimming The coast starts getting steeper as you head north, offering better swimming conditions.

1. McGregors Bay
Inside Coromandel harbour, you will find a few beaches to swim at, though all are tidal and very muddy at low tide. McGregor's is the first spot coming from town, but the oyster farm nearby demonstrates just how tidal and shallow it is. **Coromandel Town Backpackers** (07)866 8327.

2. Wyuna Bay
Similar to the above, Wyuna is a pretty and sheltered bay, and an okay spot to beach-launch boats closer to

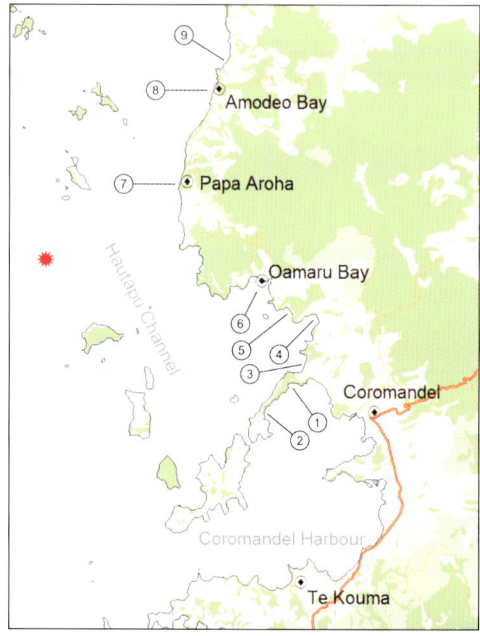

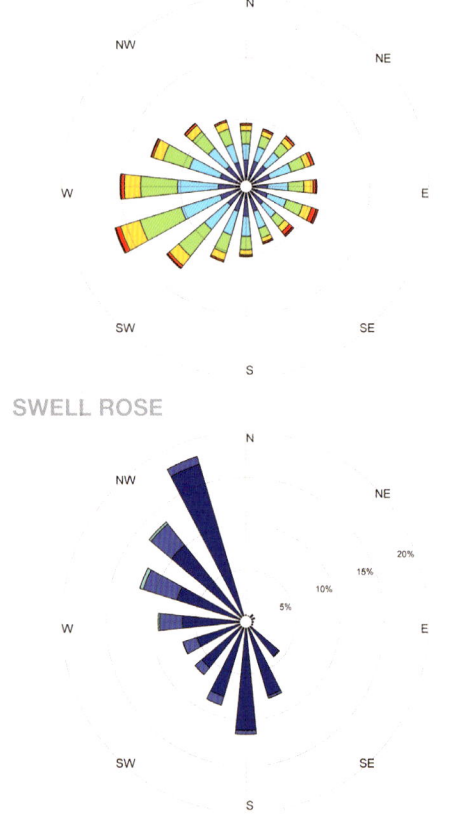

WIND ROSE

SWELL ROSE

Coromandel Harbour

Oamaru Bay

Long Bay

the islands and fishing spots further out in the Firth. You'll find toilets and bins on the foreshore.

3. Long Bay
A popular motor camp faces north on the opposite side of the peninsula from Wyuna Bay, but receives plenty of shelter from Waimate Island, so still feels like you're in a harbour. The fishing can be great here too, surrounded by mussel farms, not too far from shore. **Long Bay Motor Camp** (07)866 8720.

4. Kikowhakarere/Shelly Beach
Muddy and tidal but cute. There are a few baches and it's a beautiful bay, but completely dominated by the **Shelly Beach Top Ten Holiday Park** (07)866 8988 www.shellybeachcotomandel.co.nz

5. Oamaru Bay
It features a settlement of about a dozen baches, some cute little boat sheds, a tidal boat ramp and a camp site with cabins. Turkey Island offshore was used to film some of the scenes from the film "Sleeping Dogs". **Oamaru Holiday Park** (07)866 7750.

6. Koputauaki Bay
Backed by Maori land and farmland, this broad five hundred metre sweep of sand has a handful of baches tucked into the north-eastern corner. It's a place with a lonely feel and zero in the way of amenities, dominated by a solitary tombstone.

7. Papa Aroha
The name means "foundation of love" in Maori. "Where the fishing's great" reads the brochure from the holiday park, with several pictures of some monster snapper caught nearby. The pictures don't lie. The fishing offshore is fantastic, but the beach itself is also one of the best in the area. As a consequence a large, and loyal fishing community has established itself within the camp, which has maintained its rustic feel, reminiscent of old New Zealand. There's a specacular glade of natives including puriri, pohutakawa and kohekohe beside the main road. The camp shop provides basic supplies. **Papa Aroha Holiday Park** (07)866 8818 www.papaaroha.co.nz. Boat launching using the camp ramp costs $3 per day and includes boat washing and engine flushing.

8. Amodeo Bay
Captain Frank Amodeo arrived from Trieste to NZ in the mid 1800's as an unemployed miner, and through hard work, became one of the pioneers of Auckland's sea-trade, as a skipper with the Northern Steamship Company. This bay is named after him. You'll find more fantastic boat and kayak fishing at this beach, with Anglers Lodge being one of the best organised, dedicated fishing camps I've seen, complete with its own charter boat, a well equipped shop, cabins, van-sites and a swimming pool located right on the coast. **Anglers Lodge** (07)866 7352 www.anglers.co.nz

9. Waitete Bay
Waitete translates as "water dripping from the ground," and it's a broad bay with a tidal nature. There's another absolutely idyllic sandy cove off Waitete Beach Rd, that's pohutakawa-backed, north-facing and sheltered from the wind, where you'll find some beautiful rocks to swim off. A safer place to get wet, you won't find. Park above the beach where possible, and find some space alone. The main beach is more exposed to the west with no trees for shade.

Waitete

Papa Aroha

Colville to Fletcher Bay

This is the northern tip of the Peninsula, and the entrance to both the Hauraki Gulf and Firth of Thames. It's a spectacular piece of land that guards the convergence of these two significant water masses, dominated by the brooding Mt. Morehau. The highway north hugs the coast, at times hundreds of feet above sea level, and the gnarled and twisted pohutakawas that fringe the foreshore along its length add sparkle to an already superb oceanic playground. Where the road hits the high ridges, it offers spectacular vistas, and dotted along its length at sea level you'll find small stretches of sand between the main beaches that you can swim at. By the time you reach the Cape, the landscape is bare and burnt, but as you wind your way over the last hills, you'll reach a couple of the most superb beaches in the North Island. Their scale and beauty will surely take your breath away, as will the stunning views over the Colville Channel and out to Great Barrier Island, which on a clear day almost looks close enough to swim to. The race that's formed when the water draining from the Firth meets the current coming around from the east coast, is yet another spectacular sight.

Travelling The road heading north turns to gravel and clay a few kilometres north of Colville. Despite being steep and windy in a few spots, it's "gravel road light"; well maintained, flat and generally wide enough for two cars everywhere. There's no food or fuel north of Colville, and little in the way of accommodation other than the DOC campsites.

Surfing It's rumoured that there are waves on the western peninsula in a large north-west swell, though there's little evidence to back up this claim.

Fishing Some fabulous fishing in the Colville Channel with equally productive land-based opportunities too, the further north the better. This is kingie country.

Swimming The bays on the north coast are absolutely stunning, and even the west coast is inviting.

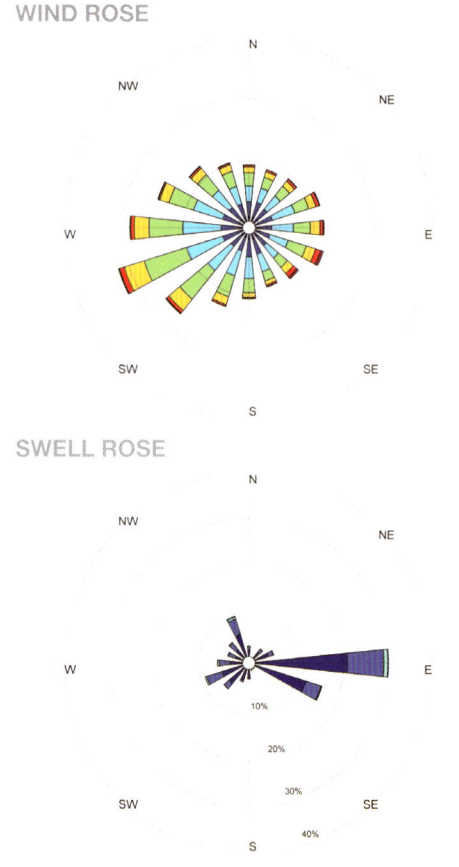

WIND ROSE

SWELL ROSE

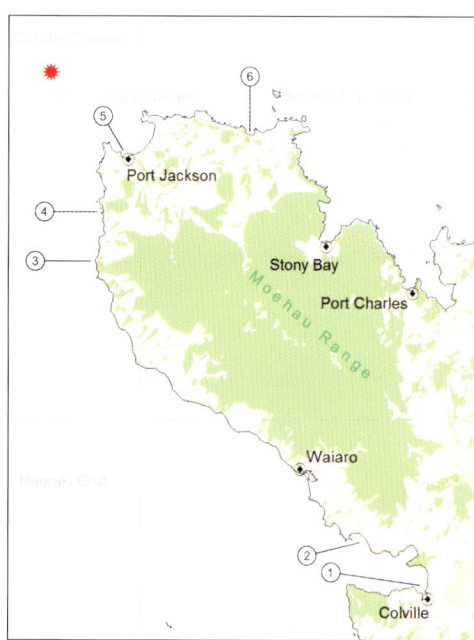

1. Colville Bay
While originally known as the location for a brace of seventies hippy communes, it is now the last source of fuel and refreshments for travellers heading north along this coast. It is home to a flat beach that's tidal, and not ideally suited for swimming, however if you take Wharf Road to the launch-ramp, there are some picturesque and sheltered sections of shingly sand backed by trees, that are both private and out of the wind. I saw significant numbers of terns and oyster catchers here on the low tide cockle banks, that are also known to produce a good feed of flounder at high tide. There's a fairly large reserve area behind the main beach with picnic tables but no bins or toilets. **Colville Bay Motel and Campground** (07)866 6814. **Mahamudra Centre** (07)866 6851 runs a range of Buddhist/meditation retreats, and welcomes casual visitors. They also offer simple casual accommodation www.mahamudra.org.nz

2. Otatu Bay
A curved beach with a wharf at the north end, a dozen or so baches, and a hard-core, fishing-focused caravan park, offering good boat access to the Hauraki Gulf and the northern peninsula. **Otatu Bay Motor Camp** (07)866 6801.

3. Granite Bay
Another small bay with a popular boat ramp at the southern end, it was named after the granite that was mined and quarried nearby. Large chunks still remain.

4. Fantail Bay
A tiny chink of sand by a stream, with an intimate DOC campsite set back off the road, that's garlanded with huge pohutakawas and which again, has a strong fishing focus. You're unlikely to stay long unless you're a fisherman, but if you are, you will notice that the current rips in and out here, and as a consequence,

Port Jackson

the rocks out front can produce many good species including kingfish. There are some other good ledges that are visible from the main road, just north of the bay. Fantail Bay is a beautiful spot to stop for a swim and a cup of tea if you're feeling road weary.

5. Port Jackson

After Fantail Bay the road climbs and winds its way to a high ridge. As you pass over it, the perfectly shaped crescent of Port Jackson comes into view, hundreds of feet below. It's not a port in the usual sense any more, though remnants of the original stone wharf are visible in the south-western corner by the boat ramp. It stretches more than a kilometre from end to end, with a DOC campsite extending in a long ribbon behind the foreshore. It's now a beach stripped down to its bare essentials, with burnt farmland behind, and hardly a tree in sight, and one of those places that when you imagine fringed with native forest, makes you want to weep for our stupidity. On a positive note, the Moehau Reserve that extends way back up behind the beach, is having some notable success ridding itself of possums and restoring kiwis to the remains of the forest. It's still a mellow place to camp, and even shaved, retains significant beauty. The steep, rocky coast between Fantail Bay and here has some prolific fishing ledges and no doubt the bay itself could produce a feed at change of light or at night. With a boat, or even a kayak, you gain access to some special fisheries nearby. **Port Jackson DOC Campsite** (07)866 6932 (eftpos available).

6. Fletcher Bay

Fletcher Bay is a small sandy cove, flanked by large protective headlands, fringed with reefs, all within a short paddle of Square Top Island, The Pinnacles, and a host of other rich marine habitats. The campsite is one of the most sheltered and laid back places you could hope to visit, with lots of space, a stunning golden sand beach out front, and vast pohutakawas offering shade along the shoreline. It also offers access to a few miles of empty coast and beaches to the east, plus boat launching is possible with a good 4wd. Sadly, there doesn't appear to be a decent bank in the bay for surfers, which would really top it off, though it is exposed to north-east swell and the wider area warrants a serious look in a cyclone. The Coromandel Coast Walkway is a fantastic 3hr walk from Fletcher Bay to Stony Bay, across the top of the peninsula. It is also a popular mountain-bike trail. For those not keen on doing the walk both ways, **Coromandel Discovery** (07)866 8175 offer pick-ups and drop-offs from Coromandel Town www.coromandeldiscovery.co.nz. The problem with Fletcher Bay is that once you get there, you'll never want to leave. **DOC Campsite** (07)866 6712 **Fletcher Bay Backpackers** (07)866 1106 has 16 bunks in 4 rooms.

Granite Bay

Fletcher Bay

Stony Bay to Kennedy Bay

Probably the least visited, yet most diverse part of the entire peninsula; the north-east isn't overly endowed with sandy beaches, but the few that you can get to certainly make the trip worth it. The coastal geography is generally rocky and steep, and the Coromandel Range pressing hard up against the sea, is often shrouded in mist, which lends an imposing air to any visit. Each of the communities here has an entirely different feel and shoreline, as do the two DOC campsites in the far north, which are almost the only services in the region. If you are seeking a bit of peace and quiet, this is a good place to start looking.

Travelling Vast sections of this coast remain inaccessible by car, and the long stretches of gravel road that separate these beaches amplifies both the driving time and sense of isolation.

Kennedy Bay

WIND ROSE

SWELL ROSE

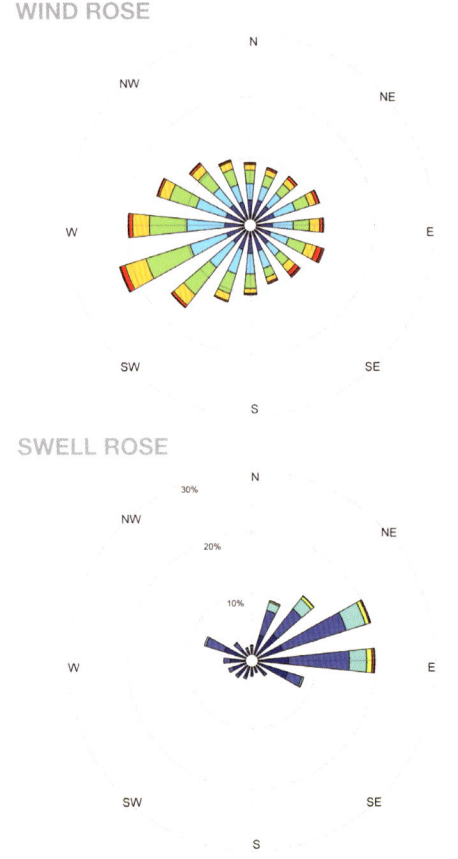

Surfing There are a few spots you can get to by land, plus a few you'll need a boat for. Waikawau Bay is one of the most swell-exposed on the peninsula.

Fishing This whole coast can fish extremely well, with the main problem being access. The steep drop-offs and rocky terrain make it ideal for snapper and kingfish, with some excellent land-based spots, and even more choices if you throw a boat into the mix.

Swimming The best places to swim are the sandy bays, but Stony Bay is delightfully clear too.

Stony Bay

1. Stony Bay

Time seems to slow markedly when you get to Port Charles. At Stony Bay, it stops. This is as far as you can go by road, and many don't get this far. It is, as its name so eloquently implies, a stony bay, that's well protected by headlands on either side. The only facilities are a DOC campsite fringed in pohutakawas that can take 200 visitors per night. But if you like your nature uncooked, that's enough. Stony Bay is exposed, and with an east or north-east swell, the shingle banks in front of the stream come alive with some punchy rights. It is a popular kayak fishing location, and the steep profile of the shingle beach also offers lively swimming, while the deep water under the cliffs to the north has produced many fish and crays. **Stony Bay Campsite** www.doc.govt.nz

2. Sandy Bay

As its name implies, it's a beautiful sandy beach; located just north of Port Charles, with half a dozen baches and a timeless air. Its flat shelf and protected nature make it a great place for a family swim, though there are no public amenities or easily accessible shade. **Trevs Bach** (07)866 6635

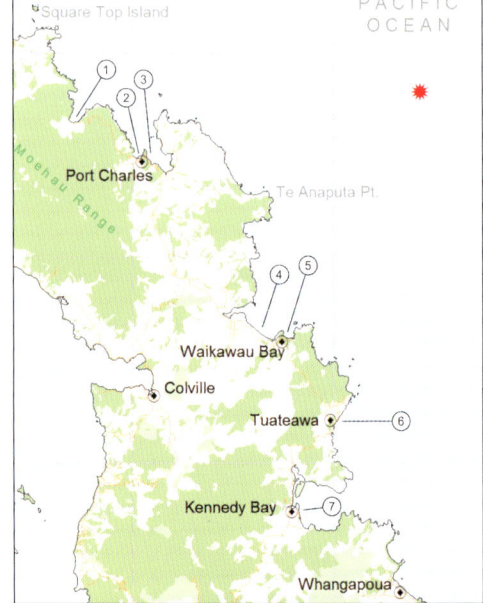

Kennedy Bay Marae

3. Port Charles

Visited and named by Captain Cook in November 1769, Port Charles is an enclosed harbour that would have given the good captain a calm and safe anchorage and a peaceful night's sleep. There's a jetty on either side of the harbour entrance now, and trailer boat launching can be easily carried out on the beach by the north-east entrance, which is also a tempting spot for a dip. **Port Charles Harbourmaster** 0800 800 401 or 027 480 9767. **Tangiaro Kiwi Retreat** (07) 866 6614 www.kiwiretreat.co.nz

Port Charles

Kennedy Bay estuary

4. Waikawau Bay

The busiest DOC campsite in the country is at Waikawau Bay; with up to 2000 people per night flocking here over the six weeks of peak season. They come here for the country feel, the glorious long crescent of sparkling white sand, the seabirds, the fishing, and ironically, for most of the year, to find some peace and quiet. The bay is a significant seabird-breeding location, and the extensive dunes are a critical part of their habitat. Other than when walking through the alotted access ways, stay off them! It is a popular surf beach and totally exposed to north and east swell. The best waves are often in the middle of the beach, depending on swell direction and state of the banks. The north end is a popular nude bathing location, so don't be surprised to see a bit of raw flesh on display. For boaties who don't fancy the beach retrieve with their car, or who get stuck, the local farmer will drag it out with his tractor for $25. **Waikawau Bay DOC Camp** (07)866 1106 (bookings are required at Christmas). A camp shop selling basics, is open from 10-12 and 4-5 on weekdays most of the year, and all day in silly season. **Kayak hire and horse treks** (07)866 6956.

5. Little Bay

It is what it says it is; a little bay that's home to ten or twenty baches, clinging to the steep cliffs which plunge to the rocky shoreline, where you'll see a tiny sliver of beach. It doesn't offer much to the visitor, with no amenities, difficult access, and not even much of a view; but it's a great place to have a home if you're lucky enough.

6. Tuateawa

Also backed by steep hills, Tuateawa is a funky bay with 3 or 4 interesting baches nailed onto the cliffs which back it. In one way inhospitable, but yet so captivating; it's a piece of rocky eye-candy that the world, or at least as much of the world that gets out this way, generally drives straight past. A slab of greywacke closely resembling The Incredible Hulk's head, sticks out of the sea at the north end of Rabarts Rd. The rarely surfed left that peels off it has a sucky take-off and a fair bit of drive, should you be looking for a wave in the area. You can boat launch by tractor at the southern end of the beach.

7. Kennedy Bay

One of the most appealing spots on the whole Coromandel features a beautiful arc of sand in an enclosed bay, with a meandering river estuary feeding onto it. Sadly Kennedy Bay is riven with internal strife regarding conflicting attitudes towards future development proposals, in what was a last bastion of Maoridom in the area. Only time will tell how it all pans out, meanwhile it's a great place to fish and swim, with access down a sandy country lane that is apparently sometimes closed for socio-political reasons. There are few public amenities, and even fewer visitors. Let's hope it remains in its current pristine state for many years to come.

Waikawau Bay

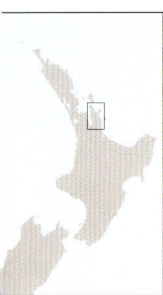

Kuaotunu to Matapaua Bay

This is actually a separate peninsula off a peninsula, that has somehow remained one of the least inhabited stretches of the Coromandel coastline. The notorious Blackjack Rd connects these diverse locations, and the fact that it is made of gravel has helped maintain a certain rawness to the area. People are less rushed and there's a certain old time feel which still permeates the air. Easy access to the Mercury Islands, and the shelter they provide, just adds to the benefits of northern aspect enjoyed on this slightly forgotten finger of land; and with such a wealth of fine beaches, it's pretty hard not to have a good time here, whatever your tastes.

Travelling These beaches are all connected by the infamous Blackjack Rd; long may it remain gravel. The ony shops and fuel are at Kuaotunu.

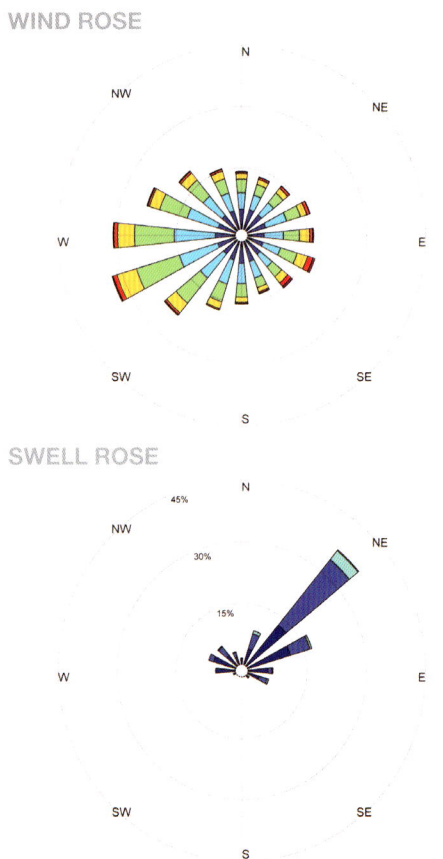

Surfing Some of the waves here are as good as anywhere in the country when they fire. Sadly that's all too rarely, as there are usually only one or two proper north swells per year. If you can get there when it's pumping, you won't be disappointed.

Fishing Beach and rock fishing is similar to the rest of the Coromandel. Trailer boat access to the Mercury Islands is a major bonus for this area. Kayak fishermen are able to access a fair amount of good terrain between Kuaotunu and Otama, likewise from all the other spots on the peninsula. **NZ Landbased Safaris (07)866 2850.**

Swimming For most of the year this is a placid coast, offering sheltered water and sparkling sand.

1. Kuaotunu

Two long sections of glorious white sand are separated by a rocky promontory called Quarry Point, with pohutakawas and reserve land at either extremity. Facing north towards Great Barrier Island, with the Mercs offering shelter from the east, Kuaotunu is a delight for travellers, offering lots of space and all the amenities you need on a holiday. Despite being the main population centre on this little peninsula, there aren't a huge number of holiday homes, which means less pressure on the beach, but more pressure on the busy motor camp. The boat ramp is really good, and located on the west side of Quarry Point. The beach can get good waves along its length, but the main surf action is centered on the reef at the eastern end of the bay. It's a long, bowly

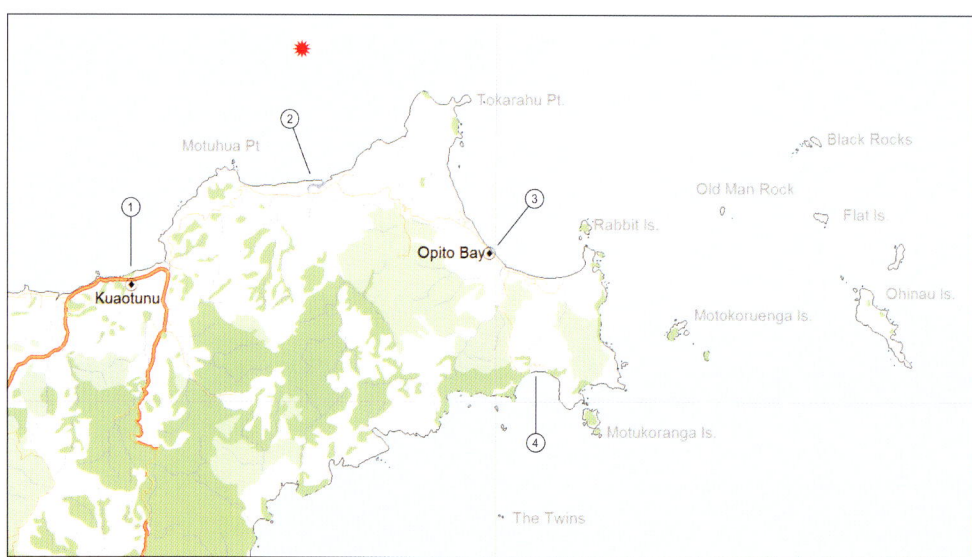

Kuaotunu West

Otama Bay

right that breaks in shallow water, then reforms. At high tide in a small swell, there's a good learner wave on the inside. This corner of the beach only gets due-north swell as anything with too much east in it will get blocked by the Mercs, but when it breaks, it's a seriously fun wave. Low tide is best and any wind with some south in it is ideal. There are tennis courts in the middle of the beach; while fuel, lpg, food and beer can be bought at the shop to the east of the beach. **Kuaotunu Holiday Park** (07)866 5628 www.kuaotunumotorcamp.co.nz **Black Jack Lodge Backpackers** (07)866 2988 www.black-jack.co.nz **Reefers** (07)866 4233.

2. Otama Bay

Blackjack Rd leads up the hill from Kuaotunu and winds its way down to Otama in a spray of gravel. Arriving at the coast you find one of the purest white beaches in New Zealand, with a recognizable rocky point to the west, and a long headland stretching out to the east. A stunning wetland divides the beach into two distinct halves. Both maintain an empty feel, though there are a few baches at the eastern end set back behind the reserve. It's hard to believe when driving down here on a tranquil summer day, but despite the shelter it gets from the Mercs, in a grunty north swell, Otama can get waves that are as heavy as any of the Coromandel's beaches, with thick barrels breaking hard on the sand just metres from the shore. Mid-tide is often best, with peaks scattered everywhere, depending on the condition of the sand. If you're after a feed, many people fish the western rocks, and the beach adjacent. There are public toilets on the reserve in the middle of the beach. **Otama Bay Camp** (07)866 2362 is open in summer, located behind the dunes before the wetland.

3. Opito Bay

More gravel road takes you to the end of the peninsula where you'll find Opito Bay, which faces east into the lee of Great Mercury Island. It's another stunningly long crescent of white sand; offering easy access to the waters around the nearby island group for small boats. Opito has been the scene of some dramatic tussles in the environment court as developers seek to increase the number of holiday homes in the area, to the ire of some. It is a settlement notable for a very affluent feel, though one of the locals was quick to help me out with his tractor one day, when my car got stuck trying to retrieve the boat on an incoming tide. It can have average waves in an east or north-east swell, but the beach here is a lot flatter than Otama, thus making it less exciting for surfing but a safer swimming spot. Facilities include toilets, a bbq and bins, in the picnic area located by the stream in the centre of the beach.

4. Matapaua Bay

Drive for ten minutes over the clay and gravel road which continues from the far end of Opito Bay. There's a gentle climb into the bush before you're offered a wee peek at the stunning south-facing bay below. It actually has a cove-like feel with a pronounced headland to the east and rocky fringe to the west. A dozen or so baches clustered on the valley floor behind the beach, set amongst manuka and regenerating native trees, constitute the settlement. It's a little slice of paradise offering great swimming and snorkeling; and the fishing off the rocks at either end of the beach can also get good, while a cluster of boat moorings in the eastern hook of the bay offer shelter from most but south winds. The one drawback is limited parking. The flip side is the abundance of shade offered by the huge pohutakawas, which drip off the foreshore. Sadly there are no public amenities.

Otama Bay

Matapaua Bay

New Chums to Rings Beach

The selection of spots covered on this page are some of the most idyllic and captivating in the country; each of the four locations completely different, each appealing to a different personality type, and each offering a unique coastal experience. The atmosphere is pretty relaxed when compared to the commotion you often experience further south, and the sense of space and peace offered on the two long beaches which sit either side of the Whangapoua Estuary is beautifully counterpointed by the intimate charms of their dimmunitive, but equally delicious neighbours.

Travelling It's a bit of a mission to drive around the harbour, and for that reason, these two distinct areas retain a separate feel. Again there's very little in the way of public accommodation on either side.

WIND ROSE

SWELL ROSE

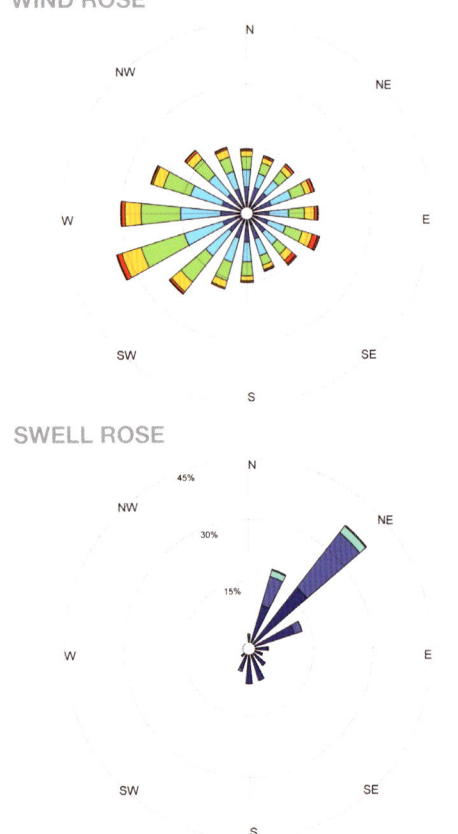

Surfing Something of a mixed bag, with New Chums the most exposed to east swell, followed by Whangapoua, which can get amazing waves.

Fishing Lots of good land-based spots off the rocks, plus the estuary and its wharf both fish well.

Swimming Matarangi and Rings are the safest, as they receive the least swell. Clear water everywhere.

1. New Chums

It was rated by a Sunday Times journalist as the fourth best beach in the world, whatever that means. But New Chums does posess significant beauty, and unlike Cathedral Cove further south, one does entertain the possibility of some peaceful time on this beach. Recent news that the land behind the foreshore had been sold for development caused cries of indignation from many, but it should be clear to all of us by now that nothing is sacred in this country, and the saga is still unfolding. The 20 minute walk through the nikau groves and pohutakawas from Whangapoua is stunning, and the squeaky white sand that greets you will hasten the removal of your shoes. New Chums is the most exposed to east swell in this part of the Coromandel, and it's steeply shelving profile creates power in the waves that should make the casual tourist wary of swimming when there is surf. There's a right that sometimes breaks off the south-eastern point, and you'll find peaks down the beach that work through the tides. It's the local wave magnet, and gets good when Whangapoua is small, but doesn't like too much size. Access is from the north end of Whangapoua beach. Walk over the stream and follow the trail. There are no amenities, so use the loo before you go, and pack any trash out.

New Chums

Rings Beach

2. Whangapoua

Sitting on a bench here one day taking photos, a woman came up to me and said, "You needn't look any further, you've found the most beautiful beach in the world," referring to Whangapoua. While that's a matter of opinion, it is certainly one of my personal favourites, home to some of the most stylish, yet unpretentious beach architecture in the country, with epic waves on its day, fabulous white sand, and a totally laid back feel. Whangapoua's hundred-odd holiday homes are nestled at the base of some low hills just north of the Whangapoua estuary. It's a long drive around from the south, but this guarantees fewer people on the beach. It offers more exposure to east swell than Matarangi, with a steeper beach profile like New Chums, giving the waves here some extra punch. You'll find peaks along its length, a high tide freak wave inside the island, and a rifling left hand sand point into the mouth of the river to the north. It's all good news for surfers but can put a handbrake on any land-based fishing, which often gets good during and after a swell. The wharf and boat ramp inside the harbour, located just before Whangapoua, will provide fun fishing for the kids, and produce a feed at the right time, with even the odd kingie turning up occasionally. Public facilities at the main beach include toilets and bins by the store, and in the reserve at the northern end. **Whare Moana IV** private accommodation www.whangapoua.com

3. Matarangi

The jury is still out on Matarangi for many, as while there's no doubt it's a fabulous stretch of sparkling white sand, Matarangi's up-market and rarified air renders the experience a bit flavourless, despite the stunning beach homes and safe swimming. And they're still trying to pack them in. Facing north/north-east, the beach picks up the smallest pulse of north swell, and can have good banks along its length, especially at the estuary end, where the fishing is also predictably good. Matarangi would be an excellent spot to deploy a kon-tiki or torpedo off the beach, and the rocks between here and Rings are also a productive land-based fishing spot, with various access points and limited parking adjacent to the road. There are plenty of private homes to rent on the internet, but little in the way of public accommodation. Other amenities of note are the supermarket, golf course, beauty salon, hardware store, conference-centre and quite a good restaurant. **Omaras** (07)866 5397 www.matarangi.co.nz

4. Rings Beach

Pretty little Rings Beach is hidden away down the short coastal road that connects Matarangi and Kuoatonu; a dimunitive bay with tons of character, and a real family atmosphere. There's not a lot to it; a hundred metres of sand, backed by protective hills, with a few dozen baches nestled behind the dunes. The rocky headlands at either extremity frame a spectacular view of Great Barrier. The beach itself is more sheltered and steeper than Matarangi, and can get peaky waves when the rest of the coast is big. The rest of the time it's a superb bathing beach and the kind of place where you wish you had friends with a place so you could go and stay. There are no public facilities and to launch a boat you have to go back to Kuoatunu. **Just Paradise** (07)866 2414 is a private bach to rent above the beach www.justparadise.co.nz

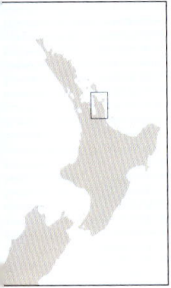

Mercury Bay

Mercury Bay is one of the most significant coastal drawcards in the country, with a full hand of beaches that includes Buffalo Bay, Cathedral Cove, Cooks Beach and Hahei. Each in their own way are significant national landmarks that have witnessed historic events of some magnitude; and on a lighter note, many thousands of happy smiles, for many thousands of kiwis, who come to enjoy these spectacular and sheltered sandy beaches. While this is an area of some beauty, the huge amount of visitors who throng to the various attractions on this stretch of the peninsula, take a bit of the fun out of it for me, but it remains a unique and stunning section of Coromandel, that's high on the "must-visit" list.

Travelling Mercury Bay is divided by the Whitianga estuary. It takes nearly half an hour to drive around, but a ferry runs between Whitianga and the stone wharf, a 5min ride away. They say 150 million metres of Kauri were taken from here over the years. Now the ferry just carries tourists www.whitianga.co.nz

WIND ROSE

SWELL ROSE

Surfing Mercury Bay is one of the most protected areas on the east coast, but Wharekaho can be ok in small swells. **Peninsula Surf School** 0800stand-up.

Fishing Obviously something of a boaties mecca, but not the best land-based area really. **Mercury Bay Gamefishing Club** www.mbgfc.co.nz

Swimming Few problems with waves means excellent and safe swimming for all. There's also some excellent snorkelling in the area. **Dive HQ** (07) 867 1580 www.divethecoromandel.co.nz

Wharekaho

1. Wharekaho/Simpsons Beach
There's not a lot at Simpsons Beach, just 500m of sand and a handful of baches, but it's a charming bay and a pleasant spot for a swim on the way north. It's less sheltered from the east by the islands, so picks up more swell than Buffalo Beach, with peaky beachies the order of the day. Boat launching tends to happen at the northern end, in front of the caravan park (open to caravan club members only). Public facilities are limited to toilets at the western end of the bay.

2. Whitianga
Whitianga is one of the most commercial, and possibly least sympathetic developments on the Coromandel. In fact if Springfield had a coastal twin, this would probably be it. The scary thing is, Whitianga Waterways twenty year plan could yet see up to 1800 new sections on 220 ha of land, along more than 6km of man-made canals, with a 255 unit retirement village, a hotel complex, a medical centre and a retail island all planned. It is the commercial hub of the eastern Coromandel, offering a range of accommodation, eating and nightlife options, supermarkets and even cinemas. There are some well priced (and well pricey), eating holes; and those wanting a beer won't find it too tough either, though nothing seemed particularly exciting. There are two sections to the bay. Buffalo Beach is the main foreshore area adjacent to the town, and curves around to the north for over a kilometre. It was so

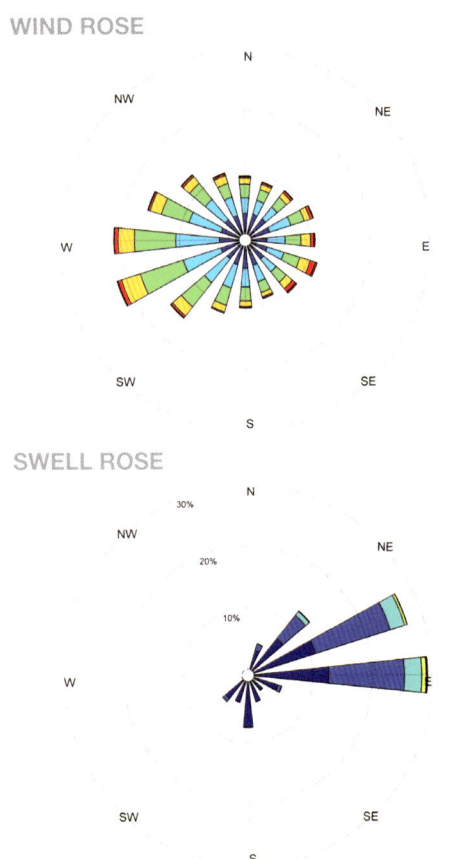

Whitianga, Buffalo Beach

named after HMS Buffalo, which was wrecked here in 1840. Ohuka or Brophy's, is the cove and stretch of sand in the far north-west corner of the bay. Both normally offer extremely safe swimming, though in a big east swell, they can have a few waves; but the advantage of this beach is the amount of shelter offered in a range of swell and wind conditions, with somewhere that's usually calm. The estuary mouth can produce fish, as can the beach itself, especially at change of light. I saw kingies rounding up baitfish and small snapper in the Ohuka hook at full tide, and the estuary also has flounder further up. Whitianga is one of the main game fishing ports in New Zealand, due to its proximity to the fishing grounds beyond the Mercs, and as you'd expect, a wide array of boat fishing charters exist here, your choice would depend on what type of fishing you want to do. If scallop debauch is your thing, the Whitianga Scallop Festival will be right up your alley. **Harbourside Holiday Park** (07)866 5746 is adjacent to the harbour. www.harboursidewhitianga.co.nz

Ohuka

The Great Navigators of Mercury Bay

It's hard not be moved by the pivotal nautical events that have occurred in Mercury Bay. Of course Kupe, one of the greatest sailors of all time, was first. The name Whitianga is an abbreviation of "Te Whitianga a Kupe" (the crossing of Kupe). It is where he supposedly first landed on the NZ mainland after an epic 2960 km voyage from Ra'iatea. On seeing clouds on Mt Moehau, his wife Hine apparently exclaimed, "E Kupe, ha aotea, kua u tatou", "Hey Kupe, it is a cloud. We have arrived!" hence the name Aotearoa. Next was the Arawa canoe in the 14th century, and its sailing master Hei, who chose the bay for his people, and whom the bay, Te Whanganui-o-Hei (the great bay of Hei), and local iwi (Ngati Hei), were originally named after. Then came Cook, 400 years later. He spent twelve days camping in the dunes to observe the transit of Mercury, before commencing his incredible 69 day voyage to circumnavigate and chart New Zealand, with his primary geodetic datum being the location of Cooks Beach. The Mercury Bay museum commemorates this history. On a less significant note, the Mercury Bay Swordfish and Mako Shark club was established in 1924 with its first recorded catch in 1925 being a 300 lb striped marlin. Then there was the indomitable Zane Gray and the controversy caused when he abandoned Roberton Island in the Bay of Islands for Red Mercury Island in 1929. There's another good fishing tale about the area and the attempts made by a couple of intrepid locals to kickstart the fishing tourism business after the war. It involves a thousand pound black marlin and several fishing rods, and takes a lot of beating.

Mercury Bay: Eastern Beaches

The beaches on the eastern fringe of Mercury Bay seem totally distinct and different from nearby Buffalo Beach and Whitianga. Hahei and Cooks may be stalwarts of the great Kiwi summer experience, but Cathedral Cove and Hot Water Beach have unashamedly been claimed by the bus companies, who cherry-pick the highlights of the Coromandel in their whirlwind tours of the peninsula, full of young Europeans or ageing Japanese. Sadly due to their influence, it's hard to enjoy the pristine beauty of the arches of the cove with 500 foreigners and a shameless Kiwi selling icecreams and drinks. Still that's the way of the world and little we can say here will change anything. If you really want to enjoy this coast, go off-peak.

Travelling These beaches are all within a few kilometres of each other, and between them offer enough facilities to cater to most people's basic holiday needs. A number of operators offer scenic tours of the marine park and Cathedral Cove by boats of varying descriptions. Cathedral Cove is a short kayak from Hahei or even from Cooks Beach. The guided kayak trips are a popular and low impact way of experiencing the area. www.haheiexplorer.co.nz or www.cavecruzer.co.nz or www.glassbottomboatwhitianga.co.nz. On busy days, it's nearly impossible to park within walking distance of the cove carpark. A shuttle can take you from the overflow carpark at Hahei. **Cathedral Cove Shuttle** 027 422 5899.

WIND ROSE

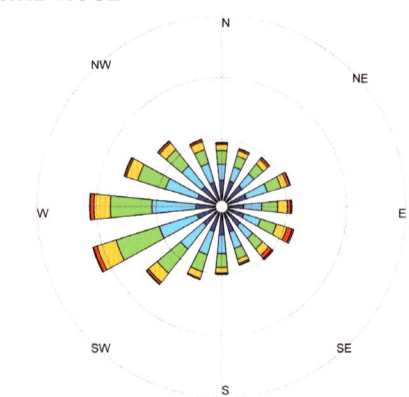

SWELL ROSE

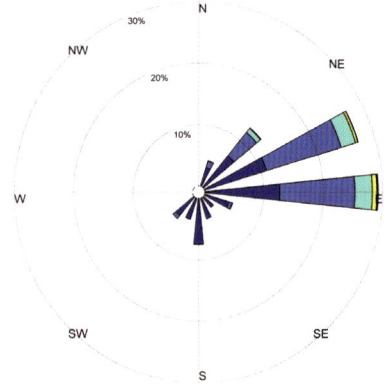

Surfing As for Whitianga, very little swell gets in here, though in massive storms there can be a wave off the mouth of Flaxmill Bay stream and Hahei apparently has a mysto bombie out in the bay.

Fishing You'll find pretty good land-based fishing off the rocks either side of the marine reserve.

Swimming These beaches rank as good a place to swim as anywhere in the world on a fine day, and the snorkelling around Cathedral Cove is spectacular.

3. Flaxmill Bay and Front Beach

Coming from Cooks Beach, the road to the ferry rejoins the coast at Flaxmill Bay, with the Purangi Estuary at the eastern end, yachts moored off its mouth, and a dozen or so baches on the ridge behind it. Front Beach is part of the same bay but faces east, with separate access points to the west of the main beach. The two are divided at higher tides by spectacular sculpted limestone outcrops, but both beaches are studded with pohutakawas and are beautifully sheltered spots to swim and cool off. **Hideaway at Flaxmill Bay** (07)866 2368 www.flaxmillbay.co.nz **Flaxmill Bay Motels** (07)866 5609

4. Lonely Bay

Take the Shakespeare Cliffs lookout road and park where the road ends. The walking track to one of our most picturesque and idyllic swimming spots starts here. Lonely Bay is a tiny cove backed by steep bush, with bleached white limestone cliffs and boulders that glisten in the sun. If you fell asleep and woke a bit confused, you could be forgiven for thinking you were in the Greek Isles, with its clear light and azure water. Ancient pohutakawas form an impressive entrance to the beach at the bottom of a short but steep walking track, and once you're down it, the rest of the world almost ceases to exist (unless it's January). There're toilets and bins at the top of the track.

5. Cooks Beach

So named by Cook himself during his historic visit; the site where he camped is 300 metres west of the estuary, and a cairn and sign mark the spot where the measurements were taken. The beach itself is a stunning crescent of white sand stretching for a few kilometres from end to end, with a large headland to the east and a smaller sandstone promontory to the west, backed by low dunes. Access is easy right along the foreshore, and while it retains its beautiful sand and sheltered aspect, the community has been rendered a bit featureless by budget seventies developments, and a sad lack of design sensitivity or planning. Due to its north aspect and the shelter offered by the Mercury Islands, there's only surf in an extreme north swell, when there will be peaky waves along its length. For boaties, there's an all tide hard ramp inside the estuary, while the Mercury Bay Boating Club is the social centre of the local fishing community. Other public facilities include a tapas bar, liquor store and building supplies store, a few streets back from the beach. **Cooks Beach Holiday Resort** (07)866 5469 has camp sites and cabins www.cooksbeachcamp.co.nz. **Bay Breeze** 027 422 7852 is a two brm unit. **Shakespeare Cliff Lodge and Resort** is maybe NZ's most luxurious beach house to rent 021 615 215 www.shakespearecliff.com

Flaxmill Bay

Cathedral Cove

Hahei

6. Cathedral Cove

Cathedral Cove is a unique section of the coast, featuring sculpted cliffs and a cathedral vaulted hole through a prominent rock in the middle of the squeaky white sand beach. It's one of the most popular locations on the Coromandel, drawing literally thousands of tourists on a busy day. The walk from the carpark also takes in Gemstone Bay (with a small sandy beach) and Stingray Bay (which is predominantly rocky). It is a fairly easy 40 minute hike with a few steep headlands to climb, but the track is well maintained, with steps in the steeper sections. When you get there, you'll find huge pohutakawas cascading down steep bluffs which back the bleached white sandy shore. Walk through the arch and you find another open expanse of sand, with a sculpted needle/sentinel watching over the western headland. It is a spectacular place at any time but particularly dawn and dusk. The entire shoreline is a part of the marine reserve, and the snorkeling trail from Stingray Bay offers the chance of an encounter with large snapper, stingrays and crayfish. Facilities include toilets in the carpark and also hidden under the trees down on the beach. Absurdly there is an icecream and drink cart in operation during summer.

7. Hahei

The name derives from Hei, the ancestor of the Ngati Hei people who arrived on the waka Te Arawa in the fourteenth century. Nearly a kilometre of squeaky white sand, and million dollar views over Mahurangi and the Mercs, plus its proximity to Cathedral Cove, all make Hahei one of the Coromandel's most popular beach towns. It becomes insanely busy over the Christmas/New Year period, but remains pretty sleepy for the rest of the year. A general store, takeaways, cafes and a wine bar and pizza parlour at the shopping complex, make it a more social option than nearby Hot Water Beach, but yet small and intimate, unlike Whitianga. Hahei is backed by quite a few baches, and also features a fantastic camping ground at the eastern end backing right onto the beach, which keeps the everyman's feel to the town. It's a charming and welcoming place, and a great place to swim, but quite a few other people share the knowledge, so don't expect isolation. Due to the shelter offered by the islands, swell rarely gets in here. **Hahei Motor Camp** (07)866 3889 has sites and cabins set just back from the beach, including some luxury options; and their website features other private accommodation in the area www.haheiholidays.co.nz. **Tatahi Lodge** (07)866 3889 is a backpackers with dorm rooms and ensuite private facilities at a variety of rates tatahilodge@xtra.co.nz.

Lonely Bay and Cooks Beach

Hot Water Beach to Pauanui

There isn't a more diverse group of beaches on the Coromandel than this lot, ranging in extremes from the teeming hordes at Hot Water Beach to the isolation of Sailors Grave; from Tairua's solid community, to Pauanui's one month a year residences; and a more satisfying section of coast to visit is hard to find anywhere. Fishing, diving, surfing and swimming are all catered for almost to excess, and if you had to choose one area to find your summer fun, this would be as good as anywhere, though this stretch of coast attracts a fair amount of swell, so it's not for the faint hearted.

Travelling The easiest way to get from Tairua to Pauanui is by the vehicular ferry, which runs between 9.00am and 5.00pm in off-season, later and more frequently in summer. It leaves from the wharf and costs $3.00 one way and $5.00 return.

Tairua

WIND ROSE

SWELL ROSE

Surfing Hot Water Beach is one of the most consistent surf spots on the Coromandel, with a steep shelf and partially rocky seafloor holding solid banks, offering hollow waves in the right conditions. Same with Tairua and Sailors Grave. Somewhere between these beaches, there'll be a spot handling most east coast swell conditions. **Hot Water Beach Surf School and Shop** 0800hangten www.hotwaterbeachsurf.com. **Outback Surf School and Shop** (07)864 7558 is in Pauanui www.outbacksurfschool.co.nz

Fishing Tairua is the hub for the fishing community. **Tairua Dive and Fishinn** are the crew to see for all your needs, including charters to the Aldermans plus fish and dive equipment for hire www.divetairua.co.nz

Swimming Of them all, Pauanui is the safest, no question. If there is swell running, the Tairua estuary can be good at high tide. If there are no lifeguards around and a swell, remember the golden rule: don't swim where there are no waves breaking. That will signal a rip! Beware of the Tairua shore break.

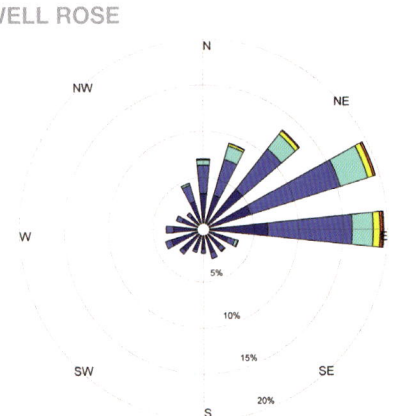

1. Hotwater Beach

World famous for the mineral springs in the centre of the beach; at low tide it feels as if half the tourists on the Coromandel arrive here, spade in hand, eager for a soak. Where they come from and where they go to is anyone's guess, but on a busy day you can barely get a park. And it's not just confined to summer. There are actually two springs known as Maori and Orua. The northern spring reaches a temp of 64C and the second spring, twenty metres south, reaches 60C. They are accessible a few hours either side of low tide, but you will need a spade, or to become a hole thief to enjoy them. The beach itself is a two mile crescent of glorious sand, arcing around to the north-west, divided by a rocky bluff in front of which

Hot Water Beach

Pauanui

Tairua

you will find the springs. The south-eastern end of the beach is where the baches, shops and surf-school are, with a few cafes open during the day, but nothing at night. This is the most popular surf area, with occasionally tubing rights off the point. Lifeguards patrol this end of the beach, and also the hot pools at designated times, as it is amongst the four worst places in the country for drownings. This is partly a result of the large number of tourists, but also due to the swell which the beach attracts and its steep shelf. The north-western end almost feels like another beach; empty and spacious, with a separate access point, toilets and parking. It also can have exceptional surf, depending on swell direction and the state of the banks. The dunes behind the beach are home to breeding dotterels and are protected, so stay off. The beach store hires spades. **Moko Artspace** (07)866 3367 www.moko.co.nz. **Hot Water Beach Resort** (07)866 3116 has camp and van sites and cabins just back from the beach.www.hotwaterbeachholidaypark.com. **Surf Sands Cottage** (07)866 3878.

2. Sailors Grave
A deviation off SH25 down a steep, bush-lined valley leads to Sailors Grave, a stunning, unpopulated bay that's protected by headlands at either extremity. In the days of sail, it was a popular place for naval ships to pick up timber for their spars, and it takes its name from seaman William Simpson, who drowned on the beach while loading kauri onto HMS Tortoise in 1842. It can offer excellent rock fishing at the northern end at low tide, and the waves can also be good, with several potential peaks dependent on swell direction and tide. An excellent stream offering fresh water swimming in the lagoon to the north of the carpark, plus shade-offering pohutakawas dripping onto the beach, completes a very seductive picture. You'll find a long-drop and bins in the grassed reserve overlooking the beach.

3. Tairua
Sprawling along the north edge of the estuary and down the length of Ocean Beach, Tairua is one half of a dynamic duo with its neighbour, Pauanui. Tairua is the gritty half; the half that has been a mill and farming town for over one hundred years, the half that's a working, living community with all the associated services. Dominating the harbour in an almost carbon copy of Hohoura Heads is Paku, an ancient volcanic cone. Once heavily inhabited by Maori, remnants of the original pa sites remain today, and the 15 minute walk to the summit from the top of Tirinui Crescent is richly rewarded with spectacular views both ways, up and down the coast. There are a number of good swimming options, both in and outside the harbour, safe anchorages and a stunning ocean beach, backed by low dunes and holiday homes, that is patrolled by Trust Waikato surf life-saving. You'll also find some good land-based fishing out on the rocks by the entrance, with kingies, kahawai and the odd snapper turning up. Tairua can also offer some of the gruntiest waves on the Coromandel when it's on, due to the ultra-steep beach profile, and exposure to east swell, with thick, board-snapping peaks that are often better at the south end by the rocks, and at lower tides. Tairua is also the gateway to the Alderman Islands. Good fishing and even better diving off them draw the boats, and have done for many years. All the big fish species get weighed in at Tairua at some stage in a season, with less of the puff surrounding game fishing than in some surrounding towns. Boat launching takes place inside the estuary by the dive shop and wharf, where there is also a cafe and restaurant. You'll find toilets and access points at either end of Ocean Beach, plus a couple of walkways onto the beach between the homes that line it. The carpark at the north end offers the easiest parking, overlooking the beach. **Tairua Beach Villas Backpackers** (07)864 8345 tairuabackpackers@xtra.co.nz. Nearby and privately owned Slipper Island also has some camping and beaching options in South Bay (07)864 7560 **www.slipper.co.nz**.

4. Pauanui
When it was initially developed, it had an appalling and possibly undeserved reputation as a bastion for rich Aucklanders with private planes, who used it for long, boozy golf weekends with their plastic wives and overweight clients. While that was true to a degree, it is has broadened as a community, and matured as a settlement and the excellent long term planning that went into the resort has begun to pay dividends, as it blends in with its neighbour and still offers all the fabulous amenities it was designed with. The surf can be excellent, and though the beach profile is less steep than Tairua, it can have good peaks along its length, that are often biggest and best at the south end. When the bar at the mouth of the estuary breaks, it can be one of the best lefts on the peninsula, though the sandbars are inconsistent, so it isn't a wave you'd bank on. Casting baits into the channel entrance produces the odd kahawai, while the rocks to the south of the beach also fish well. **The Glade Holiday Park** (07)864 8559 offers camp sites and chalets. www.pauanuionline.co.nz.

Hot Water Beach

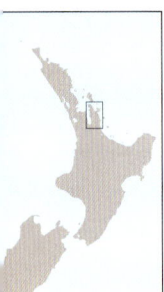

Opoutere to Whiritoa

Sandy beaches, fantastic surf, and a deeply indented coastline are the prime attractions of one of the most spectacular and exotic sections of the Coromandel. Thankfully, though highly popular, this area has retained a chilled-out atmosphere that has long ago departed some of the other more salubrious parts of the peninsula; while its diversity holds a huge attraction for a wide range of visitors. If it's a party you want, you'll probably find it at Whangamata. If it's solitude you seek, then Opoutere is the place for you. Surfing? World class. Swimming? Tick! Fishing? You bet. Natural beauty? In spades. Is there anything else we can help you with madam? Enjoy your stay.

Travelling While there are a few different accommodation options at each spot, Whangamata is almost the sole provider of fuel and entertainment. **Whangamata I-site** (07)865 8340 www.whangamatainfo.co.nz

WIND ROSE

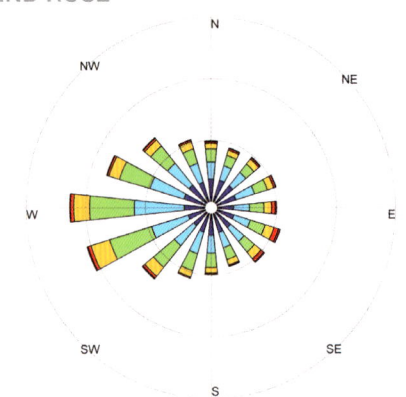

SWELL ROSE

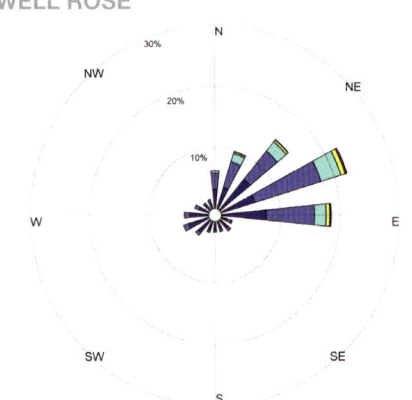

Surfing The whole coast is well exposed to swell from the east, and all the beaches shelve relatively steeply, offering good shape when the wind is offshore. Whangamata is obviously one of the surf capitals of NZ, with several surf shops and lots of surfers too. **Whangamata Surfing School** (07)865 6879 has a good reputation www.whangamatasurfschool.co.nz.

Fishing A lot of coast and some juicy rock headlands and estuarys for the land-based crew. All the facilities, including a fishing club and good tackle shop, are in Whangamata. **Whangamata Ocean Sports Club** (07)865 8704 by the wharf www.oceansports.co.nz. **Bubbas Fishing and Outdoors** stock all tackle and offer dive refills (07)865 7464.

Swimming There are lots of fantastic places to swim here, but this coast is known for powerful waves, so be wary.

1. Opoutere

At a time when our coast seems to have been carved to bits by developers, it's great to know that places like Opoutere still exist. Here you have a long, pristine sandy beach, that's close to all the main tourist destinations, yet still remains somewhere you can get away from the fuss. Driving along the banks of the estuary, with its pristine mangrove fringe, pohutakawas laden with widow-makers, and the little private wharf to fish and swim off, is like a time warp; taking you back to the days when the Coromandel was a lot less spoiled than it is now. This pristine

sweep of golden sand extends for several kilometres, with not a house in site, but the price to pay for an untouched beach is that there are access issues. Either walk out to the spit at the south end via the public walkway, or through the campsite if you're staying there. The surf can be good, with mixed peaks down its length and occasionally a wave off the estuary entrance. The dunes between the campground and

Opoutere

Whangamata

the spit are a renowned dotterel breeeding ground, so respect the fenced-off areas. Ohui, which is the tiny settlement at the north end, is 10k by gravel road from the camp. Opoutere has been commonly accepted as a clothing optional beach, especially at the north end, so don't be surprised to see pink flesh on the beach. There's a small community website which has a few private baches for rent, plus info on the dotterels www.opoutere.org. **Opoutere Coastal Campground** (07)865 9152 www.opoturebeach.co.nz. **Opoutere YHA** (07)865 9072 www.yha.co.nz

2. Onemana

Once known by the surf community as Shangri-La, back when it was an empty piece of paradise; cute wee Onemana is now home to a well maintained, but very quiet settlement, set behind the still lovely white-sand beach, that would hold little interest to the casual traveller other than as somewhere to have a picnic and a quick swim. The facilities at the main beach include tennis courts, toilets, and picnic tables at the south end, plus a private day-spa complex, as well as a dairy and cafe. It's a busy place in summer, but if you are looking for solitude, you'll find it half way down Whitipororua Rd, where there are turn-offs to two separate beach access roads. Whangamata Peninsula Rd to the right, is a 10 km forestry track that's as hard on your tyres as any road in the country, but offers access to Te Ananui Beach, plus spectacular views south over Whangamata from the loop walk at the end of the road. The road to the left is similar in nature and leads to Pokohino Beach after 7km, which is a beaut spot for a picnic or a day lazing in the sun. It is a pretty steep track down, but a popular fishing spot for the land based guys who don't mind walking. Both gates are locked in the evening at 7.00pm.
Onemana Beach Chalets (07)865 8623.
Onemana Spa and Gym 027 252 0077.

3. Whangamata

As much as anywhere in NZ, it is the presence of a world class wave that has driven the development of "Whanga". It is an out and out surf town, with a permanent population of 5,000, that swells in summer to 30,000, and is one of New Zealand's most popular holiday spots, with a long reputation for partying. While there always seem to be a few people in the surf, it's a particularly busy place in large east swells, when the Whanga Bar comes alive, with some of the country's best lefts, breaking off the sandbars created at the rivermouth at the north of the bay. It is a long, hollow, and now extremely crowded wave, that's best on incoming tides in a west wind. The beach break is as consistent as any on the Coromandel, though the quality of the waves on the beach isn't a patch on what happens out on the bar. Due to the popularity of the town and the concentration of housing it has spawned, there have sadly been a number of issues involving the health of the estuary. The first problem (as it so often is), was sewage contaminating the water. The next was more insidious as the mangroves started aggressively expanding into areas siltified by erosion, caused by deforestation upstream. And the third is the not fully realized impact of the marina development, that was completed in 2010. Whangamata wharf at the south end is a popular family fishing spot, but don't expect too many trophy fish. There's a community website for accommodation options www.whangamata.co.nz. **Whangamata Beach Hop** www.beachhop.co.nz

4. Whiritoa

Whiritoa at first glance promises to be a bit of an Onemana; cute but a bit sterile. But it's a stunner. It shelves steeply, which can create sucky, powerful waves at lower tides in peaky swells, and while that's a good thing for surfers, it makes swimming a little treacherous. Those less confident in the water should be cautious of the shorebreak when there's a swell running. At the north end is a small lagoon, from where there's a short walk to Waimama Bay, and at the south you'll find a bush walk to the blowhole. There's also a useful amount of shade offered by the pohutakawas growing along the beach foreshore. Facilities include **Ocean Curves Beach Store** to the north by the beachfront reserve, plus there's a surf club, public loos and kids play area. **Whiritoa Surf Lifesaving Club** (07)865 9045.

Onemana

Whangamata Bar

THE BAY OF PLENTY

A region with two distinctly different personalities, it occupies a significant portion of the central North Island's east coast, extending nearly 300 km in a gigantic semi-circle from Waihi to Cape Runaway, with sparkling beaches and harbours to the west, and a more moody, eastern shoreline offering a dramatic change in tone. Named by Cook in 1767, who must have felt he had found paradise when he sailed around Cape Runaway and glimpsed west, it delivers a significant percentage of the global kiwifruit crop, as well as a copious harvest of grain, dairy and timber; and if there was such a thing as a Kiwi smile harvest, it would account for a fair percentage of that too. The Coromandel may receive more attention in the tourist brochures, but the Bay of Plenty quietly lives up to its name, going about its business offering spectacular waves, sensational fishing, beautiful swimming conditions, and some of the highest sunshine hours in the country. People move to the bay for all these reasons, and visitors to the region will also quickly work out that you don't have to look too hard to find your fun here; as like a lady of the night, the bay happily displays her fabulous charms to all who pass by.

Travelling A coast road runs almost its entire length, with only a few minor diversions inland. **Bay of Plenty Tourism**, 95 Willow St, Tauranga, (07)577 6234 www.bayofplentynz.com

The Western Bay Also known as "The Sunshine Belt", the coast extending from Waihi Beach to Whakatane is about as different from its neighbour as you can imagine. The West is a study in wide open spaces, with its miles of expansive, golden beaches, split by meandering harbours, backed by low dunes, farmland and orchards. It is a thriving agricultural and horticultural province, boasting New Zealand's busiest port, offering a quality of life second to none. Visitors flock to some of the country's most lively summer holiday towns in their thousands, but while the Coromandel Peninsula lies deserted for much of the year, The Bay is populated by lifers and fulltime residents who appear to want to have their cake and eat it too.

The Eastern Bay By contrast, it's off the beaten track for most; a curious hundred and fifty kilometres of rocky shores backed by brooding mountains, with very few people and fewer facilities. Maori culture sits at the heart of the communities here, and life is centered around the Maraes. Arable land is sparse, economic opportunities few, and tourists thin on the ground. Perhaps that's why I love visiting it so much.

Matata

Ruakokere

Surfing Like the remainder of the North Island's east coast, The Bay only receives swell from the north and east, generated by cyclones, or off squash-zones between systems in the mid-Pacific. Cyclones generally occur between December and May, and in a good summer we will see several swells of two to five days duration. However some years, there may be only one or two. There is a fair old choice in the wider area on any swell if you are seriously chasing surf, but there is a bit of distance to drive to cover all the options. The orientation of the coast ranges from north-west around Te Kaha, to due east in Waihi, with all stops in between on the way around, which obviously helps in the search for offshore winds. While there's choice in the orientation, there aren't many reefs or points; but you can't have everything.

Fishing You'll find superb fishing right across the region, with a healthy share of shellfish in the sand too. Good boat launching facilities and varied habitats offer opportunities for landing all main NZ's main recreational fish species here, but land-based activities are primarily confined to beach fishing.

Swimming Without doubt you'll find some of the best swimming coasts in the country here, with some of the biggest, emptiest expanses of pristine sand in NZ. Sadly there are also some dirty rivers too. Lifeguards patrol the busy beaches in season, and prevailing winds blow offshore giving rise to consistently calm conditions. **Environment BOP** 0800 884 880 www.boprc.govt.nz

Matakana

Waihi Beach and Bowentown

Waihi Beach quite suddenly marks the start of a major change in geography from the rocky, indented and mountainous Coromandel Peninsula, to the wide open spaces of the Western Bay of Plenty. It is a long and open beach like the Mount, and it gets surf like Whangamata, but that's where the similarities end. Waihi has always been the poor cousin to these more glamorous neighbours, but it has grown in leaps and bounds in the decades since I lived there as a surf-hungry teenager in the early eighties. Waihi benefits greatly from being in a central position, from which a number of beaches either side can be enjoyed; also giving easy access to the northern reaches of Tauranga Harbour, which has its own unique coastal culture and marine habitats.

Travelling You will find quite a few different accommodation options in Waihi beach, ranging from the campground to top-end private rentals. www.waihibeachinfo.co.nz

Surfing There's surf all along the beach, with the best banks often nearer the harbour entrance, but despite its reputation, Waihi isn't the greatest spot due to its flat profile. If you're there and it's pumping, then of course go surfing, but on any given day somewhere else nearby will almost certainly be better than Waihi. **Sunshine Surf School** (07)863 4857 www.sunshinesurfcoaching.co.nz

Fishing There's plenty of good land-based fishing in the area, with access to the Tauranga harbour adding to the number of ways you can get a feed. **Bowentown Boating and Fishing Club** has a great clubroom and hard ramp facing into the harbour for all-conditions launching. Willy Priestly is club captain (07)863 5006.

Swimming With all the options including Anzac Bay and Orakawa, plus an active surf life-saving club, it's a fantastic place for families. **Waihi Beach Surf Life-Saving Club** emergency (07)863 5144, or general enquiries (07)863 5108.

WIND ROSE

SWELL ROSE

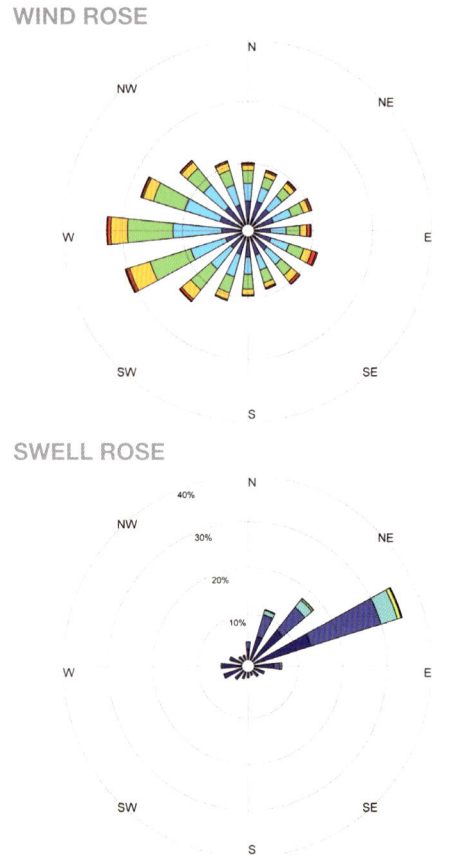

1. Orakawa

Really the last of the Coromandel spots before the landscape abruptly changes, it is fittingly one of the finest, and a contender for NZ's best beach, with gorgeous white sand, a long line of pohutakawas spread out on the slopes behind it, the little stream to the north, and rocky headlands at either extremity.

Orakawa

Located a thirty minute walk north from Waihi Beach along a well maintained track; the surf is often a foot or so bigger and a fair bit punchier than at the main beach, plus there are plenty of good mussels and snapper to be had off the rocks between Orakawa and Waihi. There is a longdrop toilet on the ridgeline, just before you descend down to the beach.

2. Waihi Beach

Stretching south for 7km, Waihi is longer than most of the Coromandel's beaches, but probably due to the influence of the harbour, has a much flatter profile than many of those to the north. As a consequence, it shows waves a lot, but few are rideable. As a swimming location it's fantastic, because even when there's surf, it breaks into crumbly whitewater way before the shoreline. The beach itself has never been a world class fishing spot; for that, you need to visit the extremities. It has a sort of twin resort (Bowentown), at its southern end, and the two are joined by Seaforth Rd, but separated by the Bowentown reserve, which is 3 or 4 km of uninhabited land in the centre of the beach. The Waihi pub and RSA are legendary, and there are a wide range of accommodation options, cafes and now licensed eateries, that are all worth visiting. To cap it off, it has a laid back and unpretentious feel that has always endeared itself to me. **Waihi Beach Top Ten Holiday Park** is a resort-style campground with every facility imaginable (07)863 5504 www.waihibeach.com. **The Luv Shack B&B** (07)863 4848. **Bill and Lyn's Beachmart** doubles as an info centre (07)863 5500.

3. Bowentown

The southern half of Waihi Beach is backed by the Bowentown Reserve; with the community of the same name clustered at the extreme end of the road, where you'll find a cafe, boating club, campground, and a mixture of permanent homes and holiday baches. The camp faces the Pacific, situated just before the headland which protects the harbour entrance. This was once a significant and strategically crucial pa, that today offers great views, and access to some highly productive, land-based fishing spots around its base. Cave Bay is the beach below it, facing into the harbour, and is a good place to find privacy; but be wary of the current. **Bowentown Beach Holiday Park** (07)863 5381 www.bowentown.co.nz

4. Anzac Bay

A sheltered, sandy, inner harbour beach with a long history as a bathing spot from yesteryear, when people were less interested in playing in pounding surf than we are today. The sheltered water is as attractive now as it was then, especially if there's swell on the main beach at Bowentown, when it's just a stroll over the hill to find this oasis of calm. It offers easy parking, public loos in the reserve, plus small-boat launching and some great fishing.

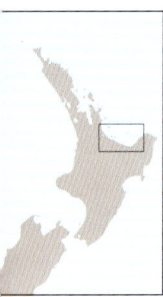

Tauranga Harbour and Matakana Island

There are several good reasons for Tauranga's location, the main one being that it sits at the head of a huge, fertile and sheltered harbour, that offers easy access to the open ocean, yet is protected by the Mount and Matakana Island from swell out of the east. It is consequently New Zealand's busiest port and also a well used recreational resource, offering safe swimming, plus calm boating, water-skiing and sailing. It has some of the best harbour fishing in the country, producing large specimens of many species, plus Matakana's world class waves, to add to the mix. For the hundred and ten thousand lucky residents of one of the country's most vibrant small cities, who have all this on the back doorstep, you would have to say, "You made a good choice!"

Travelling Tauranga I-Site, 95 Willow St, (07)578 8103 www.bayofplentynz.com **Adventure Bay of Plenty** run guided tours in the area 0800 238 267

WIND ROSE

SWELL ROSE

Surfing Matkana Island gets world class waves, but access issues restrict the crowds somewhat. Most people take private boats from the Pilot Bay boatramp at the Mount. Paddling across can be highly dangerous, especially on a big outgoing tide.

Fishing Snapper, kahawai, kingfish, mullet, mackerel, trevalley, john dory and flounder are just some of the species caught regularly in the Tauranga Harbour and its tributaries. There are a number of deep channels and holes that fish well for snapper, as do the islands and middle-harbour banks, and big snapper are not uncommon. The kingies are suckers for a marker buoy and any baitfish that hover around them, while the areas of flat water are where you'll find the flounder. It's harbour fishing; so you need lots of lead, and you need timing to line up preferred tides and change of light. Tauranga Gamefishing Club (07) 578 6203 www.tgfc.co.nz

Swimming Harbours rarely offer great swimming and this one is no exception, with marginal water quality in the populated areas. There are a few ok spots at high tide, but low tide is a bit of a grovel.

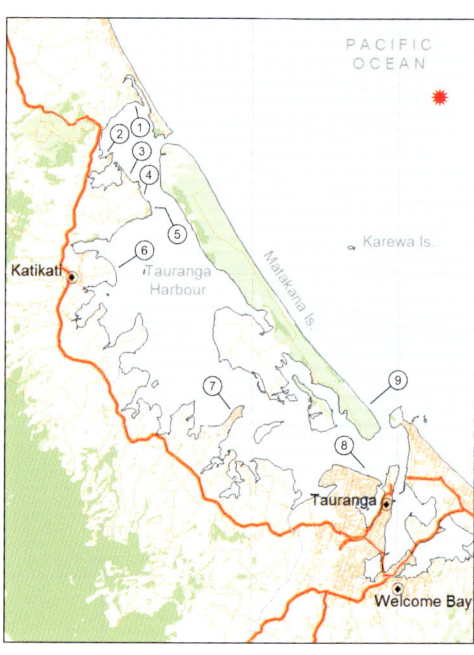

1. Athenree
Heading south from Waihi, the turnoff for Athenree leads to the first of a series of shallow and tidal inner-harbour access points. **Athenree Hot Springs and Holiday Park** has tent sites and cabins, plus two mineral pools which are free for paying guests (07)863 5600 www.athenreehotsprings.co.nz

2. Tanners Point
A sheltered wee spot with a handful of homes adjacent to a particularly deep channel of water, where you'll find one of the few moorings for larger boats in the area. There's a good all-tides ramp within sight of the north entrance, and a well maintained jetty that offers some exciting fishing prospects.

3. Tuapiro Point
Twenty five one acre sections with homes on them sit adjacent to a flat piece of foreshore that attracts the local pony club, the sailing club, and families looking for a bit of space to walk the dog and let off steam. Deeper water comes in close here, though its still only a few feet deep at high tide. **The Point** boutique winery and lodge www.thepointlodge.co.nz

4. Ongare Point
This settlement consists of 50 or so homes spread along a few hundred metres of highly tidal foreshore, that's sadly plagued by sea lettuce. It is quaint in a muddy sort of way, though hardly a destination location, with little to offer fishermen or swimmers other than a bit of company and some public loos.

5. Kauri Point
Kauri point historic reserve is a tree-lined patch of grass that is devoid of human habitation. The main feature of note here is the wharf, situated before a bend in the harbour, and adjacent to a deep channel, with a fair amount of current running past it. All of this screams kingfish, and some 50lb plus fish have been taken here. Public amenities include decent loos and bins.

6. Katikati
Beach Rd takes you to the MacMillan reserve, with its snippet of highly tidal beach, a small patch of grass and a parking area. What is unusual about this spot is the long concrete boat ramp extending far out onto the mud flats, lined by guide poles. It is a campervan-permitted spot with public loos and bins.

7. Omokoroa Beach
A peninsula juts into the harbour roughly half way between Tauranga and Waihi, with sheltered anchorage and the wharf where the Matakana ferry runs from. Near the jetty there are a couple of strips of sand where you can swim. It's a pleasant enough spot and a lot of other people agree, as evidenced by the number of homes in the area. There's a busy boating club with a beautifully situated clubroom overlooking the harbour. Their boat ramp is popular with both the water ski/wake board community (who access the ski lanes around Motuhoa island), and fishermen. Amenities include a cafe, restaurant, toilets, and picnic tables. **Omokoroa Thermal Holiday Park** (07)578 0857 www.omokoroa.co.nz

Tauranga

8. Tauranga City Beaches
Tauranga has an extensive foreshore but it flatters to deceive. At high tide it glistens and sparkles, but low tide presents a vastly different face. Starting from the north, Tilby's Rd is deep in suburban Otumoetai, and leads you to Kairero or Tilby's Point, as it is now known. It marks the start of the reserve that runs to Ferguson Park. There's a beach of sorts and a boat launch ramp here, but a rather grim sign warning against collecting and eating shellfish due to pollution was enough to put me off. It is a popular windsurfing and kite-boarding location, with toilets and a lot of grassy space, plus campervans are permitted to stay here for 2 consecutive nights. Beach road and Kulim Park are the next accessible spots. Kulim Park in particular is a lovely area but very shallow again, and plagued by sea lettuce. Tauranga Yacht and Powerboat club have their HQ here. Further south, Harbour Drive skirts a very shallow part of the foreshore, that's unswimmable really, until you get to Maxwells Road, which houses a small patch of steeper beach facing across the channel towards the marina, that's popular with families in summer. There are various other beaches towards Welcome Bay including Mangatapu, but they too are shallow and tidal.

9. Matakana Island
Matakana protects the entrance to Tauranga harbour, with 25km of rippling white sand, backed by dunes and pine-forest for much of its length. The island is a farm, but also has a number of holiday baches on it, that was pioneered as a surf spot by Al Byrne, Kevin Jarrett and others. Logan Murray's classic shots of Puni's Farm and The Bag of Granny's appeared as fold-out posters and covers in many of the world's leading surfing magazines, alerting not just those in New Zealand, but surfers all over the globe, to the quality of the waves which break at the southern end of the island. It remained an unpopulated surf spot for many years, but that's not the case any longer, as evidenced by the number of boats anchored up on any swell nowadays. It can break all through the tide, and handles plenty of swell. Offshores are south-west. The Matakana car and passenger ferry runs from Omokoroa Wharf to the inland side of the island and costs $22.50 (cars) and $3.00 (passengers) one way.

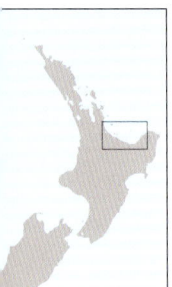

Mt Maunganui and Papamoa

The Mount, or "Mauao" as it is affectionately known, is the quintessential Kiwi summer beach town. Literally millions of holiday makers have made a pilgrimage here at some stage, and there have been many serial offenders over many generations, who have contributed to its transition from the sleepy little collection of seaside baches it once was, to the busy and built-up place it is today. Infamous for its festive season free-for-alls, New Year's Eve at the Mount used to be a riot; literally. Bogans in v8's would do wheelspins up and down Marine Parade and beer would flow conspicuously. Fights were common and at times, the air would be thick with flying bottles. It's embarrassment of riches eventually led to an explosion of interest by a slightly better heeled holidaymaker, and it seemed almost overnight The Mount morphed into our version of California, with its boardwalks, processions of yummy-mummys, cyclists, exercise freaks and surfers all doing their thing; while tourists happily laze and watch from the cafes and the beaches. The Green House has gone. The Bogans have (sort-of) gone, and while some of the architecture behind the main beach should be pulled down by public order, the atmosphere always seems really up-beat. Papamoa too has also become exceedingly popular, with beach-front homes extending almost all the way to the end of Papamoa Drive. It has a different flavour and less tourists, but it's essentially the same beach.

Travelling There are a couple of campsites at either end of the beach, numerous apartments to rent, and a few B&B's and backpackers. Mt Maunganui I-Site is on Salisbury Ave (07)575 5099

WIND ROSE

SWELL ROSE

Surfing There are quite a lot of choices without a huge amount of variety. All are sand bottom beach breaks, but neither The Mount nor Papamoa like huge swells. The council got sucked into trying to rectify this by commissioning a failed artificial reef at Tay St, which is now more of a hazard than a benefit (take a bow ASR). **Bay Boardriders** (07)576 2951 www.bayboardriders.co.nz. **Hibiscus Surf School** 027 279 9687 www.surfschool.co.nz. **The Mount Surf Museum** www.mountsurfshop.co.nz

Fishing There's some good land-based fishing off the reefy headland which protects Main Beach, and off Leisure Island. You can find tutauas all down the beach, and where there are tuatuas, there are snapper at change of light. **Mt Maunganui Sports Fishing Club** www.mmsfc.co.nz

Swimming It's home to a range of beautiful swimming beaches of all kinds: sheltered/exposed, clothed/unclothed, with lifeguards at Main Beach, Omanu and at Papamoa. Water quality is good

1. Waikorere/Pilot Bay

Stretching from Salisbury Rd to the base of Mauao, is Pilot Bay. It is a harbour beach, so is a calm, sheltered place for a swim and probably the safest in the area. Flanked by a row of large Norfolk Pines that offer useful shade, and backed by a grassy reserve with picnic tables and public loos in the middle, it's a popular place for families with small children to picnic. The Salisbury Ferry Berth Wharf and The Mt Fishing Club buildings are at the western end, and offer good wharf fishing and a good place to get a beer and a meal respectively. The beach is a popular spot to launch waka and small sailing boats, and the

boat-ramp at the eastern end near Adams Ave, is a busy little place from well before first light, especially if there's a swell, or good fishing conditions.

2. The Entrance Beach
You have to walk around the base of the mountain for 15 minutes to get to this beautiful little north-facing patch of sand, that juts right into the harbour entrance, looking over to Matakana. It's a really pretty place for a picnic, but has no amenities.

3. Main Beach, Mt Maunganui
While the east coast doesn't get as many swells as you would wish, Main Beach can often be the best place to surf due to its steep shelf, with a range of peaks down its length. Moturiki (Leisure Island), with its blow hole at the end, marks the southern end, and in a big swell you'll sometimes get good rights breaking off its north side, with the advantage that you can jump off the rocks or use the rip to get out back here. The section of beach south of the island is known as Shark Alley. It is more protected and usually smaller in a north-east swell, but it's less crowded than main beach, and popular with tourists. The old campsite located at the base of the mountain is both handy, and an iconic piece of Kiwiana that should be preserved in its current state. The nearby saltwater hot pools are open from dawn till 10.00pm most nights, and are a neat way to start or finish a good day in the sea, or as a winter tonic. Of course the beach is dominated by Mauao, and it's a well loved resource of importance to local iwi and pakeha alike. It's an hour up and down, or 40 minutes around for most fit people. **Beachside Holiday Park** (07)575 4013. **Cosy Corner Motor Camp** (07)575 5899 www.cosycorner.co.nz

4. Tay St Beach
As you leave the protective shadow of Leisure Island, you are on Ocean Beach, which runs almost uninterrupted till Maketu, with different names along different stretches. Tay St is the first named part of this long beach and it has always been one of the most consistent places at the area to find a good sandbank, though apparently the failed artificial reef has created marked rips here, so beware.

5. Omanu Beach
Marine Parade ends south of Tay St, where it turns into Ocean Beach Rd, and from here on down you'll find homes built along the foreshore, with a number of walkways to the beach between the houses, where you'll often be able to find a quiet spot to yourself. This is the start of Omanu Beach. Keep driving along Ocean beach Road and there are several different access roads to the coast. The Omanu Surf Lifesaving Club is located at the end of Surf Rd, and there are often good banks here. **The Omanu Beach Surf Lifesaving Club** is the biggest in the Bay of Plenty (07)575 4805 www.omanubeach.co.nz

6. Papamoa
Eventually Ocean Beach Rd transforms into Papamoa Beach Rd. Unsurprisingly, this marks the start of Papamoa Beach. It has always been the sleepy end of town, once known as "nappy valley," with fewer crowds and less development, though it would be difficult to make that assertion any longer, as it is all systems go at Papamoa these days. Gone are the beat-up old shacks, and rapidly going is the reserve itself which has been swallowed up by holiday homes of dubious architectural merit. The surf can be good down this end of the beach, and usually less crowded, especially in front of the reserve, where access is more difficult. The stretch in front of the Papamoa Domain from Sunbrae Rd to Domain Rd is a renown nudist beach. Papamoa Lifeguards at the end of Domain Rd, have a good surf cam on their website www.papamoalifeguards.co.nz.
Papamoa Beach Top 10 Holiday Resort has extensive facilities and an array of accommodation options (07)572 0816 www.papamoabeach.co.nz

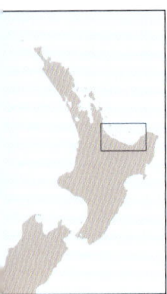

Maketu to Pukehina

This is officially the end of the Western Bay, and feels like a landscape and a province in transition. You arrive in Maketu and immediately notice the difference, both socially and physically. Gone are the high rise apartments and flash beach homes of Waihi, The Mount and Papamoa. Te Puke is a warm-up, heralding the agricultural heart of the bay. Maketu introduces you to the Tangata-Whenua. The Maketu region features several kilometres of sparkling sand either side of Town Point, with a fairly large resident population, and a more traditional lifestyle than you'll encounter in the towns further north.

Travelling The fact you have to deviate from the main road to get here is one reason it remains less popular than many surrounding areas of coastline. But it's a deviation worth making if you are the kind of person who enjoys a bit of space alone on a beach.

Maketu Estuary

WIND ROSE

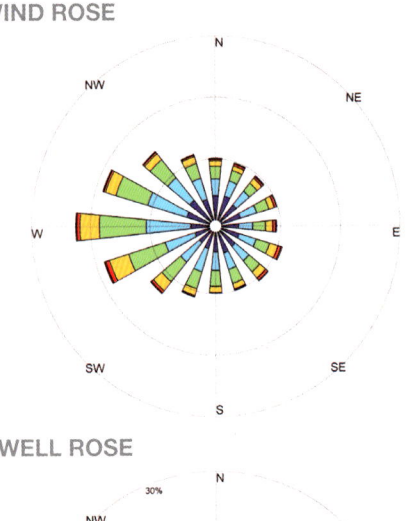

SWELL ROSE

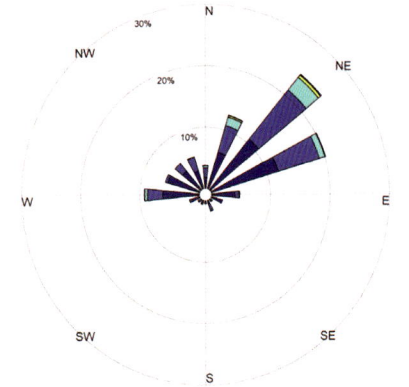

Surfing There are some great waves in the area, with the variety in the orientation of the coast presenting a fair few wind and swell options. Maketu can get a bit busy, but other than that, you'll be surfing with a handful of people. **Te Arawa Boardriders** (Maketu/Rotorua Lakes) (07)346 1685

Fishing Both Waihi and Maketu estuaries are ancient bread baskets, and the local communities are still reliant on fishing and gathering shellfish for daily subsistence. Given the mix of pressures on waterways and seafood stocks, there are some big issues here. This seems to be a critical period where we can manage this resource for the future, or lose it.

Swimming The great thing about Maketu is there will usually be somewhere out of the wind and swell, due to the headland and the harbours either side; with surf life-savers at both Maketu and Pukehina.

1. Kaituna Rivermouth/The Cut

The first spot where you can easily get out to the coast south of Papamoa is called The Cut, which is a man made deviation of the mouth of the Kaituna River. Driving down the road which flanks it, you first come to a settlement with a boat ramp and some moored vessels. Ramp fees of $2.50 are payable in front of the house there. The mouth itself features a reasonably sized breakwater which makes an excellent position to target the once sensational runs of kahawai into the rivermouth. I say "once sensational" as this is one of the worst affected rivers in the country from siltification and effluent run off from the Rotorua lakes, and the numbers of kahawai are a pale shadow of what they were only a few years back. That said, it can still turn into a bit of a rugby scrum trying to get a line in on a busy day, as the area attracts not only the local crew, but also many of the seasonal workers from the Te Puke region. It can also have grinding waves off either side of the mouth, with substantial sandbanks created by the rivers flow, that hold a bit of size. South or south-west winds are offshore. Obvious issues present themselves with fishermen casting lures from the pier and also boats launching in the river, both of which can be hazardous for surfers. It is a sandfly plagued location and the only amenity is a very basic long drop.

2. Maketu

Maketu sits on a sprawling cockle-filled estuary, protected to the south by a headland of ample proportions called Town Point. This is apparently where Te Arawa waka landed in 1340, and as such is a place of special significance for local Iwi. A memorial erected to commemorate this epic navigational feat looks out over the river and across to the multitude of seabirds that congregate on the northern spit, which is a popular bird watching area. There are a variety

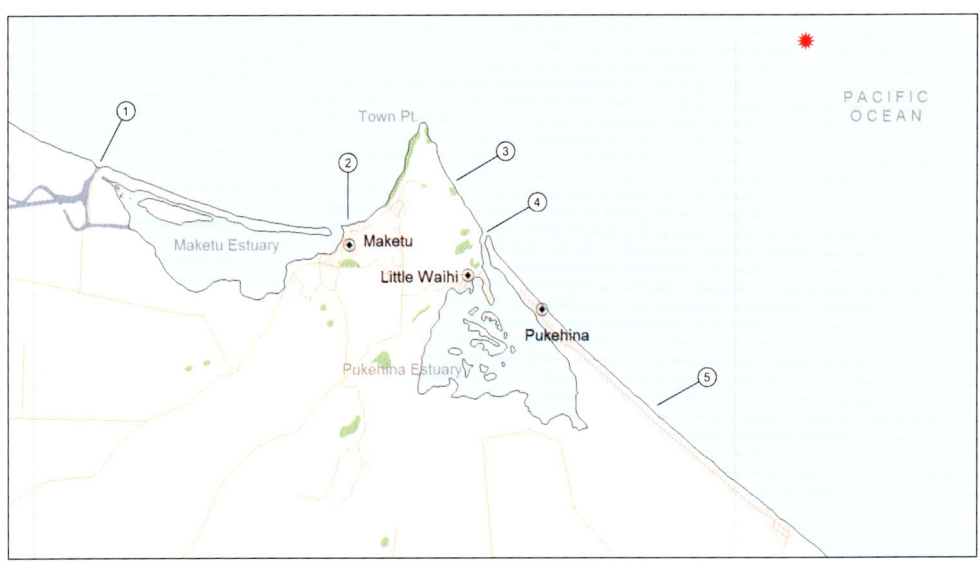

of waves in the area, including the lefts and rights peeling off the estuary mouth, plus several kilometres of beach peaks to the north that are guaranteed to be less crowded than those in front of the carpark. A mysto spot out on the headland can break in big swells, but it's a rare occurrence. Maketu faces north/north-east and receives some shelter in a big east swell. Offshore winds are from the south and you can get both fish, waves, and sheltered swimming here in a south-east wind, which is worth remembering, as it is a wind that can be a blight on the rest of the bay. The estuary is handy for launching and retrieving boats, while land-based fishermen will find some good spots out on the headland, around the mouth, and up the beach. The sleepy little town of a thousand occupants supplies most basic food needs, including a licensed cafe and fish and chip shop on the foreshore overlooking the beach. Maketu pies are the bomb! **Maketu Beach Holiday Park** (07)533 2165 located right on the beach, has cool log cabins and motel rooms as well as camping sites www.maketubeach.co.nz.

Pukehina and Little Waihi

3. Newdicks

Newdicks lies on the southern side of the headland that shelters Maketu. It is a popular surf spot that picks up all east swell going, backed by tree-lined cliffs and sheltered from west and north-west winds. The bottom is a sand covered patch of reef that continually changes, but always seems to have a range of interesting peaks, that generally pack a decent punch. Newdicks is easiest to get to by driving to the end of Town Point, where there's a gate and a sign laying down the rules, which are that to access the beach from here, you cross a privately maintained road. Hours of use are limited from 6.00am to 6.30pm in summer and 9.00am till 5.00pm in winter. It costs $4 for a car, and $6 for a camper, but walking is free; it takes ten minutes. However there has been some stress around parking at the top of the road, with one of the local residents reportedly calling police with glee if you park illegally. The alternative is by walking or 4wd from Little Waihi. There are no amenities here other than a long drop toilet behind the beach, so pack it in and pack it out. **Briars Seaside Rides** (07)533 2582, will make you giddy up with glee www.briarshorsetrek.co.nz

4. Little Waihi

At the entrance to the Waihi Estuary, you'll find a campsite and stretch of beach called Little Waihi. It is easily accessed by driving over the hill from Maketu, and once there, can in turn be used to get to Newdicks Beach. In fact the two merge seamlessly at low tide. It is a short walk out to the beach and further on to Newdicks from the carpark. There are excellent waves in front of the estuary, on both sides, with powerful peaks and an epic left that breaks in a clean swell, usually better at lower tides; and offshore in a south-west wind. **Bledisloe Holiday Park** (07) 533 2157 www.bledisloeholiday.co.nz

5. Pukehina

The spit that protects the Waihi estuary is a 5 km long stretch of sparkling white sand that's backed by a low key, but interesting little holiday settlement, of 300-400 homes, called Pukehina. There's a useful public reserve at the south end and a surf life-saving club and large carpark to the north. Pukehina can also have some tasty peaks in small to medium swell, plus offers car access to the south of the rivermouth (see above), and all are generally uncrowded. The main beach features a steep shelf, which can cause problems for swimmers; but when the surf isn't pumping, it is a fantastic swimming spot, and also produces fish at both ends. Accommodation is limited to the campsite, or private rentals. There's a shop in the middle of the beach and toilets at the reserve by the **Pukehina Surf Club** (07)533 3934 www.pukehinasurfrescue.co.nz **Pukehina Motor Camp** (07)533 3600.

The Cut

Maketu

The Bay of Plenty | 161

The Whakatane Coast

This is the beginning of the Eastern Bay of Plenty, and Whakatane sits at the gates; its capital and commercial centre. It features some of the most spectacular beaches in the country and a rich diversity of marine habitats that are both safe and accessible. The road hits the coast south of Pukehina and runs in tandem with the railway line for nearly twenty kilometres along the Matata straights, before a deviation to Whakatane and Ohope. Miles and miles of empty beaches with the most glorious white sand stretch almost un-interrupted to "The Heads", and continue south along Ohope Beach. Whakatane itself is a busy recreational port situated inside the Whakatane river entrance, with a utilitarian feel.

Travelling Camping is the order of the day down the Matata straights with several good spots (see below). Whakatane has a range of options, as does Ohope. **Whakatane i-site** 0800 924 528 www.whakatane.com www.ohope.co.nz

Surfing In what is almost a mirror of Maketu, there are a selection of spots which work in a wide range of wind and swell conditions, with a large headland offering protection, separating two good beaches. Like Pukehina, Westend at Ohope is the most surfed spot, due to its increased exposure to east swell. Then there's the Heads which pumps in big swells and south winds. The beachies on the Matata straights pick up any swell going, with more punch than Ohope. **Salt Spray Surf School** operate at Ohope (07)312 4909. **Westend Beach Longboard Club** (07)308 4625 www.westendlongboardriders.co.nz

Fishing Whakatane is one of the sport-fishing capitals of the country due to its proximity to White Island and the fish rich waters between it and the Cape. **Whakatane Sport Fishing Club** (07)307 0334 www.wsfc.co.nz. **Eastern BoP Kayak Fishing Club** (07)307 005.Whakatane Surf-casting Club (07)312 44966.

Swimming There are a ton of excellent bathing options due to the varied coastal geography; and if you don't mind swimming in the river and harbour, you can always find some sheltered water somewhere. **Whakatane Surf Life Saving Club** (07)312 4676 or a/h (07)308 4736 www.whakatane.surf.org.nz. **Bay of Plenty Sun Club** for naturists (07)322 2031 www.gonatural.co.nz/BOPSun

1. Otamarakau
State Highway 2 hits the coast at Otamarakau, with a campsite located just across the railway line that skirts the coast road from here to Whakatane. This is the start of Kohioawa Beach, a stretch of sand that runs from Pukehina, in an uninterrupted line all the way to Matata. The spots mentioned before Matata are all just different access points to the same beach.

2. Pikowai
Next stop Pikowai, a council-run campsite with some very handy shade trees, that sits adjacent to the beach and right by the mouth of the stream that gives it's name. Pikowai means "bending river" and this is a mouth that moves like a snake through the sand with

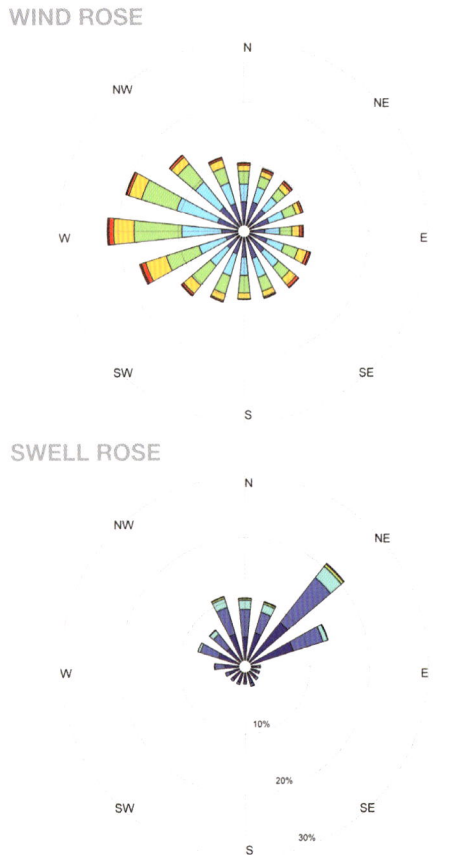

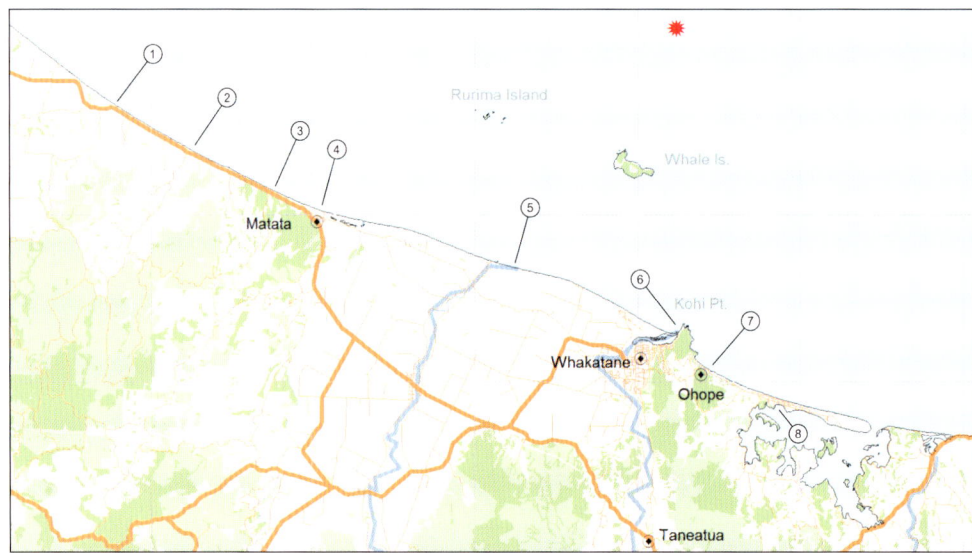

Thornton Beach

Ohope

successive storms and tides. It is a popular fishing camp, with torpedos, kites and standard beach casting all employed. It's also worth checking for waves in a swell. With such a dynamic little river, the sandbanks change constantly and anything is possible.
Pikowai Campground (07)306 0500
www.pikowaicampground.co.nz

3. Murphy's Campground
Just before Matata, you come to Murphy's campground. I didn't meet Murphy or stay in the campground, but I did get good waves and would have definitely had a fish if it wasn't 18 feet in the ocean. It is a popular surf spot, and due to its steep profile, can hold a bit of size, and has been the site of many a local surf comp in its day. There's plenty of public picnic space and parking beside (but separate from) the campsite, and even a few shade trees. As with the rest of the coast, surfcasting, kites and torpedos are popular fishing methods and snapper and kahawai are the main targets.
Murphy's Campground (07)322 2136.

4. Matata
Matata is a thoroughly unremarkable town stitched onto the side of highway 2, that was made famous after the horrendous landslides there a few years back. Turn left just after the shops heading south, and drive down the short dirt road to the beach, where you will find pretty scruffy little parking space above the dunes. There can be some good waves out the front, or nice swimming if there's no swell. **Matata Campground** (07)322 2327.

5. Thornton Beach
A developing beach community with a cluster of new subdivisions sits on the north side of the Rangitaiki rivermouth. It is a highly popular beach fishing spot, and also features a well used hard ramp inside the estuary mouth for boat launching. The waves here have extra snap due to the pronounced sandbanks formed by the river. **Thornton Beach Holiday Park** (07)304 8296 www.thorntonbeach.co.nz

6. Whakatane Heads
The town is built just inland of the river mouth on the south side of the estuary, nestled into the base of Kohi Point which offers significant shelter from south and east winds. Whakatane really feels like a port town, and the shops run right down to the water, where you will find the sport fishing club, weigh station, coastguard building, several moored boats and a slipway. It has a gritty feel to it, worlds apart from the glitz and show of the Mount, but you can get anything you could want for a beach trip here, and will find some okay restaurants and possibly some night-life as well. It's functionality as a port is aided by the fact that the bar is navigable by experienced skippers even when there's swell running. As the surf community knows, the conditions for waves at The Heads are a substantial north or north-east swell, which sadly is a relatively rare event. East swell does get in here but it will be bigger and better further north in those conditions. The main wave is a right that can peel for a hundred metres or more down the sandbars formed at the harbour entrance, but which comes and goes depending on sand flow. At time of writing, it was sectioney in parts and slow in others. There is some land based fishing around the entrance, and further out along the headland, though it is the game fishing which really draws people here.
Whakatane Holiday Park (07)308 8694 www.whakataneholidaypark.co.nz

Whakatane Heads

7. Ohope
They proudly proclaim Ohope the best beach in the world down Whakatane way, and on the evidence, they've got sufficient grounds to lodge a claim. It's certainly got a lot going for it, with nearly ten kilometres of sparkling sand, and enough facilities so you have a choice at dinner time, but not so many people so as to ruin the experience. It's a bit like Waihi Beach, except Ohope leads to the entrance of the Ohiwa Harbour. Whakatane and Ohope are divided by the Kohi Point Scenic Reserve, and if the main beach is looking too populated, you can walk from the west end of Ohope, over the hill, where you'll find a private and secluded bay out on the point called Otarawairere Beach. Westend is the most commonly surfed part of the beach, with more swell, better banks, and shelter from less than perfect winds. In a cyclone swell, there can be good waves at the Ohiwa Harbour entrance. **Ohope Beach Top Ten Holiday Park** (07)312 4460 www.ohopebeach.co.nz

8. Port Ohope
Not really a port in the traditional sense of the word any longer, but Port Ohope is a cluster of homes, with a Thai restaurant, a fish and chip shop and a busy boat ramp and slipway facing into the Ohiwa Harbour. The harbour itself is a prolific fishery with extensive shellfish beds, and all the usual issues, but all the benefits too; with kahawai, trevally and even kingies a common sight, especially in late summer. Shallow water and nearby structures mean that if you're targeting kingfish, you will lose a few before you catch a few, but its an easy and productive place for a family fish whatever you're chasing. If you keep driving past the port, you reach the end of the spit with the Otao Domain and the golf course. This is a popular picnic and shore fishing spot, where you'll find toilets, and another smaller boat launch ramp closer to the open sea. The extreme end of the spit is a wildlife refuge for breeding dotterels, and there are rumours of good waves here in big swells.
Port Ohope Yacht Club (07)312 5312.

The Eastern Bay

This is the homeland of Te Whanau a Apanui, and one of the more spiritually significant sections of our coastline to Maori. There are only a few destinations of interest to tourists with staying-a-while in mind, but even a drive-by is a visual treat of dramatic landscapes and vibrant Maori art and culture. The massive Raukumara Ranges plunge dramatically into the ocean just east of Opotiki, and the coastal topography alters significantly here, at what is essentially the start of the cape. Rocky headlands protect reefy bays, split with the odd stretch of steeply shelving sand. Local communities are predominantly Maori, and every town seems to have a more spectacular marae than the previous one. There's a sense of going back in time as you drive this coast. Life is slower. Community feeling is strong and tourists are relatively few. It emits a powerful sense of history, inspiring reverence and awe in most sensitive souls.

Travelling After Opotiki, there arent a lot of shops and gas stations, and equally not a huge amount of accommmodation choices. Opotiki I-Site (07)315 8484 www.opotikinz.com

Opotiki

WIND ROSE

SWELL ROSE

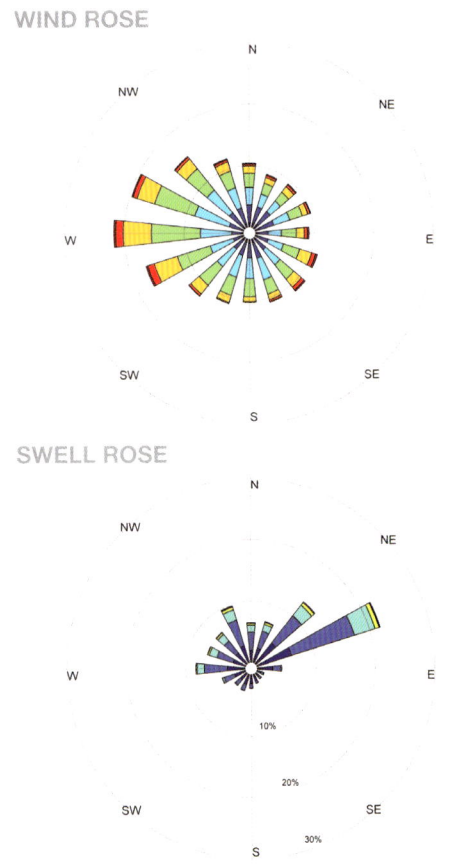

Surfing Some of the spots here can be epic on their day, but there has to be significant amount of north in the swell for it to really fire. Sadly there seem to be some really bad vibes from locals, who don't want people surfing when it gets big, as a result of the rahui that was placed on the coast after the tragic drownings of 2 surfers at Omaio during a big swell in 2004. This needs to be resolved soon before there's trouble.

Fishing All the estuaries and rivers are fertile hunting grounds, but especially the Motu River which is a particularly prolific kahawai fishery, but respect is required. Opotiki Sports Fishing Club (07)315 4859.

Swimming There is some great swimming at the sandy spots, plus the cape shelters a lot of east swell. Opotiki Surf Lifesaving Club (07)315 7526.

1. Ohiwa

On the east side of the meandering and amazingly fertile, Ohiwa Harbour, lies a section of beach sandwiched between the harbour entrance and the Waiotahi River estuary. It is divided by a rock promontory, and you'll find settlements on either side of the headland, each with separate access roads. To the west, there's an old collection of baches on Ohiwa Harbour Rd, just inside the harbour, with a fabulous campground and a few baches further east, facing the ocean. **Ohiwa Family Holiday Park** (07)315 4741 www.ohiwaholidays.co.nz. Alternatively, if you take Ohiwa Beach Rd, you'll come to another pretty beach with some private baches but no public facilities. The hillock in the middle of the spit is a burial ground and wahi tapu. **Wrightspot by the Sea** is a private bach for rent (07)315 4716. **Aurum Retreat** is a day spa with accommodation (07)315 4737 www.aurumretreat.co.nz.

2. Waiotahi

After Ohope, the first place State Highway 2 arrives within sight of the coast again is adjacent to Waiotahi

Ohiwa

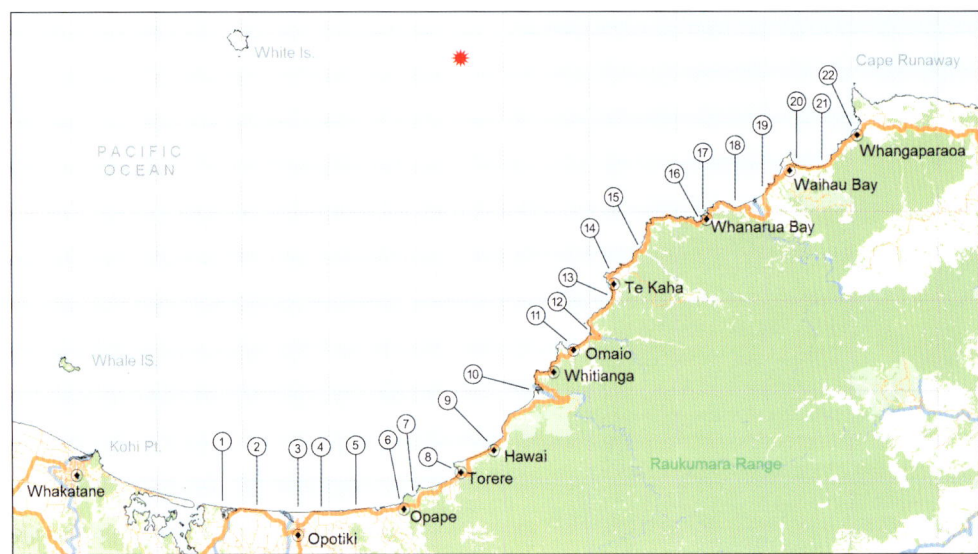

Beach. It is flat, and fairly exposed to the road, but has beautiful white sand, is backed by an incredible row of pohutakawas, and offers several pull-ins beside the beach allowing easy access. Fishing can be good especially beside the river entrance. On the eastern side of the Waiotahi stream, just before the coast, there is another great free-camping area, with toilets and a flush site. **Icon Beach Villas** (07)315 5233. **Opotiki Beach House Backpackers** (07)315 5117.

3. Opotiki
This busy little community is a living museum, with most of the buildings dating from the turn of last century, built on an estuary with a wharf, weigh-station and launch ramp at the bottom of town. It's the last real shopping hub before Hicks Bay.

4. Hikuwai Beach
Where the road hits the seashore again heading east, there's a pullover with public toilets and a sign announcing the start of Hikuwai Beach. Just before the coast, a left turn down Snells Road will take you to Te Ngaio Beach. It's just a sand road without amenities and no space to turn around, but it's a beautiful spot and more secluded than the main beach.

5. Tirohanga
With its cute little cluster of baches, beach store, gas station and campsite backing onto the Tirohanga Conservation Area, it's a great place for a sortie. There are a few access options. The most eastern point is just a pullover on the side of the road, but with a short walk over the dunes you are likely to find yourself alone on a long expanse of white sand with minimum effort. **Tirohanga Beach Motor Camp** has sites plus cabins (07)315 7942.

6. Opape
Protected by the rocky headland that forms the end of what began as Te Ngaio Beach, there's a cluster of rundown shacks with a similarly run down campsite, that's a popular beach launch spot for trailer boats. There's not much here for the casual tourist but no doubt there's good fishing off the rocks.

7. Maurices Beach
Drive down the first road on your left after Opape Rd North. It looks like it's private, but it's not! A popular surf and picnic spot that gets any swell going.

8. Torere
A shingly, open beach with few amenities, it features an impressive marae and unusual church adjacent to the main road. Some huge pohutakawas in this bay.

9. Hawai
This low key settlement features nearly a kilometre of steep, gravelly beach, with a motor camp at the north-east end, featuring a famous and fearsome looking marae. Fishing is good all round the beach, and for surfers, the eastern point by the river mouth can hold solid waves in a big north or north-east swell. South or south-east winds blow offshore and low tide is best. **Hawai campsite** (07)315 6308.

10. Maraenui/Motu Rivermouth
A powerful and historically significant piece of coast, Motu is a raging river that attracts huge schools of kahawai at many times of the year. It is a traditional bread basket, and people flock here in their hundreds at times to get a feed. The surf can also be epic, holding substantial swell when the banks are good. The river entrance has waves as does the bend in the shingle spit, which breaks like a point, but when the surf is small and people are fishing (guaranteed when its offshore), you would be insane to suit up and paddle out right where the fish are feeding. It's not a move that will endear you to anyone. There are two ways to get to the mouth. You can drive down to Maraenui, which is signposted off the main road. The access road leads past the highly impressive marae and to the shingle bank, but the last kilometre is only navigable by 4wd. Alternatively you can approach off the road to the north-east, where there's a parking area and a track leading down to the beach on the other side of the river. Be aware of the permanent rahui on fishing the mouth on Saturdays and on the 12th of the month, due to a tragic drowning in 1900. No camping is allowed and there are no amenities.

Motu fisherman

Hariki

11. Omaio
A long shingly beach with a series of reefs, connect to a small bay at the western end. The cove is sheltered from most winds and swell, and as a result you'll find a number of waka stored on the beach due to easy launching. There is a rahui on fishing in front of the Te-Apirana marae. Amenities include a large reserve, toilets, a shop/gas-station and the substantial marae.

12. Awanui
A few kilometres north of Omaio, you'll see a shingly beach protected a small island, that is connected to the mainland by a semi-submerged reef. There's a small track running off the main road at the north end as the island becomes visible, that can be used to launch small boats or kayaks. It is a beautiful spot for a snorkel or a dive, and the fishing looked good.

13. Hariki
A beautifully protected cove found just before Te Kaha, it invites you to take a dip on a hot summers day. There are no amenities.

14. Te Kaha
Te Kaha translates as "the strength" and word has it that the warriors would come here to rest after battle. Once a whaling station also, it's name refers to a few kilometres of coast that's a little oasis of north facing beaches with clear water, protected by fringing reefs. There's good fishing all year and a couple of accommodation options, as there are a few different swimming areas. Te Kaha Hotel Rd leads to a frightening modern resort that has been built for some anticipated rush by the super wealthy to come to Te Kaha and idle their summers away.

It hasn't happened and the resort is going broke. Shamefully they bulldozed the original pub to make way for this big white elephant. Further north is the beautiful main beach, called Maraetai Bay, which is protected by pohutakawa clad Wharekura Point. There is a broad grass area set aside for parking and freedom camping adjacent to the beach, with toilets and a dump station. **Te Kaha Homestead Lodge** (07)325 2194 is located in an idyllic spot amongst the pohutakawas with a spa overlooking the ocean. It is ideally set-up for fishermen, and the owner also runs a fishing charter with boat launching adjacent to the lodge. **Te Kaha Holiday Park** (07)325 2894 has everything www.tekahaholidaypark.co.nz

15. Waikawa
The name translates as "bitter water." It's a private cove, but there is a small beach north of the mouth of the Waikawa Stream with big shade trees and easy parking **Campsite** (07)325 2132. **Waikawa B&B** (07)325 2070 is spectacular with a self-contained bach also for rent.

16. Whanarua Bay
This is one of the more stunning places on the cape, a protected rocky bay with crystal clear water, with about a dozen baches adjacent to the foreshore and another handful on the cliffs above it. Access is down a one-way track with a traffic light at the top. The turn off is adjacent to the Macadamia Nut Cafe. **The Homestead** (07)325 2071 www.homesteadonthebay.co.nz. **Whanarua Bay Cottages** (07)325 2721. **Whanarua Campsite** (07)325 2132.

17. Maraehako
The ranges seem to drop straight into the sea here. Maraehako is owned, and has been for generations, by a local family. The campsite is in a large grassed area

Whanarua Bay

set behind the sand, looking out over what is in effect a private beach, watched over from the absolutely unique B&B in the cove opposite. **Maraehako Bay Retreat** (07)325 2648 www.maraehako.co.nz, is a rambling home with highly unique guest quarters, that look like something straight out of Robinson Crusoe, set flush up to the sea, in a private rocky cove adjacent to the beach, with its own private boat-ramp. **Whanarua Bay Camping Ground** (07)325 2047 is owned by the same whanau, and has clean toilets and non-potable water.

18. Papatoa Bay
A long beach with the Ruakokere River draining into its centre, but the only access is at the north-end by the urupa, where there's a grassy foreshore and some parking.

19. Patiki
Features a marae and the imposing figure of Ruakokere chapel, one of the key post colonial landmarks in the area, glowing pure white, standing alone on the end of the point. It's followed on the road east by a pretty beach, that's very rocky at lower tides.

20. Waihau Bay
Tucked into the lee of Orere Point is a cluster of buildings adjacent to a wharf and slipway. It may not be much to look at, but Waihau Bay is one of New Zealand's hottest game-fishing destinations, due to its close proximity to the northern-cape, and the deep waters beyond. It is a pretty specialized, high stakes fishing spot that attracts a hardy type of angler. They have to be because Waihau translates to windy water and this area of the cape is known for it. The Bay of Islands it is not, but on many an afternoon in summer there will be big fish on the weigh scales; yellow-fin for Christmas for the lucky ones and an assortment of large marlin the rest of the season. There are plenty of kingies around the northern tip of the cape, as well as snapper and kahawai to be taken from land. The wharf in front of the hotel is an easy spot for a family fish, and can even see the odd kingie landed in late

Waihau Bay

summer. Amenities include a pub, store, bait shop/gas station, wharf, boat ramp and weigh station. Gas here costs nearly 30% more than in Opotiki, so you would be wise to fill up before you leave town. **Waihau Bay Lodge** (07)325 3804.

21. Oruaiti
Head north-east from Waihau Bay for two kilometres. The road passes a long expanse of sand, that's backed by a few homes and some sprawling pohutakawas. It's a fabulous swimming spot that's usually deserted, and is what most people refer to as Waihau Bay when they're talking about the beach around here. It faces due north so will get surf. I've never seen it break, but it's got a fairly flat shelf so is unlikely to deliver much punch or hold any size, but the point to the north looks promising. **Oceanside Apartments** (07) 325 3699 www.waihaubay.co.nz. **Waihau Bay Holiday Park and Café** (07)325 3844.

22. Whangaparaoa/Cape Runaway
A significant and powerful region of Aotearoa, this long stretch of sand north of Waihau Bay extends to the lee of Cape Runaway, which is the western of the two capes. It marks the boundary of the rohe of Te Iwi a Apanui, with the Ngati Porou people to the east. More significantly it is known as the site where both Te Arawa and Tainui wakas first landed on New Zealand soil, and holds a position of special reverence due to this fact alone. The river of the same name drains into the eastern end in a wide mouth. This spectacular beach can be accessed with permission from Maori land owners, by taking the private road past the marae out towards the river mouth. The rocks here lead out to the cape, and the fishing is predictably good, but access is only possible half way. Ask before you go down to the beach, there are plenty of people around. If you come with respect and humility, you're unlikely to be denied. There's a tap with the most delicious spring water in front of the kura kaupapa on the main road. Visitors are welcome to drink and fill their water tanks for a small donation to the school. Other than this tap, there are no amenities here, which limits things somewhat.

Whangaparaoa

Whangaparaoa

EAST CAPE and POVERTY BAY

The East Cape is as isolated and as far from the bustle of city life as you can get in the North Island; but it is an isolation that's thick with promise and full of colour. The guarantee of pristine sandy beaches, some exceptional fishing and surfing, and the chance to be first to greet the new day, lures a steady stream of adventurous travellers from all corners of the globe. For many, the pilgrimage to the cape to see the sunrise is the only reason to visit, but those who love the ocean will find a thousand and one more. The beaches are amongst the most perfect you will see; the sense of drama and space boldly washed in crisp blue and sun-bleached white. Every corner and bend in the road seems to offer a quirky or breathtaking scene, while an air of timelessness hangs like a cloak over the whole region. Maori culture dominates the communities, and as with the eastern Bay of Plenty, each town seems to have a more fascinating marae or church than the last. Though Hikurangi Maunga is the first place in the world to see daylight, one could be forgiven for thinking that time stopped sometime last century on this coast. Many folk still travel on horse, modern amenities are few, and most of the public structures are antiques. Like the gold mine and timber towns, there is a feeling of abandonment and disrepair since the early days of sea travel. But the one thing that can never be taken by time, and that you will discover in abundance, is the majesty of the landscape and the unique spirit of the local people.

Travelling Take a bow Gisborne Council, who allow inexpensive freedom camping at a range of designated sites across the coast between September and April. You can apply online for a permit, or obtain one from the council office in Gisborne www.gdc.govt.nz/services/freedomcamping. **The Ngati Porou Visitor Centre** offers an opportunity to interact with local iwi culture www.ngatiporou.iwi.nz

Surfing One of the lesser known surf frontiers with oodles of potential and several very well known main breaks, it receives exposure to everything from northeast, to south swell. The trick is picking your spot, but it is a fair distance to drive between them, so choose well. When it is big, the various points are the places to head. On the smaller days, most of the beaches produce good peaks, with the odd river sandbar thrown in for good measure.

Fishing The variety is huge, though access to many good spots is limited and boat-launching even more difficult, with few ramps and much foul ground. The coast is renowned for crayfish and paua, though obvious pressure on the resource is keenly felt.

Swimming The beaches on the cape offer superb swimming and universally clean water, though much of the coast features a rocky, reefy foreshore, studded with intermittent patches of sand. The rocks can show through at many points, making it difficult at times to walk into the water, especially around low tide. It is easy enough to see the change in colour and worth attempting to identify sandy channels. There's not a lifeguard in sight, so exercise all common precautions when swimming.

Waihau Beach

Uawa/Tolaga Bay

Tikitiki

Lottin Point to East Cape

This is about as far as you can get from a town of substance in the North Island, and though it is the middle of nowhere, this region has a coastline that's as magnificent as they come. The huge contortions and multiple peaks of the northern cape gradually recede from the coast south of Hicks Bay, and the geography morphs into a succession of familiar cliffs and bluffs, with deeply indented bays between the headlands holding umpteen kilometres of pristine, golden sand. Statistics New Zealand estimates 2790 people live around East Cape; and Hicks Bay and Te Araroa have between 600 to 800 locals between them; so don't expect to see too much happening socially. Both towns are pretty wild and unique. Lonely Planet describes them as, "a real middle of nowhere town" and "a lone-dog village" respectively, and yet both descriptions carry too much of the negative to really reflect the character of these special places.

Travelling Few facilities and steep, winding, roads create challenges for travellers. Allow for longer than usual drive times. Te Araroa is the biggest settlement, though Hicks Bay provides for many basics and the store there seemed well priced. There's fuel at both but it's more expensive that in Gisborne or Opotiki.

Surfing Only north and north-east swell gets into this area due to the Cape, which blocks most waves from the south, but there're a lot of unexplored spots.

Fishing Some of the biggest fish in the country swim around in these waters. Lottin Point is the star attraction, a rocky location renowned for exceptional kingfish and large specimens of other species. Hicks Bay wharf fishes well for a range of table fish, as do the beaches and rocks around Te Araroa and East Cape. www.eastcapefishing.co.nz

Swimming These bays offer exceptional swimming though there isn't a lifeguard between them.

Lottin Point

1. Lottin Point

One of the most spectacular pieces of geography and marine opportunity in a country stuffed with both, Lottin Point is one of the best land-based fishing spots in the entire hemisphere. The bottom drops off to 70m nearly straight off the point, and many huge kingfish have been caught here over the years, plus it's one of the best potential spots for those targeting marlin from land. The bay itself is extremely protected from everything but due northerlies and is a divine spot for a swim, or a kayak, but the point is plagued by exposure to just about all wind directions, and thus notoriously difficult to fish. The walk in and out takes at least an hour, and as a result, if there was a location in the country to practice catch-and-release, this is it. Try lugging a big kingfish over those hills, and you may wish you hadn't caught it. There's a private boating and fishing club in an adjacent private bay just east of the main beach, but beach launching small boats with a 4wd is relatively easy adjacent to where the road ends. The only amenities are public loos. **Lottin Point Motels** sell bait and basic foodstuffs, as well as offering accommodation (06)864 4455.

WIND ROSE

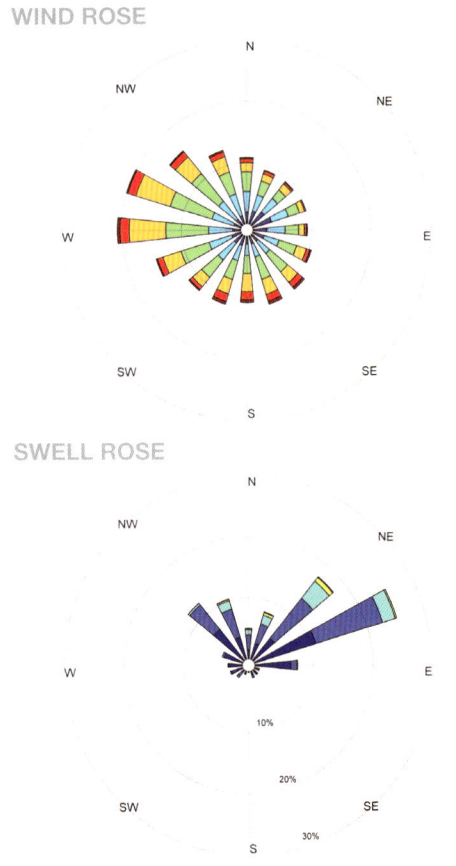

SWELL ROSE

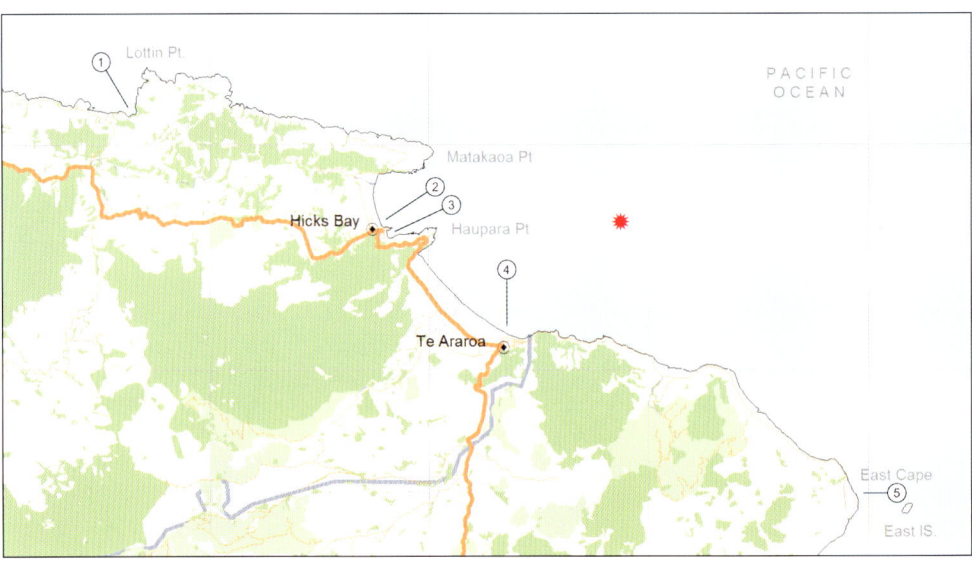

Te Araroa

Hicks Bay

2. Hicks Bay

Known by Maori as Te Wharekahika, it gained its English name from one of Cook's crew on the Endeavour. One of my favourite spots, Hicks Bay is a tiny village with a fabulous 5km long beach and a great fishing wharf at the north end. It faces almost due east, and is highly protected by extensive headlands to both north and south. The town is set back from the coast at the southern end, and public access is only possible at the extremities. The wharf consistently produces snapper and kahawai, with kingfish a common sight in late summer. It is a pretty flat looking beach with a small swell window to the due east, so waves aren't frequent and often pretty mushy. It was quite a busy place once, but no longer, with only a general store and gas station, which suits many people just fine. There aren't too many sleeping options. **Hicks Bay Motor Lodge** (06)864 4880 is a bit weird, but has brilliant views and a pool. www.hicksbaymotel.co.nz

3. Onepoto Bay/Horseshoe Bay

At the southern end of Hicks Bay is Onepoto Road, which leads to Onepoto (Horseshoe) Bay. It is a tenth of the size of Hicks Bay and features about 20 baches and ideal swimming conditions due to its sheltered nature. In an easterly there will be a few waves on the beach and the point to the south supposedly gets good in a larger east or north-east swell, at low tide.

4. Te Araroa

Te Araroa is the gateway to the Cape. It is a small, largely Maori community located at the south end of one of the most gorgeous beaches in New Zealand. Te Araroa establishes a pattern which repeats at several settlements to the south; a takeaway bar, a general store, gas station and community buildings set back from the beach, with a huge, largely undeveloped foreshore. The peaks and cliffs behind Te Araroa lend an epic quality to this charming, if dilapidated town and though limited accommodation and other tourist facilities means many keep driving after their visit to the Cape, Te Araroa is enchanting. Fishing opportunities around the river and off the rock ledges to the east will keep land based fishermen happy, and there are a range of surf spots between Te Araroa and the cape, depending on swell size and direction. The beach is steeper than Hicks and hence packs more punch, while the right point at the south side of town towards the Awatere River, is renown for grinding barrels on its day, though it needs a decent north east swell to break properly. At more than 350 years old, and featuring 22 trunks with boughs of up to 40m, the pohutakawa in the Te Araroa school ground (called Te Waha-O-Rerekohu) is allegedly NZ's biggest. You'll find public loos and a skate ramp on the foreshore road. **Te Araroa Holiday Park and Motels** (06)864 4873 is at the north end of the bay, 4 mins from the beach. It has excellent amenities, with budget facilities for backpackers, a general store and bottle shop. **Sunrise Lodge** (06)864 4854 has basic rooms and campsites.

5. East Cape

The Cape is the easternmost tip of mainland New Zealand, 20km east of Te Araroa along a gravel road that flanks some inviting stretches of pristine beach. With stunning coastline on one side and dramatically sculpted sandstone cliffs on the other, it's a visual treat all the way. After about 10 km you'll find a sparse but functional, campsite overlooking the sea, and other than the toilets at the cape, that is the full extent of the public facilities. The abundance of foul ground here presents obstacles for fishermen, but there are fish around, no doubt. Little is known about the surf here, though it must receive all north-east swell, and with so many rocks and reefy structures, anything is possible. The walk to the lighthouse from the carpark takes about 20 minutes. **East Cape Campsite** (06)864 4831. **East Cape 4wd Sunrise Tours** (06)864 4775 offer lighthouse trips, horse treks, hunting & fishing.

Hicks Bay wharf

Tikitiki to Kaiua

Sitting in the shadow of Hikurangi Maunga, this section of coast is the cultural heart of the Cape, and the social hub of the Ngati Porou iwi. Maori culture is at its most prominent here, and spectacular maraes are numerous. It's not flash, but heralds a slew of some of the nation's most spectacular beaches, that all feel like they have been chiselled out of big chunks of the coast. Most are some distance from the main road, but every one is worth a visit if your idea of fun is long, pristine and totally empty stretches of sand. Again facilities are few, and surprises are likely around every corner.

Travelling The main highway is torturous and the logging and sheep trucks present constant hazards. The roads to the beach are almost all steep and unsealed, so be on your game. Speeding anywhere is a guaranteed bad move. Enjoy the mellow vibe.

Tokomaru Bay

WIND ROSE

SWELL ROSE

Surfing A few epic spots and a host of good spots, receiving swell from north-east to south-east. Those beaches with south orientation will pick up the most swell. Cyclones or big north and east swells offer a whole new set of options according to aspect.

Fishing The same combinaton of points, and sandy beaches with foul ground scattered everywhere.

Swimming There is a huge variety of orientation and profile to the beaches. Each offers fantastic swimming, but again, there's not a lifeguard in sight.

1. Waiapu River
The small community of Tikitiki sits inland from the mouth of the Waiapu River. This isn't the most glamorous stretch of coastline in the country, but of some interest to surfers and fishermen. Take Beach Rd from Rangitukia to the coast. The road stops a couple of kilometres from the river's mouth, so to get to the best surfing and fishing spots, you'll need a 4wd. It's a steep and shelving beach, with light brown, granulated sand and plenty of midges. There are no facilities at the beach, and very few people around.

2. Reporua
It's a half hour mission down windy, steep, gravel roads to get there; and when you do, there's not much to greet you. One suspects there are hidden waves in the area, though little is known.

3. Tuparoa
When you finally get to Tuparoa, you feel a bit like Indiana Jones. Not only is the half hour drive down the gravel road both steep and windy; but for the last few kilometres it drops onto, follows, crosses and at times becomes one with the river bed that eventually

opens onto the beach. As you hit the coast, there's a camping site under the trees, with a few old caravans; but other than that, there's a lot of not much and a big open stretch of steeply shelving sand. There must be waves here, and locals fish off the beach.

4. Whareponga
Another in a long line of completely empty beaches, it's yet another 20-30 minute mission down gravel roads, and when you get there, you'll find a deeply indented bay, split by the stream bed which forms the road. The foreshore is backed by a large expanse of flat farm land, that would be ideal for camping, but for the lack of toilet facilities. Maori landowners were happy for me to spend time there, but not stay overnight for those reasons. It is quite a steep shingly beach with total exposure to south swell, a clutch of caravans to the south, and a headland to the north.

5. Waipiro Bay/Ohineaki
Waipiro is one of the jewels of the coast; a gaping ten kilometre-wide bay, with a tiny community near its centre. It is a beach of two halves, protected by massive headlands at either extremity, that once was home to thriving town based on farming and coastal shipping, but no longer. Today you'll find the

Anarua Bay

Tokomaru Bay

marae and church, a handful of homes, and a lot of empty beach. To the north, a lumpy track leads to one of GDC's freedom camping areas adjacent to the beach, then stops; offering a further few kilometres of completely untouched coast, backed by scrub and trees. If you head south along the 4wd track which leads to the farthest point, you'll find Waipiro's famed point breaks Creeks and Frog Rock. Creeks breaks off the creek to the south east of the car-park, and Frog Rock breaks closer to the beach. These aren't waves for beginners, and in a north-east or huge south swell, can get frighteningly good. In the middle of the bay are some sections of reef and sand that can hold good banks in more moderate swell, and the point way to the north is also rumoured to break. Waipiro iwi have placed a rahui on the collecting of crayfish and shellfish, but beach-fishing is fine, and the rips and sandy guts can be productive. **Te Puia Springs Visitor Information Centre** (06) 864 6853.

6. Tokomaru Bay

"Toko," as it is universally known, is one of the most colourful towns in New Zealand; deeply Maori, highly dilapidated, but intensely vibrant and completely unique. The local hapu, Te Whanau-a-Ruataupare, have four active marae in the area, all beautiful in their own way. Also known as a place where the people ride around town on horses; it features an excessively beautiful beach extending for nearly 8km, in a long arc. Beach Rd follows the coast from from the village to the north, and leads past the fabulously located pub, to the abandoned freezing works and wharf. Half way along, you will find a right reef, breaking just before the boat ramp in south swells and west winds, that can get pretty shapely. **Te Puka Tavern** (06)864 5466. **Footprints in the Sand** is a backpackers with tent sites. www.footprintsinthesand.co.nz. **The Ruins** 027 267 6561 offers two self contained units near the old works.

7. Anaura Bay

When Cook beat a hasty retreat from Poverty Bay, he sailed north to Anaura Bay, where he was warmly received by local Maori. In his memoirs, he wrote of "The profound peace in which the inhabitants lived," and you'll find it is equally peaceful and accommodating today. This is yet another breathtaking East Cape getaway that was sculpted in your dreams, and filed under the heading "unspoilt idyll". It occupies a huge scallop shaped bite out of the land, fringed with sparkling sand, and flanked by dramatic headlands at either end; offering acres of space, safe swimming and good beach fishing. No shops and only a handful of baches complete the picture. There are two campsites appealing to quite different tastes. The DOC site at the northern end is rudimentary, but perfectly located for both the beach and the Anaura Bay Walkway, which is a three hour bush walk. The private camp where the main road hits the beach is like staying in an empty school yard, but the facilities are great, and here you'll find a plaque commemorating Cook's voyage. You'll find shade at the north end but little along its length. The beach itself is too flat for good surf, but the reefs on the north side of Motuori Island produce good rights on their day, with a decent east to south-east swell and a south-west or west wind. **Anaura Bay Motor Camp** (06)862 6388. **Anaura Beachstay** www.anaurabeachstay.com. **Rangimarie Beach Stay** offers a range of options on 1.5acres of private beachfront www.anaura-stay.co.nz

8. Kaiaua Bay

Kaiaua follows the form of many of its near neighbours, but lacks some of the enchantment of the less denuded spots. It stretches for a couple of kilometres, and features free-camping along its length, with both toilets and bins strategically placed. It is a quiet spot and not unattractive, and showed most exposure to south swell and a steeper shelf; so when many nearby spots are flat, it can still have a wave.

Tokomaru Reef

Tolaga Bay to Tatapouri

Despite the increasing proximity to Gisborne, this area retains the same feel and coastal geography as the section of coast preceding it. The sense of timelessness and space remain, and the beautometer stays locked on high. It is a treasure trove of pristine bays, featuring many kilometres of empty and inviting sand, but access to the beach is limited to a few spots, that are all equally charming. Typically there are few facilities and as few people, but this turns out to be a pretty good deal if you're well organized and looking for a little bit of time and space to yourself, as you will most certainly find it here.

Travelling Before you get to Tatapouri/Gisborne, only Tologa Bay offers sustenance to travellers. Same East Cape roads, same East Cape precautions for drivers: drive to stay alive and enjoy the views.

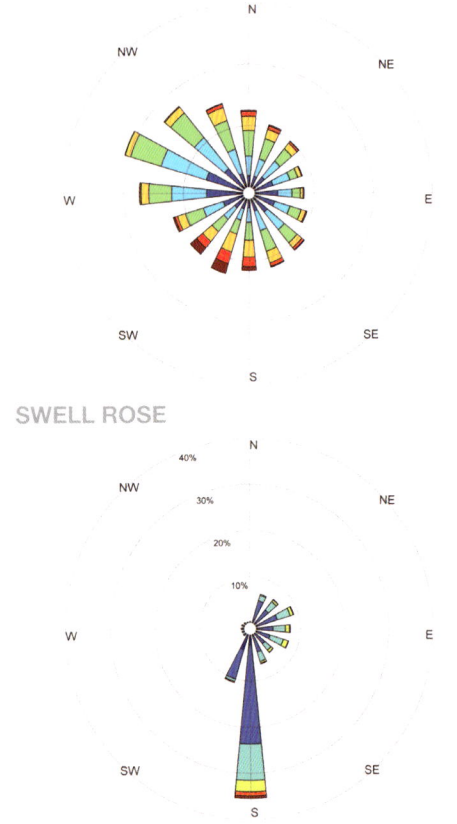

Surfing This is not the most wave-studded part of the cape, though Tologa and Waihau can be good in small south swells. Cooks Cove is rumoured to get epic waves but few have surfed there.

Fishing The marine reserve is out of bounds but the Tatapouri coast is a happy place to be a fisherman.

Swimming More sparkling, empty beaches with beautiful swimming conditions, but no lifeguards.

1. Uawa/Tolaga Bay

Childhood memories of Dad driving us all in his Vauxhall Cresta to Tolaga Bay for the weekend and watching a shark caught off the wharf, are seared in my consciousness. Revisiting Tologa 40 years later exposed the inadequacy of my powers of recollection; and for once, reality outstripped my dreams. The bay is sparsely beautiful like I remembered, but the wharf is much bigger. In fact, it is the longest wharf in the southern hemisphere. The beach is another like the others; long and white, clean and empty, but conveniently offers several access points, and has a unique and very laid back charm. It is a functional town with 3 or 4 food stores, a cafe and takeaways; and as well as the fulltime residents, there are even a few baches. In East Cape terms, that all constitutes to an embarrassment of services. The large grassed esplanade located to the north of town is a great place to laze, picnic and swim, and the surf can get really good off the rivermouth when the banks are

solid. At the south end of the beach, you will find the wharf, set amongst a tangle of driftwood, and located directly below the breathtaking cliffs which tower from the sea. Predictably, it's not a bad place to fish from. This is also where you'll find the access point to the Cooks Cove Walkway, with a campground and small shop. **Tolaga Bay Holiday Park** (06)862 6716.

Tolaga Bay

Waihau Beach

Pouawa

2. Cooks Cove

A 25 minute hike up and over the headland out to its extremity, delivers you to Cooks Cove. The walk is steep in parts though well maintained, with steps where critical. It meanders through farmland along the cliff tops, offering breathtaking views north over Tolaga Bay. When you arrive down at the coast, there's a small enclosed bay with some fascinating rock structures and a cairn to mark the presence of the great one, so many years ago. You'll find some hefty, ledging waves out here, with a point, mixed reefs and a small offshore island all warranting exploration by serious surfers in a serious swell. No doubt the same area produces fish in calmer conditions, being out on an extremity, as it is.

3. Waihau Beach/Loisells

The road to Waihau Bay, which plunges 6km off the main highway, is etched into the cliffs in a most precarious manner. It delivers you to a tiny settlement of maybe twenty baches and an open grass space for camping, directly in-front of the beach, with just a toilet, bins and some trees for shade. The spectacular descent whets your appetite; and the reality is even better. You will find is as beautiful, tranquil and unspoilt as any beach in NZ, but one that requires complete self-sufficiency. It is totally exposed to south swell and shelves steeply, so the waves are powerful. It is a good spot to look for waves when "Gissy" is small, but the shore-break is worth avoiding if you aren't a strong swimmer. Some large sections of reef in the inter-tidal zone can cause difficulties for fishermen and swimmers alike, but the sandy guts are clearly visible from above. Try and spot them and remember where they are on your way down the hill.

4. Whangara

This tight-knit Maori community, focused around the marae and church, is where the film "Whale Rider" was shot. A private road runs to the only easy access point on the picture postcard beach, which offers nothing but emptiness. It's an unknown quantity surf and fish wise, and there are no facilities at all here; so other than a fleeting visit to say you've been, most people won't linger without an invitation from local people. Nonetheless, it is a highly atmospheric spot and reminds you how great it is to live in a country where undisturbed places like this still exist. Whangara is the northern boundary of the Te Tapuwae o Rongakao Marine Reserve, which extends all the way south to Pouawa.

5. Pouawa

Pouawa is a stretch of coast adjacent to the main road as you near Gisborne from the north. It will delight you as you drive past, and delight you if you decide to linger, which is made all the easier by the GDC freedom camping site adjacent to the beach near the south end. It is a popular family camping spot that is less troubled by swell than the beaches nearer to Gisborne, thus offering safe swimming in most conditions. The north end is home to a large wetland and the southern perimeter of the marine reserve which covers approx 2450 ha of coastline. Established in 1999 as a joint venture between Ngati Konohi and DOC, it affords legal protection to at least 8 marine habitats, including inshore reef, rocky intertidal platforms and sediment flats, that are representative of the marine area between East Cape and Mahia Peninsula. The easiest place to explore is the southern tip where there's a sandy beach about 4km long, as well as the inter-tidal reef platforms around Pariokonohi Point. Crayfish numbers are getting healthier yearly, and undersea, the sponges, and kelps are just some of the delights. Snorkeling is easy in calm weather, with lots to see even on the inshore reefs. There is also an abundance bird life to enjoy. The reserve depends on the care and vigilance of all visitors. Anything threatening the integrity of the reserve is an offence. If you see anyone taking anything, please contact DOC immediately.
DOC hotline 0800 362 468 www.doc.govt.nz.
East Coast Hawkes Bay Conservancy
(06)869 0460 echb-conservancy@doc.govt.nz

6. Tatapouri

No book on the coast would be complete without a reference to the Tatapouri Hotel, which was a legendary place to get a beer, but sadly burnt down in 1996. Now there's only a campground here, with a useful boat ramp that's an out and out fishing haven, but one with significant appeal even to those whose idea of fun is doing nothing but lazing around.
Tatapouri Seaside Park www.tatapouri.co.nz.
Dive Tatapouri offers boat tours, and underwater excursions to the marine reserve and surrounding highlights www.divetatapouri.com

Whangara

Gisborne and Poverty Bay

Gisborne's place in our coastal lore was cemented from the very first moment of European contact. It was here that Captain James Cook first came ashore on New Zealand soil, after initially sighting Young Nick's Head. He named it Poverty Bay due to the highly unfavourable reception offered by local Maori, but for the beach-goer, it is far from a poor destination; offering some of the best surfing beaches in the country, some excellent fishing, and sublime swimming options. It is conveniently placed between the East Cape and Mahia Peninsula, which throws up a range of other aquatic options for those with travelling in mind, and particularly for the surf community, this contributes to its reputation as one of our surf capitals. All this, coupled with some of the highest sunshine hours anywhere in the North Island, conspire to make it a seminal summer holiday destination.

Travelling Gisborne offers all the amenities you could want, plus good campsites and easily accessible free-camping, both in town and further north. It's becoming increasingly popular with foreign travellers, and a coast road makes all the spots easy to get to. Tourism Eastland (06) 868 6139 www.gisbornenz.com

Surfing "Gissy" is home to some of New Zealand's most consistent and well shaped beach breaks, complemented by a few reefs and points, all facing in different directions. South and east swells produce a staggering variety of surf options, with prevailing west and north-west winds producing clean waves on a high number of days per year. South swells are the most common, but north-east and east swells also produce magical waves at various locations. Winter can be a particularly good season, though the water is cooler than north of the cape, due to south currents. A good selection of services and a mellow vibe, conspire to make it a fantastic place for a surf trip at any time of the year.

Fishing The predominance of foul ground and inshore reefs isn't ideal for beach fishing, but there are a lot of crayfish around for those with some snorkelling gear or a cray-pot. The Waipaoa River offers good kahawai fishing from land.

Swimming Waikanae, Midway and Wainui offer surf life-saving patrols in season. Though most spots are generally good, the water quality issues near the Wainui Stream and near the mouth of the river in town mean swimming near them should be avoided.

1. Makarori

Makarori feels like a slice of the wilderness, yet ironically is located just a few kilometres out of town. It is framed by spectacular headlands at each end, with a small, colourful community tucked into the base of the substantial hill that marks its northern boundary. The few lucky residents who live here shelter behind a spectacular flat reef that creates a unique habitat for stingrays, crayfish and paua, and also provides surfable waves in a large south swells and north or north-east winds. But the main attraction for visiting surfers is the five kilometres of sparkling sand to the south, where you'll find a range of excellent peaks, including (from north to south): Murderers, Red Bus, Creeks, Centres and the Makarori Point. Due to its orientation, the beach is most often surfed in south swells. Patches of rock extend all along its length which can be quite hazardous when entering the water, especially at lower tides, so beware. The point is legendary, but works better in an east or north-east swell, when it changes from a lazy slow mal wave into a hard breaking right of some repute. There's a great viewing point as you drive over the hill from Gisborne, and a huge carpark at the south end, plus several pullovers and access points along its length, with toilet blocks at either end.

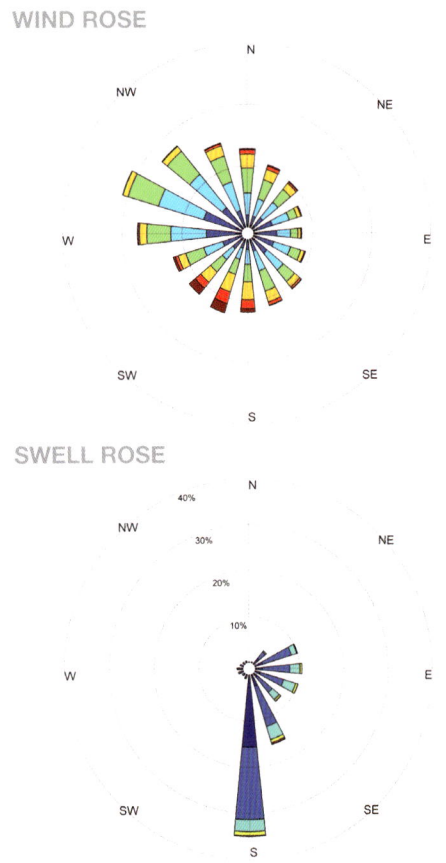

the mouth of an ancient valley that forms a cut in the surrounding hills, facing south-west. It is defined by Tuahine Point, with its impressive stratified cliffs to the east; while to the west is a small promontory that offers a perfect lookout over the bay and south towards Tuamotu Island (located just offshore). It picks up a bit of swell despite its sheltered aspect, but rarely offers good waves, though the reefs to the east can have some good longboard peaks on their day. There are a few picnic tables above the beach, and public loos in the carpark.

Makarori

2. Wainui/Okitu

One of New Zealand's most desirable pieces of coastal real estate, and as laid-back a place as you'll ever hope to visit, Wainui owns a spot in the pantheon of great NZ surf destinations due to its consistently high quality beach waves. It is separated into two enclaves, with the Wainui end to the south, while the community to the north-east is known as Okitu; though the beach itself retains the same name all down its length. The Wainui end faces further to the north, and here you'll find peaks known as (from the south): Cooper St, Stock Route, No Access, Schools, and Pines. These generally work best in east or north-east swells. The Okitu peaks, which pick up more south swell, are known as Chalets, Lone Pine and Whales (which is the name given to the northern end of the beach). Offshores vary from north-west to south-west depending on where you are on the beach. By and large, the sandbanks are pretty consistent, and it is the ability to hold solid swells and still keep its shape that's one of Wainui's distinguishing features. Facilities include two stores, plus several public loos. The surf life-saving club is in the middle of the beach, located beside the (sadly) often polluted, Hamanatua Stream. There are several reserves along the foreshore, with open areas for day trippers, and no homes on the beachfront at the Okitu end, giving heaps of picnic space and easy carparking. There's also a magazine ("Beach Life"), and a website dedicated to this coast, with plenty of accommodation options listed on it www.wainuibeach.co.nz.
Ocean Beach Motor Lodge (06)868 6186.
Wainui Beach Motel (06)868 5882.

3. Sponge Bay

One of my first ocean memories involves nearly drowning at Sponge Bay. This dimmunitive little cove is only a hundred or so metres long and sits at

Sponge Bay

Wainui Beach

East Cape and Poverty Bay | 177

Tuamotu Island

4. Tuamotu Island
"The Island" as it is known to the surf community, is an aquatic treasure, that offers a prolific marine habitat, and holds epic waves in a variety of conditions. South-west swells produce grinding lefts off the southern side (The Bowl), and in a north or east swell the rights fire up. If you don't have a boat, it's a long walk and a paddle from Sponge Bay. The best surf check point is from the top of Kaiti Hill.

5. Kaiti Beach
If you drive down Hirini St past the port entrance you end up at a kilometre long stretch of sand facing due west known as Kaiti Beach, that's protected by a fringing reef. There are a few homes nestled into the base of Kaiti Hill, and it's also home to the Gisborne Yacht Club with its quaint clubrooms, picnic tables, children's play area and public loo. This is where Cook first set foot on NZ soil, and a memorial to this event marks the spot, though it is hard to envisage today, surrounded as it is by the busy wharf complex. Gisborne Yacht Club (06)867 2004.

The Crook Cook

6. The Cut
At the mouth of the Turanginui River is a small, tree-filled public reserve that extends along the foreshore to the nearby campground. It is known as The Cut, and has public tennis courts, offers plenty of shade, and you'll see statues erected to both Cook and Young Nick along the foreshore. Due to the shelter offered by the breakwater, it's a popular spot for families with young kids to swim, though the water quality looks marginal. It's not a bad place to surf in south swells, best suited to SUPs, mals and beginners.

7. Waikanae
Probably the busiest of "Gissy's" town beaches, Waikanae extends from the camping ground to the

Gisborne

Waipaoa River

end of Salisbury Road, with access points between the beachside homes off Grey St, Roberts Road and Seaview Rd. It's popular with families and tourists looking for a dip, and has good waves in south swells. **Waikanae Beach Holiday Park** (06)867 5634 www.waikanaebeachtop10.co.nz

8. Midway
Midway faces due south and is really an extension of Waikanae. It starts at the beginning of Marine Parade and extends all the way down to the Big River. Unlike Waikanae, there are no homes on the foreshore here, giving it an open, parklike feel. Adjacent to the beach are the Olympic Pool and The Awapuni Sports Centre, plus an extensive adventure playground. Midway's main claim to fame is The Pipe. Consistent sandbars are formed on top of the town sewage outlet pipe, which extends more than 3km out to sea from here. This pipe has huge fringe benefit for the towns surfers, creating solid banks that produce some of the hollowest waves in the area in a strong south swell and north-west winds. After Stanley St, the beach begins to curve towards the east. **Midway Surf Lifesaving Club** (06)867 5500, is one of the most competitive in the country, and the club room offers a restaurant, toilets and carparking.

9. Waipaoa/The Big River
If you continue down Centennial Marine Drive to its end, you arrive at the mouth of the Waipaoa River (also known as The Big River). It is a popular fishing spot, with kahawai runs that draw locals looking to catch a feed with both rods and nets. It can also produce grinding waves in the right conditions (a huge south swell or a decent east or north-east swell), if the banks are in good nick. There are many access points to the beach along Marine Drive, but remember that the foreshore here is owned by the Kopututea Trust, so be respectful of this fact. The last few kilometres turn into clay, which cuts up quickly after rain.

10. Muriwai Beach
A gloriously empty stretch of sand, backed by a wide, driftwood strewn hinterland and the Wherowhero Lagoon, which has its mouth at Muriwai, and extends from the Waipaoa River to Young Nick's Head, with separate access points at Browns Beach Road and Muriwai Beach Rd. Either point leaves you with a few hundred metres of low dunes to cross before you get to the beach, and neither offers public amenities of any kind, but both offer splendid isolation and spectacular views, and an opportunity to swim without worrying about waves, in all but the biggest south swells. In those conditions, it can be a useful spot to check for waves. This is a breeding area for dotterels and oystercatchers so tread carefully.

The Pipe

HAWKE'S BAY

It looks like something took a giant bite out of the middle of the North Island, and created Hawke Bay. Maori named it Te Matau-a-Maui, and consider the bay to be the hook with which Maui caught the fish that is the North Island. It was given its Pakeha name by Cook in honour of Sir Edward Hawke, the first Lord of the Admiralty. These days most people think of Napier when they think of this area, but the greater Hawke's Bay region is far bigger than just Hawke Bay itself, extending as far north as the Mahia Peninsula, down to the Tararua region in the south, where it meets the Wairarapa. Hawke Bay is just the mouthful in the middle, a region famous for wine and fruit, sunny days and art deco buildings. Either side of this populated zone, the coast becomes a relative wilderness. The diversity of beachscapes on this extensive coastline is simply immense, and in many ways offers the best of all worlds to the coastal traveller. Crowds are almost non-existent, the climate is dry and hot, and while the water is chillier than the Bay of Plenty and the coast further north, it still falls into acceptable ranges.

Travelling A coast road skirts much of the main bay, making access a simple thing, though Mahia and the south coast are relatively isolated, and feature few amenities and modern comforts. Napier and Hastings are the obvious service centres. The tourist website is www.hawkesbaynz.com

Surfing When you factor the Mahia Peninsula into the equation, any surfing region is going to get the thumbs up, but even without Mahia's established pedigree, the range of different waves on offer across the province is as diverse as any on the east coast. As well as some spectacular rivermouths in the north, the southern coast offers long exposed beach breaks and untold secrets to find around the miles of empty reefs, for those with the desire and persistence to go looking. The surf population is small in number, though be warned, the "Mahitians" can get fierce!

Swimming There is such a massive diversity in the nature of the coastline, that there are almost an unlimited number of options with good water quality at most of the spots.

Fishing The crayfish and paua are plentiful, and land-based fishermen can generally get a feed of a wide variety of table fish from the obvious spots. Beach fishing is less popular than further north, but a multitude of headlands offer access to deep water and good results, and the substantial rivermouths are fertile fisheries offering prolific kahawai numbers and whitebait in season.

Mahia

Wairoa District

Rivermouth perfection

The Tooth

Cape Kidnappers

Hawke's Bay

The Mahia Peninsula

Mahia is almost an island; a long, chiselled, bleached white peninsula jutting out into the sea, that forms a perfect break between Poverty Bay and Hawke's Bay, and though geographically similar to the East Cape, emotionally, it is land unto itself. Mahia is an abbreviation of "Te Mahia mai Tawhiti" which means "the murmuring of home". This beautiful and poetic name refers to the ever-present echo of the ocean that resonates all over the peninsula, especially when there's a good south swell running. It is a superb place to spend some quality time in the sea, with a series of spectacular sandy beaches and some of the most consistent and challenging surfbreaks in the country, plus crays, paua and a host of fin-fish all around its varied shoreline. Add to this its wild countenance and glorious sense of isolation, and you'll see why it's one of my personal top ten beach locations in NZ.

Travelling The main issue for travellers is the shortage of commercial accommodation. Other than the campsite at Mahia and a few private rentals, it's all pretty sparse. There is plenty of space if you're in a camper, but few public toilets and only a few shops. www.voyagemahia.co.nz

WIND ROSE

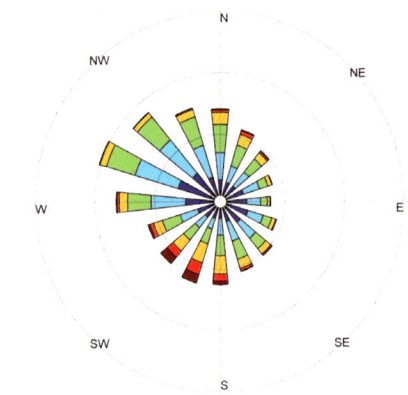

SWELL ROSE

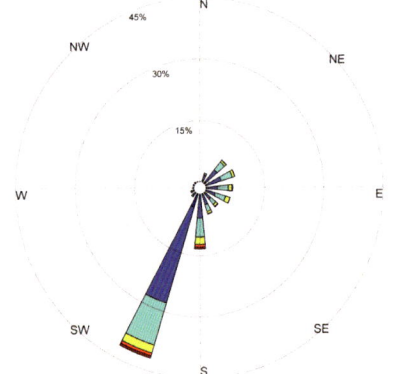

Surfing The Mahia Peninsula occupies a seminal place in NZ surf culture, with a host of spots catching swell from north-east to south-west, and quality breaks of all kinds holding all sizes of swell, with remarkably few people around. You've gotta love that; though north swells are depressingly rare, so it's the south of the peninsula that is the most surfed side. Luckily, if the winds are right, it can handle anything that the ocean throws at it. Don't be undergunned.

Fishing Both beach and rock fishing can be remarkably good, with snapper and kingies to add to the good crayfish and paua populations in the area. Mahia Boating and Fishing Club (07)836 5560.

Swimming There's clear water and sparkling sand everywhere, with the advantage here that you can switch coasts if the swell or wind is bothering you. Very convenient indeed!

1. Last Chance
So named, due to the fact that if you didn't get a wave anywhere else, and were heading back to Gisborne, it was your last chance. It is an excellent left point break that picks up most east and even some

Oraka

south swell, though access is an issue, requiring you to walk through a farmer's field at the end of Happy Jacks Rd to get there. There is an overpowering sense of being unwanted here if you're not from the peninsula, so don't expect to bring a van full of frothing grommets and have a good time, because it is likely you won't. Best to go with a local.

2. Mahunga Beach
The first spot you see as you drive from the north is Mahunga. The beach is a broad crescent of gorgeous white sand arcing nearly 5km to the east, where it finishes at Oraka. Mahunga is the western most

the hollowest barrels in the country. It requires a big north-east swell and southerly winds to light up, and even then, can be really difficult to make, with lots of people pulling in but not too many making it out of the deeper sections. A right breaks off the end that can also be fun, though it's a pale shadow of the left. A lot of boards get broken here, be warned. Further east there's a section of coast with a series of short patches of gorgeous white sand, protected by fringing reefs that are fabulous places to swim, even when there's swell. The nearshore reefs can also have good waves in small, clean swells.

5. Boat Harbour

As its name implies, this is where the locals launch their boats on the north side of the peninsula. The ramp drops off into the river, which can be a bit tricky to navigate on very low tides, but with the advantage of a deep channel out to the ocean, it is usable regardless of swell conditions. It is also home to a fantastic right-hand wave that breaks onto a reef just offshore, that can get incredibly hollow on a good north-east swell with a southerly wind. The pronounced channel means you'll be sitting in the line-up with macking waves, and the local cray boats will be motoring out and staring in as people pull into the tube. It just seems to add flavour to an already colourful surf experience, though this spot also gets very crowded.

settlement and features a handy little stream and beautiful rocks to explore, with a small boat harbour, and a host of waves when there's a big east or north swell, including the point, and peaks along the beach. You'll find public loos and parking at the western end of Happy Jacks Road. **The Quarters** is a self contained apartment between Mahunga and Mahia (06)8375 751. **Remoana B&B** and self-contained units (06)837 5898 www.remoana.co.nz

3. Oraka

On the eastern side of the Maungawhia Lagoon, which marks the end of Mahunga Beach, you'll find a settlement of about a dozen baches nestled into the hill, with a small turnaround and parking area adjacent to the coast. This is Oraka beach. No doubt the lagoon entrance fishes well, and the sandbanks created there can hold some good waves too. The public loos on the right as you turn into the beach access road appear to be the last ones heading east on this side of the peninsula.

4. Te Waipera/The Spit

As you head east over the hill from Oraka, you'll see a collection of about a dozen homes set behind the beach, facing over a long finger of rock which juts out into the sea for nearly a hundred metres. This is known as "The Spit," and on its day hosts some of

6. Aurora Point

East of Boat Harbour there's a headland that can also get some rideable waves, plus the rocks all around here are a popular land-based fishing spot, attracting kahawai in numbers, the odd gurnard, and even a few kingies in late summer. It is an extremely pleasant place to fish with easy parking and lots of space.

7. Little J Bay

Further around from Aurora point there is a range of rocky terrain with beautiful patches of sand in between, then a private feeling beach backed by farmland. Keep heading east and you come to one of the most bizarre reef structures in the country, that literally looks like spare-ribs, which can have some okay rights peeling down it on its day.

8. Dinahs Beach

Drive east for about 15 mins from Boat Harbour on the gravel road, and you come to a turnoff on your left. Wainuiorangi Rd delivers you in a precipitous manner down to Dinahs Beach, which is the last place you can drive to on the north side of the peninsula. It is a stunning beach, with patches of reef offshore creating punchy waves, but with no public facilities. Public parking is back from the foreshore, from where you can walk over the dunes to the beach. There are a few old shacks on private land to the east, which give it a ramshackle feel. The road east from here is tortuous and dusty, offering spectacular views but there is no public access down onto the coast from this point on. Many people drive up the beach from further south, but it's not encouraged.

Dinahs and Table Cape

9. Taylors Beach
A cute stretch of sparking sand over the hill from Mahia is home to a couple of dozen holiday homes, and while there are few public amenities, the tranquil ambience is highly inviting. **Private Beach House** (04)473 0072 www.beachhouse-mahia.co.nz

10. Mahia Beach
The main township on the peninsula, Mahia lies at the northern end of Opoutama Beach, where it hooks around to face almost west. It is a collection of a hundred or so real kiwi baches, with a large campground, fishing club, pub and general store. This is the main boat launch spot on the south side of the peninsula, and is extremely sheltered from swell and most wind, though it's an off the beach affair. Swimming here is excellent and safe, and you will find public loos, a childrens play area, and a large grassy picnic area on the foreshore. **Private Home to rent** (06)8375 088 www.mahiabeach.com. **Mahia Beach Motels and Holiday Park** (06)837 5831 www.motelscabinscampmahiabeach.com

11. Opoutama
Oputama is one of our more glorious stretches of sand, backed by low dunes with several walkways onto the beach, and substantial grass parking areas allowing easy public access. It is almost completely uninhabited, save for a tiny settlement at the western fringe, where you'll find the spectacular marae, a handful of homes, and a petrol station. It is a great place to swim, with a flat profile, and can have mellow, longboard waves that are suited for beginners. The absence of public loos is a bit of a hassle.

12. Tracks
The first of Mahia's southern trio of point breaks, Tracks is usually the smallest, with less exposure to the south. Located between Waikokopu and Oputama, it can be accessed from either location.

13. Point Annihilation
Is there a more intimidating name for a surfbreak anywhere in the world? Drive down Waikokopu Rd to the old wharf, where there is an abandoned jetty and seawall structure, and a short beach, with a parking area adjacent to a few homes. Point Annihilation is a freight train right point break out off the end of the headland, that can hold huge swell, and breaks best at lower tides. Crowds can be a factor in peak season.

14. Rolling Stones
As for Point Annihilation, take Waikokopu Rd, but after a few hundred metres you will see an old tractor on the grass, adjacent to a short, sealed section of road. To the right there's a gate and a path leading

Rolling Stones

Point Annihilation

through a gap in the hills. This is the walkway to Rolling Stones, one of the country's heaviest right point/reefs, that can hold big, powerful waves when mega south swells push up from the roaring forties. It got its name from the huge round stones that roll and grind around on the sea floor in big swells. They make a particularly daunting noise as you contemplate jumping into the vicious, pounding shorebreak. It's at its best at lower tides, with offshore winds from the north-west. When its breaking well, you can hear it well before you can see it!

15. Blacks Beach

After Opoutama, Blacks is the next real beach you can get to heading south, and signals the end of the peninsula. From here, the long and wild expanse of coastline stretching to Wairoa begins; unruly, driftwood strewn and empty. Named after a local farming family, Blacks is possibly the most consistent surf spot in the whole country; a sand covered right hand reef, facing due south, that is either offshore or sheltered from wind a fair amount of the time. It used to be really hollow and punchy, but due to siltification, it seems to be more of a longboard wave nowadays, with a mellow takeoff, sometimes gathering intensity, with some bowley inside sections. Whatever the condition of the sand and whatever you ride, it's a fallback option when there isn't a wave anywhere else on the coast, that has provided hours of enjoyment for thousands of surfers over the years. It also happens to be surrounded by beach peaks of varying quality, which are also worth a look if it's crowded. A conveniently located public toilet in the carpark makes life easy for travellers.

Blacks Beach

Wairoa District

This is the wild north, and doesn't in any way fit the standard impression people have of Hawke's Bay, with a geography and seashore more akin to the East Cape than Napier. The coastline features a series of massive rivers that force their way to the sea between high cliffs and bluffs, interspersed by wild and empty driftwood strewn beaches of dark granulated sand. Socially it's worlds apart from the genteel, old money towns of central Hawke's Bay, being both deeply rural, and deeply Maori. I found it exciting and empty, and a real treat to explore. If you're looking for something different, here's where you may find it.

Travelling There's lot to explore but not a lot of accommodation in the area and Wairoa is the only real town of substance. I-Site, cnr State Highway 2 and Queen St 0800 924 762 www.wairoadc.govt.nz.

WIND ROSE

SWELL ROSE

Surfing You'll find miles and miles of empty, steeply shelving beaches, with one or two epic rivermouths that are well protected by the local crew. It is the usual story; politeness and respect is a must, and full car loads won't make too many friends.

Fishing Good land-based fishing around the river mouths and headlands.

Swimming It is wild and exposed to any south swells running, with all the beaches featuring steep profiles, so isn't a region for the less confident on any but the calmest of days.

1. Whakaki
A 400 metre long gravel track leads off the main highway, over the railway line and down onto the coast. There is nothing there of substance, but it allows easy access to several miles of untouched driftwood-strewn beach, backed by extensive low dunes, and a small lake and wetland which extends west towards Wairoa from here. This beach faces due south, so can be blustery, but is an extremely beautiful, if isolated spot, and a riot of colour in spring.

2. Wairoa Rivermouth
The community of Wairoa sits upstream from one of the most expansive river mouths in the country. It is a town that marks the northern end of the Hawke's Bay region, though feels more like the "wild west" than like the old school towns further south. The main street skirts the river and eventually delivers you to the coast at Whakamahi, about a kilometre west of the actual mouth itself. It is another vast expanse of dark shingle backed by low dunes, that's absolutely covered in driftwood. A 4wd or a determined walk is required to get out to the river entrance, where there are good runs of kahawai offering fine spinning opportunities. It is also a primo whitebaiting river, with keen fishermen scattered around the entrance and staggered all the way up the river towards town in season. The surf can be epic, though it's a fairly fiercely protected spot, so don't expect a warm reception. South swells and north winds are required, with hollow rights and lefts peeling off the mouth, and at low tide, Wairoa can be absolutely world class.

3. Waihua Beach
A cute spot just off the main road, but it is very difficult to turn around at the bottom of the gravel road and there are no facilities. 4wd recommended.

4. Mohaka Rivermouth
The Mighty Mohaka is a sight to see; a vast and sprawling river delta with a wild and savage feel. There are two separate beach roads, one to the east and one to the west, and both lead you to huge stretches of driftwood cluttered, dark shingle. Take East Beach Road, then the beach is signposted from it. The road, like at Wairoa, doesn't actually lead to the mouth; a 4wd or quad bike is required for that. Alternatively take West Beach road to get to the other side of the river, where there are also no facilities, but plenty of space to park up.

5. Waikare
Another of Hawke's Bay's hidden delights, the gravel road turns and winds through bleached and tortured hill country, before descending down to the DOC riverside reserve, featuring a covered picnic space, a grassy parking area and a longdrop. From there it's a 2km hike up hill and down dale to the beach, but though poorly marked, is well worth the effort; just follow your nose towards the sea. Alternatively, with a kayak or surfboard, you could take a short paddle down the river. If you want to find a bit of unspoilt NZ coastline, then this is it. Huge stacks of driftwood are scattered along a massive expanse of golden sand on either side of the rivermouth; that's as inviting as anywhere on the coast. Beach peaks unload for miles each way, and no doubt the fishing off the beach, and around the mouth would be epic on its day.

6. Waipatiki
You descend steeply from the unusually shaped hills that surround Waipatiki, into a virtual Garden of Eden, leading to a few hundred metres of golden brown sand. The valley floor is an oasis of subtropical native trees including one of the few remnants of coastal forest left in the entire region. It's home to the southernmost coastal nikau palms on the east coast, plus a collection of other gems including old growth matai, kahikatea and kanuka. When you stop and look around, it almost feels like you've been transported to another part of the country. Native birds call out as you drive the last few hundred metres to the beach, which is flanked by steep cliffs on either side, with a stream bisecting it in the centre. There are 30 or 40 old baches discreetly tucked away on the northern fringe of the valley, and sadly a dozen or so new, (and totally obtrusive) holiday homes just behind the foreshore, that now dominate the landscape, typical of the insensitivity shown towards coastal development in many other parts of the country. The surf here can be good, though it's a beach, with all the vaguaries that implies. Fishing can also be excellent at the extremities, with photos of some huge snapper and even a few kingies at the excellent campsite to prove it. **Waipatiki Beach Farm Park** (06)836 6075 www.waipatikibeachfarmpark.co.nz

The Napier Coast

Napier sits almost smack bang in the middle of Hawke Bay, with a coastal walkway extending from Clive, far to the north of the city. It's a busy little port town wedged between the ocean on one side, and a rich horticultural hinterland on the other, that's gained a reputation both as an art deco shrine, and an epicurean paradise, both of which are true. It is also blessed with a variety of waterfront gems to the north and south, and while the coast for many kilometres either side features steeply shelving shingle beds, it is not without charm, and posesses a host of other amenities to keep a wandering seabird happy, whatever the weather.

Travelling There isn't much you can't get or do in Napier, and there are a huge variety of accommodation options for all budgets. The I-Site at 100 Marine Parade is both conveniently placed, modern, and well appointed. www.hawkesbaynz.com (06)834 1911.

WIND ROSE

SWELL ROSE

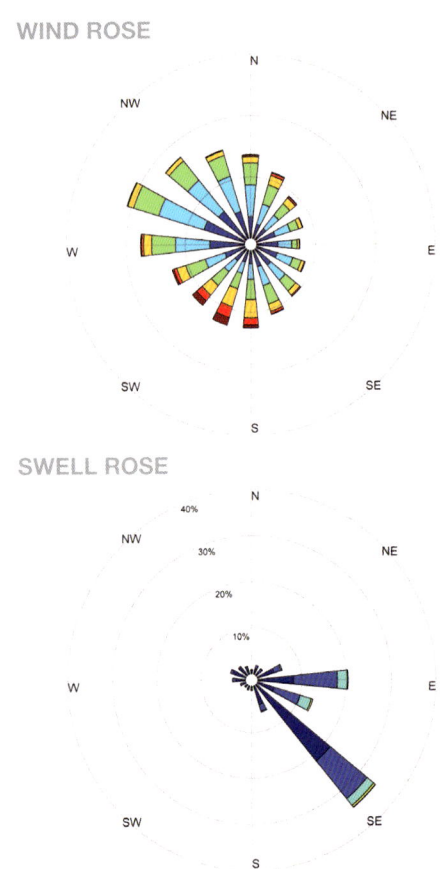

Surfing Huge south, or moderate east and north-east swells are the best conditions for the Napier spots. Boardzone Surf Co (06)835 7362.

Fishing There is pretty good beach fishing all around the city, in particular directly south of the port where a reef structure sits just offshore, leading out to the famed Pania reef, which to this day still supports a healthy shellfish and cray population. Further south, the rivermouths are the centre of activity for targeting fin-fish and whitebait in season. Common species are kahawai, the occasional snapper, gurnard, doggies and a few bigger sharks in summer. Hawke's Bay Sport Fishing Club (06)835 8911 www.hbsfc.co.nz

Swimming Beware the steep shelf off Napier's foreshore when there is swell Pacific Surf Life Saving Club (06)835 3821.

1. Stingray Bay
You need to walk the track from Tongaio for about twenty minutes through the gap to get to Stingray Bay, but its well worth it for the quality of the point/reef waves you'll find there; which include a left to the north-east and a quality right at the south-western end, that can offer grinding barrels on a good east or north-east swell, best at higher tides. Its orientation means it picks up a lot of south swell too, and shelter offered by the cliffs also has its advantages. The whole area can fish well as headlands and points do, though south swell can cause problems.

2. Tongaio
It's a hickory little collection of about a dozen shacks set back from the beach at the northern extent of Hawke Bay. You will find a small area to park near the cliffs and that's about it.

3. Whirinaki
Whirinaki is a cute, tight-knit seaside community adjacent to the gas-fired powerstation north of the Napier-Taupo Rd turnoff. It is just a simple row of houses across the road from the beach, which is similar to the miles of coast to the south, but the fishing is rumoured to be excellent, with many large snapper attracted to the mussel beds just offshore, and kahawai are also in abundance. The shorefront vegetation here has to be seen to be believed, especially in spring. The photos don't do it justice. Facilities include a public loo, but that's it.

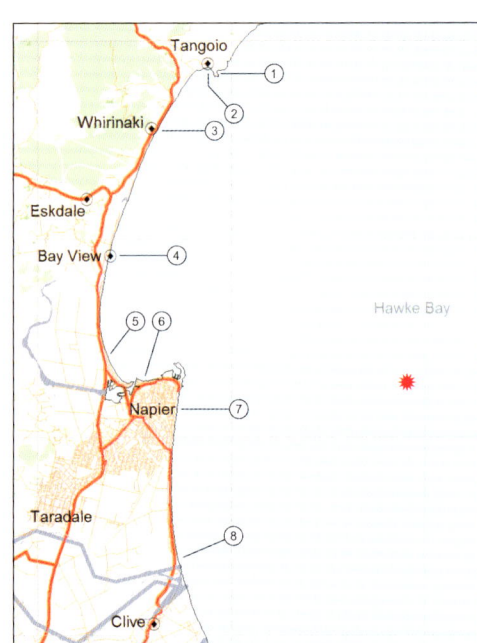

4. Bay View
Bay View heralds the start of the Napier city coastline proper, with its steep shelving shingle banks accessed by a series of dead end roads. The fishing can be good here, as evidenced by the name of the local campsite. Bay View Snapper Holiday Park is well located and friendly 10 Gill Rd 0800 287 275 www.snapperpark.co.nz

5. Westshore
A seaside suburb north of Napier adjacent to the Airport, with extensive grass reserves adjacent to the beach, featuring a surf-lifesaving club overlooking the shingle beds that stretch for several kilometres

Napier foreshore

north. The coastal walkway passes along its entire length, and continues after the road dead-ends. It is a treacherous piece of the coast to swim at, due to the steep profile, so stay near the lifesaving club. **Westshore Surf Life-Saving Club** (06)835 9553 www.westshoresurf.org.nz. **The Beach Cottage** 021 890041 www.thebeachretreat.co.nz. **Westshore Holiday Park** www.westshoreholidaypark.co.nz

6. Ahuriri

Ahuriri is the Maori name for what is now Napier. These days it's a cool community on the north side of the estuary and just west of the port. Located around the old port sheds and up Hardinge Rd, you will find a conglomeration of bars, restaurants and hotels opposite the water, and despite being a heavily modified shoreline, and somewhat overshadowed by the ever expanding new port, the little stretch of beach in the middle of the Perfume Point Reserve offers the safest swimming in the central bay. There are several fishing platforms around Nelson Quay for kids looking to land a trophy sprat, plus you'll find the **Hawke's Bay Sport Fishing Club** and boat ramp here. Hardinges Rd used to have some good waves in a big east swell, but as the port breakwater has got bigger, the swell window has got smaller. It is now a rare event indeed. City Reef can also have good waves in the same huge south-east, or north east ground swells, though there would generally be somewhere better in the area to surf on those conditions. **The Crown Hotel** is on the beachfront www.thecrownnapier.co.nz (06)833 8300. **Portside Backpackers** (06)833 7292 www.portsideinn.co.nz

7. Marine Parade

You wouldn't call the foreshore along Marine Parade pretty, especially below the Bluff where it hits the Port. Scrappy and a bit unloved was my impression, though there is a well maintained walkway that runs almost all the way to Clive, and makes for an interesting stroll and an excellent place to run and suck in some salty air. The locals refer to the stretch of beach adjacent to the bottom of town as "the kiddie snatcher", because it seems that every year a child gets pulled down by the ferocious shore break which results from its steeply shelving profile. The shingle beds that make up the coast can also lead to a potentially fatal loss of footing, so if you are going to get in for a swim, take care. If it all sounds a bit too dangerous, the warm saltwater pools of the waterfront **Ocean Spa** with its lap pool, spa pools, gymnasium, sunbeds and cafe are a luxurious and safe alternative www.oceanspa.co.nz. There are plenty of public facilities along this long stretch of foreshore, and other attractions include the statue of Pania and the magnificent **National Aquarium** (06)834 1409 www.nationalaquarium.co.nz

8. Clive

The first major interruption to the perfect crescent of the bay south of Napier is the Clive River, with its meandering mouth and driftwood strewn shingle beds. It is a hotspot for local fishermen who reap a steady harvest of kahawai, shark and whitebait from its jaws. It can be a social, and sometimes competitive spot to get a line out, drawing punters from far and wide; and can also get blisteringly good waves in the right swell conditions and when the sandbars are lined up. Sadly the sign warning not to eat shellfish from the river is a sign of the neglect shown by the farming community further upstream, so swimming around it should be treated with caution. Access is down a gravel road just north of the bridge that crosses the river. The actual town is located on the south side, where access to the beach is restricted by the lagoon which meanders southwards behind the shingle berm for nearly 4 km.
Clive Colonial Cottages (06)870 1018

Ahuriri

Pania of the reef

Hastings District

Hastings tends to lay claim to these spots, despite the fact that it is anything but a seaside town, unlike its neighbour Napier. It is, however the closest commercial centre to all of them, so it's fair enough to concede the title. From the shingle banks of lower Hawke Bay to Waimarama's broad sweep of silver sand, you'll struggle to find more variety in a single segment of New Zealand's coast, and with good waves, surprisingly good fishing and vineyards producing world class wine directly adjacent to the beach, there are plenty of reasons to find yourself wandering these shores.

Travelling Oddly, there isn't a huge amount of waterside accommodation in the area, though there are a few coastal wineries with fantastic eateries attached. Clearview and Elephant Hill at Cape View are the notable ones. **Hastings I-Site** is located on the corner of Russell and Heretaunga St, in town. 0800 Hastings. www.hastings.co.nz

Surfing There are some remarkably good waves in the area, including the rivers around Hastings that work in east swells, while south swells push into the coast south of the cape. **Boardzone**, Hastings (06)876 0171. **Hannah Surfboards and ding repairs** are on the foreshore at Cape View 027 3168749.

Fishing There is a good range of fishing in the area, from the whitebait, kahawai and sharks found around the river mouths, to the broader mix of species offered near the cape.

Swimming The expansive beaches to the south of the region are the best by a long shot, with lots of space and fine golden sand; but on a hot summers day, you would enjoy a dip at all of these spots.

1. Haumoana

Just south of the Tukituki River, you will find the most densely populated of the coastal settlements south of Napier. It has a comfortable, lived-in atmosphere, more suburb than beach town, but happily signals the start of the coast where sand replaces shingle, at least below the high tide line. Consequently, it offers more pleasant, and generally safer swimming than further north. The river mouth can have epic waves in a moderate south-east or east swell, and like all the rivers in the bay, produces prolific kahawai and whitebait runs in season. The foreshore is backed by heaped shingle banks, with a number of pullovers offering easy access to the beach. Ongoing erosion, over many years, led to a rough attempts at foreshore stabilization using steel girders roughly jammed into the beach, with limited success. Recent discussions between local residents and council about efforts to prevent the changes to the coast seem to be (misguidedly in my opinion) leading towards building a series of groynes. Avoid driving on the shingle berms and if interested in the issue, visit www.capecoast.co.nz

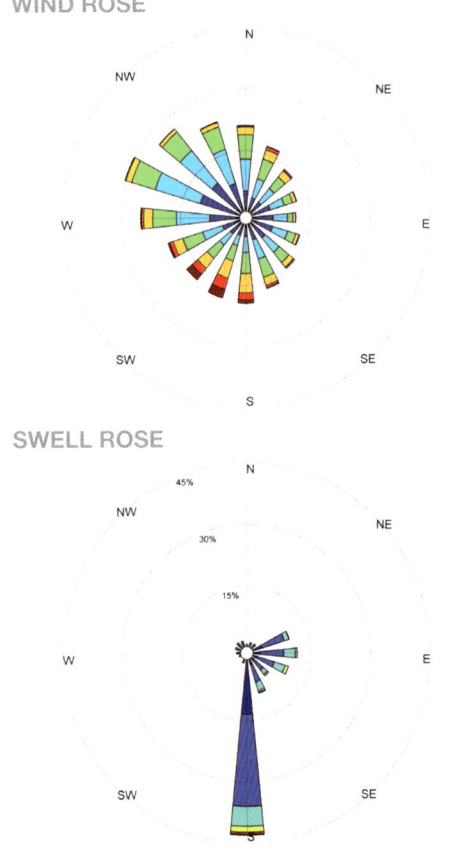

Haumoana

Waimarama

2. Cape View
Called Cape View for obvious reasons, it is now just another kilometre in the unbroken line of baches that stretches between Haumoana and Te Awanga, with little to differentiate it from its neighbours other than its store, takeaways and bottle shop. **Sea Spray** beach front accommodation 027 443 2168

3. Te Awanga
"TA" as it is known, is the most colourful of the Hawke Bay beachside communities, located at the mouth of the Maraetotara River. It sits adjacent to a distinct bend in the shingle with a patch of reef holding consistent sandbars in place, that has strongly endeared it to the local surf community over the years. It's a mellow right hander in a south-east swell, but gets a bit more poke when a north-east pushes in, though it doesn't hold too much size. There's not bad fishing off the rivermouth, and you will find a few whitebait here in season also. The only amenities are the public loos on the cute foreshore reserve.
Te Awanga Cottages (06)875 1963 www.teawangacottages.co.nz.
Te Awanga Point Holiday Park (06)875 0334.

4. Clifton
Clifton features a quirky motor camp and a boating club, tucked into the base of the cliffs adjacent to the southernmost point of Hawke Bay. It is notable for the totally unique way that the locals launch their boats here i.e. still attached to the trailers, which are kept afloat by buoyancy aids. On a busy day, there will be 20 trailers anchored up a hundred metres offshore. You have to see it to believe it. There is a small stretch of beach for public swimming, but no real amenities other than the campsite. **Clifton Marine Club** (06)875 0518. **Clifton Motor Camp** (06)875 0263.

5. Cape Kidnappers
The name refers to an incident during Cook's first voyage when an attempt was made to trade with the occupants of an armed canoe. Tiata, the Tahitian servant of Tupaia, Cook's interpreter, was seized by the Maoris and escaped by jumping into the sea when their canoe was fired on. Cape Kidnappers is an extraordinary landform extending nearly 10 kms from Clifton out to "the Tooth". In Maori legend, it was the point of the hook that pulled the North Island from the ocean. It now holds the largest mainland gannet colony in New Zealand, which is one of Hawke's Bay's leading tourist drawcards, and an absolutely stunning diversion on any holiday to the area. **Gannet Safaris** offer guided overland tours (06)875 0888 www.gannetsafaris.co.nz. The reefs and beaches below the Cape are accessible below half tide and used to be a prolific fishery, well sheltered from south winds and with a completely different biodiversity than the rest of Hawke Bay. Sadly they are suffering from years of overfishing, but it is still a great place to go for a walk or a swim. The DOC walkway starts at the north end of the Clifton campsite. Though I don't play, no mention of The Cape would be complete without reference to its luxury golf course, consistently rated as in the top 100 in the world. www.capekidnappers.com

6. Ocean Beach
Ocean Beach heralds a significant change in coastal geography after the shingle-lined beaches of Hawke Bay. Its magnificent sweep of sand extends in a long arc from just south of Cape Kidnappers to the headland that separates it from Waimarama. The access road turns to gravel a few kilometres from the coast then descends steeply for the last kilometre, but don't let this deter you. It is a total gem and worth every dusty metre. An extensive foreshore reserve leads north from the stream that divides the beach, and the road that follows it ends at the surf club and public toilets (which are the only amenities). There is a pocket of houses to the south down a private road, but the beach both ways can be walked with impunity. The surf can be excellent either way, with pronounced banks near the rivermouth in most swells and tides. 4wd access to the north opens up a whole new range of options for both fishermen and surfers, and due to the south-east orientation, the north end picks up more south swell, but equally, is more exposed to south winds. Access onto the beach is granted by the Pukepuke Tangaroa trust, so respect the rules: no driving on the dunes, and adhere to the 20km speed limit. **Ocean Lifestyle Accomodation** offers 4 self-contained cottages and powered van sites approx 5km from the beach. (06)874 7894 www.oceans7.co.nz

7. Waimarama
One of Hawke's Bay's coastal icons, Waimarama has been a centre of Maori culture for more than 500 years, and in many ways is a beach divided in two. The pakeha community, store, gas station and baches are concentrated around the south, while the local iwi have a strong presence along the northern stretch, which is accessed from Waitangi Rd. At the south, there are several access points leading down to the beach, and a large reserve sitting just back from the dunes that was gifted by local iwi, featuring the surf club, picnic areas and public toilets. Waimarama has a flat profile that offers safer swimming than its neighbour Ocean Beach. The waves are generally better in a north-east or east swell, with various peaks along its length, but often good shape at the south end, and either side of Kuku Rocks, which also provide a handy channel for boat launching. Like Ocean Beach, the north gets more exposure to south swells. **Hakikino Maori Tours** offer a totally unique local experience that's thoroughly recommended 021 0570 935 www.waimaramamaori.com.
Waimarama Seaside Resort/campsite (06)874 6813.
Jarks Licensed Café (06)874 6813 www.jarks.co.nz

8. Karamea/Cray Bay
Either walk over the hill from the south end of Waimarama, or around the rocks below mid-tide, and you come to one of the best kept secrets in the area. Cray Bay is one of the hottest surf spots in the region, with a few surfable options on the way around. First there's Paua Point, then the bay itself, which features a long hollow left. All the waves are best at higher tides. The coast walk is a delight even for non-surfers with some beautiful sandy spots between Waimarama and Red Island. The area is a prolific food basket, with the reefs and foul ground holding a variety of sea life.

Central Hawke's Bay

Quite why it's called Central Hawke's Bay I never found out, for clearly it is a misnomer, but when you head south of Waimarama, everything changes; landscape, population density and even the personality of the beach settlements. Big bluffs and cliffs are split by wide rivers and deep gorges. Farm follows farm; hill follows hill, and not much breaks the pattern all the way to Wellington. The sense of isolation that permeates the coastal communities right down to Cape Palliser starts here. As the distances between beaches increases, the services available decrease incrementally. The old boy-scout motto seems highly appropriate: "Be prepared."

Travelling The absence of facilities and shops can be a real hassle, with virtually no decent food stores at any of these beaches, and few gas stations. www.centralhawkesbay.co.nz (06)858 6488.

WIND ROSE

SWELL ROSE

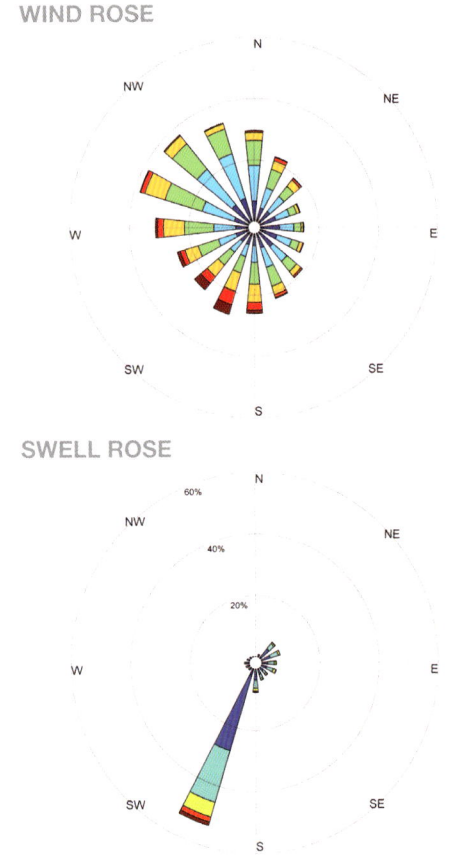

Surfing Not the most obvious surf coast in the country, but the truth is, there are plenty of good waves down this coast and a few discoveries yet to be made, with exposure to a huge amount of swell from south-west to north-east and many empty miles of coast with interesting rock structures. Prevailing winds are offshore and crowds almost non-existent.

Fishing Paua and crays are the main attraction, though a few fish get pulled off the beach and around the rivermouths. Sadly the fishery here seems to be in marked decline as evidenced by the annual charts recording heaviest weighed fish at the Porongahau fishing shop. Boat launching is generally by tractor.

Swimming Not a surf lifesaver on the coast and there are definite water quality issues around most of the streams, as is now the case in many parts of the country. Swim Safe Line (06) 878 1368.

Kairakau

1. Kairakau
Kairakau is a real beauty, backed by spectacular bluffs, and located an hours drive south of Waimarama. It couldn't be more different than the Hastings beaches, with a real "outpost of the empire" feel, consisting of a raggedy collection of baches and a simple campsite set just above the beach. There is also a freedom-camping area reserved for self-contained vans tucked into the base of the spectacular bluff that backs the beach, and a public loo, but no other facilities. It features good, peaky waves down its length at all tides, plus another little beach called Waterfall Bay to the north, which offers more good surf potential, but can only be accessed below mid-tide. **Kairakau Beach Camp** (06)858 4245 is open from 25 September till April. **Kairakau Boat Club** has tractors for beach launching (06)858 4245.

2. Mangakuri
A kilometre of sand between fringing reefs, which stretch both ways up and down the coast, is what you find at the end of Williams Rd. There is nothing here for the casual traveller, as it was a family owned spot for nearly a hundred years, with a collection of baches that were not for sale. In the last twenty or so years this has changed, but it still remains an extremely tight-knit, insular community, that is popular with cray and paua divers from around the area. Scattered foul makes it an unlikely surf destination. You'll find some baches available for rent on **Book a Bach**.

3. Pourerere
On 22 October 1773, Captain James Cook, in HMS Resolution, hove to off Pourerere to receive visitors from shore. He presented them with spike nails, seeds, pigs and fowls which Chief Tuanui promised not to kill so that the country might be stocked. Pourerere went on to hold the first sheep station in Hawke's Bay, and the rustic old farm buildings still lend an historical air to the place. The beach is long and expansive, leading all the way south to Muddy Point, which is where boat owners will find a convenient gap in the reef that offers safe launching. Beach fishing can produce moki and kahawai, and while

the flat shelf doesn't offer great surf prospects, it does provide tons of safe swimming. Beachside camping is allowed along the foreshore to the south with a permit from the **District Council** (06)857 8060 or 027 446 3796. **Pourere Beach Caravan Park** has small shop (06)857 8802.

4. Aramoana/Shoal Bay
Another mint spot that has recently seen the money move in and a development of modern homes sprout where until quite recently there were just a few old baches and a campsite. The quid-pro-quo is that there are now public loos, with some space set aside for free-camping vans. Aramoana signals the start of the marine reserve, and the incredible reef structures that are typical of this unique stretch of coast, and which provide such a prolific variety of marine habitats. There are bound to be waves off the end of the reef to the south, plus beach peaks at higher tides.

5. Parimahu/Blackhead
It is 3km to Aramoana as the crow flies, but an arduous hours drive by road if you're coming from the north. Apparently 4wd vehicles can get around at low tide, though I didn't try. A gap in the hills following the ancient river valley takes you plunging down to Blackhead Beach, which is another chink of sand cut out of the reef system, that continues from Pourerere to Te Paerahi. There are a couple of dozen baches to the north and down McHardy Place, plus a private resort across the bridge over the river to the south, and a large grassed area for picnicking. The surf can be epic, with little low tide peaks to the north, and a right hander that winds down the edge of the reef at the southern end of the bay that can hold size and get hollow. **Blackhead Campsite** is open all year, though is generally booked out by long term residents (06)857 7335. There are public loos located in the campsite, with showers $2.00 for non-campers.

6. Te Paerahi/Porongahau
The most developed of the southern Hawke's Bay beaches, and also the longest by a country mile, Te Paerahi seems to stretch forever, with the settlement at the southern end backed by a headland and hills offering protection from the wind. The rest of this glorious golden arc of sand is wide open and backed by farmland, with a gravel road running parallel for most of its length, though public access is restricted to the south end only. There is a fabulous free-camping area off Te Paerahi St, at the northern extent of the settlement, with parking under the pine trees and a public toilet. The surf can be good along its length, despite the flat shelf. **Beach Marine** (06)855 5131 www.beachmarine.co.nz. **Beach Rd Holiday park** (06)855 5821. **Porongahau Lodge** Fishing charters, accommodation and meals (06)855 5386.

7. Whangaehu
It's a tiny, intimate beach with twenty or so little baches, a stream down the middle, rocks to the north, and a large headland with a long finger reef protruding off the end of the point to the south. It is extremely charming, with golden sand, a timeless, almost forgotten feel and a distinctly fishy vibe, but the sign warning that the stream was polluted sort of broke the spell for me.

8. Wainui/Herbertville
Named by pakeha after Joseph and Sarah Herbert who settled in this district in 1854, it is a spectacular mix of contrasts. The village is as nondescript and un-interesting as any in the country, but the beach itself is gigantic and awesome, stretching for nearly 10km down Seaview Rd, which skirts its southern extent. There is something almost prehistoric about Herbertville, with the massive bluffs and cliffs of Cape Turnagain visible to the north, its wide expansive dunes, and deserted feel. Advantages for travellers are the huge amount of space for free-camping to the south, public toilets on the left before the beach, a very basic pub which serves meals in summer season, and a campsite which has recently been bought by a syndicate of long term patrons. **Herbertville Motor Camp** (06)374 3466 herbertvillecamp@xtra.co.nz. **The Cock & Pullett** is a small cafe (06)374 3840.

9. Akitio
This is yet another vast swathe of sand at the mouth of a gigantic river valley, with patches of rock and foul ground along its length, and a broad flat reef marking its southern extent. Akitio has around 50 or so dinky old baches at the south end, where you will find the campsite and a small store and boat club, plus a set of public loos on the foreshore reserve, that stretches for much of its length. With its flat shelf, driftwood strewn wildness and empty countenance, it's another absolute gem. Waves can be good at all tides and fishing is popular off the stream mouth; or for the kids, from the bridge before town. **Akitio Retreat** Self-contained accommodation (06)374 3519. **Akitio Motor Camp** (06)374 3450. **Akitio Boating Club** (06)374 3587.

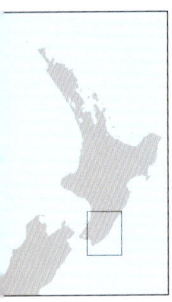

THE WAIRARAPA

The name Wairarapa derives from the Maori words wai (water), and rarapa (glistening). It is a region of dark, shingly beaches, immense cliffs, big skies, broad valleys and small towns full of character. It is almost crushingly huge, and scarily beautiful on a scale that's not for the faint hearted! All around it, a series of spectacular ranges soar out of the sea, with the Rimutakas separating it from the Wellington coast, and the Aorangi Range guarding the south coast, creating an appropriate frame for the vast fertile plains that stretch north for many miles. Palliser Bay is considered the mouth of Maui's great fish (Te Ika a Maui), with Lake Wairarapa its eye; and while there is some doubt about who named it (legend offers several choices), there is no doubt about the areas primeval beauty. Its history is equally impressive, home to some of the earliest dated Maori settlements in NZ, and a single 12th century stonewall that asks many questions of our known prehistory. This was also the first part of NZ to suffer the indignities of intensive farming by Pakeha settlers, yet the severe coastline itself proved far less amenable. Many shipwrecks attest to this fact. The people you'll meet are a unique breed, alone and unto themselves, fashioning their futures in a remote and hauntingly appealing region of the country; battered by the wind, rarefied by their isolation, almost forgotten by time.

Travelling To call it isolated is somewhat of an understatement. It breaks into two distinct parts: the east coast, and the south coast. The east coast is vast and prehistoric, and the accessible spots are well spaced and are without exception, well off the main road. Much driving is required to get to each and every beach, and facilities when you get there are even fewer than on the East Cape. Plan your journey well and remember, almost all the roads leading to the coast are gravel, steep and tortuous, and gas stations almost non-existent. The south coast by contrast has a convenient coast road offering simple access to most of it. Destination Wairarapa, 7-13 Church St, Masterton www.wairarapanz.com.

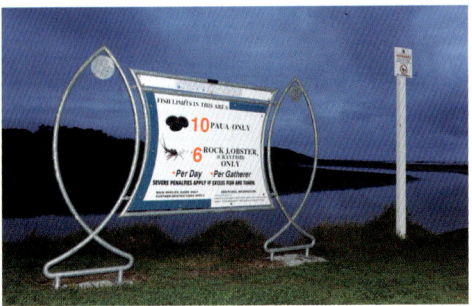

Surfing It's a coastline for the adventurous, with an abundance of some of the heaviest, ledgiest waves in the country; the east coast favouring rights and the south coast offering choices going both ways. South swell is the most common, but east and north-east swells are always welcome, and though infrequent, can produce the best waves of all. The predominant north-west wind blows hard and at times way too hard, but it's offfshore at many spots. If you like your waves thick and fast, make the pilgrimage at least once in your surfing career. Wairarapa Bush Boardriders have a facebook page.

Fishing You wouldn't call it the most popular beach fishing region in the country, with cool waters keeping some desirable species offshore, and regular swell making it hard to get a line out off the rocks. Before being almost fished out, grouper were a common land-based catch, but nowadays it's cod, moki, gurnard, dogfish and kahawai that are commonly targeted. Crayfish and paua are still abundant, and prime delicacies for divers and snorkellers. The boating culture is highly individual, particularly the method of launching, with bulldozers and trailers featuring outsized drawbars (some up to 20m long), being the norm.

Swimming This is a heavy coast, with cool waters, regular lashings of swell, and steep shelving beaches; so if it's a gentle dip you're after, choose your location well. The only lifeguards are at Riversdale.

Lake Ferry

Castlepoint

South coast shingle bank

The Wairarapa | 195

Masterton District

The most populous and well known stretch of the Wairarapa coast is possibly the most spectacular, featuring one of New Zealand's most recognizable coastal landmarks, and home to a good percentage of the holiday houses and baches in the entire south-east. Proximity to Masterton is partly what has fuelled development in the region, though people would invariably seek out these spots, no matter how far from a population centre they were. There is a huge geographical variety down these two main roads and the side-roads that run off them, making it an area that's definitely worth a drive-by at least once. It is classic Wairarapa; big, steep, powerful and inviting.

Travelling These beaches are all accessed off the Masterton-Castlepoint Road, which forks at Awatoitoi. It's roughly 60 km to the nearest point on the coast either way, and while the roads are windy, they're breathtaking; but make for a long day trip.

Surfing "The Gap" at Castlepoint is the main focus, and one of the most consistent spots on the coast, though there can be rideable waves at all the places mentioned. **Kiwi Surf School** 027 4RAGLAN

Fishing While crayfish and paua are the most lauded catch; blue cod, gurnard, kahawai and terakihi are the main table fish, and if you're lucky, you'll run into a few stray snapper in late summer. The reef at Castlepoint is the most popular land-based spot. Mid-summer is the easiest time to get crays close-in; and at that time you can almost walk a cray-pot out to some spots along this coast and get a feed. **Uruti Point Fishing Charter** Nigel Skeet (06)377 3552. **Riversdale Fishing Club** Darryl Payne is club chairman 027 454 9777.

Swimming It can be a great swimming coast, with clean seas, though at times gets wild and funky. The lagoon at Castlepoint is no doubt the safest spot, and after that, there's safety in numbers at Riversdale. The rest is wilderness, so be on your best behaviour.

WIND ROSE

SWELL ROSE

1. Mataikona
Take a left turn when the Castlepoint road hits the coast and head north. The road skirts 10km of sandy beaches, rivermouths, little headlands and outer reefs that can all have waves when it's small. The settlement is no more than a few old shacks populated by local fishermen, with no amenities at all.

2. Whakataki
Where the road arrives at the beach, there's a small settlement by a short beach called Whakataki. It is notable for a left reef at the north end that can get good in clean swells. It's called Slipperies, and is right in front of the hotel. **Whakataki Hotel** (06)372 6747 is a great place to stay www.whakatakihotel.co.nz

3. Castlepoint
So named in 1770 by Cook, who was struck by the similarities between Castle Rock (which marks the south of the bay), and the battlements of a castle. The fossilised limestone reef which protects the foreshore, and the 162 metre-high Castle Rock, are separate parts of a conglomeration of outstanding natural features protected as the Castlepoint Scenic Reserve. It's a lively aquatic environment offering outstanding surf, good land-based fishing, and some of the safest bathing and boat launching you'll find anywhere. Frequently visited by several species of dolphin, as well as fur seals, the reserve is also home to numerous sea birds as well as being the only known location of a rare shrub, the Castlepoint Daisy. The crumbling limestone reef is a popular fishing spot, allowing anglers an easy cast into the deep water below, but the warning signs at its base should be heeded. Southerly swells regularly break over it, sweeping aside all in their way, and many deaths are proof of the potential dangers here. The main beach is a popular swimming and surfing location facing north-east adjacent to the main road into town. To the south of the main settlement and the lighthouse is Deliverance Cove or "The Gap", as it's known by many. It was given its English name by William Colenso after a ship in which he was sailing found safety in a storm here, and nowadays it is where you'll find some of the most consistent beach peaks in the country. Facing south-east, the horseshoe-shaped bay picks up most swell and offers protection from wind due to the high cliffs that encircle it. The surf is often better at low tide, when the peaks break a lot closer to the entrance. Walk a further kilometre south, along the Deliverance Bay track and you'll come to Christmas Bay, a

Deliverance Cove

secluded and charming spot where you'll most likely find yourself alone with your thoughts. Putangirua Pinnacles is a spectacular formation of sandstone just behind Palliser Bay that's also well worth a hike. **Castlepoint Holiday Park and Motels** www.castlepoint.co.nz (06)372 6705 is an absolutely classic and perfectly located camping ground, with tent sites, cabins, van sites and spectacular sea views; plus internet access and a whole lot of character. There's a store at the main beach that's open till mid-afternoon in winter, but it is poorly provisioned and not much more than a gas station shop. **The Berley Pot** bar opens up in summer, when Castlepoint comes to life. For much of the rest of the year, it's a very quiet place.

4. Otahome

The road winds around and at times runs adjacent to the coast, with rocky headlands, little beaches, stream mouths and reefbreaks. There is no settlement here, and the road ends at Castlepoint Station.

5. Riversdale

This is the community hub of the East Coast, featuring 3 or 4 km of granulated sand, with an exposed feel, backed by a string of beach homes adjacent to the foreshore. This is probably the only piece of the Wairarapa that's un-threatened by the steep terrain that lurks behind the coast, which is a predominant feature of the rest of this region. It's an established holiday destination but also a busy community, with a healthy population of residents giving it a lived in feel. Fringing reefs sit just offshore and these are an obvious fish attractor, but pounded by swell so hard to get to for most of the year. The north end of the beach is where you will find the surf-lifesaving club, and if you want to swim, all signs lead you here due to the flatter profile of the shelf, and the presence of lifeguards in summer, making it safer. Ironically it's right next to a river mouth that's had significant water quality issues in the past, that are hopefully being remedied by the public works due for completion as we go to press. There are three or four boardwalks between the homes as you drive south down the superbly named Blue Pacific Parade, plus a further public reserve at the south end with parking and loos. Riversdale has a well supplied grocery shop and gas station, which also doubles as a burger bar and does monster cooked breakfasts. Accommodation is limited to a few private baches and a campground by the store. www.riversdalebeach.com. **Cobweb B&B** (06)372 3445. **Haystacks Cottage** (06)372 3473. **Riversdale Surf Lifesaving Club** (06)372 3461. **Riversdale Campground** (06)372 3482.

6. Uruti Point

Uruti has a steeply shelving section of beach to the south of the point, backed by an extensive spinifex dune system. It's a favourite spot amongst local land-based fishermen, due to the rocks here, and the differing orientation of the coast as it bends away south, which also offers some good waves for surfers when Riversdale is small. You'll find it just south of Riversdale and you reach it by taking the turn off a couple of km's down Waiorongo Road. The road ends in a gate and a 4wd track through private land. Either park and walk the few hundred metres from there to the beach, or drive on and close the gate if you've got the traction. There are no amenities.

Riversdale

South-East Wairarapa

This is the least populated stretch of the Wairarapa, and for most of its wide expanse, farmland borders the coast. It's home to several absolutely solid gold beaches, set against some of the most spectacular coastal cliffs in the country, and as well as having some of the most productive paua and cray fisheries in the North Island, it offers stunning and well organized walks, productive beach fishing, and a couple of absolutely epic surf spots. The trade-off for this abundance is that it's about as remote as it gets, each location a long drive off the main road; made more challenging by the gravel and threat of slips in winter, a fact that keeps many would be visitors away. You wouldn't come if what you found on arrival wasn't breathtaking, but it is; all of it. Each spot is different, everything is huge and inspiring.

Travelling The gravel roads, howling north-westers, lack of facilities and some badly placed locked gates leave many problems to be solved by travellers.

WIND ROSE

SWELL ROSE

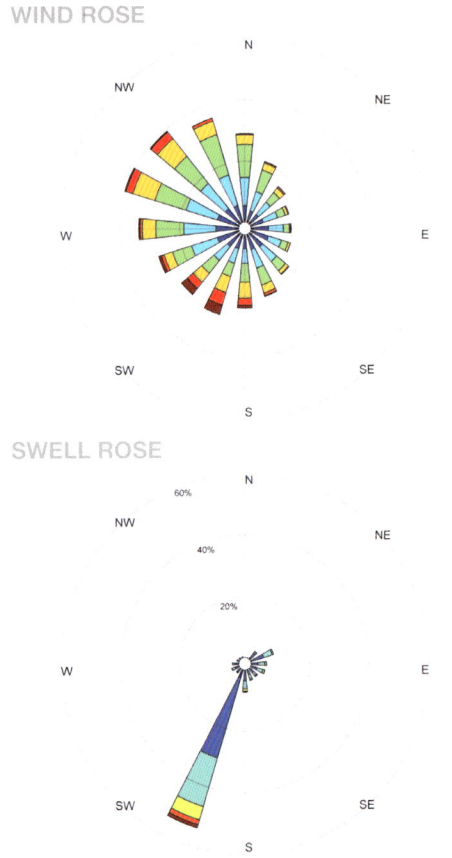

Surfing There are some epic waves on this coast if you can deal with the long drives, which makes a surf check a half day mission. South swell is consistent, and often big, but the wind rarely blows gently.

Fishing It's a hard coast to fish, with lots of foul, a steep shelf, and much water movement. That said, a feed can be still be got. There aren't too many boat launch locations, but there are plenty of paua and crays, and fish of several species to be had.

Swimming This is a wild and untamed coast, with fantastic water, but many rocks and steep, shingly beaches. Less confident swimmers won't find it too welcoming. Tora is the most accommodating.

1. Flat Point

A wide flat plain sitting in the lap of plunging cliffs and ravines forms an oddity that extends for thirty kilometres, from Honeycomb Rocks in the south, to Flat Point further north. The road splits when it hits the coast, with the northern fork leading to the point referred to in its name, which is a triangular promontory facing north-east, that's protected by fringe reefs offshore. For most of our European history it's been an almost empty stretch of coast, with farm land to the water and no public access. However, there has been a recent subdivision at the point itself, with a further swag of sections currently being marketed. It is a very odd place with a cluster of divergent, modern homes clustered together without much landscaping or continuity; looking very out of place. The quid pro-quo for this development has been the provision of public access down a narrow right of way leading from the carpark to the beach. The river gorge before the coast is a beautiful convergence of some of the clearest green waters you'll see, and where this river meets the ocean, you'll sometimes find a surfer blown this way by the vagaries of the wind. There's an odd, thatch covered toilet in a field halfway along Flatpoint Road, that constitutes the only public amenity. **Reefpoint Lodge** (06)372 7527 offers a mix of accommodation at the extreme north end of the bay www.flatpoint.co.nz. If you take the south fork, Glenburn Road hugs achingly close to the foreshore, however all the properties that border the beach have riparian rights with difficult public access. Some stunning patches of cabbage trees, karakas and other mixed natives offer a glimpse of the former glory of the region's coastal forests, before the road ends at Glenburn station. This is where you'll find the DOC walkway for those

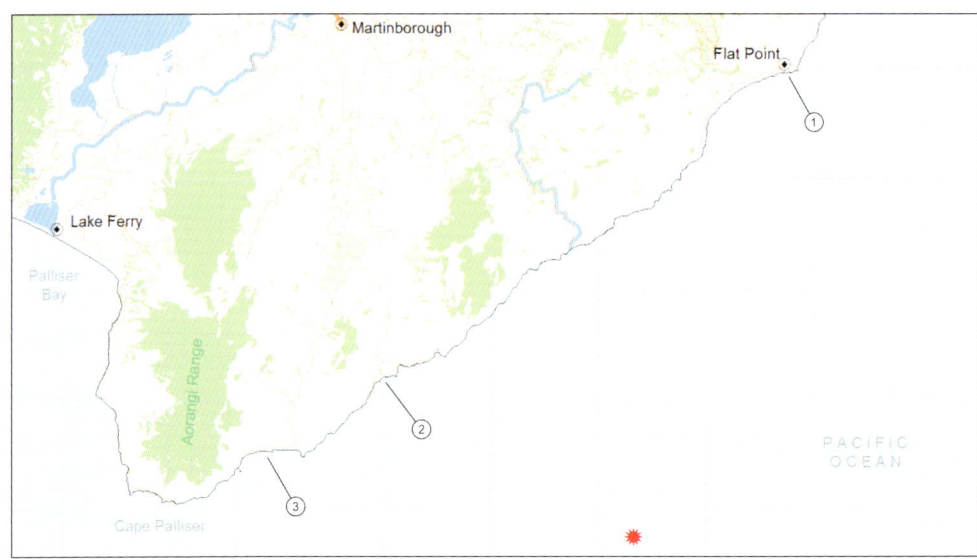

Flat Point

Tora

wanting to make the three hour return hike to the Honeycomb Rocks. **The Scrubcutters Cottage** (06)372 7732 on Glenburn Rd is a quaint old cottage offering self-catering and a charming old style. It's adjacent to Waimoana Station, and just a short walk to the coast.

2. Tora

The word Tora is presumably a reference to the Maori word meaning "rough water" and it is as grand and dramatic as its unusual name implies. Like Flat Point, it features spectacular cliffs behind the beach, and a road that splits to the north and south when it arrives at the coast. The left fork takes you past an expanding coterie of holiday homes that face a jagged and indented few kilometres of coast, culminating in Awanui Station and a locked gate. There's a boat ramp of sorts here, plus an area that used to be one of the prettiest free-camp sites in NZ, owned by the Wairarapa District Council, but recently closed due to lobbying from a kill-joy local resident. The fishing opportunities are many all around the various bays here, and in between the points, there are some useful sandy stretches for those seeking a swim; though Tora is best known as a surf destination. The main spots, which include several right hand reef breaks, are all adjacent to the road south of the Awhea River. South to north-east swell brings waves; south-west to north-west winds create shape. All spots are rocky and powerful and are for intermediate to experienced surfers. Inside Point, also known as Tora Stream, is the first spot you see heading south, and the most consistent. It's a powerful right that bends back to the shore and despite its name, it's a reef break. There's an excellent free-camping spot with a long-drop toilet conveniently located adjacent to it. Outside Point (aka Tora Tora), features a right peak with long walls. It's a super long wave that will connect with Inside Point on a huge swell. Shippies is another right hand, flat-shelf reef-break with barrel sections making it one of the best in the bay. It's so named after the shipwreck that you paddle over to get there, and you'll find it south of the stream. There are other waves with a variety of names breaking on the various reefs in the bay, depending on swell size and direction. As well as world-class surf, Tora has a renowned walk through private land (06)307 8115 **www.torawalks.co.nz**. **Tora Cottage** Alistair(Tora) Boyne (06)307 8869 is adjacent to the main surf spots toraboyne@xtra.co.nz. **The Beach House** (06)307 8864 offers a choice of two self-contained buildings adjacent to the coast www.thebeachhouse.co.nz

3. White Rock

White Rock gets its name from the huge chunk of white limestone evident at the north end of the bay. It's one of the most stunning and best known sections of the Wairarapa coast, that's home to one of the best waves in the country; but it's also the most frustrating, due to issues surrounding access. It's 65 km from Martinborough to get here, and if washouts on the road don't stop you, one of the Wairarapa's biggest landowners will, with locked gates and farm fences making it almost impossible to enjoy without a certain amount of discussion and payment of a fee. There are two main waves, both at the south end of the bay. The Spit is a rock structure extending several hundred metres into the ocean, culminating in a T-shape reef at its head, not unlike its namesake on the Mahia Peninsula. Rights and lefts peel off either side of it, though the right is the most sought after. It likes an east or north-east swell and west to south-west winds. There is a gate several hundred metres before The Spit but you need to pay a $15 fee to have it opened, and should you want to camp, the fee is $20.00 per person per night. There's a toilet at the cabbage patch adjacent to the waves, but that's it as far as facilities go. Contact Frank, Ngapotiki Station Manager (06)307 8212. Seconds is a right point, breaking further to the south that can handle solid south swells. Access to it is either on foot from The Spit, or by a long and difficult 4wd track from Cape Palliser. There's a hut on DOC land, adjacent to Seconds owned by NZ Deerstalkers Assn called **Ngapotiki Lodge**. It's a shack at best, and costs $4 per night, payable at DOC offices, Greytown Auto Repairs or Adamson's service station, Featherston.

White Rock

The South Coast

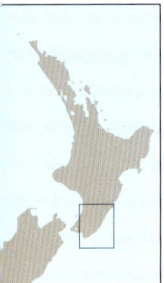

The south-facing Wairarapa coast is a land of its own, populated by some of the most eccentric and colourful characters and coastal dwellings in the country. At times moody and violent, at times peaceful and playful, it is raw New Zealand in its finest incarnation, featuring a towering set of cliffs and some crunchy beaches, divided by Lake Ferry's sublime charms. It feels like you're walking around on a buttress set resolutely against the malevolence of the Southern Ocean. At its eastern extremity is Cape Palliser, a magnificent and poignant point of land that takes some ferocious weather, but also offers spectacular coastal views and stunning walks in the surrounding areas. Guarding its western border are the Rimutakas, that form an abrupt divide between the Wairarapa coast and the Wellington Bay; and to the south, you'll see the The Kaikouras winking at you on a clear day, almost inviting you over.

Travelling The coast road from Lake Ferry to Cape Palliser is spectacular but highly slip-prone, taking you past world-class surf spots, families of fur seals, and a few odd clusters of baches, ending at an iconic lighthouse. The only place to get groceries and fuel on the coast is at the 160 year old Pirinoa Store.

Surfing The coast between Te Kopi and The Cape features world class waves adjacent to the road along much of its length. The main spots are named, but it's a bit like Taranaki here; when it's firing, there are lots of un-surfed breaks. South-east and south swells are required for surf. Offshore winds range from east to north-west, which is a handy fact.

Fishing Fishing action consists of pauas and crays; cod, kahawai and dogfish off the beach; and whitebaiting in Lake Ferry in season. It's a tough land-based coast to fish due to swell and steep beach profiles, but you'll get a feed if you know what you're up to.
Marco Polo Charters Garth Gadsby (06)307 8000.
Cape Palliser Fish and Dive Charters Keith Banks (06)307 8086. **Ngawi Fishing Club** (06)377 0596.

Swimming The beaches are dark shingly sand, and all shelve extremely steeply, so beware the shorebreak along this coast. It is particularly powerful and highly treacherous for all but the most experienced ocean goers. Lots of people swim in Lake Ferry; it's the safe bet, though water quality can be marginal.

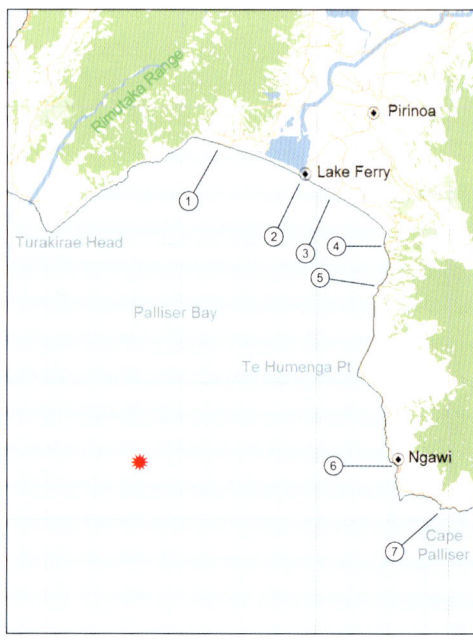

WIND ROSE

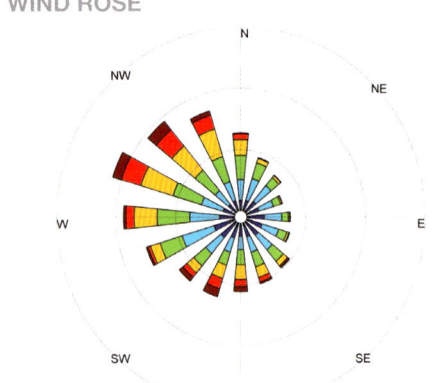

SWELL ROSE

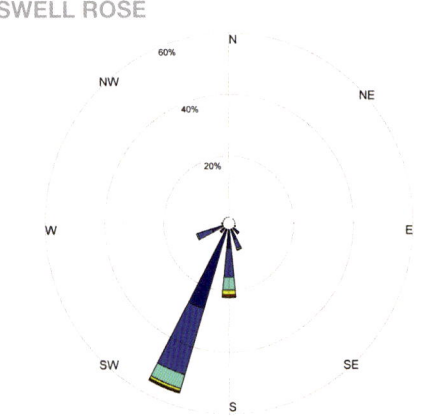

Ocean Beach

Ngawi

1. Ocean Beach
It's a fair drive along the western side of Lake Ferry and down to Ocean Beach, a forlorn feeling stretch of sand that's home to one of the oddest collection of baches in the country, and backed by steep cliffs that prevent many of these rustic little dwellings from seeing any sun in mid-winter. The track that runs parallel to the coast leads to the base of the Rimutakas, which collide with the sea at the western fringe of the bay. Here, there's a DOC camp (Corner Creek Campsite), which is also where the locals launch their boats. You will need a 4wd to get around all the way to the campsite, as the last river often becomes too difficult for normal cars to cross. The cliffs and valley at the southern end are a spectacular hang-gliding and parasailing location, plus if you're a surfer, you'll find a sand point here that works in a south-east swell, and is offshore in the raging northwesters which regularly sweep the Wairarapa. It is tempting to think that with a 4wd you can drive from here all the way to Wellington, as the maps show a track, but it's a dubious undertaking, especially after rain when the streams become impassable. **Wharekauhau** is a luxury lodge on the hill before the beach (06)307 7581 www.wharekauhau.co.nz

2. Otoko/Lake Ferry
A slightly scruffy but deeply charming settlement of a hundred or so houses with an old hotel faces directly onto the lake, near its entrance to the sea. Lake Ferry is filled by the catchment from the Rimutakas and the Tararuas, but during dry periods, a sandbar closes its mouth, preventing water (and fish) from leaving. It is home to flounder and eels, plus whitebait in season, and offers calm and protected water for small boats and kayaks, as well as safe swimming. Fishing off the beach can yield cod and kahawai, though it is hard work dealing with the swell. The beach adjacent to the mouth runs south for a few miles to Whangaimoana, and it's a safe bet you'll find yourself alone here after a few minutes walking. It is a popular summer holiday destination, but in winter it's quiet and windswept by the huge southerly storms that blow through on a regular basis. These deliver some of the hollowest waves in the country onto the shingle banks at the mouth, but it only works when the entrance is open, which happens after rain. Offshores are north-west to north-east. **The Lake Ferry Hotel** is the southernmost hotel in the North Island and enjoys one of the best bar views in the country (06)307 7831 www.lakeferry.co.nz. **Lake Ferry Camping Ground** is located right on the lake.

3. Whangaimoana
A short road (called "The Street" by locals), leads off the main coast road and heads down to the sea. A string of twenty or so houses and baches are tacked on to its south-eastern footpath. Where the road ends, you'll find an extensive public domain behind the dunes that back the beach. From here you can clearly see Wahatarangi across the chiseled cliffs, which mark its eastern boundary. There are no public amenities other than the immaculate foreshore, and the crashing of the waves along its sandy fringe; but for the locals, that's enough. **The Cottage at Whangaimoana Station** offers a self-contained cottage plus palatial B&B in the grand old house itself. Contact Jacqui and Alastair Sutherland (06)307 7736.

4. Te Kopi
Consisting of a handful of ramshackle baches that appear to be falling into the sea by slow degrees; it's a settlement that offers little for the interested tourist, other than a photo or two.

5. Whatarangi
It is a settlement of maybe one hundred homes, set on the landward side of the road. A substantial reserve fronts onto the rock-lined foreshore that's a good spot for a picnic, offering easy parking close to shore, but no other amenities. There are two popular surf/windsurf spots here (Whatarangi Point and The Bombie), which work when the coast is huge.

6. Ngawi
A wild community with a unique fishing culture on the south-eastern tip of the island, the "Ngawigians" are renown for using bulldozers to launch huge tinnies down steep shingle banks in atrocious weather, on trailers connected by the longest drawbars you can imagine. Aside from the boat culture, it is also a good spot to fish from shore, and happens to have some legendary surf spots all around it too. Craps (aka Ning-Nong) is the best known and most surfed, named after the public toilet located in front of it. Clearly visible as you approach Ngawi, it's a left that can have occasional rights off the peak, which breaks through the tide. Further east there are other peaks like The 19th Hole and Dee Dees. These spots all face nearly due-west so easterlies are offshore, and all are visible from the road.

7. Cape Palliser
The lighthouse at Cape Palliser is one of the most majestic in NZ, set atop a jagged, weather battered pinnacle looking resolutely into the teeth of the southern ocean. Commanding views south towards The Kaikouras are an absolute gem on clear days, especially in winter when there is snow on the peaks. The 4wd track east from Cape Palliser eventually ends up at one side of the locked gate at White Rock, near the ramshackle DOC hut, but is unadvisable for all but the most confident off-road drivers. Aside from the untamed rivers which course from the hills behind the coastal plain, the rocks are tyre shredders and the track tortuous and narrow. **Washpool Coastal Retreat** (06)307 7823 offers a self-contained house with sea views www.washpool.co.nz

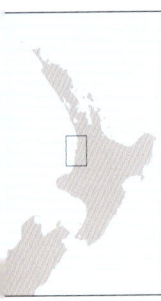

THE KING COUNTRY

You are unlikely to know too many people who've taken their beach holidays in the King Country, because not many people have. But the numbers shouldn't deter you, because the King Country coastline offers a great dollop of adventure and oozes character with a flavour all of its own. Steep hills crash into the sea on black sand beaches, interspersed by sprawling rivermouths and harbours that punctuate the coast all the way to Taranaki. The experience is intensified by ones almost complete isolation, which is good news for aquatic life and even better news for those who live here. Summer sees snapper off the beach, crayfish in the pots, game-fish and tuna further out, and kahawai at the harbour mouths. Winter sees whitebaiting and deep water snapper fishing for those with boats, while surfers will appear at any time of the year when the wind blows offshore and the ocean cleans up. But whichever way the wind blows, there's always a powerful sense of drama on what is possibly the wildest and most primitive stretch of the North Island's west coast.

Travelling Kawhia at the north and Mokau to the south are the two biggest settlements, and there is a lot of not much in between so come prepared! All the roads that connect these spots are gravel and clay, so expect longer than average travel times. The scenic route that connects Waitomo and Awakino, is one of the loneliest roads in the North Island, and is gravel packed clay for about half the 75 or so km from Marokopa south; but is one of the nicest roads you'll ever drive. www.kingcountry.co.nz

Surfing For surfers it's a kind of lost paradise; an empty, swell drenched coastline with some very kindly land features which aid the creation of perfect waves. The truth is there is virtually nobody surfing many spots on this coast due to its isolation. There are a lot of beach breaks, waves off the rivermouths and a couple of points, of which Kiritihere is the easiest to get to. East or north-east winds are critical.

Fishing It's one of the more challenging coasts in New Zealand to fish from land, due to continual swell and prevailing onshore winds, which is why torpedo fishing is so popular in the area. Boaties also suffer from difficult launching conditions but as a consequence, this coast is not overfished, so when you can get a line out, it's generally well worth the effort, no matter how you get it out.

Swimming Not a lifeguard in the whole region, which may deter some, but shouldn't. The idea is not to get into trouble by following all basic beach safety rules. Obviously it will be safer swimming inside the harbours and river mouths.

Marokopa

Consevation success story Marokopa is a fantastic example of environmental restoration through local vigilance and perseverance. Ten years ago the dunes north of the mouth had all but disappeared due to heavy foot traffic and inconsiderate use. The spinifex was the first to go, and over the years, with the aid of some big winter storms, the sand followed close behind. With nothing to hold this natural storm barrier together, the Tasman was threatening to bust through. The Ngati Toa Tupahau trust, working in conjunction with DOC and Environment Waikato, began a restoration programme involving PD prisoners performing community planting, which has been highly successful. When previously the dunes were a virtual dead zone, they now support a group of 15 dotterels and two seals. There are up to 5 volunteer wardens on busy weekends, patrolling the estuary to ensure that the good work isn't undone. A community group, led by Kahu Hohaia (watching like a hawk from her home overlooking the water), liaise with the harbour-master by RT and don't miss a trick!

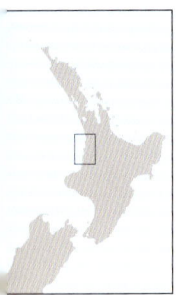

Aotea and Kawhia

The coast south of Raglan is indented by two beautiful tidal harbours, each with a very different countenance, separated by some of the wildest stretches of beach in New Zealand. This is the home land of Te Rauparaha, most feared of Maori warriors, and composer of the now globally recognized Ka Mate haka. This territory marks the start of the King Country and was long impenetrable to Pakeha, but now a series of gravel roads connect the various spots covered on the map. Pre-European Maori lived in abundance on these coasts; the oceans alive, with fish of all species even coming up the tidal streams. There are still plenty of fish to be had, good waves, some huge stretches of pristine beach, and still not a lot of people living in a uniquely invigorating piece of New Zealand.

Travelling Other than route 39 from Otorohonga, all the roads in this area are gravel and generally winding, and it's a very bad place to speed. Be prepared for washouts after heavy rain. The only places to get fuel are Kawhia and Raglan.

WIND ROSE

SWELL ROSE

Surfing There are a couple of outstanding surfing options, but both are out of bounds for most people. Albatross Point south of Kawhia is a legendary spot in huge swells but inaccessible unless you know local land owners, and Aotea Reef is a big wave tow-in spot that is strictly for those with a jet ski and large nuts. Ocean beach at Kawhia gets okay waves, but is rarely surfed, and usually a bit smaller than Ruapuke.

Fishing Kawhia is a legendary fishing harbour and home to a substantial fleet of commercial boats. The wharf is an easy place to fish from land as is the harbour entrance, which has accounted for some huge fish over the years. Dove Fishing Charters (07)871 5854 are the best known and well respected.

Swimming There's sheltered harbour swimming at both Aotea and Kawhia. Kawhia's Ocean Beach is a wild and woolley spot, but easier to get to than Aotea.

1. Aotea Harbour/Maukutea Beach

Aotea Harbour lies 50 km south of Raglan, and a small, pretty, but dilapidated settlement lies nestled on the south side of the estuary approximately 5 km from its mouth. The beach there, called Maukutea, but signposted as Ocean Beach, is wild and spectacular, but the Otorohonga council in their wisdom have locked the gate which allows vehicle access, due to

issues regarding dune erosion. This only leaves the inner harbour as a swimming spot for casual visitors, which is okay at high tide, but hardly spectacular. Add to this the lack of amenities of any kind, and it

Aotea Reef

adds up to a place most won't bother visiting. Maybe that's what the council wants. You can nonetheless walk to the heads from the carpark, a thirty minute each way excursion, and the sight of Aotea's huge black dunes makes it worth it. Aotea has recently been the scene of a new big wave discovery; with a reef breaking offshore holding monster waves, that are only accessible with a jet-ski. As you would expect the fishing both in the harbour, at the mouth, and in the surrounding ocean is very good.

2. Kawhia Harbour/Ocean Beach

Kawhia is a slightly dusty feeling port town with a permanent population of about 700, facing onto the water a few km from the harbour mouth. It is an especially important place to local Maori, as it was in Kawhia that the Tainui waka made her final landing. History tells us that when its two leaders stepped ashore, they tied the waka to a pohutakawa tree which still stands to this day on the foreshore between the wharf and the Marae, behind which the canoe is said to be buried. It is a busy fishing hub with a rich maritime history, out of which operate several charter boats catering to the general public. The fishing out of Kawhia is as good as anywhere on the West Coast, and some would say better, given the huge variety of terrain accessible from here. There are fish close in during summer and autumn for land-based guys, with the wharf at the bottom of town a convenient and popular place for visitors to throw a line out. The inner harbour produces a wide range of species from kahawai, trevalley and snapper, to flounder, mullet and the odd kingie. Fishing the entrance also has a a long reputation going back through time, with some monster snapper landed around it over the years. There are some patches of sand adjacent to the wharf and out towards the entrance that offer safe swimming, while the only open ocean beach is called, funnily enough, Ocean Beach. It is flanked by

high spinifex tufted dunes, and stretches nearly 20 km north to Kahua Pt and Aotea Harbour. You'll find it 5km west of the main street, by following Te Puia Rd. Like most west coast beaches, it sufffers badly in the prevailing south-west winds, with no shelter of any kind. But Ocean Beach holds a fantastic surprise; a hot spring to match anything the Coromandel has to offer, and at low tide you can dig your own pools, which are at the perfect temperature for a soak. There's a delicious pleasure to be found when sitting in a black sandpit in steaming thermal waters. It's feels even more delicious in winter, when its freezing, the surf is huge, and the wind is howling onshore. You need to take a shovel and then dig as deep as you can to really enjoy the experience. The location of the pools is almost directly in front of the public walkway from the carpark, though for precise directions ask a local. The beach here can get good waves, though it's usually smaller than Ruapuke, the result of Albatross Point's swell shadow. The only amenities out here are cold showers and toilets in the carpark behind the beach. The drive from Raglan is about 50 km, of which about thirty are bone jarring, rutted, windy gravel, and seems to wash out frequently after rain. Alternatively come via highway 39 south of Pirongia and save your spine and vehicle. It is home to a range of ammenities including three campsites, a pub, cafes, fish and chip shop, petrol station and a store. **Kawhia Beachside S-Cape** (07)871 0727 is a well located holiday park on the edge of the harbour as you come into town, with cabins and a basic backpackers block. www.kawhiabeachsidescape.co.nz

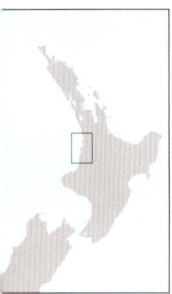

Marokopa to Mokau

It's a region of tight, quiet little coastal communities, with a mix of summer homes and a few permanent locals. The holidaymakers generally come from across the Waikato and from farms in the King Country, and for the month of Christmas festivities, all the homes are full and the campsites are busy. People come for the fishing and wild-west beach life, which in mid-summer involves big barbies, boxes of beer and fish of all kinds cooked all ways. For most of the rest of the year, it's an area that sees few lingering visitors. The northern beaches, while spectacular, are virtually ghost towns for much of the time.

Travelling Be aware there are no services between the Marokopa campground store and Awakino. There are a few accommodation options at Mokau and the odd bach for rent in Awakino, but otherwise only a few campsites. This is the New Zealand back country.

Waikawau tunnel

WIND ROSE

SWELL ROSE

Surfing There are a host of different waves on this section of coast, with the harbour mouths all holding good banks. Kiritihere has a sand bottom point, plus there are good beach peaks everywhere, and a few spots to find for the intrepid seeker.

Fishing The harbour mouths all offer exceptional spinning for kahawai, and are also a well known and prolific whitebait fishery in season.

Swimming Swell pounded and isolated ocean beaches offer intimidating conditions, but the harbours offer an easy set of choices for families.

1. Marokopa

Marokopa presents itself as a speckled, rather scruffy cluster of baches, and that is what it is. It is unashamedly a fishing community with few pretentions, and at low tide, the entire town seems to flock to the entrance of the harbour for a shot at the kahawai feeding around the mouth, armed with surfcasters and heavy silver spinning lures. You'll find good snapper fishing off the beach to the north, though access requires a vessel of some kind. Boats can be launched in the river, and the open ocean accessed a few hours either side of the high tide in low swell conditions, but be warned, it is a pretty wild bar. The memorial to HMS Albatross attests to this fact. Marokopa is also a good surf spot in smaller swells and north-east or east winds, with good banks both to the north and south of the mouth. Access

to the north requires a short paddle followed by a walk up the beach. Same goes for fishermen, but please don't walk over the dunes! Swimming in the harbour before the heads, presents fewer risks than at most other spots on this coast. **Marokopa campground** (07)876 7444 and store are open all year marokopacampground@xtra.co.nz

Marokopa

Kiritihere

Awakino

2. Kiritihere

The gravel road south from Marokopa climbs the hills and after five or so kilometres, drops back to the coast. Soundy road follows a cabbage tree studded river bed that leads you to the ocean. Kiritihere is unassumingly beautiful, in a desolate, wind battered way, and though devoid of trees, the point at the south end offers some protection from south-west wind and swell. It is a popular free-camping spot for wandering surfers who come looking for a quiet wave on their own, and Kiritihere often provides that. When the swell is smaller, the inside reef called Kenny's will break. When it's bigger, waves break off the outside point. This spot is called Kinas and in ideal conditions, it can connect through. The beach can also have some pretty hollow banks. Fishermen will find good snapper in late summer off the rocks at either end of the beach, and sprats can be caught off the bridge for bait or for the kids. It is a popular beach launch spot for boaties from Marokopa wanting to avoid the bar. Swimmers should be wary of the rips around the stream especially on outgoing tides. Kiritihere is also a popular fossil finding spot with the cliffs to the south showing an abundance of 12 million year old scallops and other shells. There's a good long drop and bins in the freecamping area at the south end.

3. Waikawau

Waikawau is all on its own, halfway between Awakino and Kiritihere, down a dead end road in one of the most isolated spots in the North Island. I put an "x" by it when I saw it on the map for all those reasons, took a right turn, and followed the road till it ended. There you find a ribbon of sand, backed by sheer cliff, but uniquely, access to the beach is gained by way of a 50 metre long tunnel through the cliffs. It was hand hewn by early farmers, who found it easier to perform this back breaking task, than to drive their stock over the hills every season after a muster down the beach. The tunnel is high and wide enough for a man on horseback and feels faintly church like. The beach itself is a couple of km long with a point to the north end and a reef fringed headland to the south, but there isn't much sand at high tide. It produces good fish in late summer when you can get to the points to fish from the rocks. There are toilets, bins and picnic tables on the landward end of the tunnel.

4. Awakino

To call Awakino humble wouldn't be stretching things, but what it lacks in finesse, it makes up for in character. Awakino Point Rd leads to small, driftwood lined stretch of sand inside the harbour, where it is safe to swim. Continue south along the gravel road and up the hill and you can look north over the estuary and south towards of Taranaki, plus you'll find a track down onto the beach, offering 4wd access for fishermen and surfers. It's a common spot to find torpedoes deployed, and a good place to spin for fish, with kahawai and snapper caught all around the entrance. There is a pub in the main settlement and tearooms on the main road a couple of kilometres to the south. The pub is legendary and if you're keen to meet the local fishermen you'll find members of the 260 strong Mokau fishing club cooking lunch here on the first Sunday of the month. **Awakino Hotel** (06)752 9815 www.awakinohotel.co.nz.
The Seaview Holiday Park (06)752 9708 is situated right on the coast between Awakino and Mokau.

5. Mokau

Mokau is the largest of the rivers on this part of the coast and the biggest coastal settlement in the King Country. It meets the ocean at a turbulent and dangerous mouth, and a settlement has developed on the north side with a history built on river trade. Mokau is well known for whitebaiting, and the fritters at the Whitebait Inn beside the highway are a travellers standard. The rivermouth produces fish, as do the beaches to the north and south. The surf community has long been aware of Mokau's charms and on both sides of the river you may find some of the ledgiest waves in the region. It's a heavy coast, but for safety, many local swim inside the mouth. **Mokau River Tours** (06)529 036 www.mokauriver.co.nz

6. Mohakatino

A quaint and unusual cluster of half a dozen bachs pressed hard up against the river banks, upstream from the Mohakatino mouth and adjacent to the main road. The reef system which begins just south of here, which you need to go through Mohakatino station to access, is one of the most dynamic land-based fishing spots in the area, though tricky to get to, but apparently difficult to fish.

Seaview Holiday Park

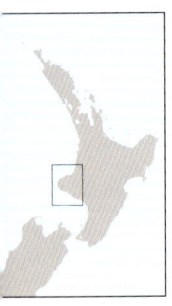

TARANAKI

One of New Zealand's most rugged and at times violent stretches of coastline, Taranaki is dominated by the mountain which gave the province its name, brooding over the region with an implacable countenance; sitting, watching, waiting. Its volcanic geology is responsible for the black sand that colours the coast all the way up to the Kaipara Harbour, with the big plate like shields on its flanks incessantly eroding black iron-ore particles down the streams that variegate its sides. Taranaki changes dramatically as you head south, as does the coastline, with the sculpted, mixed stone cliffs of the north giving way to the volcanic reefs and black sands south of Waitara, where boulder-strewn rivers course through rolling farmland to the sea. And everywhere you look, there's the mountain dominating the horizon. Known as a "hard-core" place; it is often dark and windy, socially conservative, and steeped in some difficult history. The massive oil and gas projects that, combined with farming, are the regions economic mainstays, have had a large impact on the collective psyche, though New Plymouth in particular has broadened culturally in recent years. It has a gritty but healthy reputation as a fishery, producing anything from whitebait to marlin, depending on season; and as a province in which to chase waves, is unbettered in New Zealand. To cap it off, it has some of the most accessible and spectacular coastal walks in the country along its fractured shoreline, offering truly stunning views right around the peninsula, giving it significant appeal for those of a less dynamic disposition. Unsurprisingly, world-class waves, epic fishing, and the range of other outdoor activities on offer in the region, have attracted a large community of lifestylers. With New Plymouth a decent sized town giving some good career options, you'll see why a lot of people are choosing to live the dream here.

Travelling Highway 3 covers the north coast, skirting inland before it hits New Plymouth, where it becomes the evocatively titled Surf Highway 45; tracking the coast all the way south to Hawera. This legendary road is like a wheel, with spokes heading off it to the coast, and crazy as it sounds, pretty much all of them lead to a world class surf spot. After New Plymouth, there are only a few small rural service towns, and in between there isn't too much of anything, except for acres of green grass dotted with cows. **New Plymouth District Council** (06) 759 56060 www.newplymouthnz.com

Patea

Surfing To be a surfer in Taranaki is to be blessed indeed, as this is surfing's answer to Disneyland. The base of Mt Taranaki conveniently projects into the wrath of the Tasman; its foreshore studded with reefs and protective headlands, fanning both into and away from the swell, which pounds the coast with mechanical repetition. The spots are, with a couple of notable exceptions, reef or point breaks of varying intensity, ranging from Ahu Ahu Rd's more mellow offerings, to the thick ledges at Stent Rd, with all stops in between. Beginners and intermediates will enjoy the less threatening waves on offer at the beaches like Fitzroy, Back Beach and around Oakura. There's a real country feel to surfing in "Taras" and most of the locals are super-friendly and seem happy to oblige with information. There are hundreds of potential surf options on any particular day, given the diverse orientation of the coastline, but travellers probably only need to know a handful of spots, considering the difficulties of getting all the elements lined up at the same time. The key is getting to know the vagaries of coastal winds, reading the swell, and then factor in all the choices available off Surf Highway 45.

Fishing You have to be a scrapper to fish from either the shore or a boat in Taranaki. The swell-pounded coast is littered with foul ground and that's where you're likely to find the fish close-in down here, though there are a range of river and stream mouths which make the going easier, and can produce good results. The combination of continual waves and the rocky foreshore present problems for boat fishermen too, though New Plymouth harbour is a "launch in all conditions" spot. The Cape Egmont Boating Club has a good facility that can handle a bit of swell, as does the Opunake Boat Club at Middleton Beach.

Swimming The Taranaki District Council has been the first district in Oceania to sign up to the blue flag scheme, a European method of classifying beach integrity. Bathing water quality at the 3 designated sites (Fitzroy, Oakura and Opunake), is tested for fecal coliforms and fecal entrococci fortnightly, and the results posted on the signs adjacent to the beach in question. **Blue Flag NZ** (04)920 7640 www.blueflag.org.nz. **Taranaki Regional Council** (pollution hotline) 0800 736 222. **Surf Life-Saving Taranaki** (06)758 2555 www.taranakisurf.org

Winter cloak

Stent Rd

North Taranaki

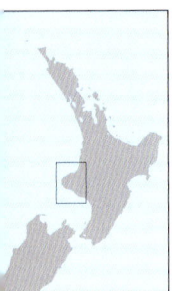

The Three Sisters at Tongaporutu mark the border of North Taranaki, as witnessed by the radical change in coastal geography that occurs here. Steep cliffs and odd, wind and wave chiseled shapes in the pale sandstone rocks lend a distinctive feel to a coastline which offers some problems with access, but extreme beauty when you can get to it. There are far more people here than further north in the King Country, but it was a revelation how beautiful this coast still is, and how productive it can be for surfers, fishermen and other ocean lovers. All different, these beaches individually and collectively possess a character that surprises most visitors. The White Cliffs walkway is a national treasure, and the adjacent Parininihi Marine Reserve, while controversial, will only benefit the local community in the long run. It's not the most dynamic surf coast in the country but can offer some shelter in huge winter swells, and Waitara in particular can get world class. There are some fabulous places to swim and no shortage of fish in the sea.

Travelling Being the most sheltered, this part of Taranaki has traditionally been the most populated, especially by non-surfing types. There's an old colonial feel to the area that is unique and charming, and a greater density to coastal settlements here.

Fishing Inshore reefs make torpedo fishing difficult here; rods only from the land. **Waitara Offshore Fishing Club** and **Waitara Surfcasting and Angling Club** have healthy memberships www.wofc.co.nz.

Surfing This is the least surfed part of the Taranaki Coast, but is a good place to look for manageable conditions in big winter swells. **Waitara Bar Boardriders** (021)255 6859 kava@clear.net.nz

Swimming Plenty of good spots to swim, just avoid the rivermouths for obvious reasons.

1. Tongaporutu

Tongaporutu feels like it belongs in the King Country. Actually, it is the geographical dividing line between the two provinces, and a walk out to The Three Sisters will demonstrate how markedly the coast changes at this point. Looking south you can see New Plymouth in a straight line along the White Cliffs which run 14km to Pukerahue and Pariokiwa Point. The village itself is one of the quirkiest settlements in New Zealand; a long line

WIND ROSE

SWELL ROSE

5. Onaero
Tiny Onaero can only really claim a hundred or so metres of beach, but it's a pretty chink in the coast with a clutch of baches and a man-made boulder bank protecting the foreshore from the Tasman's moods. **Onaero Bay Holiday Park** (06)752 3643.

6. Waitara
One of the less hospitable beach fronts in New Zealand, Waitara owes its existence to the deep channel at the mouth of the Waitara river. A service town twenty minutes north of New Plymouth, it supports a hardy fishing, boating and surfing community, who may not live in the prettiest place in the country, but who profit from the sheltered, northerly aspect of the coast here. The Waitara reefs, and river bar are somewhat mythical winter surf spots with a fearsome reputation for localism. Give respect. East Beach can also have good shingle banks for surfers, with lefts and rights up from the rivermouth depending on conditions. The rocky western foreshore is backed by a park and coastal road, with parking and public facilities near the mouth. There are a few tiny strips of black sand on West Beach, but it is unlikely to be the cleanest place to swim. You get there by taking Princess St off State Highway 3, and it's got a classic municipal outdoor swimming pool if you don't fancy the ocean. **Marine Park Motor Camp** (06)754 7121 is close to both the beach and river. **Waitara Boating Club** (06)754 8099

of fibrolite baches parked right on the river, leading to the spectacular, and highly photographed rock stacks further west. These coastal icons and the beach surrounding it, are only accessible below mid-tide, by driving to the end of Clifton Rd and walking about 15 minutes from the riverside reserve. The fishing around the mouth is said to be very good, and the odd tale of occasional big snapper caught upstream keeps everyone guessing. Further north, the Rapa Nui conservation area has been established to preserve a remnant mutton bird colony. It is also rumored to be a good fishing spot. You can find bins and toilets in the council reserve and carpark at the end of the Pilot Rd.

2. Pukerahue
Pukerahue is the southern portal to the White Cliff Walkway, and a stunning stretch of sand and rock, backed by the spectacular cliffs, that offers unlimited space to enjoy the coast alone. Beach fishing can be excellent here, and it is also a popular boat launch location, suitable for 4wd vehicles. The controversial Parininihi Marine Reserve lies offshore here and joins the coast walkway half way up the beach. Be aware of its boundaries. www.doc.govt.nz

3. Wai-iti
A small bay with a shingle and sand foreshore and a few baches, it offers quite a bit of shelter from south winds. A feature of the beach is the fossilized remnant of a puriri forest that was burnt and covered in ash during the last eruption of Mt Taranaki. The stumps have been preserved by being covered with sand and saltwater. **Wai-iti Beach Retreat** (06)752 3726 offers powered and non-powered sites plus cabins and a weekend cafe www.wai-itibeach.co.nz

4. Urenui Beach
Urenui is a popular resort at the mouth of the river of the same name, that feels like a tamer and more highly populated version of Mokau. Built around the beautiful river mouth and beach, with stunning headlands at either extremity; before the growth of surfing, this was where the New Plymouth establishment used to holiday, and many still do. The caravan park is a good one, and there's even a golf course. **Urenui Beach Camp** (06)752 3220.

New Plymouth

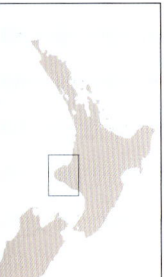

New Plymouth presses up against the relentless Tasman, in an heroic gesture of resistance to the oceans vengeance, its high concrete breakwater offering both physical and psychic protection from the elements. It is a sea town with a long history of fishing, that is home to a keen boating community, which chases everything from crayfish to marlin off its shoreline. If you're a surfer, you can usually get a half-decent wave somewhere between Bell Block and Back Beach, even on the hugest days. And there're also some great places to swim, just a stone's throw from town. If the ocean is in chaos, there's the incredible Govett Brewster Gallery and Puke Ariki Museum, plus quite a few good eating and drinking holes to boot. So where the bloody hell are ya?

Travelling It can get a bit confusing navigating the back streets around the citys beaches; get a free map from the i-site and hang on to it. The 7km New Plymouth coastal walkway extends from Lake Rotomanu to New Plymouth, and is a great way to get the feel of the town and surrounding coast.

Surfing A phenomenal choice of orientation and exposure offers possibilities in almost any sea state. Beach St Surf Shop (06)758 0400 is in Fitzroy. Go see Arch and Daisy for everything, including lessons.

Fishing The Lee breakwater has seen some massive snapper and kingfish landed over the years. New Plymouth Sport Fishing and Underwater Club (06)7583901 www.npsuc.org.nz

Swimming Despite the rocky shoreline adjacent to town, the beaches at either extent offer great swimming, though consistent swell means you have to be on guard. Ngamotu beach is usually calm. Surf Lifesaving Taranaki 24 hr call out number 027 496 2888.

1. Bell Block
A kind of satellite suburb, come retirement village for New Plymouth residents, with a pohutakawa-lined foreshore and a speck of sand that counts as a beach. At high tide it is pretty limited, though at lower tides a fair amount of coastline opens up to the north that is a good place to walk and swim. There's a much discussed reef break visible out to sea that works in large swells and south winds. Come here on a summer evening and you'll find families bbq'ing and enjoying the air around the reserve. Facilities include toilets, bins and picnic tables on the beach front.

2. Waiwhakaiho
An epic spot, it gets a bit more swell than Fitzroy and features well shaped rights breaking into the northern edge of the rivermouth, and lefts peeling the other way that can handle some solid swell. It is also one of the best fishing spots in town, especially if spinning for Kahawai. This is the beginning of the superb walkway to the port, and a new foot-bridge crosses the river, allowing easy access from Clernow Rd.

3. Fitzroy Beach
The most prominent town beach, Fitzroy is a suburb of New Plymouth, fronting a kilometre long curve of driftwood scattered, black sand. It's tucked in behind

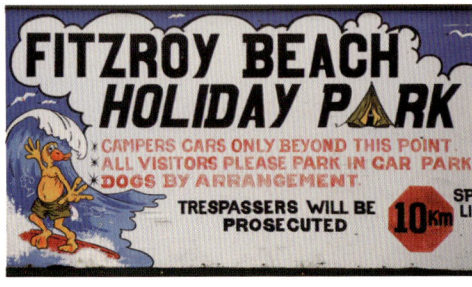

WIND ROSE

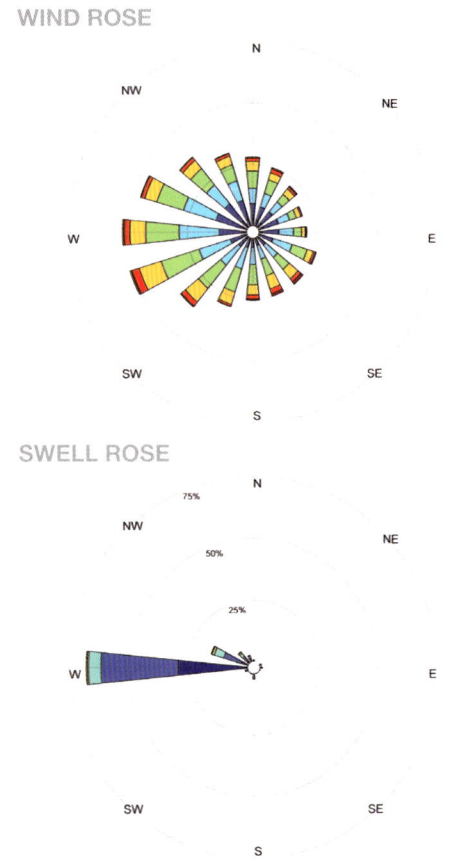

SWELL ROSE

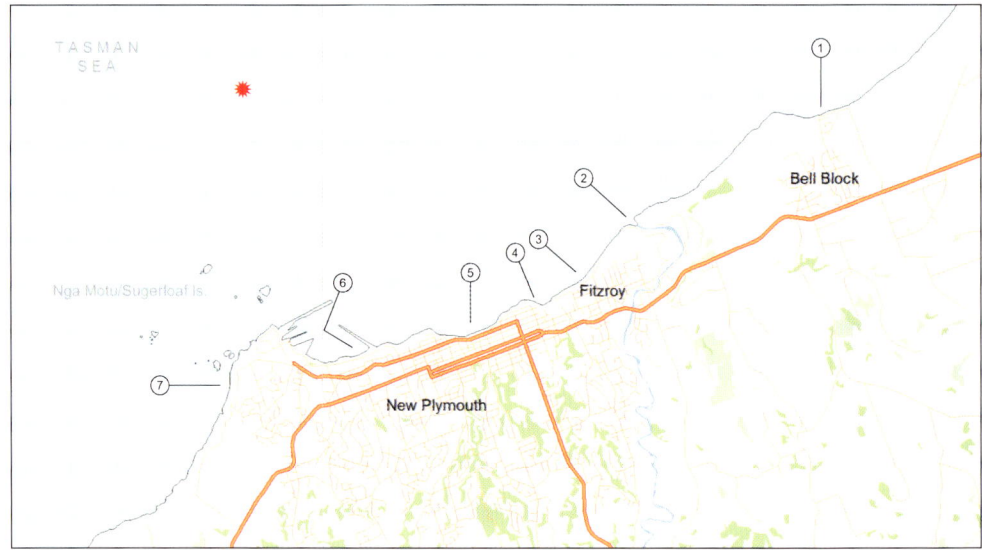

Fitzroy Beach

Ngamotu Beach

the headland and harbour entrance, and the shelter it receives from these make it a good place to swim, but an even better spot to get surf when the coast is too big and the wind blowing hard. Fitzroy can have hollow waves on its day, with peaks all the way to the groyne at the western end, plus the campsite is one of the most handily located in a New Zealand city, right on the beach, just a short walk from town. A large carpark at the bottom of Beach St has public loos plus a kids play area. This is where you'll find the surf life-saving club and campsite entrance. The extremely active **New Plymouth Surfriders Club** (06)758 1489 occupies a prime position in the middle of the beach www.npsurf.co.nz. **Fitzroy Beach Holiday Park** (06)758 2870. **Fitzroy Beach Surf Life-Saving Club** (06)758 2870 www.fitzroysurfclub.org

4. East End Beach

East End Beach is at the other end of Fitzroy. It is a sheltered spot in a southerly wind that also has good beach peaks, generally better at higher tides, though is always a bit smaller than Fitzroy. There is a left point here that can also get good. Access is from the East End/Purakau Beach Reserve with parking, shade trees and public toilets at the bottom of Buller St.

5. Bog Works

Located in front of Woolacombe Tce, adjacent to the bottom of town just north of Puke Ariki, it is an excellent, mainly right reef break that can be rideable when elsewhere is unsettled or too big. Access is via a set of steps below the carpark at the intersection of Pari St and Buller St. It's a long paddle out.

6. Ngamotu Beach

A sheltered swimming and boating beach inside the port, it is home to New Plymouth Yacht Club, fishing shops, dive operations and several cafes and restaurants. There's a grass verge with seats and easy parking on Ocean View Parade, just behind the sand. In the hugest winter swells, there are waves in here too. **Chaddys Charters**, located nearby, offer expeditions to the nearby Sugarloaf Islands Marine Reserve in a restored Liverpool class "C" lifeboat (07)758 9133. Paritutu Rock stands guard over the south end of the beach, and it's a good place to enjoy the views up and down the coast. **Belt Rd Seaside Holiday Park** (06)758 0228, sits on the coast just north from here www.beltroad.co.nz. It also has a wave adjacent to the breakwater that's popular in huge south-west swells.

7. Back Beach

A sandy strip of coast that sits in the hook of the Port Hills, Back Beach faces west/south-west and is one of the most consistent surf spots in the country, known to regularly have good banks, with a good profile that gives the peaks punch. Host to many a surf contest over the years, it is a New Plymouth daily staple, and while often busy, it's generally a pretty relaxed spot to surf, despite its popularity. You'll find well maintained toilets and bins in the various conveniently placed carparks above the beach.

East End Beach

Back Beach

Oakura to the Cape

Just south of New Plymouth, on the appropriately named Surf Highway, is Oakura. It signals the start of a long expanse of lightly populated countryside, and also another shft in coastal geography, as the foreshore becomes rocky and reefy. The variety of surf breaks in the vicinity put it on a par with Gisborne and Raglan, as one of the absolute best places to go in NZ for a surf trip, and one where you're almost guaranteed to get waves of high quality. There is somewhere for all ability levels on this coast, from the mellow peelers on Oakura Main Beach to Stent Rd's freight trains. Fishing is a mixed bag for the land-based guys, but exceptional if you can get out in a boat. Great swimming at a few of the beaches completes the menu for a feast in the ocean around Oakura.

Travelling Wavehaven Backpackers is a legendary spot if you're travelling on a tight budget. **Ahu Ahu Rd Villas** are at the other end of the spectrum price wise but are right on the beach. Further south towards the cape, there's the **Stony River Hotel** (06)752 4253.

WIND ROSE

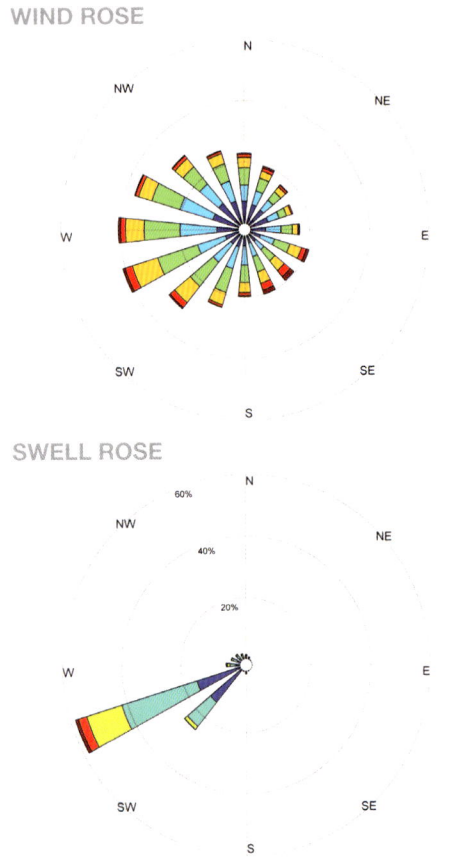

SWELL ROSE

Surfing This is the most wave-rich stretch of coast in the country, with huge variety, though it can be fiendishly difficult to predict the best place to be. If the wind has south in it, stay close to Oakura or New Plymouth. When the wind turns east or north-east, the spots further south do their thing, and the choices become almost overwhelming. **Oakura Boardriders Club** (06)752 7126 www.oakuraboardriders.co.nz. **Vertigo Surf Shop**, Highway 45, Oakura. (06)752 7363 surfboard and wetsuit sales, rentals and repairs.

Fishing Not an easy coast to fish from, with near continuous swell, and rocks galore, but there is some excellent fishing off the stream mouths and the various headlands. You would be well advised to connect with the local crew if you want to fish seriously off this coast. **Oakura Surfcasting and Kayak Fishing Club** oakurasurfcasting@paradise.net. **Cape Egmont Boating Club** Viki Loveridge (06)763 8860.

Swimming Oakura Main Beach and Ahu Ahu Rd offfer the most shelter from swell and wind, and also the most sand, though the streams should be avoided. Water quality reports are posted on the signs by the surf life-saving club. **New Plymouth Old Boys Surf Lifesaving** (06) 752 7776 www.npob.co.nz

1. Oakura Main Beach

One of the three blue-flag monitored locations in Taranaki, it is a popular sandy beach, with some Malibu style homes behind it, accessed by taking either of the right turns as you drive into Oakura from the north. The town itself is a handy little spot with a pub, garage, a few cafes and a surf shop, plus a convenient location at the beginning of Surf Highway 45. There are a range of accommodation options nearby, plus it's close enough to New Plymouth should you need anything major. The main beach gets surf, but it is rarely epic, usually best around the stream mouths. The good thing about Oakura is that it is offshore in south winds when spots further south are hating it. On an unusual note,

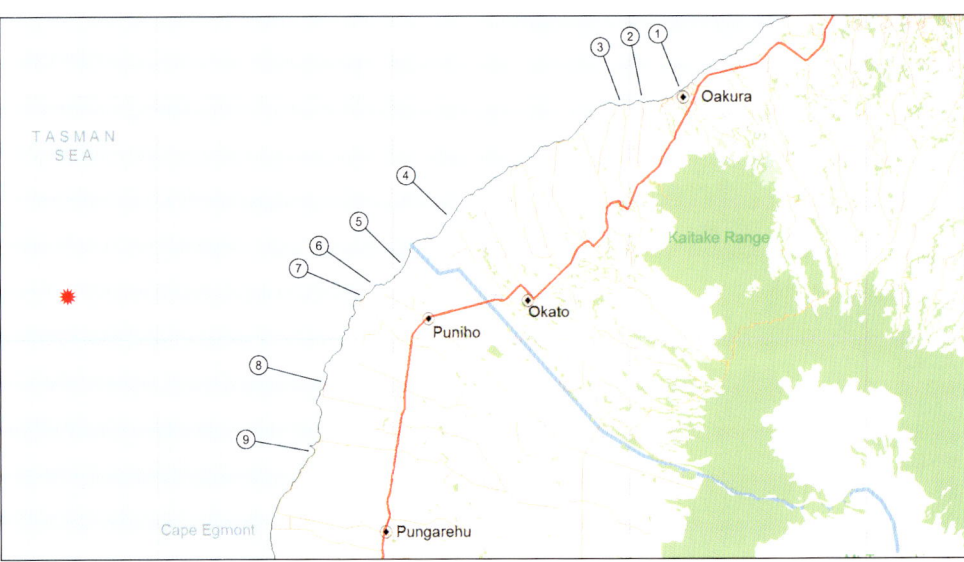

Oakura

Ahu Ahu Rd

the bombora that breaks offshore was the host to thirteen people on a surfboard, in an epic Guinness Book of World Records feat. It is the home of the Oakura Boardriders Club and a well established surf life-saving club, both of which have good public facilities including showers and changing rooms on the foreshore. As usual, the best swimming is at high tide, but the middle of the beach is still sandy at low tide. Many local families swim with their kids in the stream just north of town, where there looked to be a good sand bank with waves at low tide too, however conflicting reports on the quality of the water in surrounding streams make me nervous about this, and while the testing for the blue flag was carried out in the centre of the beach, the fringes are unmonitored and may be less clean. **Oakura Beach Holiday Park** (06)752 7861 www.oakurabeach.com

2. Ahu Ahu Rd

Ahu Ahu Rd is one of my favourite spots in the whole country, a small north facing oasis that's protected from the wind by both its orientation and the hills which back the beach. The aspect is critical for fishermen and surfers seeking offshores, in an area suffering from a lot of south and south-west winds, which can really kill the fun further south. There are a variety of waves to choose from, with the reef to the south picking up the most swell. Inside that, there's another long mellow left breaking into the bay. The beach can break well at high tide with various peaks, though this area is highly dependent on sand bank formation and changes regularly. This is a popular stand-up paddleboard and kite-boarding area, offering easy launching and a wide range of peaks to choose from. Some good snapper have been caught off the ledge to the north of the beach at low tide, and further south you'll find an abundance of foul to fish off at lower tides. It's got great park-up spots with public loos on the grass reserve behind the beach, and no matter what you want to do in a day at the beach, you can probably do it here. The area is one with long iwi history for many of the reasons it has appeal today, and in particular the knoll and pa site south, between here and Lower Weld Rd, are sensitive areas. **Wavehaven B&B** (06)752 7800. **Ahu Ahu Rd Villas** (06)752 7370 www.ahu.co.nz

3. Lower Weld Rd and Timaru Rd

Both these roads converge on the coast a hundred or so metres along from Ahu Ahu Rd, and share the same features on the foreshore. They are separated by a rocky spit, and Weld Rd seems to get less people. It's a good longboard spot offering a mix of peaks with lefts and rights breaking around the rocks in the middle of the bay. It's got a small strip of sand between the rock fringes, and is sheltered in westerly winds. There's a large reserve area behind the dunes with bins and toilets that's an accepted free-camping location, so a great spot if you're in a van, and also well used by day-trippers. Despite the existence of roads on your map, public access to the beach and coastline south of here isn't possible till Kahihi Rd, but it is a wonderful place to explore on foot.

Weld Rd

Ahu Ahu Rd low tide

4. Kahihi Rd
Kahihi Rd leads to one of jewels in Taranaki's crown, the Kumara Patch. "The Patch" as it is affectionately known, is a super-long, left point, that likes any wind with an east in it, and works through the tide. It breaks from north of the Stony River mouth and into the bay adjacent, with the main access at the end of the official road and through a farm. While it is private land, apparently it's a paper road to the beach, so access can't be refused. It is about a 15 minute walk south from where you park your car. Expect crowds and wobbly legs when it's pumping.

5. Komene Rd
On the southern side of the Stony River there's another bay with waves breaking into it on all sides. The left to the south west can get good as can also the rocky beach. The Stony River mouth is also a summer kahawai and trevalley spot, with some good size fish close in by the mouth, and in the waves.

6. Puniho Rd
"Punihos" is one you can't pull up to and check from the car. You have to cross farmland over the stile and head right. It's got a long left with a short right breaking off the peak. Both are fairly shallow and get hollow, working best from mid to high tides in smaller swells. You can get out either side of the peak.

7. Paora Rd
Another road where you hit the jackpot at the bottom, with a choice of world-class waves and a really mellow feel, with vehicle parking on the foreshore overlooking the surf. Rocky Lefts is the first spot you'll see. It's a left point with a sucky temperament, that peels to the shore from directly in front of the carpark, with a steep take off and a super hollow section on the inside. Rocky Rights, and another left which break off it, are a hundred metres to the south. You just follow the line of people with surfboards heading into the scrub. Then there's Graveyards, a long twisting left with a short bodyboarders right off the peak. It is located north of Rocky Lefts, and though an ugly grovel over the sharp rocks to get out to to the peak, it's totally worth it when you do. There are toilets beside the foreshore.

8. Stent Rd
One of New Zealand's few truly world class surf spots, Stent is a heaving right hand point that holds some pretty hefty size, and in a good swell peels for over a hundred metres, usually best at lower tides. Parking right out in front, and easyish entry and exit guarantees a crowd; and when it's pumping, expect to have to compete for waves with a pretty hard core and committed local posse, plus every travelling wannabe in town. The road sign is always getting stolen by souvenir hunters; but it's there on your map, the next road after Paora Rd heading south. There are actually a bunch of waves in the vicinity, including a left on the north side of the main peak, plus another left across the bay to the south.

9. Bayley Rd/Coast Rd/Anglers Lane
This is the road that leads down to the Cape Egmont Boating Club, with its miniature lighthouse that's a replica of the real one, just across the stream. When they automated the original lighthouse in 1986, the unwanted bits and pieces were re-housed in the replica here. There's not much sand, but there are some beautiful lay-bys along the coast that get used as free-camp spots. Public amenities include toilets and bins, plus the Boating Club has its own facilities for members, including a useful launch ramp.

Rocky Rights

Stent Rd

Rocky Lefts

Opunake

After Cape Egmont, the landscape flattens markedly, the access points to the ocean are fewer, and the sense of windswept isolation increases with every mile you drive south. This part of the coast feels the full force of winter southerlies, and few trees stand in its face, which lends an austere tone. There are long stretches that are seemingly unreachable, with large headlands and points, and numerous potential secrets for both fishermen and surfers. Population density is low, and attractions are thinly spread. Opunake is the main centre, and looks like a period film-set with the clock set back, only now there's tarmac and cars instead of drays and dusty tracks. It's not a sophisticated place but very much heartland New Zealand.

Travelling Opunake is the obvious place to look for a bed, with few private accommodation options in the region, and nothing on the coast road south until Manaia and Hawera. **Opunake I-Site**, Main Road (06)761 8663 www.southtaranaki.com.

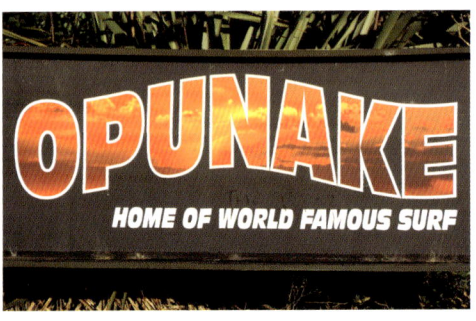

WIND ROSE

SWELL ROSE

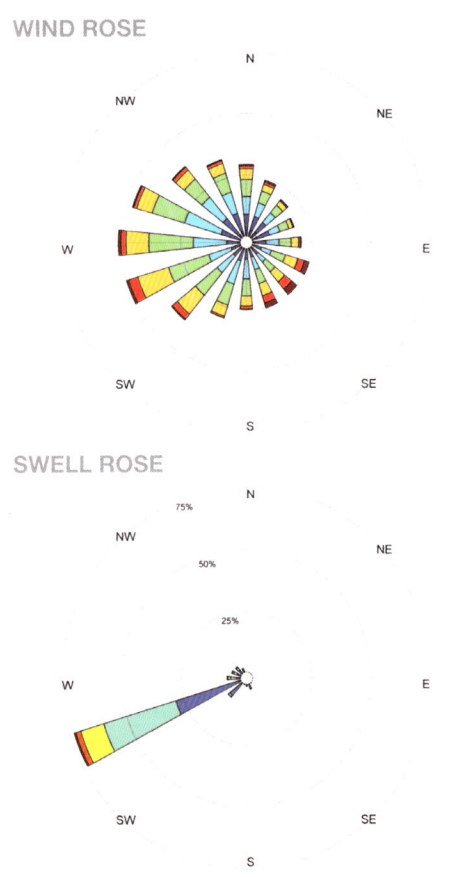

Surfing There are surf spots of some description at the end of all the roads where you can get access to the beach. It's all about the north-easterlies; south winds pretty much kill the spots around here.

Fishing Opunake Boat and Underwater Club has its HQ at Middleton Beach, just north of Opunake main beach. VHF Channel 84 is monitored by Cape Egmont Coast Guard. VHF Channel 77 is the unmonitored club channel. A casual users launch fee of $2 applies. The club owns a tractor for members to use, that's housed in the boat sheds by the beach.

Swimming The only easy swimming on this coast is around Opunake's town beaches.

1. Cape Egmont
The westernmost tip of the North Island gives a visual reference to the word desolate. Take Cape Rd to the end. Set back half a kilometre from the most windswept and rock-strewn stretch of foreshore in the country, sits a fabulous, once manned, though now electrified lighthouse, that serves as a warning to nearby shipping; "stay away...there be rocks here!" Cape Egmont lighthouse was originally erected on Mana Island north of Wellington in 1865, but was dismantled and rebuilt here in 1881. The cast iron tower stands 20m high and the beam can be seen for 22km. There are no amenities and little shelter here; just a bare piece of grass to park on. There's no sand, so it's not a great spot for general swimming, but waves and fish in the region will continue to draw people to the cape. It is absolutely beautiful and yet totally unforgiving in nature, with a long history of Maori occupation and use.

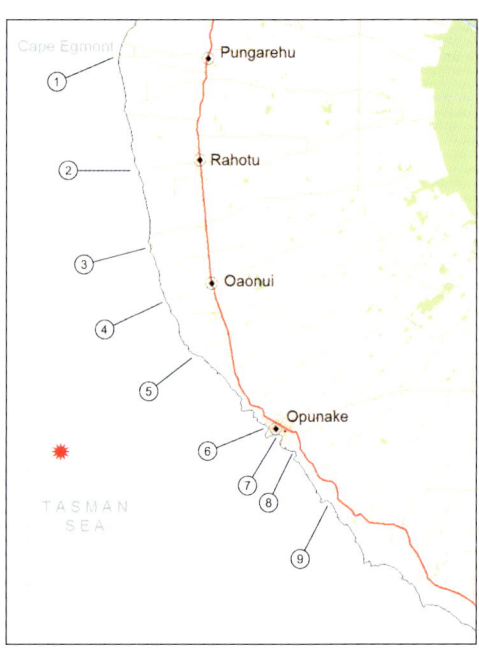

2. Lower Kahui Rd
A short road ends behind extensive low sand dunes, approximately 500 metres from the shoreline. It is popular for both fishing and surfing, with fishermen heading south, to the mouth of the Pungarerere Stream and Mussel Rock, and surfers taking advantage of the beach peaks and reefs in the area which can be good in tiny swells. It's extremely beautiful and very quiet, and makes a lovely place to camp in or behind the dunes.

3. Manihi Rd
Desolate and striking, it's sandy at high tide, rocky at low, with no real shelter. It offers easy 4wd access to the coast, and can fish well at lower tides. Sadly, there are no facilities.

4. Kina Road Beach
A sandy beach with rocky fringes, one cute shack and a public toilet. The waves include good rights to the north, and good lefts to the south, that can both hold serious size. It is an exposed spot with little protection from the wind, hence popular with windsurfers and kiters, with good access to the coast for beach fishermen.

Mangahume

5. Arawhata Rd
A right hand point/reef that's good in smaller swells and clean conditions, is located down this road, with offshores blowing from the north and north-east. A peak forms to the north which then reforms into a bowly inside section breaking close to the rocks. It works through the tide but it's a bleak, exposed spot that hates any south in the wind, and is only of interest to surfers and maybe fishermen. There are no amenities but it's an easy spot to pull up and check.

6. Middleton Beach
It is home to the local boat club and a sheltered neighbour to Opunake, with significantly less swell getting in here. Middleton Beach totally lacks charm, but would be one of the safer spots to swim in the region, though unpatrolled. There are public loos.

7. Main Beach
Opunake has long been favoured as a recreational beach by pakeha, with bathing facilities including a pagoda located where the surf club now stands, dating back to the thirties. Once seen as potentially the biggest port on the west coast due to the protection it receives from large headlands to both north and south, two attempts were made to build wharves at Opunake in the early part of last century. Both failed and the last remnants of one can still be seen off the north point, (known as Desperation Point by local surfers). The council in their desperation to generate surfing dollars, recently embarked on another folly, and in a futile effort to harness the ocean for cash, paid ASR to build an artificial surfing reef here. Predictably, it failed too. Remnants of their 2 million dollar investment can be seen on the clifftop, creating an eyesore to this day. **Opunake Beach Holiday Park** 0800 758 009 or (06)761 7525 www.holidayparks.co.nz/opunake

8. Mangahume/Sky Williams
A spectacular cove can be found a few kilometres south of Opunake, with an impressive headland to the north of a wide bay that's pierced by a long fringe of reef. In this cove you'll find two of South Taranakis better waves. Sky Williams is the long left which breaks into the bay to the north; Mangahume, the shorter, punchy right reef which breaks into the little bay to the south. Both hold size, and deal power. Sky Williams prefers low tide, "Mangas" mid to high tide. Access is through the gated but public road visible from highway 45, just after you see a shed with the "kneeboard world title" signs on it. Park on the cliff above the coast, and walk down the track onto the beach. There are no amenities.

9. Greenmeadows
Well known but tricky to find, and possibly not worth the effort; take highway 45 till 8 km after Watino Road and follow the stream to the coast through farmland. Check with the farmer to be polite. Greenmeadows is best surfed at low tide in a big swell with a light north-east wind.

South Taranaki

Driving south of Opunake, you hit the "Deep South", with Taranaki at its plainest; a great slab of treeless, rolling, dairy land stretching all the way to Whanganui, that gradually bends into the lee of the South Island. Access to the beach in the south of the province is limited due to the chiseled cliffs which line the coast in its entirety. As a result, all the beach locations are at the mouths of streams and rivers, which sadly are amongst the country's dirtiest; a fact that will surely hinder the growth of any meaningful tourist revenue in the future. That said there is a fair amount of pristine coast, and a stunning set of walks amongst other things to do. One word of caution that is worth remembering at all these locations: the cliffs are in a constant state of erosion, so be very wary walking either above or below them.

Travelling Accommodation is limited to the main centres (Manaia and Patea), which don't have much to offer themselves; or campsites, of which there are several, in good locations. Highway 45 seems to skirt the coast exactly three km inland, as every sign in its direction reads exactly the same: Surf Beach 3 km. **South Taranaki Visitor Centre**, 55 High St, Hawera, (06)278 8599 www.stdc.govt.nz

Surfing There are some remarkably good waves given the shallow shelf that is a feature of the coast, with long sandy points and some epic river bar breaks; though the area is reliant on big west swells and north to east winds for clean conditions, and that's not a common combination. Patea is the most surfed spot, with a selection of peaks in the area working in different conditions. The swell gets smaller as you drive south, and the shelf gets even flatter, reducing wave power and size. **Patea Boardriders and Surf Club**, Secretary L. Niu (06)273 8801.

Fishing If Taranaki is for scrappers, here's where you have to scrap the hardest, with a rocky shore, raging streams, and an abundance of swell. Cool water and a shallow shelf keep many desirable fish species well offshore for much of the season, though late summer can see a few big snapper caught by various means. The rivers offer boat launching, but the bars are turbulent; though they're not shy of a bit of swell down this way. Out deep there's cod, shark, kahawai, trevalley and snapper in summer. Winter sees leaner pickings, made up for when the whitebait come on. **Ohawe Boating and Angling Club** Malcolm Hurley (06)278 5661. **Patea and Districts Boating Club** (06)273 8398. **South Taranaki Fishing Charters** 027 2899 929.

Swimming A flat shelf and less swell than further north offer good swimming conditions, but the highly dubious water quality around all of the rivers is a big issue here. I wouldn't let my kids swim within 50 metres of any of them.

1. Kaupokonui Beach
Lower Glen Road takes you to the first easily accessible spot south of Opunake. Heads Road takes you to the mouth of the river and the beach there, which is the first of several access spots to the coast around Manaia. It's a fantastic and underrated spot, dominated by the campground; with a large reserve area adjacent to the river, and a tiny clutch of the oddest baches, in their own separate community, named Maraekura. There's good fishing for kahawai in the stream mouth, snapper from the beach with either torpedos or kayaks, and whitebait in season. **Holiday Park** (06)274 8577 has all facilities

2. Ohawe
Famous as the first place where moa bones were discovered in NZ, this little gem deserves a visit. It's another rivermouth that's gouged out a pathway to the coast through the two hundred foot cliffs, and is backed by the Rangatapu Reserve. The beach is a mix of sand and stones, offering good land-based fishing,

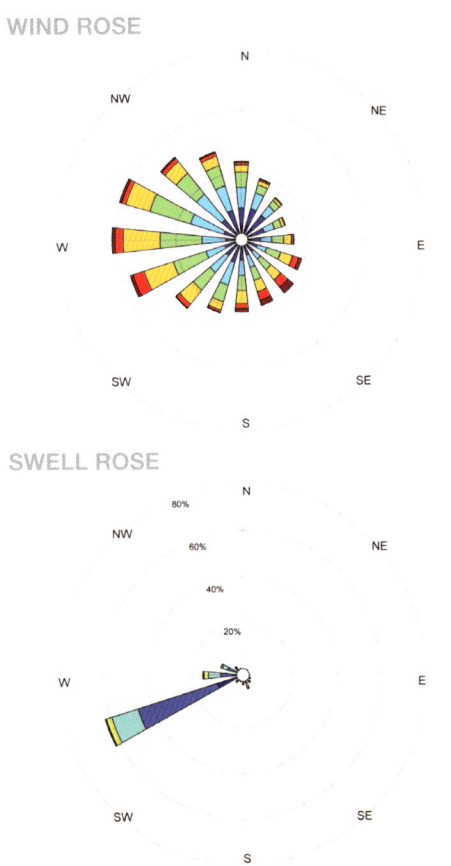

WIND ROSE

SWELL ROSE

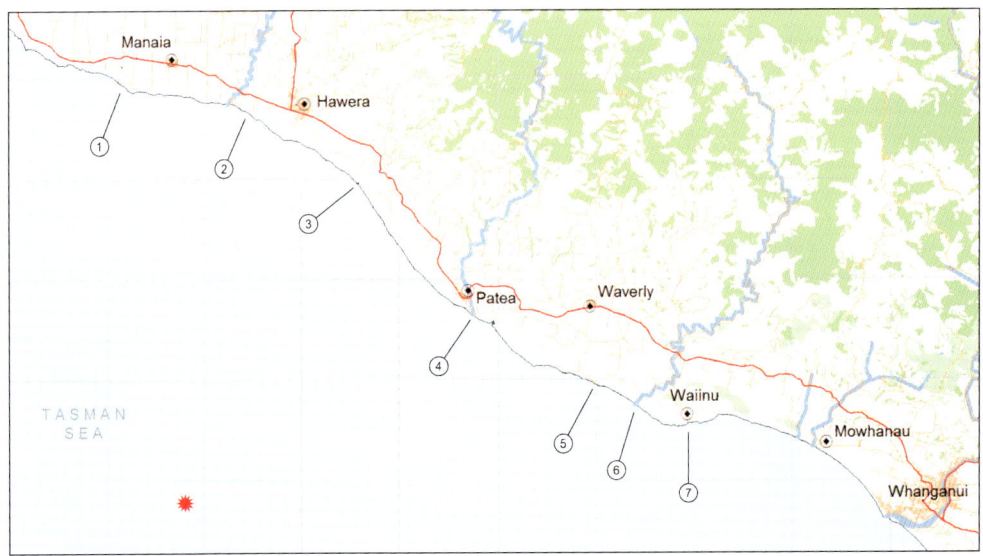

Patea

Waihi

and some good waves both at the stream mouth and up the coast. **Ohawe Beach Motor Camp** (06)278 6939 has 24 acres of prime beach land, left in trust, and administered and maintained by volunteers.

3. Waihi Beach Park
Yet another sign announces a "surf beach 3km." It's a freak canyon, with a steep descent to the beach between the twin peaks, and about as shady a stretch of sand as you'll see, with some areas receiving no sun at all during winter. Its very black, but very beautiful in an imposing, almost gothic way. There are no amenities, but good parking above the beach.

4. Patea Rivermouth/Carlyle Beach
The replica of Turi's waka in the main street commemorates the settlement of Taranaki by Turi and his hapu, who travelled overland from Kawhia. Historically known as Carlyle beach by Pakeha, Patea River mouth features a groin-protected river entrance, that produces good waves on both sides. It can work at all tides, with better conditions usually found to the south. Access is by walking out and jumping off the rock walls, which are also popular with fishermen, offering an easy way to get a bait into some deepish water with relative ease (see pic). The cliffs in the distance offer a little surprise too, if there is a solid swell. The wreck of the Waitangi can clearly be seen on the beach to the north, which is where you head for Mana Bay. Sadly the sign announcing sewage contamination in the river is obviously used so much they've got one made up with a hinged front, so that if it is ever clean, they can just flick it up and cover the bad news. Shame on the council! **Carlyle Beach Motorcamp** (06)273 8620. The **Patea Surf Lifesaving Club** amenities include toilets and a cold shower, plus an extensive parking area, a children's playground and picnic tables.

5. Waverly Beach
Waverly Beach Road leads to the coast where you will find two beaches. Cave Beach is the one in all the pictures, with a cathedral type arch of moderate proportions, sheltering a pretty little sand cove, which as well as being a great place to swim, is also home to the boat ramp. Long Beach is the area to the north. The coast is flat here and while low, the cliffs should still be treated with extreme caution. Coleman Ave skirts the beach with 50 or so baches making a funky little community. The developers have moved in a couple of km up the coast at Waipipi Beach, which is the first (private) access point you see as the road hits the coast. **Waverly Beach Campsite** (06)346 6013 or 0800 111 323 (24/7) operates on an honesty system; pay at the Waverly Library or send to STDC.

6. Waitotara Rivermouth
The totara part of the name refers to an ancient fossilized forest, that is buried at the mouth of the river. This is a nature reserve, protecting the different wildlife that enjoy the unique habitat, including a multitude of sea birds and waders. There's good kahawai fishing at the entrance, occasional snapper off the beach, whitebait in season and flounder in the estuary. Access (by 4wd only) is down the track that begins at the end of Hawken Rd.

7. Wai-inu Beach
Wai-inu is the centre of the Nukumaru Recreational Reserve, and while the geography is less dramatic than at many of the big rivers nearby, access to so many coastal features both north and south, plus safe swimming, and mellow waves on the sandy beach are all good reason to come here. The name means "water coming up from the ground," because of the water coming up through the sand in places. Nukumaru/Snapper Rock is the focus for fisherman, with deep water attracting a variety of fish species, and even the odd kingie in late summer. Just before it on the coast south you can see remnants of an old fishing camp, which also housed the local waka from the late 1800's till the 1970's. It is now at Pakaraka Marae in Maxwell. This is also a quality south facing surf spot, known as Fences, the NZ version of Malibu. You'll find long rights breaking down the sand and rock point, that need a hefty swell and north winds to produce the goods. The local farmer is happy enough for people to drive down his access road, but remember to close farm gates.
Wai-inu Capsite (06)346 5938 or 0800 111 323.

Cave Beach, Waverly

THE SOUTH-WEST

It starts with an immense set of cliffs and ends with an immense set of cliffs, and whilst it isn't considered the most desirable part of the North Island's coastline, and often neglected by travellers rushing south to Wellington, it does offer miles and miles of space, and a sense of freedom and peace that's worth gold if that's what you're seeking. It is such a big area, with such a huge diversity of landforms and aspect, that generalisations can fall flat on their face, so one really has to examine each area on a case-by-case basis. If you consider the geographical variation between Whanganui and Mana Island, including the phenomenal river systems that drain into the sea along this coast, the huge expanses of sand between them, and the spectacular beauty of Pukerua Bay and Paekakariki, there is a lot going on; and though it doesn't possess some of the glamour of other parts of the country, it offers a lot of choices, each with a ton of charm. The Kapiti Coast is considered almost a part of Wellington these days, but geographically it is very much connected to this coastal region, so I have resisted the urge to treat it as a chattel of the city.

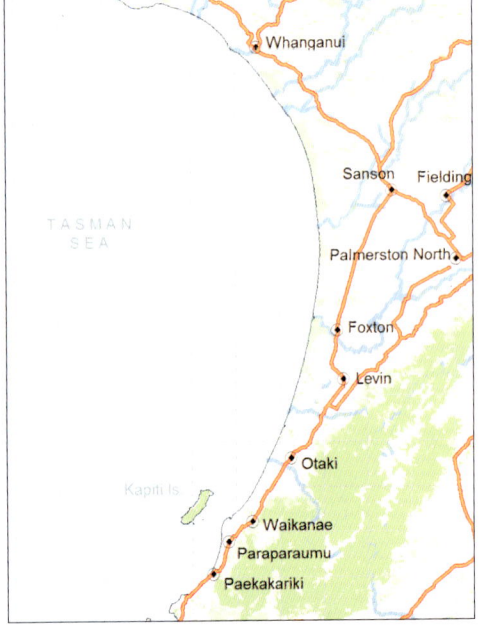

Travelling This is a lightly populated area of coast, with a cluster of settlements to the north around Whanganui, and south around the Kapiti Coast, with not much in between; which is fine if you're in a camper, but less so if you need a solid roof over your head.

Surfing Despite the endless expanse of flat, swell sheltered beaches that makes up the majority of this region's coastline, the occasional good session can be had by seeking out the pronounced sandbanks at the numerous river estuaries. The reef breaks around Pukerua Bay and the spectacular waves rumored to break around Kapiti Island, all spice up the offerings in a north-west or west swell, though it's not really a destination worth focusing on for travellers.

Fishing There is no question that land-based fishing with a rod is at its most difficult and least productive along this shallow coastline, when compared with other areas of the North Island. However kontikis and torpedos are often successful and the rivermouths can offer good spinning, and a harvest of whitebait in season. Boat fishing offers much better results, allowing access to the deeper water snapper grounds offshore. If you're after a feed, you'll find pipis in abundance at many spots.

Swimming Shallow water and prevailing onshore winds don't help, but on a fine day with an easterly blowing, it can be fantastic, and the water is generally a bit warmer than on the Wellington coast.

Himatangi

Paekakariki

Kai-iwi

Manawatu and Horowhenua

The longest continuous sand-dune system in the country runs from Whanganui to the Kapiti Coast, and while it is interrupted by several rivers, its essential characteristics remain the same down its length, so I have grouped it as one region. This huge stretch of beach was once the main road from Wellingtom to Whanganui, and became the birthplace of the locally renown Cobb and Co, which was New Zealand's version of the Pony Express. It is home to a phenomenal amount of different seabirds and a surprising array of fish life too, and though it doesn't have a reputation as the most spectacular coast in the North Island, it surprised me with its, at times, breathaking beauty and substantial charms.

Travelling Access is relatively easy at all spots, but the accommodation is pretty basic, consisting mainly of camping grounds. The main road is rarely too far from the coast, which makes it fairly easy to visit a few spots on your way past.

Surfing It's hardly the most exciting bit of coast for surfers, with a significant swell shadow created by the South Island, and a shallow shelf that sucks both power and size out of the waves, and while it does get ridden in decent south-west or west swells, it is longboard or SUP territory for most of the time.

Fishing The rivermouths tend to be the main focus for land-based fishermen, seeking either fin-fish or whitebait in season. **Foxton Beach Sports Fishing Club** (06)363 6143.

Swimming The water is rarely clear, but the shallow shelf which reduces its appeal for surfers, creates a safer swimming environment. Avoid the notoriously dirty rivermouths for the sake of your health

1. Totoka Beach
A more neglected beach you'll struggle to find, and though there are two toilets, I can't see too many people coming out here to do anything other than burn out cars. The stream was the dirtiest I've seen, which was a real shame, as it could be an amazing spot.

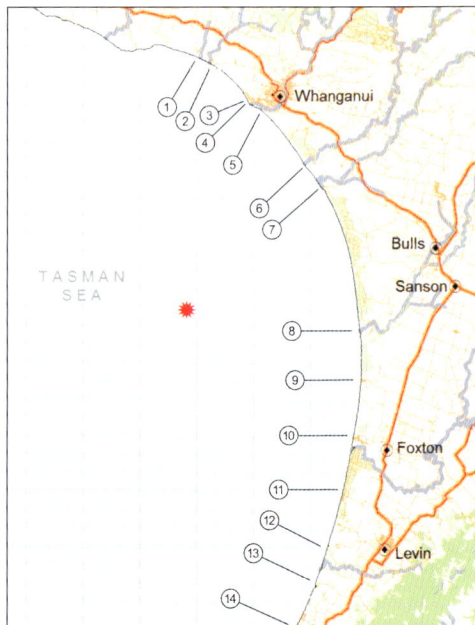

WIND ROSE

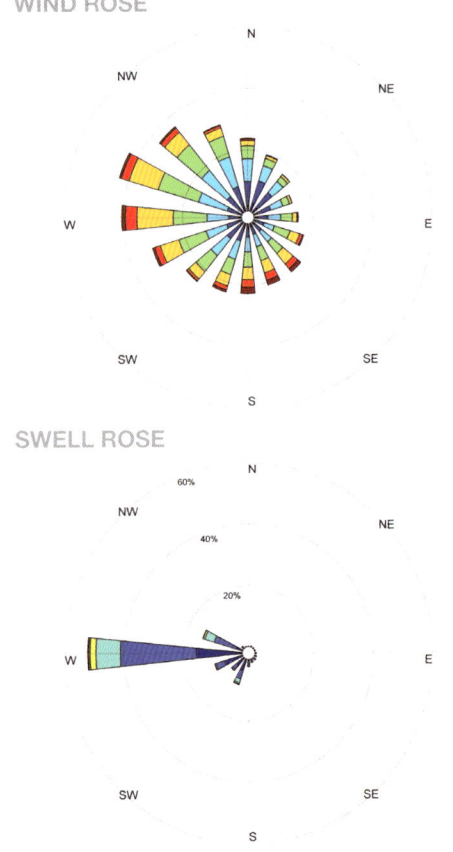

SWELL ROSE

Kai-iwi

Castlecliff

beaches. I wouldn't swim here though, and would be very careful surfing; ear plugs a must and don't swallow the water if you can avoid it.

5. South Beach
Airport Road leads to the coast. Park and walk over the dunes and you'll generally find yourself alone on a beach that leads to the south side of the Whanganui River entrance, offering access to some of the best surf in the region. Offshore is north-east, wave quality better at lower tides.

6. Whangacheu
5km of gravel road and 3 farm gates leads you to a beach settlement that can best be described as a coastal ghetto, with about a dozen squatter shacks and broken down caravans hidden in the dunes, set back from a broad river of the same name. The coastline features a sprawling mouth, dark shingly sand that is completely littered in driftwood, and a wide spinifex hinterland. It is beautiful in the most desolate sense of the word, but the sign warning of acid water that comes off the volcanic plateau, and the snarling dogs, were enough to deflect any enthusiasm I had for a swim or a fish. There are no amenities.

2. Kai-Iwi Beach
After Totoka, you could almost call Kai-Iwi Beach and the settlement of Mowhanau, gentile. It's a satellite suburb of Whanganui really, with most of the few hundred homes occupied all year, their residents taking advantage of the long stretches of coast to both the north and south that can be easily accessed from here, plus close proximity to the city. Safe swimming, and a real family atmosphere are the norm, though the stream mouth looked pretty mucky. **Camp Mowhanau** (06)342 9658 has just had a major revamp with new cabins and a cafe operating in summer www.campmowhanau.co.nz

3. Castlecliff Beach
One word. Grim. It doesn't help that you have to drive through the appropriately named Gonville, one of Whanganui's bleakest suburbs to get there; but when you do, it's as spartan an experience as you could imagine, at what is essentially the main town beach. It stretches from North Mole for several kilometres north, but no effort has been made to beautify the foreshore or public amenities along this forsaken stretch of sand, and regardless of any excuses, this is a major town resource gone begging. The main access point to the beach offers access to miles of empty coast, and is far enough from the detritus pouring from the mouth of the river to offer the possibility of safe swimming, plus the surf can also be okay on a big south-west swell. A reserve area well behind and above the beach has some sculpted landscaping, but not enough to make a real impact. You missed the mark here Whanganui council. The only amenities are a big carpark and toilets (which were locked when I was there). **Castlecliff Seaside Holiday Park** (06)344 2227 is adjacent to the beach www.castlecliffholidaypark.com

4. North Mole
It's an interesting place North Mole; bleak, post industrial and grey, but it holds a lot of attention from a fair few people including both fishermen and surfers. Long breakwaters extend out both sides of the Whanganui river where it hits the sea. North Mole is the one on the north side, and stationed along the last kilometre of the access road are tables and areas set out for fisherman. Commonly caught species are red cod, kahawai and shark. Again because of the channel scoured by the river, the banks seem to have a bit more punch here compared to the surrounding

7. Turakina Beach
Apparently Turakina is the midpoint in the longest sand dune system in NZ stretching from Patea in the north to Paekakariki on the Kapiti coast. It is a friendly and intimate coastal community at the mouth of another river, which totally changes the coastal landscape depending on its moods, in response to rain and swell. Consequently, the stretch of water between Koitiata and the beach can be a river estuary, a tidal lagoon or a landlocked lake depending on recent weather conditions. It is a significant wildlife habitat with curlews, sandpipers, terns, herons,

North Mole

oystercatchers, spoonbills, dotterels and pied stilts all in evidence. Fishing off the beach can be good, mainly for kahawai and rig, and there are a few waves on its day, but nothing spectacular. Fusilier Beach, named after a famous shipwreck, is 7km south, but the beach is growing at up to 4m per year and the wreck has been swallowed by the advancing sand. **Koitiata Camping Ground** (06)327 3770 is well located and quiet most of the year.

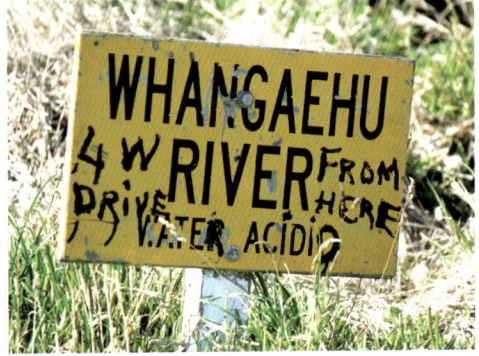

8. Tangimoana
It is a 22km drive off the main road to get to the mouth of the Rangitikei River, which is the site of an interesting coastal settlement called Tangimoana, set behind a broad wetland several hundred metres from the ocean. The name implies a lament for the ocean, but it is a beautiful and fertile spot that attracts a lot of land-based fishermen, who weren't doing too much lamenting when I visited. There are two access points onto the beach, the closest leads to a boatramp which lets you into the river inland from the mouth; the second leads to the dunes and ends a few hundred metres from the coast, with 4wd access only from there. There are public loos in the small park by the intersection as you arrive into the village and a motorcamp down Koura St, but no shop.

9. Himatangi
This is one of the most popular beaches on the coast, with a few hundred homes and a well-loved feel. As well as a surf club, there are a wide range of other facilities including a health centre, a cosmopolitan club which doubles as the fishing club, plus a good store and cafe. Himatangi is popular for fishermen, families from around the lower North Island, and travellers going north or south looking for a place to crash, out of Wellington. The coast here is a listed road with a 30 km speed limit, and is used by quad bikers and 4wd cars seeking fishing access up and down the beach. www.himatangi-beach.gen.nz is the community website with local accommodation details. **Himatangi Beach Holiday Park** (06)329 9575 is conveniently located and well set up. www.himatangibeachholidaypark.co.nz

10. Foxton Beach
A surprisingly large settlement 5 km off the main road on the north side of the Manawatu River, enjoys access to Foxton Beach, which on a fine day can be absolutely divine. The shelf is shallow here, so waves tend to break long before they get to the foreshore, making it a popular place to swim for families of all ages. There is one main access point, where you will find a well maintained foreshore reserve and surf life-saving club, with public toilets, cold showers and plenty of parking. Foxton has two fishing clubs and a launching ramp into the river before its mouth. Kahawai are commonly caught around the mouth, as are whitebait in season. The river is also a popular bird watching site. Other facilities include **Simply Balmy** cafe and wine bar, **Mr Grumpy's** takeaways, and two large caravan parks, plus some private rentals and motels. www.foxton.org.nz is the local community website. **Manawatu Caravan Park** (06)363 8016. **Foxton Beach Motor Camp** (06)363 8211.

11. Waiterere
A continuation of Foxton Beach but without the foreshore amenities, however, easy drive-on vehicle access makes it popular with land yachts, and also a popular boat launch spot. There is plenty of parking by the surf club above the coast, but many people park on the beach itself, where the sand is hard. History records the wreck of HMS Hyderabad, an iron, square rigged sailing ship on 25 June 1878, though nowadays, it is the "Sail On Inn" restaurant and takeaways that will make more of an impression on visitors. There is also a four square and café for travellers needs, plus **The Hyderabad Camping Ground** (06)368 4941. www.waitererebeach.net.nz has details of private accommodation listings. **Waiterere Surf Lifesaving** emergency response number 027 259 3241.

12. Hokio Beach
Named by Hau after a giant invisible bird in Maori mythology (The Hoikioi), it achieved prominence for Europeans as a stop over for the Cobb and Co mail coach, which used this beach as a highway between Whanganui and Wellington. It is yet another rivermouth, with a small, rustic settlement located by the sprawling estuary that attracts seabirds, whitebait and kahawai. Large shell middens point to the presence of pipis and mussels nearby, which would

obviously help the fishing. There are two main access points. Follow the main road and it leads to a gravel carpark several hundred metres back from the beach on the wrong side of the stream. Alternatively, take a right by the childrens play area, and go over the bridge. This route allows you to drive on to the beach without having to navigate the stream, and thus get access to some privacy or fishing spots to the north. The surf looked good, with pronounced banks by the rivermouth picking up the most swell.

13. Kuku

Kuku is an area sensitive to local iwi, that sits on land designated as wahi tapu, and borders ancestral land with riprian rights. While public access isn't prohibited, or even discouraged, with a stile and track from the end of the road leading through the trees and dunes to the beach, respect and care is requested, and only fair. A large sign by the road-side clearly points this out.

14. Waikawa

Yet another small rivermouth, with access from the road to the south side, and by foot over the bridge to the north. There's a domain with public loos and a boat ramp at the end of Waikawa Beach Road.

Kapiti Coast

So named after the spectacular island offshore that was once a base for Te Rauparaha during his many turbulent years in the south-west, and which still remains a dominant visual icon for miles around. This twenty or so mile stretch of seafront that's now an established part of the Wellington commuter belt, marks the transition from the flat coastal plain and sand dunes which stretch from Whanganui, finally ending with the cliffs and rocks at Pukerua Bay. Kapiti Island is a spectacular marine and wildlife reserve, while the waters surrounding it offer some highly productive fishing, good diving and even a few good waves.

Travelling The coast road runs almost parallel nearly all the way, so access is easy, though accommodation options aren't overly numerous. www.tourism.net.nz

WIND ROSE

SWELL ROSE

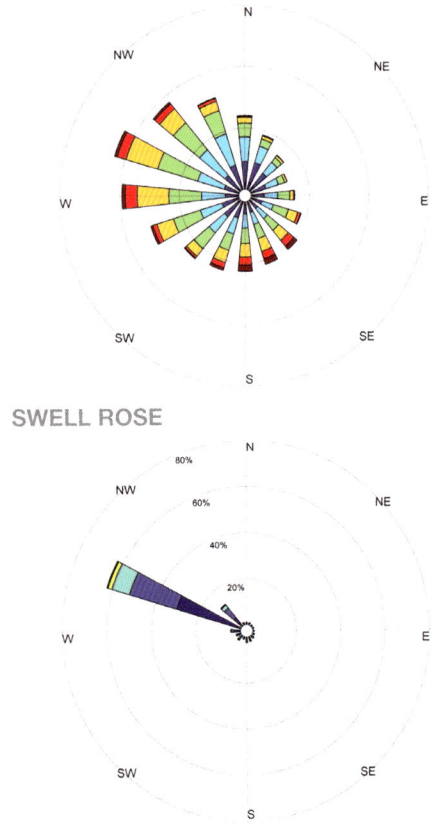

Surfing Paekakariki and Pukerua Bay have the steepest profiles on this coast, and get waves with good shape in a large west or north-west swell, when the wind turns southerly. The beaches to the north feature shifty peaks, and rarely get sizeable. Crowds are almost non-existent.

Fishing There's epic fishing around the coast for a range of species including snapper, kahawai and kingies, but most of the action is from boats or a kayak. Shore fishing around the rivermouths is likely to be most productive, in particular for kahawai. Pipis are plentiful at many locations. www.kapitifishing.co.nz

Swimming On its day, divine, with few large waves. The water is always warmer than the Wellington coast, with lifeguards patrolling the main locations on weekends and holidays. It is usually nicer in an east or south-east wind.

1. Otaki Beach
It may be a continuation of the beach that started miles to the north, but Otaki marks an increase in population density, that gets even greater as you head south. The most popular public access is near the surf club and along Marine Parade, which features a large grass reserve on the seaside, with an elegant public toilet and changing block dating back to the thirties. The south end of Marine Parade leads to the Otaki River estuary, which is surrounded by a park with regenerating native vegetation that's a cool spot for picnicking. The estuary itself is popular for fishing and whitebaiting, and pipis are surprisingly easy to find all along the beach. **Byrons Resort** (06)364 8121 has motels, holiday park and a beach-front cottage www.byronsresort.co.nz.
My Serenity luxury accommodation 0800 995 577.
Seaview Cottage (06)364 6076.

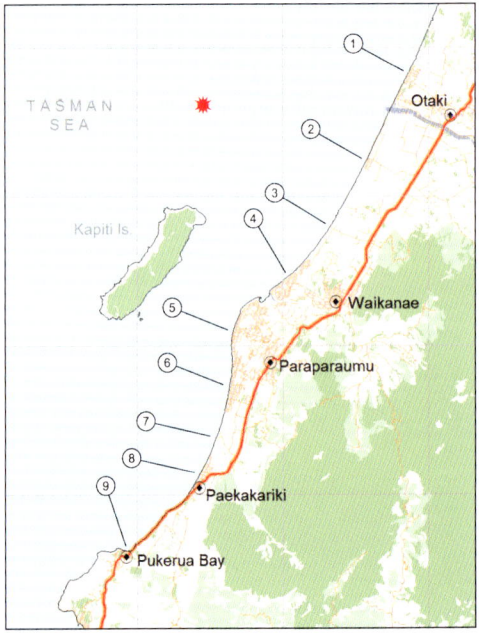

2. Te Horo Beach
Yet another small beach settlement located at a stream mouth, but here the beach is shingly and stony in the vicinity of the stream, though gives way to sand to the north and south. The main road leads straight on to the beach itself, with packed stones to park on; while Rodney Ave runs parallel to the coast, with another large grassy area and parking space set behind the foreshore. There are some large macrocarpas here, offering good shade, but no amenities. Further south Te Hapua St leads you to another coastal access point, but it is 400 metres or so through the foreshore dunes down a well maintained track to get to the beach.

3. Peka Peka Beach
Considered the northern part of Waikanae, it is not a huge settlement, but one with a close-knit feel, offering easy access onto the beach for trailer boat launching. There are no amenities for the public, other than the well known **Sandcastle Motels** (04)293 6072 www.sandcastlemotel.co.nz

4. Waikanae Beach
Waikanae marks the beginning of a long stretch of coast that lies directly in the lee of Kapiti Island, and runs south to Raumati, punctuated only by the

Waikanae River. To all intents and purposes, it is all the same beach, with a flat profile and abundant pipi beds, but the river divides the separate communities. The Waimea domain is the main public resource, with childrens play areas, shade trees, public loos, a couple of cafes, and a four square. The Waikanae Boating Club is at the end of nearby Waimea Rd, with cold showers and toilets. The club offers counter meals and bar service to all-comers on weekends, and is a great place to meet the local fishermen. Tutere St leads down to the Waikanae Estuary scenic reserve, which marks the landward border of the Kapiti Marine reserve. **Waikanae Beach Motel** 0800 048 6533. **Waikanae Boating Club** (04)293 6885 www.waikanaeboatingclub.org.nz

5. Paraparaumu Beach

South of the estuary lies Parapararaumu Beach which is where you will find the largest conglomeration of shops, cafes, bars and restaurants on the entire coast. The northern half of the beach features holiday homes down to the foreshore, and though there are a couple of access points further up Manly St, it is Marine Parade that's the most prominent spot for visitors, offering uninterrupted views out to Kapiti and southwards, plus a couple of parking spots which offer free-camping, and a foreshore walkway south to the beginning of Raumati Beach. **The Kapiti Boating Club** (04)298 8428 has a good ramp, located at the intersection of Manly St and Marine Parade www.kapitiboatingclub.org. **Barnacles Seaside Inn** (04)902 5856 www.seasideyha.co.nz

6. Raumati Beach

It isn't immediately obvious where Raumati starts and Paraparaumu ends, but one can safely assume it is where Marine Parade morphs into Wharemauku St. Raumati faces due west, and probably suffers worst from the wind and swell than its northern neighbours, but also has more character due to the low cliffs behind the beach. It features one main public access point at the bottom of Raumati Rd, and several smaller gaps between the houses with parking space for a few cars only. Garden Rd forms a semi-circle in front of Marine Gardens, and here you'll find the excellent heated swimming pool, plus a clutch of cafes back up on Raumati Rd. The beach ends at the south end of The Esplanade, which is the northern access point to the Queen Elizabeth Park. Tourist info www.raumatibeach.co.nz. **Raumati Sands Resort** (04)299 0155 offers boutique hotel accommodation www.raumatisands.co.nz

7. Whareroa Beach/Queen Elizabeth Park

When The US Marines needed to prepare for their Pacific campaign during WW2, they chose the area north and west of Paekakariki, which John Wayne refers to in his 1949 epic "The Sands of Iwo Jima." The park and its wild beach receives nearly 500,000 visitors a year and features regenerating native vegetation in what is the last area of natural dunes on the Kapiti Coast. www.gw.govt.nz/QEP

8. Paekakariki

This distinctive coastal community of around 2000 residents sits on a tiny sliver of coastal plain pressed hard up against the Akatarawa Range. The main trunk railway and state highway one pass directly behind it, yet despite this fact, few people seem to stop and enjoy its tranquil charms. The beach extends for nearly a mile from end to end, though the southern section offers less access points and virtually no parking other than at the extreme end where you'll find the Paekakariki Domain and The Fishermans Table restaurant. The northern section of the beach is accessed by turning right onto The Parade, which runs beside the seawall and a thin strip of sand. The widest section of beach is at the northern fringe, where there's a surf life-saving club. Paekakiriki can get some ok waves in a huge west or north-west swell, and is offshore in a southerly or south-east wind. There is a cool café half way down the Parade called **The Beach Store** that's open Thurs, Fri, Sat, Sun. **Paekakariki Surf Life-Saving Club** (04) 292 8085. **Paekakariki Holiday Park** is on Wellington Rd (04)292 8292 www.paekakirikiholidaypark.co.nz

9. Pukerua Bay

Stunning Pukerua Bay is really three small bays nestled into the base of the hills south of Paekakariki, adjacent to where the main highway leaves the coast and climbs through the valley to Porirua. The beach is located at the bottom of a steep, winding, and at times one lane road, and is sometimes called Brendan Beach; but whatever you call it, it is one of the most beautiful swimming and snorkelling spots in the entire south-west region. Pukerua Bay benefits greatly from its northern exposure, but sadly its ease of access and sheltered nature has led to a serious degradation of paua stocks over the years. Now there is a marine reserve in place in the region to prevent harvesting of kaimoana, and line fishing is the only permitted activity. A shop at the top of the hill and two public loos alongside the beach, are the only amenities. For surfers, there are some interesting waves in a north-west swell and south winds, with reef breaks at either side of the bay and Wairaka Reef 2km to the west, all of which seem to prefer higher tides, but break rarely.

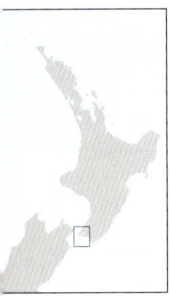

WELLINGTON CAPTIVATING BRACING SURPRISING

New Zealand's "capital of cool" is not widely known as the country's best beach destination. A city of culture is how they usually try and sell our administrative centre. You hear a lot about theatre and restaurants, Weta Workshops and funky nightlife, Te Papa and the Wellington sevens. You don't hear that much about the ocean. Its reputation as being wet and windy doesn't help matters either, if you are an outdoor person. But the truth is that Wellington is a seaside town through and through, where most suburbs are within sight of the ocean, and sits on a truly spectacular coastline that few appreciate. It is vast and incredibly diverse, spanning several geographical environments, facing in several directions, offering a staggering array of choices depending on the weather and your preferred activity. The city beaches are out of this world on a fine summers day, and the south coast unrivalled for its raw and pristine appeal. Eastbourne feels like a little slice of England, and the wild west coast posesses all the drama one would expect. With surprisingly good fishing, good surf on its day, and the acclaimed restaurants and nightlife to keep you amused when the weather turns sour, you might find Wellington a town full of surprises, all of which will make you smile.

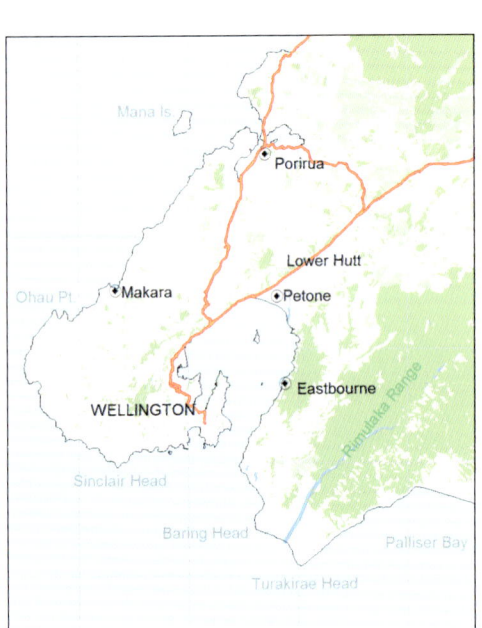

Travelling It is a fantastic city to visit for the cultural reasons one normally hears about, with all the amenities one would associate with a vibrant metropolis. The restaurants, bars and theatres are among the country's best, and then there's Te Papa! If there is one drawback for beach-goers, it would be that tourist accommodation out of the centre was a bit sparse. www.wellington.com

Surfing The majority of the good waves come off south and south-east swells that push into the south coast through the narrow window between the South Island and the Wairarapa, with the rocky headlands and reefs holding hollow waves from Wainuiomata right across to Red Rocks. The west coast spots like Titahi Bay and Paekakariki can also get good surf, but due to the sheltering influence of the South Island, rely on north-west swell from the Tasman, which is a fairly rare event. The shallow shelf off this coast doesn't help much either. Wellington Boardriders Club are a pretty active crew, and worth hooking up with if you're in the area. www.wellingtonboardriders.com. They also have a facebook page.

Fishing Believe it or not, Wellington Harbour has produced the biggest variety of fish of any harbour in New Zealand, with 56 species weighing over 500 grams, having been recorded by local fishermen. The differing habitats are immense, and to cap it off,

Titahi Bay boatsheds

South Coast

Oriental Bay

there's a good amount of paua and crayfish off all coasts for those who care to go looking. The major fishing clubs of the area are the Wellington Surfcasting and Angling Club, which is over forty-five years old, and the Port Nicholson Sport Fishing Club.

Swimming It is unquestionably the chilliest part of the North Island, and for much of the year one has to deal with water that's not in the temprature range to make many people want to get wet; however on a fine day, Wellingtonians flocks to their beaches to enjoy the admittedly "cool," but often crystal-clear water. The beauty of Wellington Harbour, is that with the wide array of coastal aspect, you can generally find somewhere to swim out of the wind, whatever direction it is blowing from.

Lyall Bay

Titahi Bay

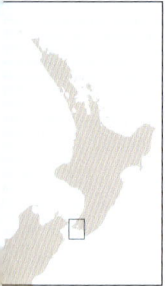

Mana Coast

Named after the island that sits just off Titahi Bay, the beaches that occupy Wellington's north-west are all completely unique, each facing in different directions and offering a totally different coastal experience, each with an individuality and charm all of its own. They share a relatively windswept countenance and on a grey day can feel pretty barren, but all demand a closer look with the wind blowing from the east, when they sparkle and show their best features. This isn't the most salubrious section of the Wellington region, but is well loved and well patronised by a huge range of people.

Travelling There's no common theme here, as all are uniquely different, but they all share a certain fringe feeling, and a sense of being off the commonly beaten tourist path, which appeals to many people.

WIND ROSE

SWELL ROSE

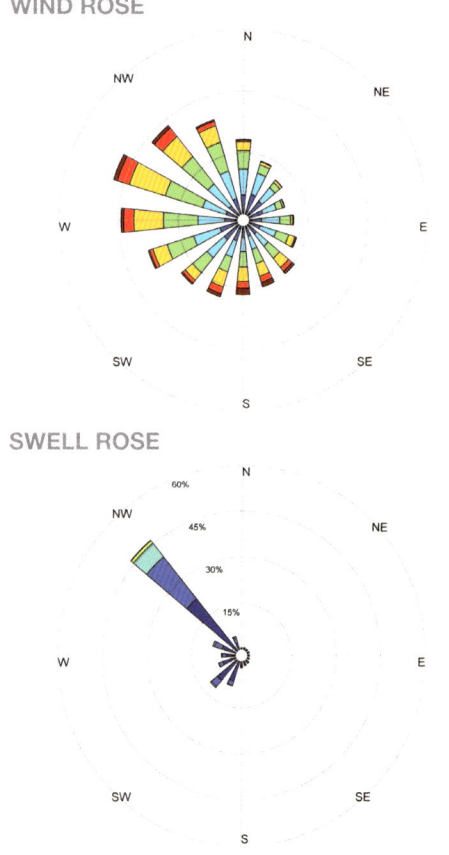

Surfing Titahi Bay is the spot on this map, but shelter from the South Island and Mana Island, means only the largest west or north-west swells get in here.

Fishing There are plenty of paua and good fishing off the west coast, with Titahi Bay and Makara the likeliest places for land-based guys and divers, though Plimmerton and Onehunga Bay are worth a look. **West Coast Charters** (04)236 8605 or 027 207 9159 are based in Mana, and can leave from any of the west coast spots www.wellingtonfishing.co.nz

Swimming Pick the right wind direction and they can all offer beautiful swimming conditions, especially in late summer. Titahi Bay has life-savers in season.

1. Plimmerton

Historically notable as place where Te Rauparaha was abducted in 1846, there are in fact a handful of beaches on this very British feeling piece of coast. Plimmerton Beach is the first, but at high tide there isn't much to it, with the water lapping up against the seawall. There is a popular short strip of sand at its south end called, unsurprisingly South Beach, with public loos and parking on the roadside. Further along, there are a couple of other streets that intersect with the seawall, and at the western end there's another little beach with a small boat-ramp. The road heading west hugs the foreshore, where there are a series of finger reefs with a couple of sandy patches at the beginning of Moana Rd. Karehana Bay is the main swimming spot in the area, and offers a couple

of hundred metres of fine sand, sandwiched between a reef to the east and the Plimmerton Boating Club, which occupies the promontory to the west, with a jetty and boat ramp on its tip. There are public amenities here, but after this the road becomes private at the historical Hongoeka Marae. **Plimmerton Boating Club** www.plimmertonboatingclub.org.nz. **www.plimmerton.org.nz** is the community website.

2. Porirua Harbour

Porirua Harbour is a broad, sheltered body of water, making it popular with small boat owners and a convenient anchorage for larger boats, offering easy access to Mana Island and the Marlborough Sounds beyond. At the Mana causeway there's a handy swimming spot on the northern side of the harbour, with a boat ramp that gets pretty busy on fine days. Onepoto Road, just before Titahi Bay, leads to another small beach with some cute boat sheds, that's home to the Wellington Powerboat Club and the Porirua Rowing Club. There is a walking track from here to Onehunga Bay. **Titahi Bay Boating Club** (04)236 7637 is the local sailing club with clubrooms at Onepoto and a good slipway www.tbbc.org.nz

3. Onehunga Bay

If you follow the road to Titahi Bay and head up the hill and into the Whitireia Reserve, the road eventually leads to a group of beaches with a sandy foreshore, that are popular with those looking for a lazy swim. A couple of beautiful reef-studded bays to the west offer excellent shallow-water snorkelling and diving. All face north, and are sheltered from a south wind by the large hill behind them.

4. Titahi Bay

Kupe reportedly landed at Komanga Point, 3 km west of Titahi Bay, leaving an anchor stone that can be seen today at Te Papa. This is Porirua's beach, and a fitting spot for Wellington's blue-collar workers to enjoy time-out. It's one of the most charismatic and friendliest coastal communities in the country, notable for its unique boatsheds at either end of the bay. In particular, those at the northern end that have been brightly painted and converted to weekend sleepover baches, are a national treasure. The close community spirit that has developed here is a joy to experience, and most weekends it's got a distinctly festive feel. There's a concrete boat-ramp in the sheltered hook at the northern end, where there are also two sets of public loos. The southern end also features boat sheds, a grass reserve and public amenities. The surf life-saving club is one of the most successful in the country and can be found with its own ramp onto

Titahi Bay

the sand in the middle of the bay. It is a popular surf beach, though extremely sheltered from any other than north-west swell. The best waves are the lefts at the southern end, offshore in a south or south-east wind, though the north side of the bay can have okay rights in the biggest swells of the year. A surf cam shows current conditions on the surf2surf website.

5. Makara

One of Wellington's many hidden surprises, this stunning piece of near wilderness is located at the end of a winding river valley west of Karori. It's only 20 minutes from one of the busiest suburbs in the region, yet surprisingly remains a place apart from the rest of the city. It is like entering a time warp as you leave Karori and drive down the hill. Even the holiday homes have a feeling of time passed-by, with none of the expensive baches or modern commuter homes that you find in places like Eastbourne. The bay is deeply indented and south-west facing, looking directly over to the Marlborough Sounds, and is as close as you can drive by public road to the South Island. The fishing of all kinds is predictably good, with paua and crays still relatively easy to find, and good boat and kayak fishing relatively close-in, with pronounced headlands and deeper drop-offs both north and south offering the possibility of a land-based kingie, amongst other species. A launch-ramp into the river at the north end of the bay is usable at all tides, but the mouth is narrow and can get very shallow at low tide, which would present issues for those launching large boats. The beach is shingle, so the water stays clear, offering good visibility for freedivers and also sparkling conditions for those just looking for a swim. There are good tracks both ways around the fringes of the coastline for walkers, with bays either side if you are looking for some privacy, while to the north are a series of ramshackle baches on farm land that look like they are from a whole different universe. As far as access goes, there are two ways to get here. Takarau Gorge Rd leads to Makara Beach Rd, and runs in a loop from Johsonville to Karori, and it can be accessed from either suburb. A fairly basic cafe that opens in the weekends is the only public facility, which may account for the limited numbers of visitors.

Makara

Petone to Wainuiomata

Petone and Eastbourne share the upper-harbour coast, and yet the two are like chalk and cheese, with Petone's long straight foreshore bordering one of the busiest light-industrial areas in NZ, while just a few miles east, the rocky coves and craggy shoreline stretching out to Muritai ooze charm and are genteel by comparison. Wainuiomata is a world unto itself; solitary and imposing, more Wairarapa than Wellington in feel, and majestic in its lonely isolation. This coast offers an interesting counterpoint to the wide variety on display throughout the rest of the Wellington region, and is much loved and well used by many.

Travelling There's a strange lack of accommodation, on offer, though a coast road offers easy access to all of it. The Days Bay ferry is a popular method of getting here, both for commuters or day-trippers, and leaves from Queens Wharf in the city. **East by West Ferries** (04)499 1282 www.eastbywest.co.nz

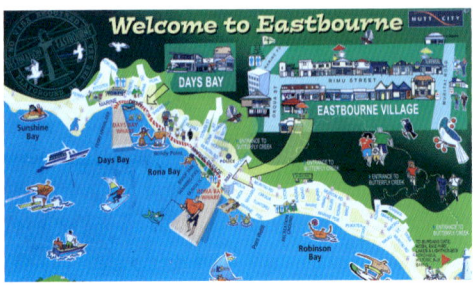

WIND ROSE

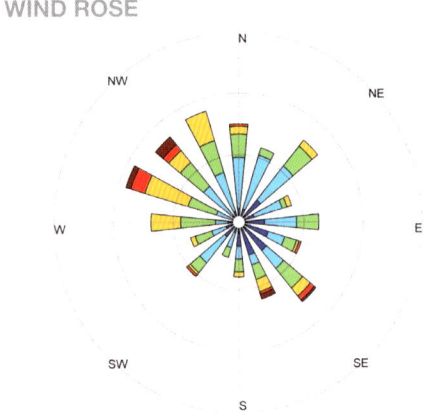

SWELL ROSE

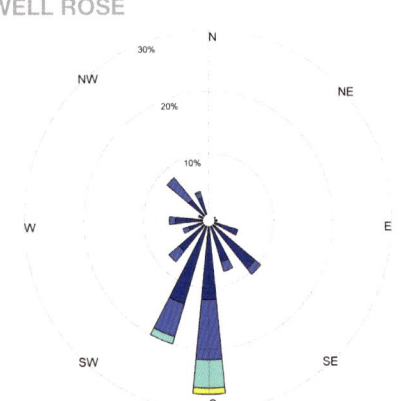

Surfing Wainuiomata gets some epic waves in a big south swell, and the Eastbourne shingle banks can have a few too, but good days are rare, so you are unlikely to feature this area too highly on any agenda for a hard core surf trip.

Fishing The rocks and beaches around the Eastbourne coast can produce fish in late summer, and there are a few paua to be had around the Wainuiomata coast. The Point Howard wharf is one of the best land-based spots in the whole harbour, with casual anglers usually catching kahawai in the morning and mackerel at night. Other more serious fishers will target particular species including red cod, red gurnard, snapper, horse mackerel, kingfish, tarakihi, and blue cod to name just a few.

Swimming The further you get from Petone, the cleaner the water gets, but a bomb off Petone wharf is a fun thing to do on a hot summer afternoon.

1. Petone Foreshore

Petone is a busy industrial centre at the head of Wellington Harbour, and blessed with a fantastic beach stretching for several kilometres from The Korokoro Gateway on the western fringe, to Hikoikoi Reserve adjacent to the Hutt River, which joins the sea at its eastern boundary. The most distinguishing feature is the extensive though redundant wharf, which due to the shallow nature of the coastline extends way out into the harbour, and used to provide ferry access to the city and Days Bay; but for many reasons, this is no longer a viable service. It also used to be a popular as a fishing wharf, though

doesn't seem to produce as well as it once did. The Esplanade runs adjacent to the foreshore and it is a frighteningly busy road for most of the day, though there are a couple of well-placed parking areas and grass patches along its seaward side. Hikoikoi Reserve is a large grassed area at the eastern boundary, which is home to the famed Petone Rugby League Club, who enjoy what must be the best view of any rugby ground in the country, but who in turn must encounter extreme difficulties under the high ball

Days Bay and Eastbourne

Lion Rock

in a strong southerly wind. The beach is covered in pipi shells and one suspects there are still a few to be had, though I would be cautious about eating them. **Heretaunga Boating Club** www.sailhbc.org.nz

2. Whiorau/Lowry Bay
Driving east from Petone along the foreshore, Port Rd takes you behind the Seaview Marina before it morphs into Marine Drive, then passes the extended finger that is the Seaview Wharf projecting hundreds of metres into the harbour. As well as offering some of the easiest land based fishing in the area, it shelters the western side of Lowry Bay, where there is a tiny strip of beach known as Sorrento Bay. The main beach further south, is a few hundred metres of shingle and granular sand with an old boatshed in the centre, but no public facilities.

3. York Bay
There isn't too much to it, with a 50 metre strip of sand thats only one metre wide at high water, plus a swimming platform just offshore and half a dozen homes behind it. At high tide in a strong westerly wind, waves splash over the road that passes directly beside the reinforced foreshore here. It's a pretty and intimate spot, but offers no public amenities.

4. Mahina Bay
It is just a short stretch of beach with a high tide concrete ramp for launching small boats and a couple of homes behind it, surrounded by fringing reefs, with a small rocky promontory to the north.

5. Oruamotoro/Days Bay
While Eastbourne is the best known of these beaches, Days Bay is the most popular with visitors, its enclosed semi-circle of fine sand offering an intimacy that isn't shared by the other bays in the vicinity. The Dominion Post Ferry draws lots of day-trippers, out for an excursion to the beach from Wellington, who come to enjoy the cafes and some excellent swimming conditions in summer. **The Pavilion Cafe** (04)562 7377 is an old favourite for visitors and locals alike, located in Williams Park just behind the beach. Other public facilities include a heated swimming pool, excellent grass tennis courts, public loos, and a swimming platform moored just offshore. For general information, there's a useful community website www.daysbay.homestead.com. **Days Bay Boatshed** (04)494 3339 rents kayaks, row boats, fishing gear, tennis racquets etc. **Fern Tree Hideaway** (04)562 7692 is a lovely bush home for rent.

6. Eastbourne
Eastbourne village sits on the coast just south of the wharf at Point Webb, flanked by two separate stretches of sand, and while they have unique names, they are essentially the same beach facing in different directions. Rhona Bay lies to the north-west and Robinson Bay sits to the south. A foreshore walkway runs almost its entire length, though vehicle access is somewhat haphazard, with a number of different access options. There can be waves off the shingle banks at the head of the point in big southerlies, but don't expect 5 star quality. The village is the commercial hub of the surrounding area, with a strong community feel and a multitude of shops including groceries, cafes and galleries. Heading south the road passes Lion Rock (a point break of variable merit), the old bus terminal and assorted stretches of sand, before finishing at the East Harbour Regional Park. This popular walking spot offers access to the beautiful, but exposed Pencarrow Coast, which is a renowned paua fishery. Despite the fact that this was the old coast road to the Wairarapa, vehicle access now stops at Burdens Gate.

7. Wainuiomata
No bleaker place exists in the North Island than Wainuiomata, though its primitive and windswept beauty draws many people 25 km over the hill from Petone, attracted by the promise of an empty walk, a view of the seal colony, or a dive for a few paua. It's a bit of a mission, though the road is sealed all the way, which significantly eases the pain compared to when I was a nipper, and used to come over the gravel road to stay at Papa Day's batch. For the surf community, the lefts by the rivermouth are a significant drawcard, though they need a solid south swell and north winds to fire. There's a carpark in the centre of the beach in front of a large solitary rock, but no toilets. "Wainui" is the end of the East Harbour Regional Park, that begins at Burdens Gate, with the southern access point just before you arrive at the coast. There you'll find the walkway to Baring Head, the lighthouse and other historic sites, including some popular climbing boulders. **DOC** (04)830 4413 or 027 467 3076.

Wainuiomata

City Beaches

The inner harbour beaches offer spectacular diversity, including the urban joys of Oriental Bay, Evans Bay's picture-book qualities, and the Miramar Peninsula with a handful of its own stunning spots. Most feature an array of the city's unique architecture, providing an intriguing backdrop to the coast, and reinforcing its reputation as an urban centre of significant charm. Wellington has also done a fine job of its foreshore maintenance, retaining a strong sense of history, character and a personality all of its own. The beauty of this city, is that you don't have to travel far if you want to go for a swim on a hot day.

Travelling Again a coast road leads directly past all these spots, and the only major consideration is parking, which can be difficult around the inner-city beaches, especially on a fine summer weekend.

WIND ROSE

SWELL ROSE

Surfing There are no real surfable waves inside the harbour, but there are a few good spots for kite-boarders and windsurfers.

Fishing The Miramar Peninsula offers the best prospects for land-based fishermen; in particular off the various headlands and from the Seatoun ferry wharf, which has seen many good fish landed over the years, including snapper, warehou and kingfish. Oriental Parade has also proved a successful kingfish location as well, which may surprise many.

Swimming A wide range of options present themselves in various winds, without worrying about waves of any significance. If the weather is too cold, there is always the Freyberg Pool.

1. Freyberg Beach
The closest beach to the CBD is a small stretch of sand facing north-east, adjacent to the Freyberg pools. It's backed by a beautiful little park, with a childrens playground just off the main road, and public loos behind the beach. The seawall to the west is a great piece of urban coastal design, with good platforms to jump off and a funky, modern feel. It looks like an okay fishing spot as well.

2. Oriental Bay
The best known and most spectacular of Wellington's city beaches, it faces north-west and is divided in two by the Fishermans Table restaurant. On a fine day it can feel a bit like the Riviera here, with its spectacular fountain, wide foreshore promenade, an array of apartments and beautiful homes on the hills behind it, and a truly cosmopolitan atmosphere. It is patrolled by lifeguards on summer weekends, when it can get incredibly busy, and parking here in particular can be extremely difficult when the sun shines.

3. Balena Bay
Oriental Parade turns into Evans Bay Parade and leads towards the broad area known as Evans Bay, which harbours a number of small beaches. The first is Balena Bay, a beautiful 50 metre stretch of shingly sand facing due east, with boat shed styled toilets towards the southern end.

Freyberg Beach and Oriental Bay

Evans Bay boatsheds

4. Hataitai
Similar in both size and feel to Balena Bay, Hataitai suffers from not having much sand at high tide. It is flanked by some beautiful boatsheds to the south, and a large grassy reserve to the north.
Royal Port Nicholson Yacht Club (04)839 6702.

5. Cobham Drive/Evans Bay
You'll find a few patches of sand amongst the rip-rap on the north side of the isthmus, which connects the Miramar Peninsula to the mainland, that are popular in a southerly wind, especially with kite-boarders. It is hardly the most scenic place in the country, located right opposite the airport and backed by a busy road, but people do swim here nonetheless.

6. Shelly Bay
There's not really a major beach, but a small stretch of shingly sand near the site of the old naval base gets late afternoon sun, and is protected from strong easterly winds.

7. Mahanga Bay
A tiny but beautiful cove, covered in shingly sand with no facilities and an odd berm like structure just offshore. There is limited parking on the roadside.

8. Scorching Bay
The jewel of the Miramar Peninsula features dazzling white sand, with an extensive grass verge adjacent to the road. There isn't a lot here other than a small collection of eclectic baches and old homes, and though it has a remote feel, still features a good set of public conveniences, with The Chocolate Fish cafe also located across the road from the beach. Bathing sheds were first erected here in 1931, and Scorching Bay has lost none of its appeal with the advance of time. The rocks at either end are pretty sharp but would be a good fishing spot.

9. Karaka Bays
The name refers to a series of tiny bays and dispersed patches of sand, inbetween the jagged rocks that divide them. It's an area that extends for a few kilometres, punctuated by the old wharf, and ends at the Worser Bay Boat Club. There are some stunning old colonial buildings and the odd shade tree behind the foreshore here, all of which gives this little chunk of the Wellington coast significant charm and aesthetic appeal. East-facing like Scorching Bay and those further south, it's nicely protected in a west or north-west wind, and if there is an issue here, it is the parking, which sadly is in short supply.

10. Worser Bay
Another popular swimming beach with beautiful white sand like Scorching Bay. Intriguingly, Worser Bay features a good surf life-saving club with beautiful clubrooms, adjacent to an extensive grassed foreshore reserve, where there are pohutakawas for shade, and well placed public loos. It's also the home of the Worser Bay Boating Club (04)972wbbc www.wbbcwellington.net.nz. Worser Bay Surf Life-Saving Club www.worserbayslsc.org.nz

11. Seatoun
Perhaps best known as the home of Peter Jacksons Weta Workshop, Seatoun is the longest of the beaches on the peninsula, extending for nearly a kilometre, with fine shingly sand and an extensive pier jutting out from the middle the bay. The ferry that pulls in here is one stop on the trip from the city to Days Bay, but only on selected sailings. Seatoun is an extensively built-up suburb with a school and shopping centre, and has some great features, but lacks some of the intimacy and charm of Worser and Scorching Bays. The wharf is one of the best spots to fish off in the entire Wellington region, allowing land-based anglers to cast baits into quite deep water, with a wide variety of species landed here. www.eastbywest.co.nz

Scorching Bay

Seatoun

The South Coast

The few miles of rocks and sand facing south into Cook Strait, are one of my favourite pieces of the entire North Island coast. They posess a raw beauty that is at times violent and at others as sublimely beautiful as anywhere in the world, ranging from Island Bay's almost antique charm, to the wilderness quality of the region extending west towards Red Rocks. This extreme range of environments is what makes it so unique, and for me it ranks as one of the most spectacular drives in any city, anywhere in the world. The surf can be excellent, there are good fish to be caught, and you won't find a fresher breath of air anywhere.

Travelling Again blessed with a coast road that allows uninterrupted access to almost every square metre, yet the accommodation options are few. Beware of penguins on the road, especially at night.

WIND ROSE

SWELL ROSE

Surfing This is Wellington's primary surfing area, attracting the most swell and generally the best quality waves, but it is a pretty challenging coast to surf, with strong winds and lots of rocks. There are two surf shops at Lyall Bay: **Real Surf** (04)387 8798 near the eastern end www.realsurf.co.nz and **Wild Style** (04)387 7182, with its coffee bar near the surf clubs.

Fishing There is a wide range of special marine ecosystems along this coast supporting a huge array of sea life. Fishing access to the centre of the coast is impeded by the 854 hectare Taputeranga Marine Reserve, but that in turn is a resource for rec divers.

Swimming There's no question it can get stormy, but in northerly winds and small swells, this is a stunning swimming coast with shimmering, clear water.

1. Breaker Bay
The road from Seatoun climbs through The Pass of Branda, a narrow cleft in the rocks that offers extensive views to the south and west. Below you lies a group of bays collectively known as Breaker Bay, though the title is only accurate for the sandy beach directly below the road. The local community consists of a collection of homes to the west of another shingly beach fringed with unforgiving reefs. The homes are actually spread between Eve Bay and Flax Bay, and the road continues south past Reef Bay, Ranger Point and Palmer Bay before Palmer Head. Both Breaker Bay proper and Eve Bay offer easy swimming, with simple access and shelter from westerly winds. There are waves here in a powerful south swell and a north wind, when you'll find grinding rights barrelling off the rocks, generally better at higher tides. If you walk around Dorset Point, which lies to the east of Breaker Bay, you'll find Wellington's naturist beach.

2. Tarakena Bay
A tiny strip of shingle and sand is protected from the east by Palmer Point, with a concrete boat ramp that's a convenient launch spot for those diving the wreck of the HMS Wellington, which is located just offshore here. The propeller from the Wahine is permanently lodged at Palmer Head, and serves as a monument to the loss of life from that fateful day. In a proper south swell you'll find a right breaking off the eastern side of the point that pitches and throws out some ledgy tubes at lower tides.

3. Moa Point
Continuing west, you'll see what looks like an island that's connected to the mainland, before coming into the wider opening of Lyall Bay. This is Moa Point. There's a small shingle bay here, just before the airport, but the town sewage outfall is located nearby so it's possibly not the best spot to swim at.

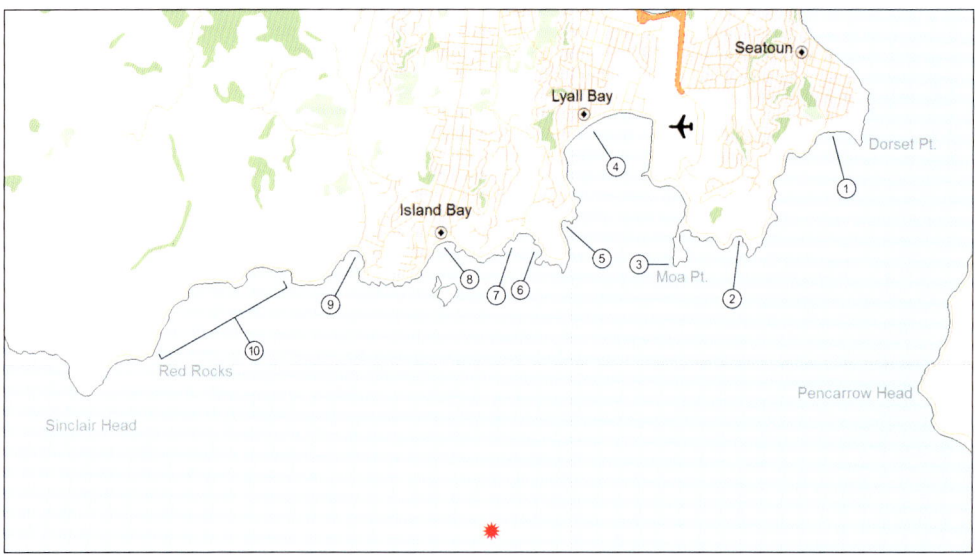

4. Lyall Bay
A deeply indented, golden sand beach with a flat profile has a reputation as a good surf spot. It is home to two surf life-saving clubs, a couple of good cafes and two surfshops; and while it does get rideable waves in a south or south-east swell, it is rarely epic due to its profile, and almost guaranteed to be crowded when it does break. You'll find peaks along its length, with the seawall next to the airport offering the best quality banks. It's offshore in north winds, though the western end picks up swell with more east, and is cleaner in a north-west wind. It is a popular swimming beach due to the fine sand, easy parking on the foreshore, the lack of rocks and the presence of lifeguard patrols. Just before Arthurs Nose, you'll find a good boat ramp.

5. Waitaha Cove
As you drive west of Lyall Bay, you pass a small cove filled with shingle and pebbles, backed by a handful of homes, with a foreshore reserve at either end. It is a protected spot for a swim in a strong westerly wind.

6. Princess Bay
A series of finger reefs project southwards into Cook Strait, interspersed with small patches of sand, directly in front of a large public carpark. This is the access point for Princess Bay, a wide stretch of beach extending west towards Houghton Bay that's one of the most popular of the south coast's swimming spots. It also marks the start of the Taputeranga Marine Reserve that extends west from here.

7. Houghton Bay
Houghton Bay is a shingle and sand beach, with a collection of homes pressed up against the cliffs that back it, constrained by points on either side. It is a popular swimming location and it's exposure to south east swell makes it a consistent surf spot too, with peaky rights off the western end. Offshores are from the north west. A sign advising of poor water quality wasn't exactly a confidence builder.

8. Island Bay
A deeply charming cove that began life as a fishing village, still remains a popular anchorage for boats working the south coast. These days, however, it's better known as an artistic community, and attracts a steady stream of day-trippers from Wellington, with a range of amenities including **Island Bay Marine Education Centre** and the **Bait House Aquarium** (04)383 8285 www.octopus.org.nz. The beach has a sea-wall protecting the foreshore from the pounding surf, but the best waves are the rights that break at high tide off the east side of Tapu Te Ranga (Rat Island), located just offshore. There can be a grinding left as well that breaks below high tide in a huge south-east swell, but beware currents in the channel on the dropping tide. Offshores are northwesters. The nearby **Bach Cafe** is a popular lunch spot overlooking the coast. **Splash Gordon's Dive School** (04)939 8101 is the local dive shop and info centre www.splashgordon.co.nz.

9. Owhiro Bay
West of Island Bay are a series of reefs and shingle patches leading to Owhiro Bay, which arcs around in a deep semi-circle. It has a good carpark behind the beach, plus a small boat ramp, and while it feels like a poor cousin to some of the other nearby communities, I found it beautiful, quiet, and a sheltered place to swim, with crystal clear water.

10. Red Rocks
The sealed road ends at a gate at the entrance to the Te Kopahou Reserve, which extends out past Red Rocks to Sinclair Head/Rimurapa, and the Devil's Gate seal colony. The track is suitable for 4wd vehicles though car access is not permitted on a Sunday between 9.00 am and 6.00pm. It is a popular walking destination, and a hike to Sinclairs Head will take two to three hours return, leading past some beautiful swimming beaches. There are a couple of surf spots out along this track, like Happy House and Sunset. Ask locals for details if you're around on a huge south-east swell. This is one of the most spectacular pieces of coast in the country and on a clear day, is absolutely breathtaking. As it isn't in the marine reserve, it's also an epic place to fish and dive.

BEACH INDEX

A
Ahipara	26
Ahu Ahu Rd	215
Ahuriri	189
Akitio	193
Algies Beach	73
Amodeo Bay	135
Anaura Bay	173
Anawhata	113
Anchor Bay	72
Anglers Lane	216
Anzac Bay/Waiheke	101
Anzac Bay/Waihi	155
Aotea Harbour	204
Aramoana	193
Aranga Beach	49
Arawhata Rd	219
Arkles Beach	81
Armour Bay	119
Army Bay	80
Athenree	156
Aurora Point	183
Awaawaroa Bay	100
Awakino	207
Awana Bay	106
Awanui	166
Awhitu Regional Park	125

B
Back Beach/Ak	85
Back Beach/New Plymouth	213
Baddleys Beach	72
Balena Bay	236
Bay View	188
Bayley Rd	216
Baylys Beach	50
Bell Block	212
Bella Vista Rd Beach	89
Bethells Beach	110
Big Bay	124
Big Oneroa Bay	98
Big Manly	79
Blackhead	193
Blackpool	101
Blacks Beach	185
Black Stump	67
Bland Bay	53
Blind Bay	104
Blockhouse Bay	120
The Bluff	25
Boat Harbour	183
Bog Works	213
Bowentown	155
Breaker Bay	238
Browns Bay	83
Bucklands Beach	92
Buckletons Beach	72

C
Cable Bay	36
Cambells Beach/Rodney	72
Cambells Bay/Auckland	84
Cape Egmont	218
Cape Kidnappers	191
Cape Palliser	201
Cape Reinga	22
Cape Runaway	167
Cape View	191
Carlyle Beach	221
Castlecliff Beach	225
Castlepoint	196
Castor Bay	85
Cathedral Cove	147
Cheltenham Beach	87
Church Bay	58
Clifton	191
Clive	189
Cobham Drive	237
Cockle Bay	93
Colville Bay	136
Cornwallis Beach	119
Cooks Beach	146
Cooks Cove	175
Coopers Beach	36
Cray Bay/Karamea	191
Cremorne Reserve	89
The Cut/Gisborne	178

D
Daniels Reef	71
Days Bay/Oruamotoro	235
Dead Dog Bay	101
Deadmans Bay	100
Devonport	87
Dinahs Beach	183
Dolphin Bay	59
Doves Bay	43
Duder Regional Park	93

E
East Beach	33
East Cape	171
East End Beach	213
Eastbourne	235
Eastern Beach	93
Elliots Bay/Far North	41
Elliots Beach/Northland	52
Enclosure Bay	98
The Entrance Beach	159
Evans Bay	237

F
Fantail Bay	136
Faulkner Bay	120
Fishermans Cove	80
Fitzroy Beach	212
Flat Point	198
Flaxmill Bay	146
Fletcher Bay	137
Forestry	68
Foster Bay	118
Foxton Beach	226
French Bay	120
Freyberg Beach	236
Front Beach	146

G
Gentlemans Bay	91
Glinks Gully	51
Grahams Beach	125
Granite Bay	136
Great Barrier Island	102
Green Bay	120
Greenmeadows	219
Gulf Harbour	81

H
Hahei	147
Hamiltons Gap	125
Haratonga Beach	106
Hariki	166
Hataitai	237
Hatfields Beach	75
Haumoana	190
Hawai	165
Hekerua Bay	98
Helena Bay	53
Henderson Bay	33
Herbertville	193
Herekino Harbour	28
Herne Bay	89
Hikuwai Beach	165
Hillsbrough Bay	121

Hobson Beach	43	Kukurau Bay	101	Mataikona	196		
Hohoura Heads	33	Kuruanui Bay	132	Matakana Island	157		
Home Bay	89			Matakatia Bay	81		
Horseshoe Bay	171	**L**		Matapaua Bay	141		
Hotwater Beach	148	Ladies Bay	91	Matapouri	58		
Houghton Bay	239	Laingholm	120	Matarangi	143		
Howick Beach	93	Laings Beach	63	Matata	163		
Hicks Bay	171	Lake Ferry/Otoko	201	Matauri Bay	41		
Hihi	37	Last Chance	182	Mathiesons Bay	71		
Himatangi	226	Leigh	70	Matiatia Bay	98		
Hoklo Beach	226	Little Bay	139	Maukutea Beach	204		
Hudsons Beach	125	Little Hula	117	Maunganui Bluff	40		
Huia	117	Little J Bay	183	Maurices Beach	165		
Hukatere	26	Little Onoroa Bay	90	Mellons Bay	93		
		Little Manly Beach	81	Midway	179		
I		Little Shoal Bay	87	Mission Bay	90		
Island Bay	239	Little Waihi	161	McGregors Bay/Coromandel	134		
		Loisells	175	McGregors Bay/Whangarei	61		
J		Lonely Bay	146	McKenzie Bay	61		
Jacks Bay	44	Long Bay/Coromandel	135	McLeods Bay	61		
Judges Bay	90	Long Bay Regional Park	83	Medlands Beach	107		
		Long Beach/Russell	44	Middleton Beach	219		
K		Lottin Point	170	Milford	85		
Kahihi Rd	216	Lower Kahui Rd	218	Mill Bay	119		
Kahokawa Beach	22	Lower Weld Rd	215	Mimiwhangata	53		
Kaiaua	95	Lowry Bay/Whiorau	235	Mitimiti	29		
Kai-iwi Beach	225	Lyall Bay	239	Moa Point	238		
Kairakau	192			Mohaka Rivermouth	187		
Kaitarakihi	118	**M**		Mohakatino	207		
Kaiti Beach	178	Mahia Beach	184	Mokau/King Country	207		
Kaitoke Beach	107	Mahina Bay	235	Mokau/Northland	53		
Kaituna Rivermouth	160	Mahinepua	40	Motairehe	105		
Kaiaua Bay	173	Mahanga Bay	237	Motu River mouth	165		
Kakamatua	119	Mahunga Beach	182	Motutara Farm Park	55		
Kapowairua	23	Mahuta Gap	51	Moureeses	55		
Karaka Bay	105	Mahurangi	74	Mt Maunganui	159		
Karaka Bays/Wellington	237	Main Beach, Mt Maunganui	159	Muriwai/Auckland	109		
Karamea	191	Main Beach/Oakura	214	Muriwai Beach/Gisborne	179		
Karekare	115	Main Beach/Opunake	219	Murphy's Campground	163		
Karikari Beach	35	Mairangi Bay	84	Murrays Bay	84		
Katikati	157	Makara	233				
Kaupokonui Beach	220	Makarori	176	**N**			
Kauri Point	157	Maketu	160	Narrowneck Beach	86		
Kawakawa Bay	94	Manaia Harbour	133	New Chums	142		
Kawa	105	Mangahume	219	Newdicks	161		
Kawau Island	72	Mangaiti	55	Ngahau Bay	53		
Kawerua	31	Mangakuri	192	Ngamotu Beach	213		
Kawhia Harbour	205	Mangawhai	67	Ngarimu Bay	132		
Kelly Tarltons	90	Mangonui	37	Ngarunui Beach	128		
Kennedy Bay	139	Mangere Bridge	121	Ngawi	201		
Kennedy Park	85	Manihi Rd	218	Ngunguru	59		
Kereta	133	Man 'o' War Bay	100	Nikau Bay	55		
Kikowhakarere	135	Manu Bay	128	North Mole	225		
Kina Road Beach	218	Maori Bay	110	North Piha	115		
Kiritihere/Waikato	125	Maraenui	165				
Kiritihere/King Country	207	Maraetai	93	**O**			
Kohimarama	91	Maraekaho	166	Oakura/Northland	53		
Komene Rd	216	Marine Parade/Napier	189	Oakura/Taranaki	214		
Kopua Domain	127	Marine Parade Reserve/Ak	89	Oamaru Bay	135		
Koputauaki Bay	135	Marokopa	206	Ocean Beach/Hawke's Bay	191		
Kowharewa Bay	58	Marsden Point	62	Ocean Beach/Kawhia	205		
Kuaotunu	140	Martins Bay	73	Ocean Beach/Wairarapa	201		
Kuku	227	Matai Bay	35	Ocean Beach/Whangarei	61		

Beach Index | 241

Ohawe	220	Paradise Bay	38	**S**		
Ohineaki	172	Paraparaumu Beach	229	Sailors Grave	149	
Ohiwa	164	Parekura Bay	45	Sandspit	72	
Ohope	163	Parengarenga Harbour	33	Sandy Bay/Coromandel	138	
Okahu Bay	90	Pareparea	54	Sandy Bay/Far North	23	
Okitu	177	Parimahu	193	Sandy Bay/Northland	57	
Okoromai Bay	80	Parnell Baths	90	Sandy Bay/Waiheke	98	
Okupu	104	Parua Bay	60	Scandrett Regional Park	73	
Omaha	71	Pataua	61	Scorching Bay	237	
Omaio	166	Patea Rivermouth	221	Scotts Point	25	
Omamari Gap	49	Patiki	167	Seatoun	237	
Omana Beach/Auckland	93	Pauanui	149	Sentinel Beach Reserve	89	
Omanu Beach/Mt Maunganui	159	Peka Peka Beach	228	Shakespear Regional Park	80	
Omapere	30	Petone Foreshore	234	Shelly Bay/Auckland	93	
Omiha Bay	101	Pikowai	162	Shelly Bay/Waiheke	101	
Omokoroa Beach	157	Pilot Bay	158	Shelly Bay/Wellington	237	
O'Neils	111	Plimmerton	232	Shelly Beach/Coromandel	135	
Onaero	211	Point Annihilation	184	Shelly Park Beach	93	
Onehunga Bay	233	Point Chevalier	89	Shipwreck Bay	26	
Onemana	151	The Poor Knights	59	Shoal Bay	193	
Onepoto Bay	171	Porirua Harbour	233	Signal Station	125	
Onerahi	60	Port Jackson	137	Simpsons Beach	144	
Onetangi	100	Port Ohope	163	Skudders Beach	43	
Ongare Point	157	Pouawa	175	Sky Williams	219	
Opape	165	Pourerere	192	Snells Beach	73	
Opito Bay/Bay of Islands	42	Pouto	50	South Beach	225	
Opito Bay/Coromandel	141	Porongahau	193	South Head/Hokianga	31	
Opononi	30	Port Fitzroy	105	South Piha	114	
Opoutere	150	Port Waikato	125	South Titirangi Beach	120	
Opotiki	165	Pouto	50	Spirits Bay	23	
Opoutama	184	Princess Bay	239	The Spit/ Te Waipera	183	
Oraka	183	Puheke	34	Sponge Bay	177	
Orakawa	154	Pukehina	161	St Heliers	91	
Orakei Wharf	90	Pukenui	33	St Leonards Beach	86	
Orapiu	100	Pukerahue	211	Stanmore Bay	78	
Orere Point	95	Pukerua Bay	229	Stingray Bay	188	
Orewa	75	Puniho Rd	216	Stent Rd	216	
Oriental Bay	236	Putaki	101	Stony Bay	138	
Orua Bay	124			Sunkist Bay	93	
Oruaiti	167	**Q**		Sunset Beach	125	
Oruawharo Bay	107	Queen Elizabeth Park	229	Surfdale	101	
Otahome	197					
Otaki Beach	228	**R**		**T**		
Otama Bay	141	Raglan	126	Taiharuru	61	
Otamarakau	162	Rangiputa	34	Taipa	36	
Otatu Bay	136	Rangitira Beach	109	Tairua	149	
Otitori Bay	120	Rarawa Beach	33	Takapuna Beach	86	
Otoka	101	Raumati Beach	229	Takou Bay	41	
Otumare	55	Rawene	30	Tamaki Beach	90	
Owhanake Bay	98	Rawhiti	45	Tamaterau	60	
Owhiro Bay	239	Red Beach	78	Tangimoana	226	
		Red Rocks	239	Tanners Point	156	
P		Reporua	172	Tapakakanga Regional Park	95	
Pacific Bay	59	Rings Beach	143	Tapeka Point	44	
Paekakariki	229	Riversdale	197	Tapuaetahi	41	
Paihia	43	Rockall	55	Tapotupotu Bay	23	
Pakiri	68	Rolling Stones	184	Tapu	133	
Palm Beach	99	Rothesay Bay	84	Tarakena Bay	238	
Palmers Beach	106	Ruakaka	62	Taramake Wildlife Reserve	95	
Paora Rd	216	Ruapuke Beach	129	Taronui Bay	41	
Papa Aroha	135	Russell Main Beach	44	Tatapouri	175	
Papamoa	159			Taupiri	53	
Papatea Bay	167			Taupo Bay	39	

Tauranga City Beaches	157	**W**		Whangapoua Beach	106	
Taurikura	61	Waharau	95	Whangapoua Estuary	106	
Tawhitokino	95	Waiake Beach	83	Whananaki North	55	
Tawharanui	72	Waiapu River	172	Whananaki South	55	
Tay St Beach	159	Waihau Bay	167	Whangaimoana	201	
Taylors Beach	184	Waihau Beach	175	Whangaparapara Harbour	104	
Teal Bay	53	Waiheke Island	95	Whangaparaoa	167	
Te Arai Point	68	Waihi Beach	155	Whangape Harbour	28	
Te Araroa	171	Waihi Beach Park	221	Whangapoua	143	
Te Awanga	191	Waihua Beach	187	Whangara	175	
Te Haruhi Bay	80	Wai-inu Beach	221	Whangaroa	39	
Te Henga	110	Wai-iti	211	Whangaumu Bay	59	
Te Horo Beach	228	Waikanae/Gisborne	178	Wharekaho	144	
Te Kaha	160	Waikanae Beach/Kapiti	228	Wharoponga	172	
Te Kopi	201	Waikare	187	Whareroa Beach	229	
Te Kouma	133	Waikawa/BOP	166	Whatarangi	201	
Te Mata	133	Waikawa/Horowhenua	227	Whatipu	117	
Te Ngaere	40	Waikawau/King Country	207	Whatuwhiwhi	35	
Te Paerahi	193	Waikawau/Thames Coast	133	Whirinaki	188	
Te Paki Stream	25	Waikawau Bay	139	Whiritoa	151	
Te Puru	132	Waikorere	158	White Rock	199	
Te Uenga Bay	44	Waikowhai Bay	120	Whites Beach	113	
Te Werahi Beach	22	Waimarama	191	Whitianga	144	
The Cut/BOP	160	Wainamu/Ocean Beach	127	Winstones Cove	83	
Thornes Bay	86	Wainui/Gisborne	177	Wood Bay	120	
Thornton Bay/Coromandel	132	Wainui/Hawkes Bay	193	Woodside Bay	100	
Thornton Beach/BOP	163	Wainuiomata	235	Woolleys Bay	57	
Ti Point	71	Waiomu	132	Worser Bay	237	
Timaru Rd	215	Waiotahi	164	Wyuna Bay	134	
Tindalls Beach	80	Waipatiki	187			
Tirohanga	165	Waipiro Bay	172	**Y**		
Titahi Bay	233	Waipu Cove	63	York Bay	235	
Tokerau Beach	35	Wairangi Wharf	89			
Tokomaru Bay	173	Wairoa Rivermouth	186			
Tolaga Bay	174	Waitara	211			
Tom Bowling Bay	23	Waitata Bay	44			
Tongaio	188	Waitete Bay	135			
Tongaporutu	210	Waitotara Rivermouth	221			
Tora	199	Waimamauku	30			
Torbay	83	Wainui Bay/Far North	40			
Torere	165	Waipaoa/The Big River	179			
Totara North	39	Waipapakauri	25			
Totoka Beach	224	Waitaha Cove	239			
Tracks	184	Waiterere	226			
Tryphena	104	Waiwera	75			
Tuamotu Island	178	Waiwhakaiho	212			
Tuapiro Point	156	Wattle Bay/Auckland	120			
Tuparoa	172	Wattle Bay/Waikato	124			
Tuateawa	139	Waverly Beach	221			
Turakina Beach	225	Wenderholm	74			
Tutukaka	58	Westshore	188			
Twilight Beach	22	Whaiangaroa	126			
		Whakaki	186			
U		Whakanewa	101			
Uawa	174	Whakataki	196			
Urenui Beach	211	Whakatane Heads	163			
Uretiti	63	Whakatete Bay	132			
Uriti Point	197	Whale Bay/Northland	57			
Urqharts Bay	61	Whale Bay/Raglan	129			
Urupukapuka Island	45	Whanarua Bay	166			
		Whangaehu/Hawke's Bay	193			
		Whangaheu/Manawatu	225			
		Whangamata	151			